WHEN GIANTS STUMBLE

ROBERT SOBEL

PRENTICE HALL PRESS

Acquisitions Editor: *Doug Corcoran*
Production Editor: *Eve Mossman*
Formatting/Interior Design: *Robyn Beckerman*

Printed in the United States of America

10 9 8 7 6 5 4 3 2 1

ISBN 0-7352-0059-9

PRENTICE HALL PRESS
Paramus, NJ 07652

On the World Wide Web at http://www.phdirect.com

For
Murray Henner
Who Made a Difference

CONTENTS

INTRODUCTION

BUSINESS BLUNDERS

I n 1899 *The Commercial & Financial Chronicle* waxed rhapsodic over the future of several large, dynamic companies with strategic leadership in promising industries. The American Bicycle Company, it predicted, would "control 95 percent of the bicycle making industry in this country." The American Hide and Leather Company "controls about 85 percent of the total upper-leather output of the country." In analyzing the American Ice Company, the magazine wrote: "The intention is said to be to bring under one control all the leading ice companies of the country."

These companies no longer exist. In came electrical refrigeration, out went the thousands of ice companies (many of which converted to home heating-oil delivery). American Hide and Leather produced leather for shoes; it was gobbled up in 1922. Chances are that the bicycles you see in the streets were manufactured abroad, the reasons for which will be analyzed in the last chapter of this book

While the utter collapse of a major corporation is unusual, the failure of products is not. A 1993 study by Kuzmarski & Associates, a Chicago-based consulting firm, indicated that of the 11,000 new products put on the market in 1987, only 56 percent were still there five years later. The firm found that most products don't even get beyond the test-marketing stage; they have a 1 in 13 chance for success by that criteria. Such has always been the case on the American scene. Consider this roster of initial public offerings for one month in 1961, admittedly a boom period for these kinds of new issues.

THE NEW ISSUES MARKET IN JANUARY, 1961

Company	Offering Price	Price on May 15, 1961
Automatic Concessions	4	10¾
Avery Adhesive Products	17	28½
Brothers Chemicals	3	11½
Chemtronic	2	3¼
Click Chemical	3	2
Cold Lake Pipe Line	3½	⅝
Colwell Co.	10	22
Cove Vitamin & Pharmaceutical	3⅛	55½
Cyclomatics	1	1⅝
Designatronics	2¼	5
Edlund Engineering	3	3½
Garsite Products	3	10
Geotechnics & Research	2	4⅛
Glassco Instruments	5	45
Great American Industries	2⅛	2
Heinicke Instruments	7½	41
Henry Engineering	2½	2¼
Holden-Day	1	3
J-F Machine-Diesel-Electronics	3	2¾
Long Island Plastics	1	4
Madigan Electronics	4½	8
Marine View Electronics	3	6¼
Measurement Systems	1	5
Medco Co.	5	28
National Trust Life Insurance	3	3¼
National Research Associates	1½	8
Pathe Equipment	5	8
Peerless Tube	4	7¼
Plated Wire & Electronics	4	8¼
Pneumodynamics	9	19½
Pocket Books	26	39
Reser's Fine Foods	7	24
Restaurant Associates	11	15
Reynolds & Reynolds	15	29

Company	Offering Price	Price on May 15, 1961
School Pictures	9⅞	24¼
Speedee Mart	6	15
United Automotive Industries	3	2½
Universal Electronics Labs	4	11½
Vacuum Electronics	15	30½
Varitab	2	12½
Vim Laboratories	3¾	3⅝

Source: *Barron's*, May 15, 1961, p. 5.

Few of these companies are around today in their original forms. They were merged out of existence, or they simply failed. Also note, by the prices their stocks went to in three to four months that many of these companies were perceived as having excellent chances of making the grade in a big way.

This is not unusual. Most failures in American business are not of the giant-sized, devastating variety, and the reasons for them are not difficult to understand. When a company is attempting to do or produce something new or to respond to important changes, those involved in leadership positions have to make presumptions and act on assumptions that can't be verified in advance. Their actions and the failures of products and services they produce shouldn't be classified as blunders, but rather as opportunistic misplays or plausible concepts that miscarried, sometimes due to some combination of misfortunes beyond the control of the businessman or company. In small companies the slightest misstep can lead to disaster. The loss of a contract, the departure of a key person, rises in interest rates, an uninsured loss, a patent problem, an offense to an important client, the wrong guess about the market for products and services, changes in prices charged by suppliers—the list of what can go wrong is almost endless.

Sometimes the timing isn't right for a wildly improbable idea. In 1952 George Cukor directed a film entitled *The Marrying Kind*, which was the simple story of a young couple, portrayed by Judy Holiday and Aldo Ray, who married in the immediate postwar world, found an apartment in a New York project, and started out with hopes for the future. Ray was a postal worker, with dreams of becoming an entrepreneur. He had an idea for a new take on an old product, but couldn't interest anyone in it. Without the services of a venture capitalist, he got nowhere. The idea, thought up by an imaginative screenwriter, doesn't seem so implausible close to half a century later. It was in-line roller skates. Clearly that fictional character of 1952 was on to something but had been born too early.

There are times when failure is almost inevitable because the product or service introduced is so simple that imitation is all but invited. There are some such inventions, however, that in the hands of a superb businessman could be identified with his company. The safety razor is such an invention, which in the hands of a King Gillette became identified with his company, and the same is true for soaps, toothpaste, breakfast cereals, and many others. More often than not, however, this does not occur, but to my way of thinking, this is not a blunder of the kind from which we can learn. Such would be the case of the ballpoint pen. Milton Reynolds is often portrayed as its inventor, or if not that, its first important promoter.

Reynolds, who was born in Albert Lea, Minnesota, in 1892, where his father was a threshing-machine salesman, was always seeking the main chance. After failing out of high school, he became an automobile salesman, and at the age of 20 was an independent tire dealer. Reynolds experienced great success in this business. By 1918 he was a millionaire, only to lose all of his money within four years. This was a preview of what was to come. During the next eight years Reynolds rode a financial roller-coaster, which resulted in three bankruptcies.

Reynolds moved to Chicago in the early 1920s, where he became a stock-market speculator and was wiped out in the 1929 stock-market crash. After two days searching for new business ideas he came upon a printing shop that sold commercial signs. He purchased the shop, intending to manufacture the equipment used in sign making, which he marketed as "Print-a-Sign." This was another of Reynolds' successes, and he was liquid once more. He was nothing if not serendipitous. During World War II Reynolds engaged in several businesses, the most successful being the importation of silver cigarette lighters from Mexico, which earned him at least $500,000.

While on a business trip to Buenos Aires in 1945 Reynolds came upon an early ballpoint pen invented by Ladislas Biro, a Hungarian journalist. While ballpoint pens were new, the idea went back to 1888, when John Loud, of whom nothing is known but his name, patented a version but never went into production. A different kind of ballpoint pen was invented by Frank Klimes, a Czech, in the early 1930s and manufactured by him and another Czech, Paul V. Eisner. The first of these instruments, called the Rolpen, was produced and marketed in Prague in 1935. Their patent ran out during World War II, when Klimes was in a concentration camp.

Meanwhile Biro, who fled to Paris when Hitler invaded Hungary, met a Hungarian woman who was married to a wealthy Argentinean, who took an interest in Biro and his invention. When attempts to sell the patent rights to Philips failed, the trio went to Argentina and sold the rights to Henry George Martin, a British promoter, who then organized a company to manufacture the pen, which was then called "Eterpen." Some of them were turned out and given gratis to the United States government for distribution to servicemen. The pen was something of a novelty. Not only could it write on almost any surface as well as under water, but it was leakproof, which made Eterpen a favorite with those who flew in military airplanes. The Biro interests licensed its patents for American production to Eversharp, Inc., and to Eberhard Faber in May 1945. Stories of the new pen were now featured in the press, but Eversharp and Eberhard Faber did not move swiftly into production.

Saying nothing to Biro or to Martin, Reynolds returned to the United States, where he had his attorneys study the Biro patent. It turned out that the Biro pens supplied the ink to the ball by means of capillary action. Reynolds developed a pen whose ink was delivered by gravity flow, which his attorney told him was different from the Biros and so was patentable. He obtained a patent on this method and swung into production before the Biro interests could enter the American market.

Reynolds capitalized his company, Reynolds International Pen, at $26,000. He started production on October 6, 1945, turning out 70 pens that first day. Reynolds decided to market the pens through Gimbel's Department Store in Manhattan, where they went on sale on October 29 for $12.50. The pens were an instant hit. Gimbel's sold $100,000 worth in one day and then notified Reynolds it would take all he could deliver. In the first three months Reynolds was able to sell two million pens through 60,000 retail outlets in the United States and 37 foreign countries, for total revenues of $5.7 million, with a net income of $1.6 million. Gimbel's alone accounted for 100,000 of the sales. It was one of the most successful new-product introductions in American history.

Stung by Reynolds' success, Eversharp and Eberhard Faber moved into production in December, and their South American subsidiary was able to ship Argentinean-manufactured ballpoint pens to the United States in March, where they were sold as Biros at R. H. Macy & Co. for $19.95. This prompted Reynolds to seek a preliminary injunction against them for harming his sales. The injunction was denied, with Judge Paul Leahy concluding there were too many conflicting questions to act without a jury trial, and as a result, Eversharp and Eberhard Faber were able to market their new American-made Repeater Pen, in May 1946. Reynolds responded that he soon would introduce a second pen with an improved ink chamber that would permit it to write for four years without refilling.

Other companies also entered the field, which by the fall of 1946 showed signs of saturation. In February 1947 Macy's was able to advertise the sale of a Reynolds pen, the Rocket, for 98 cents, or three for $2.79. The next day Gimbel's advertised the Rocket for 94 cents, or three for $2.59. The great ballpoint pen bonanza had ended.

Reynolds was undismayed. As legal threats faded and production slowed, he turned to other interests. In mid-1947 he announced that he intended to break Howard Hughes's record of a round-the-world flight of 91 hours and 14 minutes. Reynolds claimed the flight was also scientific in nature, since he intended to investigate rumors of mountains higher than Mt. Everest in Tibet.

Reynolds reoutfitted a surplus Air Force light-attack bomber and then teamed up with veteran flyer William P. Odom to make the flight in 1948 in under 79 hours. At refueling stops along the way Reynolds mingled with well-wishers and distributed more than 1,000 ballpoint pens. By then the pens were retailing for 39 cents.

Soon after his return Reynolds sold his pen business and returned to Print-a-Sign, manufacturing machinery and signs, but more as a hobby than anything else. He soon dropped from sight.

Did Reynolds blunder? When I started out on my research I had second thoughts and decided to drop this chapter from the book. After reflecting on those episodes of business blunders offered, you might try to figure out how Reynolds could have succeeded better than he did with his ballpoints.

Established companies, such as most of those discussed in the following pages, made larger bets, and in prospect they were plausible. One might have made a credible case for the Edsel, for example, or the reformulated Coca-Cola, Polaroid's Polavision, the IBM PC Jr., or RJR Nabisco's Premier cigarette, all failures resulting from unanticipated events, misperceptions, and marketing gaffes. These failures by themselves are not indications of poor management, shoddy thinking, or foolishness. It might be argued that the lack of failures is in itself a sign of deficiencies in management, which is supposed to take risks.

This certainly has been the case in the fast-food industry, which is constantly innovating since the public expects novelty along with the old favorites. McDonald's has had a host of failures, the most recent being with fajitas, fried chicken, pizza, pasta, the McLean Deluxe, and even carrot sticks. There will be more. But then consider the successes. McDonald's first attempts to woo customers to its outlets for breakfasts failed. In time customers took to the idea, not only providing the company with a new area for profits, but allowing it to use its facilities longer hours at little extra cost.

Lessons may be learned from all of these failures, but it should be considered that each of them was unique, although the morals that may be derived have application in other industries, companies, and circumstances.

It is possible to offer a generalized explanation of why some companies and products succeed and others fail. Success occurs when the company presents customers with products they feel they want and need at attractive prices that will return a decent profit. They fail when companies err in the products produced and can't sell them at a price the customers are prepared to accept.

Of course, it is more complicated than that. No company willingly turns out products or services they believe will not meet with approval. Nor are they always capable of judging customers' tastes or what economists call their elasticities of demand, which is to say, how much they truly want that product. They can't always gauge correctly the appeal of substitutes for their offering. A good deal of product planning and creation involves peering into the future, and as Mark Twain noted, it is most difficult making predictions, especially about the future.

Americans love success stories, or at least this is what we have been led to believe. So why then talk so much about failures? One reason is that so few do. Yet at least as much may be learned from why businesses fail as from why they succeed. After all, medical people study diseases in order to learn how to keep people healthy. Why not apply the same logic to the study of business blunders?

In point of fact, I start out with the belief that a large number of businesspeople actually do think in this fashion. I came to this conclusion in a serendipitous fashion. Early in my career I came upon the writings of Peter Drucker, whose works I have devoured since. What struck me as unusual about Drucker (in addition to his insights, which have informed my generation and those that follow) was his use of case studies and warnings regarding errors that beset businesspeople. This was present in his early works, such as *Concept of the Corporation* and *The Practice of Management*, and continue into his essays, talks, and collections. While Drucker is not alone in this, he is the greatest practitioner of the craft of learning from the mistakes of others. In several places in the chapters that follow, Drucker's "rules" will be introduced and illustrated. Those who want more of this are urged to read his collections of articles, *The Changing World of the Executive* (1982), *The Frontiers of Management* (1986), *Managing for the Future* (1992), and *Managing in a Time of Great Change* (1995). Of particular interest, in an area beyond the scope of business but a demonstration of how the blunders can occur in political life, see *Six Rules for Presidents* in his most recent collection. In this article Drucker indicated the blunders that beset Presidents Carter, Johnson, and Clinton and how Truman and Reagan avoided errors. He also illustrates the reasons for FDR's successes and one of his failures.

In addition to the inspiration I derived from Drucker, for many years, in the course of listening to businesspeople, I have been struck by their impatience and even boredom with what people whom they consult have to offer by way of analysis and advice. In the 1970s and 1980s they had become accustomed to talks and seminars on what the Germans or Japanese are doing right, and how their successes might be replicated in the United States. Every few years another theory of management was offered to instruct them on how to become successful. They listened politely, but more than a few noted how strange it was that people who had never run a business were telling them how to operate companies at which they had arrived in important positions, presumably because they had a measure of success.

I am neither a consultant nor a specialist in the area of management. Rather, I am a business historian whose expertise is in what has been, not what should or will be. Perhaps this is why I rarely if ever offer advice to businesspeople. Rather, I try to analyze decisions made by corporate leaders, their alternatives at the time, the knowledge they acted upon, their assumptions, and the consequences of their actions.

When I first started writing histories of companies, I learned that businesspeople were at least as much interested in how to avoid mistakes as in how to achieve success. It might have been the human desire to watch a fire that has gone out of control. A few have suggested that they liked to learn of such dismal failures to feel better about themselves. "I may not have done so well on the Buzzkirk deal, but at least I didn't act as foolishly as that bozo." I well remember relating J. P. Morgan's miscalculations with International Mercantile Marine and how one banker remarked, "Why, he was just a human being after all," which seemed to please him greatly.

It was then that I started offering talks on what I called business blunders. In these I attempted to re-create the atmosphere of the time and place, display alternative courses of action known by and open to the individuals involved, and indicate why the path taken seemed reasonable enough at the time. After all, no sensible person deliberately courts disaster.

Always I tried to indicate that one must guard against the second guessing made possible by hindsight. As H. Stuart Hughes wrote, the historian "cannot give the full sense of events as reality in the process of becoming—*because he knows the outcome*. By no literary device or trick of false innocence can he recapture his historical virginity; it is idle for him to pretend to an unsophistication of judgement which fools nobody."

Which blunders interested these executives? Perhaps you will be surprised to learn that they had no desire to learn my views on why IBM stumbled, Coca-Cola's error with its new version of its popular soft drink, the decline of Apple Computer, or any of the familiar sad tales of recent times. The saga of the Edsel was so well covered that there was nothing new that I could offer. They already knew about these cases and didn't need me to rehash or analyze failures they read about in the business press. Instead, they wanted studies of collapses of companies of which they had little or even no knowledge. They also preferred to know, in advance, what it illustrated, probably because they could in this way hold a silent internal discussion or discuss with me after the presentation was over and the question and discussion period began.

At the time I thought that there must have been several books and articles on the subject. There were articles, such as "Why Companies Fail" by Kenneth Labich in the November 14, 1994, issue of *Fortune*, but there was only one book I could uncover that dealt specifically with blunders (in the plural) and not with one specific case, such as a company history. That would be *Big Business Blunders: Mistakes in Multinational Marketing* by David Ricks (Dow Jones-Irwin, 1983). Clayton Christensen has written *The Innovator's Dilemma: When New Technologies Cause Great Firms to Fail* (Harvard Business School, 1997), which is on a related, narrower aspect of the matter than I wanted to address.

In his article Labich was more interested in developing his six reasons for failures than in showing precisely how they were realized. The six are: a failure to understand the nature of the business, or a falling away from a previous knowledge; failure of vision; a misperception of the company's financial situation; passive management in the face of rapid change; isolation of customers; and finally, failure in the care and nourishment of the labor force. As will be seen, I accept some of these but reject others, while adding a few of my own.

Successful companies often fail in attempts to enter new areas of opportunity, which is illustrated by some of Christensen's examples. All of those he discusses are in the area of new technologies, as the subtitle indicates, although he does allude to other industries as well. For those interested in this area, it can prove a rewarding read.

Ricks also had taken a different path from the one I was interested in traversing. As it turned out, he had compiled a series of blunders American businesspeople made in their dealings with foreigners. For example, in one vignette he wrote, "In most parts of Asia gifts should be given privately to avoid embarrassing the Asians, but they need to be offered publicly in the Middle East to reduce the possible impression that bribery is being attempted." Such a book is quite valuable, but not what I had in mind. Yet in his preface Ricks indicates that we had the same experiences and had come to similar conclusions. "We often hear of business success stories," he wrote, but "we tend to forget them and consequently learn little of value. Mistakes, on the other hand, are seldom admitted, are easily remembered, and can be used to illustrate valuable lessons."

I agree that mistakes are seldom admitted, but the ones discussed here were on such a scale that explanations fairly begged to be made, if not by the participants, then by others among the many who knew what had happened and why. Furthermore, they should be explored in the context of the times, the company's history, and the concepts of involved individuals. For example, without a knowledge of IBM's past and future as perceived within the company in 1980, CEO John Opel's concept of the nature of the computer industry, and the perception of the scope of the challenge from Apple, one cannot appreciate why the IBMers blundered as they did in the negotiations with Microsoft, enabling Bill Gates to become the tycoon he is today. Microsoft has a stronger position in operating systems than IBM had in hardware. This need not have been had IBM realized at the time that the industry was undergoing a major change in product mix and customers. Like the Edsel and Coca-Cola, this story has become a part of blunder lore, and so will not be discussed here.

After the fact, in the post-mortem, analysts often can identify the reasons for the failures and can try to avoid errors in the future. Of course, they will continue to experience their shares of failure, but they try to learn from mistakes, which in itself can be a major blunder. As the old saying goes, a cat that is scorched on a hot stove may not sit on one again—but that cat won't sit on a cold one, either.

Quite different are the botches caused by foolishness, pride, or short-sightedness. These are the kinds of blunders discussed in this book. Adam Osborne was considered one of the deep thinkers of the early personal computer age. He had some good ideas, but not the financial wherewithal required or the foggiest idea of how to transform them into practical results. Osborne Computer became one of the hundreds of failures in that industry. Gene Ferkauf, a success at making E. J. Korvette a force in discounting, knew little about department-store operations and lacked the personnel to carry off his ambitious foray into that field against the likes of Macy's and Gimbel's. E. J. Korvette is no longer with us. Henry Kaiser knew there would be a tremendous demand for automobiles after the war, and he gambled on beating the established companies in the field with the first true postwar product. Like Osborne, he was underfinanced, and in common with Ferkauf, didn't have sufficient personnel with experience in the industry. Moreover, he might have believed his press clippings, for in this period he had a great reputation for achieving success in a variety of businesses. Kaiser-Frazer is on the dustheap of the American automobile industry.

RCA fell apart largely due to Bob Sarnoff's feeble attempts to put his brand on the company he inherited from his father. A strong predecessor as CEO can be a blessing, for such a person usually leaves behind a company in fine shape. It can also be a curse, for it puts pressures on the new CEO to perform at least as well, and having the same surname doesn't help. RCA is still around, but as a wholly owned part of General Electric.

After having achieved a magnificent success in turning W. R. Grace from South American interests to chemicals, Peter Grace thought he could walk on water and set out on an ill-conceived acquisitions strategy. Moreover, like Sarnoff, he had a reputation to surpass, that of his grandfather. More so, perhaps, since his name was the same as that of the company he headed. Grace's blunders in fast foods, retailing, and a misbegotten attempt to create a "General Foods of Europe" were compensated by earlier and later successes. W. R. Grace is still there, but Peter Grace's career ended in sadness and remorse.

Faced with a dwindling market during the Great Depression, Packard's executives produced a less expensive car, which was a success, but in the process the company lost its grip on its wealthy clientele. Yet, had they not acted as they did, Packard might not have survived the 1930s. Some Packard cars are collectors' items today, but not the cheaper versions. Likewise, Schlitz and Pabst once had premium beers that sold for premium prices. Tinkering with winning products enabled the companies to realize economies, but also caused them to lose their cachet. Today both are off-priced brands.

Not all of these examples were utter foul-ups, and we can have some compassion for those involved. One might empathize with James Ling of LTV, who stirred the ire of government and paid the price. Once one of the nation's glamour companies, today's LTV is a factor in the more stagnant part of the steel industry. There might be less pity for Drexel Burnham Lambert, a bank that played hardball with some of the most powerful businesspeople in the country and through its actions alienated many in the financial community. When the established business interests, in alliance with government, came after the bank, others in the investment-banking business would not come to its defense or offer assistance. Drexel Burnham bit the dust, and its 7,000 employees had to look elsewhere for work.

The Penn Central failed in 1976 due to a misbegotten merger that was chockablock with blunders, but its fate may have been sealed many decades earlier by governmental actions that crippled the nation's railroads. Some of the rail lines of the Penn Central are still in use, but the company is no longer among the living. In a quite different way, Pan American World Airways was born with government support and thrived so long as that support and encouragement was present. Then came deregulation, and it was as though a deer raised in a zoo were set loose in a jungle. So, quite naturally perhaps, Pan American failed to adjust gracefully. Then its founder and CEO gambled and lost in placing a major airliner contract, and one of his successors mishandled a takeover. The company vanished in the graveyard of failed firms.

Timidity and a view of the future adhered to when evidence to the contrary mounts can prove the downfall of a company and its executives. When a critic informed John Maynard Keynes that his proposals during the 1930s were quite different from those he had advocated a decade earlier, the great economist replied, "When the facts change so do my opinions. What do you do, sir?" So it was with Sewell Avery and Montgomery Ward, which went downhill after World War II, when Avery refused to give up on a vision that was proving false. Montgomery Ward is a shell of its former self and may be in liquidation by the time you read these words. It was somewhat different with American Tobacco. Faced with assaults on the health front in the 1950s, the other tobacco companies reacted by attempting to produce products that were acceptable to smokers fearful that smoking caused cancer. American Tobacco held back, thinking the fears would pass, as they had on earlier occasions. Moreover, it already had the nation's leading smoke, Pall Mall, for which it claimed health qualities that clearly did not exist. The company's tobacco business declined, and in the end had to be sold off. American Tobacco became American

Brands, but its cigarettes now belong to Brown & Williamson, a subsidiary of British American Tobacco, which ultimately split itself into two companies, neither of which is called American Brands.

Then there is the blind arrogance informed by a narrow view of self-interest. In the 1930s, members known as specialists took command at a moribund New York Stock Exchange, and they held on for dear life after World War II, when a slow and then accelerating revival enriched them beyond their most sanguine hopes. In the process they attempted to freeze procedures in order to protect their own stakes. The specialists fought technology, failed to realize the potential of attractive new financial instruments, and when they did, opted to preserve their system rather than make adjustments. More so even than the airlines, the NYSE failed to comprehend the implications of deregulation. It survived, but acceptance of these three forces in a timely fashion would have enabled the institution to be more powerful than it is today.

Finally there was the case of Schwinn, once the premium name in bicycles. Indeed, for several decades it was the only name nonbikers recognized, and the one bikers preferred. Schwinn provides examples of many blunders already explored, plus a few new ones. It is a fitting conclusion for such a study.

At first readers may be jarred by the order of the chapters. It is not chronological or topical. Rather, the placements were made with a thought to continuity. They were structured so as to flow logically from one example to another. Deciding how to order the cases was one of the more difficult problems in this book, second only to the decisions on which topics to select. It is for the reader to decide whether one or both of these determinations was one of my blunders.

Robert Sobel
Long Beach, NY
October 31, 1998

CHAPTER ONE

OSBORNE COMPUTER: THE BLUNDER OF INEPTITUDE

At the dawn of new industries scores of pioneers appear hoping to cash in on bonanzas. This is particularly true as it becomes apparent the industry is catching on and money is to be made and fame achieved. In the 1950s there were scores, perhaps hundreds, of franchised fast-food companies, in hamburgers, hot dogs, pizza, and sandwiches; then ethnic foods arrived, led by Mexican, followed closely by every imaginable cuisine. Franchisers entered into areas such as motels, rental equipment, temporary services, hospitals, carpet cleaning, and other businesses. Most ended in failure. For every McDonald's there are scores of Burger Chefs; each Holiday Inn left behind the wreckage of a Motel World.

The automobile often is considered the most important product of the first half of the twentieth century. As for the second half, that rank is sometimes afforded to the computer. Perhaps so, but unlike the automobile, the computer had two radically different births, first as mainframes, then as personal computers. These are fundamentally different kinds of machines, with different applications (at least initially). They also had strikingly different sets of parents, one of whom resembled the automobile pioneers.

Mainframes have been likened to railroad trains—large, powerful, and suited to heavy hauling. The personal computers were compared, in their early days, to automobiles—relatively small, not much power, but highly flexible, capable of being used by the descendants of the people who drove Model Ts. The mainframes did "serious" work for corporations and required the services of highly trained technicians. The leading companies were either old-line business-machine companies (IBM, Remington Rand, Burroughs, NCR), electronics firms (General Electric, RCA, Honeywell), or start-ups (Control Data, Cray, Amdahl). The leaders of these companies were mature executives and earnest scientists, the general run of whom would be uncomfortable if not working in business suits, or at least in long-sleeved white shirts and conservative ties.

The personal-computer innovators were entrepreneurs rather than managers, quite young, and known as "hackers," a term that never would have been used to describe Seymour Cray and Eugene Amdahl, and certainly not the Watsons, father and son. Since they appeared in the 1960s, a number of them seemed to outside observers to be flower children, but despite appearances, not many of them were moonstruck by the Age of Aquarius. Few wore ties, many affected sandals and long hair, and the looks in their eyes seemed to alternate between intensity and languor. They were a driven set of people, middle class in origin, many well educated, often arrogant, but also playful. Steve Wozniak, the cofounder of Apple, said, only partly in jest, "Our success was due to a number of factors. First of all, we had never manufactured a computer before."

Into the mix that produced that generation of pioneers came a liberal dollop of the ideas associated with the then California chief executive, Jerry Brown, who was known to some as "Governor Moonbeam" for his sometimes off-the-wall ideas, and with philosopher E. F. Schumacher, whose "Small Is Beautiful" motto might have but did not refer to desktop computers.

Often the pioneers would eschew those corporate designations that were chosen in the 1950s, such as the name of the founder or a clear statement of what the purposes and intent of the enterprise were, and selected what to older people seemed fanciful designations. The most famous of these was Apple, but there also was Altair, the industry's pioneer, whose name came from the bright star in the constellation Aquilla, which in the popular *Star Trek* television series was the sun of a fictitious planet. Altair was followed by Chicken Delight, Itty Bitty Machine Co., Atari, People's Computer, and the like. There even was a Kentucky Fried Computers, the name of which was changed to North Star when the founders were threatened with a lawsuit.

This is not to suggest that hackers and playful names were the norms, but rather that they were tolerated and accepted in personal-computer land while they were not in the mainframe business. Even the leaders of the personal-computer world—the Radio Shacks, KayPros, Commodores, and Cromemcos—would have seemed out of place in the original computer industry. There was a world of difference between IBM's fortress in Armonk, New York, and Steve Job's garage where the Apple was born.

The microcomputer movement may be said to have begun in 1971, when Marcian "Ted" Hoff, who worked at Intel, a manufacturer of electronic gear, designed and then created the first microprocessor, or computer on a chip. Known as the 4004, it was little more than a curiosity. Even then Hoff knew the 4004 could become the heart of small computers.

Some scientists at the small, New Mexico-based electronics firm of Instrument Telemetry Systems realized this as well, and in 1975 created the Altair, a kit from which could be assembled a device which sold for $400 and contained the 8080 microprocessor. With another $2,000 for peripheral equipment, hobbyists might assemble a true computer.

Other kits followed, most sold from small stores catering to hobbyists. In the late 1970s Commodore International came out with the PET, a preassembled computer, while Heath offered equipment ordered from catalogues and Radio Shack, a chain-store operation, offered the TRS-80, which sold for $499.

The hobbyists and others simply interested in small computers gathered in groups to share information and ideas. There was nothing in the world of mainframes like the legendary "Homebrew Club," that group of young hackers who first met in Gordon French's garage in 1975.* Wozniak calculated that 21 business entities sprang from this group, including Computer Faire, Commodore, Mountain Hardware, IBEX, and the Bay Area Computer Stores, as well as French's own Processor Technology. The companies proliferated, in much the same way as they did in the young automobile industry. In 1983, according to the industry's monitor, Dataquest, there were more than 800 firms turning out desktop computers in the $1,000 to $3,000 range.

By the mid-1980s readers of business pages, subscribers to technology-oriented publications, and especially owners of desktop

---

*For some reason, garages figured importantly in start-ups, just as barns did at the turn of the century for automakers.

computers had become accustomed to stories of the bright young men involved in the industry. They seemed to range from M.I.T. and Stanford graduates to East European and Asian emigres to college dropouts. While only a handful started out in those garages, their new companies—if one could even call the tiny setups companies—usually began with little capital. All of their leaders seemed to know one another, and hopping from one alliance to another was usual. In time some would achieve wealth and fame, appear on magazine covers and TV talk shows, and hobnob with businesspeople from older industries, who often seemed at a loss as how to behave toward these often irreverent representatives of the future.

Even then, observers of the business scene knew that not many of these people and their companies would survive, and the betting was that once the old-line firms entered the fray, most would be yesterday's news. If the newcomers believed this, they didn't show it. As far as they were concerned, the founders of the mainframe industry were dinosaurs on their way to secondary roles, if not outright extinction.

What couldn't have been realized at the time was that this reborn industry was one of many that would be organized in what appears to be at least the next turn of the wheel in the industrial revolution and may be something even more portentous. Entrepreneurs in what has been called the age of "proprietary capitalism" started and then successfully ran their own companies, often to the applause and admiration of the public and the benefit of their own fortunes. There are many such individuals, but perhaps the most famous are Bill Gates of Microsoft and Michael Dell of Dell Computer. Not only were they celebrated (and feared by rivals) but fabulously wealthy. During the week of February 17–25, 1998, Dell and Microsoft stocks rose, enriching Dell by $830 million and Gates by $3.8 billion. Such are the rewards of success in new industries. Andrew Carnegie, Thomas A. Edison, and Henry Ford, who did as well during their periods of greatness, would not have been surprised at this development. Nor would those eager scientists, engineers, and would-be entrepreneurs who set out to accomplish just this a generation ago and their present-day counterparts have the same idea in mind. Needless to say, most of them won't make it much beyond the starting gate. We tend to remember and lionize the winners and forget the losers.

Adam Osborne was one of those bright men who swarmed over Silicon Valley and its environs during the early 1970s. Tall, gangly, with a large moustache and a pronounced upper-class English accent, Osborne stood out from the crowd. He was as arrogant as most and combined this attitude with a vivid vocabulary and a biting wit.

Osborne was born in Bangkok in 1939, the son of a professor of religion at the university there and of a Polish Jewish Holocaust survivor. The father spent part of his time attempting to convert Christians to Hinduism, which repelled young Adam. When he was still quite young, the family moved to Tamil Nadu in southern India to live in the ashram of Sri Ramana Maharishi, and Adam was raised in a village known as Tiruvannamalai, where he became fluent in Tamil. His parents sent him to a Catholic school, where he converted to Catholicism because, as he later said, the nuns treated Catholics better than they did the others. From there he went to an English university and after graduating emigrated to the United States to be with his lady friend. Osborne earned a Ph.D. in chemical engineering at the University of Delaware, after which he took a job with Shell Oil. His travels took Osborne to Northern California, where he became involved with those who were attempting to reinvent the computer and make it accessible to everyone who wanted one. In the world of Californians and New Yorkers with middle-class backgrounds and technological educations, he was certainly exotic.

Bob Jones, the publisher of *Interface Age*, one of the many small magazines devoted to computers and electronics that were springing up in Silicon Valley, was among those who noticed Osborne. In 1975 Jones invited him to write a column for the magazine. Osborne accepted, and in keeping with the arrogance that was to become his trademark, he titled the column, "From the Fountainhead." He would write for *Interface Age* for five years. "I specialized in scuttlebutt and exposing frauds," he recalled when his time there was over. "I had a lovely time."

These columns were Osborne's playpen, where he tried out ideas and toyed with notions regarding the future of computers and the ways they might affect society. It seemed that the bigger the company, the more scorn he would heap upon it. Once a firm reached a certain size, he thought, it started to ossify. He wasn't certain just what that size was, but Osborne clearly believed that smaller was better. Thus, IBM was a menace, and Fairchild Semiconductor and Hewlett Packard weren't much better.

Osborne wasn't overly sympathetic to most small firms either. He criticized them for inflated claims, being underfinanced, and making product announcement too early, which was certainly the case in this period. But they did so for good reason: The start-ups usually had no recourse to venture capitalists and couldn't obtain bank loans. They would advertise products still in the planning stages. Customers would send in their orders with payments, and the money thus obtained would be used to complete the design and go into production. "It was not uncommon for companies to have accounts receivable equal to five percent of their accounts payable," Osborne would write in his 1984 self-serving history of his company: *Hypergrowth: The Rise and Fall of Osborne Computer Corporation*. "It was also not uncommon for people to finally receive shipment of ordered products nine months to a year after their checks had been cashed. If they were very lucky, the product they received worked."

Osborne was one of a large number of futurologists who believed America's best hope of besting Japanese industry rested in electronics, desktop computers in particular, but he thought the desktop companies of that period were on the wrong track. While the leaders at the small companies often shared information and ideas, each was intent on building his own machine, which was not compatible with the others. It had been that way in automobiles prior to World War I, when there were 287 different sizes of tires.

Osborne believed the new companies that were emerging as leaders were going about their business as did those early auto manufacturers. Apple had its Apple II and Commodore its PET, while Radio Shack was pushing the TRS 80. None of the software in these machines was compatible with the others. Commonality was the key to success, he thought. Each of these companies was behaving as though it could oblige the others to bow to it. "What made the personal computer industry happen in the first place was that different people were using basically the same components and the same software, so they could amortize costs and drive prices down," he told a reporter in 1982. "But the leaders of the industry today—Radio Shack, Apple, and Commodore have strayed off that track. They're just like big computer companies—they want to lock companies into their own systems, so they spend heavily to create new hardware and software." What was needed, said Osborne, was standardization. If the big companies were dinosaurs, the small ones were magpies, chattering away endlessly without doing much of consequence. What Osborne was calling for IBM soon would succeed in doing by opening its architecture to the clones like Compaq and Dell, while Apple failed in its bid to oblige the industry to adopt its approach.

Osborne was also critical of the pricing policies of computer companies. The precedent should be Ford, not Packard, which is to say the manufacturers should strive to simplify and lower prices, not extract high profits from a small customer base. Just as Ford lowered prices as he improved performance, so should computer manufacturers. "The industry has lost its drive to push prices down," he complained in 1980. Osborne liked to say, "We are not in the business of serving the privileged few, but rather the masses. We're in the commodity business." Not for him were state-of-the-art machines, but rather those that could get the job done, no more than that. A product need not be on the cutting edge of technology to be accepted. As he put it, IBM had shown that "to be number one you don't have to be the best. All that is necessary is that the product be adequate, properly supported, and readily available."

Audacious, irreverent, and self-assured, Osborne seemed to think he alone had the ability to understand the present, as well as the knack of being able to peer into the future. Rarely did he have anything good to say about the journalists who covered the industry, almost all of whom he considered hacks, fakes, or worse. "Adam is sometimes brilliant, sometimes eccentric, and always outspoken," thought one observer, and Osborne himself cheerfully admitted that those within the industry considered him "either a visionary or an obnoxious jerk."

In the process of speaking his mind, Osborne made a reputation within the small industry in which a host of its members wished him no good. Yet he was also respected, for he clearly understood the business and its technology. He wrote books, mostly technical ones at first, with titles such as *Sixty-Eight Hundred Programming for Logic Design*, which he self-published and peddled at fairs and Homebrew Club meetings. Osborne's biggest hit was *An Introduction to Microcomputers*, a densely written book comprehensible only to those with engineering or related backgrounds, which over the years sold more than 300,000 copies and enabled him to expand his operations. By 1978 his publishing business, now called Osborne Associates, had become quite profitable, publishing some 40 books, of which he wrote 12, and it appeared that he might become not only the industry's first media magnate, but one of its most visible spokesmen as well.

That year Osborne published his manifesto, *Running Wild: The Next Industrial Revolution*, the kind of futuristic book that later would become identified with Alvin Toffler, with touches of Tom Peters and George Gilder thrown in for flavor. Read 20 years later, it seems more a product of its time rather than the guide to the future its author hoped it would be. But it also was prescient.

This was a period of gloom in America, the close of a decade that saw the energy crisis, stagflation, humiliation in foreign policy, and the seeming inability of the presidents and congresses of the period to lead effectively. Scores of books appeared purporting to tell what the Japanese were doing right and Americans were doing wrong, and they attracted large followings.

In Osborne's view there would be massive technological changes that would render a good part of the workforce obsolete. Those who mastered the new technologies would enjoy immense power and wealth, while those who did not would suffer grievously. Old companies would come crashing down, their places at the pinnacle of industry taken by newcomers, most of which would be involved with technologies. It sounded very much like what had happened during the commercial and industrial revolutions of the late eighteenth and early nineteenth centuries, hence the title and the approach.

This angry book has all the earmarks of being written hastily by a man convinced of his vision. It was badly edited, repetitive, had spelling and grammatical errors, and rambled into diversions. But Osborne was on to something. He wrote about the coming of the modem and electronic mail, though not by those names, of course, and he foresaw stock trading over computers at far lower commissions than were then being charged. He forecast sharp declines in the prices of word processors and of color printers that would produce photographs made with digital cameras. Electronic newspapers. Laser disks. And more.

Unsurprisingly, not all of his predictions have come about. The profoundly deaf do not hear with the aid of electronics, and bank fraud is not rampant, as Osborne forecast. Still, his record was better than most. More to the point, reading it today is one of the best ways to understand the mood among the Silicon Valley set in the late 1970s, and the mind-set of someone who would soon become one of the most talked-about businessmen in the industry, if only for a season or so.

As indicated, Osborne thought IBM's domination of computers would soon end, a daring prophecy. In 1979, the year of the book's release, Radio Shack had revenues of $150 million, most of that from items other than computers, while runner-up Apple's revenues were less than half that amount. That year IBM's revenues came to $22.8 billion. Osborne wrote:

> Soon IBM will be facing stiff competition, not from its traditional rivals such as Burroughs, Univac, Honeywell, and NCR, but from such upstarts as Apple Computer Corporation, Radio Shack, Commodore, Pertec, Texas Instruments, and the whole wolf pack of little guys. And when the IBM computer salesperson shows up at an office trying to interest the office manager in a new computer, that office manager may well be looking over a variety of computer systems at a local computer store.

Osborne criticized the young computer companies for their vision of the computer becoming ubiquitous in the classrooms and homes of America. While believing this would occur in time, Osborne thought at that stage of the industry's development the office market was much more attractive. In his columns he urged the manufacturers to target small businesses, predicting that in time, those desktop computers would become sufficiently powerful to challenge the smaller mainframes being produced by Data General and Digital Equipment.

Osborne also thought there was a market for a transportable computer, one that businesspeople could take with them on their trips. This was not the kind of product that struck people as bizarre or original. Portable typewriters had been on the market since 1907, when the Bennet Junior, which sold for $18 and could be carried in a man's inside jacket pocket, made its appearance. Portable typewriters that weighed as much as 30 pounds were standard equipment for reporters and businesspeople in the 1920s and afterward, and in time electric portables made their appearances too. The desktop computer was replacing the typewriter. Why shouldn't transportable computers replace the portable typewriters? Several companies had made forays into this area, but not with anything that resembled the computers then on the market, or with the computing power needed for most business applications. Unlike the home computers, the transportable would have to be rugged and simple, since in moving about it might be shaken or even dropped.

This was another theme Osborne stressed at this time. The potential customer base was not looking for elegance, but rather easy-to-understand, inexpensive boxes that could run software, which he correctly realized was the key to the industry. "Without acceptable software a computer is nothing but an expensive sea anchor," he would tell his readers. Osborne expressed his admiration for English inventor Hugh Sinclair, who in 1980 came up with the ZX80, selling 100,000 of the small handheld machines for less than $200 in its first year. It was little more than a toy with a cheap membrane keyboard that had to be hooked up to a TV screen for visuals. It was too weak for practically any serious application, something Sinclair rectified in subsequent more expensive versions; the more powerful ZX81 went for $149.95, but it still lacked a screen and couldn't run word processing software or play most games.

No one in America seemed to be thinking seriously along all of these lines. There was a gap in the market that was not being filled, and Osborne intended to do just that. In 1979 he sold his publishing business to McGraw-Hill for a reported $5 million and prepared to use some of this money to found a computer company of his own. But not on a full-time basis. As part of his contract Osborne had to continue working for McGraw-Hill, and so could not devote all of his time and energies to the company.

Osborne intended to go about it differently from the other desktop groundbreakers. Most of them started with the vision, then designed the machine and software, tried to drum up financing, and then produced the prototype. Osborne was not short on vision, but for all of his criticisms and commentaries, he was not capable of contriving a workable computer. For this he called on the talents of Lee Felsenstein, an owlish-looking young man who had the conventional credentials for the Silicon Valley of the time. Felsenstein tried working for others for a while, winding up at Ampex, then an exciting company with an apparent unsurpassable lead in tape technologies. This was not to his taste, so he quit Ampex to become a reporter and commentator for the *Berkeley Barb*, a well-known publication that lauded the counterculture, criticized the Administration's handling of the war in Vietnam, and offered strong views on the virtues of drugs. When internal dissension divided the staff, Felsenstein left for a post at another publication, *The Tribe*. In short order he became disillusioned with that publication and journalism itself and returned to Ampex, where he was put to work on computer design. Now intent on concentrating in this area, Felsenstein completed his engineering studies at Berkeley and in 1972 moved into a "computer commune" where he became involved in a wide variety of projects, none of which amounted to much.

In the process Felsenstein was learning more about computers and developing a social vision. He was one of a group that organized Community Memory, which intended to provide free access to terminals to all. This didn't work out well; most people didn't know how or why to use them, and the machines had a great deal of downtime. If computing couldn't be free, Felsenstein came to believe, it at least could be inexpensive. Clearly Osborne and he were on the same wavelength.

Felsenstein spent the second half of the 1970s drifting from one project to another, most of which were along the lines of Community Memory, which is to say attempts to bring computing to the common man and woman. Working for Processor Technology in 1976, he had designed the Sol-20 and Expander, a desktop that was actually manufactured in small numbers, and Felsenstein did some consulting work in order to survive financially. Nothing seemed to have turned out right. "I was running into the ground," he later recalled. "I was just waiting for the opportunity to do what I wanted to do and closing my eyes to the monetary considerations."

Felsenstein needed work, and Osborne needed a computer. They were made for each other, and the moment was right. They were not strangers. Osborne and Felsenstein had had dealings earlier, when Felsenstein had reviewed books for Osborne's publishing ventures, and in addition they had consulted each other on technical matters.

They met again at the West Coast Computer Faire in March 1980, at which time Osborne told Felsenstein of his ideas for a transportable computer. By then Osborne had come up with another concept. Until then computers came with operating systems, but not software. Knowing that the machines were of little use without software and that most buyers wanted at least a word-processing system and perhaps a spreadsheet, he proposed to include them, and possibly more, with the machine. Osborne intended to work out a deal with existing software companies, so that would free him from having to commit capital and manpower to that enterprise. Moreover, to make the portability even more attractive, he wanted to include a battery so the machine would be usable in areas where electricity was not available, such as airport terminals and out-of-doors. The idea of using the computer on an airplane was not even considered—the package would be too large for that—but it had to fit under an airliner seat, so that it could be carried on a passenger plane and not have to go into the storage compartment, where it could be banged up. This meant the computer would have to have a small screen. Osborne told Felsenstein he wanted a 40-column, 24-line display. Felsenstein objected, wanting 64 columns. They compromised on a 52-line display and what Osborne said was a five-inch screen, but was really a quarter of an inch smaller than that. In time Osborne users learned how to hitch the computer to a television screen by means of an adaptor, which could cost anywhere from $39.95 to $79.95 depending on the manufacturer.

All the while Osborne was on the prowl for investors. He invested only $5,000 of his own money initially. Most of the start-up financing, an estimated $40,000, came from venture capitalist Jack Melchior, a former Hewlett Packard executive with a reputation for sniffing out promising companies. Additional funding came in the next few months, so that by the time Osborne was ready to demonstrate his product, he had raised $900,000.

Felsenstein was busy with his end of the business. After he contrived the computer, he scrounged around for parts. The machine was to have two 5.25-inch disc drives, each with a capacity of 92 Ks, and would utilize a Zilog Z-80A processor with 64Ks of RAM. He and one assistant would come up with a design and then try to locate parts that were affordable. If these were not available, the design would be changed. Osborne had asked for a prototype within four months, and Felsenstein was able to deliver on time, and for his effort received unregistered Osborne shares. A few years later, recalling the experience, he asked "Do you know the feeling of toad sweat, when you wake up in the middle of the night knowing that you've overcommitted yourself? That's how it was."

The machine weighed 23.5 pounds and looked like a large suitcase. Felsenstein came up with some ingenious solutions to the problem of size. The software produced a full page, which could not be displayed on the screen. But the information could be stored, and then the user could scroll through it. Felsenstein still had doubts about the technology, however, to which Osborne replied, "Adequacy is sufficient."

Osborne next set out to strike deals with software companies. In those early days of desktop computing this was not a difficult task. MicroPro, a leader in the small field, had developed WordMaster, which in the late 1970s was generating revenues of less than $20,000 most months. The company had recently come out with an improved version, WordStar, one of the first to feature "WYSWYG," an acronym that would become well-known for "what you see is what you get." Osborne wanted WordStar and got it for 75,000 shares of stock in his company, worth perhaps $130,000 based on the cash he had raised, and $4.60 for each unit bundled with the computer.

From Bill Gates's fledgling MicroSoft, Osborne obtained BASIC, a computer language produced originally for the Altair. Gates took stock, but turned down the offer of a place on the board. Osborne tried to strike a deal for Personal Software's popular VisiCalc spreadsheet, but was rejected. Instead he commissioned another firm, Sorcim to develop a similar program, and that company came up with Super-Calc. There was more. Osborne acquired Mailmerge, which provided the means for mass mailings and Cbasic-2, for those who might prefer it to the MicroSoft version.

To manufacture and market the machine, Osborne had organized a company that he called Brandywine, Inc., because he liked the sound of the name, but that was later renamed Osborne Computer Corp., which was incorporated in January 1981.

Osborne realized he needed a manager for his company, this because he was still working for McGraw-Hill and also recognized he lacked managerial talents. He offered the presidency of his firm to Seymour Rubenstein, MicroPro's president, who turned it down, but was sufficiently impressed with what he had been shown to invest $20,000 in the company. Osborne then ran a blind ad in *The Wall Street Journal* and, of those who answered, found Tom Davidson, who once ran a taxi company and then managed a branch of a manufacturing concern. Davidson had no experience with small computers, but then,

not many did in this period. Osborne was quite high on Davidson in
the beginning, but soon cooled on him, as he would on Davidson's successor. When it was all over, Osborne would place most of the blame
for failure on the men he had selected to run the company.

The prototype in hand and acceptable, Osborne set up shop in
Haywood, across the Bay from Silicon Valley, where he could take
advantage of low rents and cheap labor. There wasn't much to assemble. After a short course of instruction semiskilled workers could cobble together the few parts with precisely 68 screws and present a
completed computer in about half an hour. It was not a particularly
attractive package, the case made of pebbled, cheap-looking pressboard covered with plastic, the name "Osborne 1" affixed as would be
a bumper sticker. The top was held in place by brackets, which when
released and unfolded revealed the keyboard, the screen, cables, and
disk drives. If the operator looked carefully, he or she would realize the
power cable was held in place by two small pieces of Velcro. Peter
McWilliams, whose *The Personal Computer Book* was the standard buying guide for neophytes seeking to learn more about personal computers or to purchase one, described the Osborne 1, which he
criticized sharply:

> Folded, the Osborne 1 resembles a drunken portable sewing
> machine: the bottom of the carrying case is slanted and the unit,
> when standing on end, list dramatically to one side. Unfolded, it
> looks like something out of Army Surplus. And the screen, the
> video screen, is *the smallest* thing you've seen coming out of an
> electronic box *that big* since the early 1940s.

I imagine that, several years from now, we will look back upon
the Osborne 1 with the sense of fond amusement we currently reserve
for, say, the first Ford, or the first $300 handheld calculator.

Undeterred by criticism, Osborne plowed ahead. There remained
one more piece of his strategy to put in place: distribution. He had
been critical of the way the major desktop companies had handled this.
Typically they worked through retailers who might place large orders
and then peddled the product to the mail-order houses that were
springing up in this period. Osborne was prepared to work with the
retailers, but would require them to take the warranty card from the
customer after it was filled out to be returned to the company. Failure

to do this would cost the retailer a substantial amount of profit and might lead to an end of the relationship. In this way, Osborne would be certain the person to whom he sold the machines did not resell it to those mail-order shops.

Osborne unveiled his computer at the West Coast Computer Faire in April 1981. It was the hit of the show, easily the most talked about new product. Visitors to his display, who knew something about computers, recognized the Osborne 1 offered nothing technologically interesting. They were impressed instead by all of that software and the price, which was $1,795, about half of what desktops were going for in this period. Those who took the trouble to figure it out concluded that Osborne's software alone would have cost at least $1,400.* It was as though Osborne had sold the software package and then thrown in the computer as an afterthought. One computer critic wrongly compared Osborne to King Gillette, who would practically give away his safety razors in order to sell blades. This was not Osborne's intent. He was telling potential customers that they would need nothing else to start writing or doing spreadsheets. Not quite. They would need some floppy disks, but Osborne was not going to enter that end of the business.

Osborne took 90 orders at the show, all for July delivery. The first unit was shipped to the Digital Deli in Mountain View, California, on June 30, 1981, and others followed. Soon Osborne would have a $6 million advertising campaign. One showed the torsos of two men, one carrying an attaché case, the other an Osborne. The caption read, "The Guy on the Left Doesn't Stand a Chance," referring, of course, to the one without the Osborne.

Even Adam Osborne, who had a pretty good opinion of himself, was surprised by the reception that greeted his computers once they hit the stores. Salespeople reported that buyers didn't even ask for demonstrations, that they had been shown the machine by proud owners. "The hardest thing about the sale is asking the customer whether he'd like to carry the thing home in the shipping carton or by the handle." Osborne had its first million-dollar month in September, three months after the first machine had been sold.

---

*In this period one might purchase a new Chevrolet for this price. This will give the reader an idea of how much computer prices have fallen and performance boosted since the early 1980s.

Success in start-ups does not mean profits, however. Initial costs and advertising were costly, and payments were usually slow. Inventories had to be built up, and there was the learning curve to consider. Osborne had a $10 million line of credit at the Bank of America. While impressed by the strong demand, officials there were becoming nervous regarding the casual way he conducted business. In early September the credit was withdrawn, and the company was strapped for cash. Not for long. Osborne Computer was a hot item, and Jack Melchior was able to raise $1.6 million by selling treasury stock at $40 a share—up from $17, the price when the initial $900,000 was in place. The money arrived even though the company had lost $1.2 million in 1981, a showing Osborne attributed to start-up costs and one-time charges.

More than 11,000 Osbornes were sold in the company's first eight months in business, and Adam Osborne claimed he had an orders back-log for 50,000 more. By then he was telling people that he intended for Osborne to be a billion-dollar company by 1984, and when in August 1982 the company did $10 million in sales, the goal seemed possible of being realized. Osborne plowed ahead. He opened a second factory in Monmouth, New Jersey, to serve the eastern market, and soon was turning out more than 200 machines a day. But the success was not unalloyed. Defects turned up in 10 to 15 percent of the early shipments, and Osborne had to spend more than $140,000 to rectify them.

From the start Osborne had known that he couldn't be successful with the Osborne 1 by itself. Improvements were coming on line frequently, and the half-life of a small computer was terribly short. Osborne recognized this before most in the industry. Looking ahead, he and Davidson planned for two more powerful computers, code-named the Vixen and the Executive, geared for release in 1983. More important, something had to be done about that small screen and the 52-column display. The disk drives were single density and could hold only 100,000 characters, and this was inadequate. He wanted to move to an 80-column display and double-density disks as quickly as possible.

In mid-1982 Osborne predicted his company would post revenues of $250 million for the year and show a pretax profit of $9 million. This figure was off the mark. In 1982 Osborne claimed to have sold 120,000 transportables for a volume of nearly $200 million and told reporters he had a profit of more than $1 million, but as it later turned out these figures were far too high.

It was dawning on the press and the industry that the reality at the company sharply differed from the picture Osborne had tried to present. Given the company's low overhead and labor costs, the declining prices of components and economies of scale, Osborne's profit margins should have been higher than he claimed they were. At that, audits later revealed the company was never profitable. The problems with defects continued, and at one point Osborne had to shut down the plant in order to correct them. While not fully recognized at the time, quality control was virtually nonexistent: One retailer who sold 225 Osbornes had to make 400 repairs on them. Within the industry it was recognized that Osborne was an indifferent manager, and he didn't seem to bother to hide the fact. In addition, his harsh treatment of retailers earned him their enmity. "I'm not much of a diplomat; I make enemies," he conceded.

So long as Osborne 1s were selling and there was no competition, the dealers would accept this treatment. When the situation changed they would turn their backs on Osborne. This development, as much as any other, caused the company to decline. He was overwhelmed, ironically by developments he had advocated and the arrival of new forces in the churning industry.

In order to understand the sudden transformation of the market, one must understand the impact IBM had on it in this period. In the minds of most people during the early 1980s, IBM was synonymous with computers. Why it held back from personal computers for so long was something of a mystery, but on August, 12, 1981, shortly before the Osborne 1 was introduced, IBM announced its PC (which had an operating system and microprocessor purchased from two upstart companies, Microsoft and Intel) with a great deal of fanfare. While the PC was not a transportable and its price was close to triple that of the Osborne 1, it did draw some sales from them, as it did from perhaps all the other companies. It appeared to most casual observers that IBM would become the dominant force in the field. Not to Adam Osborne, however, who went on record predicting Big Blue would run into many unforeseen problems.

Osborne always knew that success would breed competition. "I'm not foolish enough to think we're going to own 100 percent of the market," he told reporters at the West Coast Computer Faire. "I welcome those who are in effect endorsing our concept, but business is business—they'll find I have a few cherry bombs in the way."

The following year several transportables made their debuts, two of which came from new firms and stood out from the others. One of these was Compaq, which was organized by former Texas Instruments engineers headed by Rod Canion and backed by venture capitalist Ben Rosen. Earlier Rosen had invested in Osborne, and now he wagered $20,000 on Compaq's success.

This company was not a product of Silicon Valley, but rather the electronics complex that had developed near Houston. The atmosphere there was quite different. Canion and those around him were mature, businesslike, and highly focused. Perhaps the people at Compaq were not as imaginative as those in the Valley, but they worked away at computers with as much dedication and seemed to know just what they wanted: to build a better IBM machine than IBM could produce.

The Compaq people believed IBM would be a sure winner, and they acted on this thought. According to the company legend, Canion and two of his associates sketched their computer on a restaurant placemat. They wanted to produce a transportable that would run as much of IBM's PC software as possible, including the DOS operating system, and so would be a machine that soon would be known as an "IBM compatible," or more simply, "compatible."

The first Compaqs appeared late in the year and looked and worked differently from the Osborne 1s. The California machine was a compromise; no one would confuse it with the IBM PC. The Compaq was really an office machine that could be transported. It weighed 28 pounds, and so was heavier than the Osborne 1, but the finish was far superior, the display better, and the looks professional. It was designed for the person who had an IBM in the office and wanted an IBM on the road or at home. A computer geek might love the Osborne 1; the corporate manager would approve of the Compaq, and once the Compaq appeared it became the computer of choice for such people, just the ones Osborne had hoped to win over.

Compaq succeeded admirably. For 1983 the company posted revenues of $111 million, phenomenal for a start-up. IBM took note, and a year and a half later it delivered its first transportable. By then, however, Compaq was too strong to defeat. In December Compaq made its initial public stock offering, raising $66 million. Even so, it was not an industry leader. Two million microcomputers were shipped that year, and between them IBM, Commodore, Apple, and Radio Shack had 75 percent of the market.

Then IBM stumbled. In 1986 the company decided to stay with the Intel 286 chip rather than go to the 386. Why? Because the 386 would make the IBM PC competitive with the company's expensive midrange computers and destroy sales. IBM was in the unhappy position of having not one but two computer businesses in which there was an overlap, and benefits to one would be liabilities to the other.* Compaq, which had no such conflict, went to the 386 and almost immediately stole sales from IBM. By the time IBM realized the mistake, it was too late to recover. The joke within the industry was that Compaq was making the best IBM desktop.

Apple, which was the other challenger, had gambled by retaining its unique operating system and refusing to bow to IBM. The company rejected the Compaq approach, because its leaders were certain their software was superior to anything IBM could offer and in the end would prevail. Already it appeared a business, technological, and cultural war was brewing between IBM and Apple. It seemed at the time that all the others would join one or the other, but it didn't work out that way. By making its architecture open, IBM invited the "clones," such as Compaq, to join them. In refusing to accept clones and then clobbering another small company, Franklin, when it came out with a compatible, Apple opted for all or nothing. In effect IBM adopted Adam Osborne's approach, which is to say, it provided a single standard for the industry, based on DOS, while Apple rejected it. This also would mean that Commodore, Radio Shack, and the others would either try to put out their own compatibles or go out of business.

In the fall of that year a California company called KayPro introduced its transportable. KayPro was not a start-up, but rather had been organized a quarter of a century earlier as Non-Linear Systems, the first manufacturer of digital voltmeters. At the time it was manufacturing test equipment for the aerospace industry, including the world's smallest oscilloscope. Andrew Kay, its founder and CEO, was

---

*As Peter Drucker has noted in *Managing in a Time of Great Change*, GM stumbled in a similar fashion, when the lines between its cars became fuzzy, so that Chevrolet was stealing sales from Pontiac, and so on up the line. But there was a difference. This came at a time when brand loyalties were dissolving. IBM's error came when it was synonymous with computers and after a brilliant entry into the desktop field, which it seemed destined to control.

a graduate of M.I.T. This was a highly competitive family-run operation whose owners seemed content with what they had. Andrew and
Mary Kay ran the company with Andrew's two brothers and their son,
daughter, and son-in-law. It provided a decent if not ornate life for all
the Kays. In 1982, perhaps inspired by Osborne's success, they produced their own transportable. A year later Kay was asked whether he
had intentionally tried to replace the Osborne 1. "No," he replied.

> About two or three years ago I thought it would be good to have a
> portable computer for engineers. We've done a lot of work for the
> aerospace industry, and I thought a good, solid portable computer
> would go over well within the technical trade. About two months
> into the project someone came in with the announcement for the
> Osborne 1. We've followed the Osborne 1 closely, and decided
> that our computer had a broader audience than just engineers.

KayPro's approach was sensible enough. If the public liked the
Osborne 1, it would produce machines, loaded with software, that
were superior versions of that computer, and so it did. Kay had experience, an organization, and a knowledge of marketing. Osborne had
none of these when he started out. Potential purchasers, looking at
and working on both, would usually opt for the KayPro II. (There was
a KayPro I, but it was never produced.)

At first blush the KayPro II seemed a knockoff of the Osborne, and
to a certain extent it was, but clearly represented an improvement. It
weighed about the same, but it had a gray metal case rather than the
pressboard one in the Osborne 1, but like the Osborne 1 the top was the
keyboard. The price was also the same. Like the Osborne, the KayPro II
ran on the CP/M operating system, not DOS, and had two 5.25 floppy
drives, but these held 191 K of information each, more than twice that of
the Osborne 1. It came with a bundle of software more extensive than
that offered by Osborne. As much as Osborne devotees could praise their
machines for its virtues, they had to admit it was difficult to work on that
small screen. If users attached their Osbornes to television screens, they
were no longer transportable. KayPro rectified this problem with a nine-
inch screen that was almost as large as those that came with the desktops
and was four times larger than that offered by Osborne.

McWilliams, who disliked the Osborne 1, was rhapsodic about
the KayPro II. While purchasers of the Osborne 1 "think of it as an

acceptable second computer, or an inexpensive way station en route to a full-sized computer," the KayPro II was quite a different kind of machine.

> The KayPro II, on the other hand, is all the personal computer many people may ever need. The keyboard is good. The 9-inch video screen, close up, is as comfortable to work with as most 12-inch monitors two or three feet away. The disk drive capacity is more than adequate. One may find themselves buying a KayPro II as an inexpensive, portable first computer—and never buy a second.

KayPro had good relations with its retailers. Kay had lined up some 900 independent dealers and shipped to them directly, thus eliminating distributors. KayPro surged ahead, and within a year was the fourth largest manufacturer of small computers, behind IBM, Apple, and Radio Shack. In August 1983 KayPro would be taken public, raising $30 million for the company, the funds used to finance expansion.

KayPro's success was also made possible by the decline of Osborne. By late 1982 Adam Osborne was moving in two directions. In the first place Tom Davidson had not worked out as manager; in part, Osborne later claimed, because he had developed interests in other computer companies, and Osborne suspected him of self-dealing, which is to say, awarding contracts in ways to benefit him personally. Davidson was also boasting that he, and not Osborne, was behind the company's successes, while Osborne alone was responsible for shortcomings. Davidson was fired in September, with Osborne taking on the tasks of trying to find someone capable of running the company while he concentrated on products and marketing. The second direction was to mount an initial public offering of Osborne stock.

The executive he tapped for leadership seemed impressive: Michael Schulhof, recently president of Sony of America. But Schulhof declined, telling Osborne that a new president might mess things up by trying to recast what could be a fine operation in his own image. This was not the time for such a person.

The next choice was just the kind of person Schulhof had warned against. Robert Jaunich II, executive vice president of the $6 billion Consolidated Foods Corp., had amassed a fine record in marketing, but didn't have much of a background in technology or computers. He was responsible for a successful advertising campaign while vice president for sales at audiotape manufacturer Memorex, but had no input into the product itself. Jaunich's most important field assignment had been as product manager for Shasta, a soft drink. Later, when Apple's Steve Jobs selected Pepsico's John Scully as his successor as CEO, some remembered that Osborne had done something very much like this.

In making the announcement Osborne described Jaunich as "a good listener who comes up with good solutions." The reasons Jaunich took the job were obvious, and similar to those that would attract Scully to Apple. He was at least five years away from the CEO job at Consolidated Foods, and there were no assurances that at the end of that period it would be his. He had the chance to make the switch from the mundane world of foods to the glamorous one of computers.

Even so, it appeared Jaunich might not come after all when he was named president of Consolidated Foods. Osborne had offered him the post of chief operating officer. Now that he had more leverage, Jaunich asked to be made chief executive officer. Osborne agreed. In effect, he was turning the company over to an outsider from the food business. Osborne would remain at the company, however, and felt he had more than enough influence with the board to block or even dismiss Jaunich should this become necessary. As for Jaunich, he must have felt that Osborne was small enough so that he could make a difference—and a reputation. Finally, although his remuneration was not released to the press, Osborne was in the habit of awarding stock options to those who worked with him. Jaunich arrived in January 1983 with a salary of $150,000 a year and options to purchase 100,000 shares of stock at $16 a share.

Soon Adam Osborne realized the selection of Jaunich had been a mistake. "Jaunich and I are as different as two men can be," he wrote in 1984. "This became abundantly clear within weeks of his arrival and was subsequently reinforced in the few conversations we ever had as one human being to another. Jaunich is closed, analytical, and intense. I am open, intuitive, and generally easygoing. Jaunich has a vicious temper that constantly simmers just below his carefully controlled exterior. I rarely get angry."

By then it had been decided that Osborne 1 owners who wanted the double-density and 80-column upgrades could get them by bringing their computer back to the dealers, who would ship them to the factory. The plan was for Osborne workers to make the changes and get them back to the stores within a week. It didn't work out that way.

Insufficient upgrade boards were delivered, and in the end boards had to be removed from the production line where the new machines were being manufactured. Then it turned out that the 80-column boards didn't work the way they were supposed to, and in March the company stopped performing upgrades altogether. Everyone was angry—the old owners who didn't get their machines back in the promised time, the dealers who had been promised delivery, and Jaunich, who was dismayed at the performance.

In this period Osborne announced it was prepared to release the new Executive machine, more powerful and with a larger screen than the Osborne 1, and priced at $2,495. A year earlier Osborne had complained that "the industry has lost its drive to push prices down." Instead, he was pushing them up.

The announcement had an opposite effect to what Osborne had expected. Now that the new machine was supposed to be ready, the dealers canceled their orders for the Osborne 1 and held back on those for the Executive. Then the release of the Executive, scheduled for April 1, was delayed, and then delayed again, this time because Jaunich wasn't convinced their quality was acceptable and wanted to wait until he was certain there would be no need for recalls. This precipitated a crisis at the company, for it not only caused a decline in sales for the existing machines, but completely destroyed Osborne's credibility. Osborne and Jaunich discussed the matter, and the talk almost ended in blows.

While Adam Osborne could spin fantasies for reporters, he could not do the same for the Securities and Exchange Commission. Jaunich went over the books and learned the fiscal 1982 financials were out of line. The loss of that $1 million for fiscal 1982, which ended in November of that year, now became public knowledge. In April Jaunich told investors that "preliminary results for the quarter ended February 26, 1983, indicate revenues of approximately $34 million and profits at approximately break even." But a few weeks later the financial press reported a leak that the company had really lost $4 million in fiscal 1982 and $2.5 million in the first quarter of 1983. Then the figures were revised once again, to a loss of $8 million on sales of $80 million for 1982 and another of $5 million for the 1983 first quarter. As a result of all this double-talk, both Osborne and Jaunich lost credibility with both Wall Street and those investors who by then had poured more than $30 million into the company.

Osborne later claimed that in late 1982 investment bankers were beating down his door seeking to take the company public, but in January he and Jaunich announced that potential underwriters said they wanted to wait until the transition to the new management team was completed, the new products were introduced, and the financial situation was clarified. With this, the plans for a public offering were scrapped, leaving Osborne Computer short of cash and close to illiquidity. Jaunich was able to extract another $12 million from those venture capitalists who had come in earlier, but that was about all the company could hope for. The more he delved into the books, Jaunich later reported, the more he realized that Osborne Computer was in no position to appear before the SEC.

Desperate, Osborne slashed the price of the Osborne 1 to $1,295, but sales continued to decline, as potential Osborne 1 buyers purchased KayPro IIs instead. The price now went to below $1,000 and the not-yet-available Executive to $1,995. Osborne took this occasion to proclaim that an Executive II was in the works and that it would be IBM-compatible. Customers reacted by concluding the action indicated the old machines would become obsolete, or the company was about to collapse, and not wanting to be stuck with "orphan" machines, sales continued their decline.

In mid-May Osborne laid off 92 workers. More would follow, as it became evident that the company was sliding. The New Jersey plant was shuttered on August 2, and much of the California workforce was laid off a few days later. By early September there were only 80 employees left.

ITT approached the company with the thought of a buyout, but decided it would be better to take over after it went bankrupt. Some of Osborne's creditors came together to lend him $600,000, in the hope this would save the company. Sensing road kill ahead, liquidator Robert Leviton contacted Jaunich and offered to purchase 4,000–6,000 machines for $980 each. TWA knocked on Osborne's door. It wanted to advertise Osborne 1s for $1,495 with 20,000 frequent-flyer miles thrown in.

On September 12 one of the suppliers of PC boards sued Osborne for the $4.5 million owed him, and two others followed. Within two days Osborne Computer filed for Chapter 11 bankruptcy, listing assets of $40 million and liabilities of $45 million, with 600 creditors out in the cold. This prompted investors to sue the company and its officers for $8.5 million in damages, and in the filing they accused them of deliberately deceiving them regarding the company's finances, operations, and earnings. With this, Adam Osborne went into seclusion.

When IBM came out with its transportable in 1984, critics judged it inferior to the Compaq, which had a better screen and was easier to attach to a printer. The IBM machine was two pounds heavier than the Compaq and $200 more expensive, but Ben Rosen, now Compaq's Chairman, thought IBM's reputation would win many customers. "We are being tarred with the failure of others," he said, perhaps thinking of Osborne. The following year, *Fortune* noted that the Compaq was outselling the IBM transportable by a margin of five to one. This was due to one simple fact, said writer Brian O'Reilly. "Compaq has yet to make a serious mistake."

What could be said of Adam Osborne? O'Reilly went on to note that Compaq executives were reluctant to discuss plans for future computers. "Canion and Rosen remember what happened to Osborne Computer Corp.'s hot-selling portable: customers stopped buying it after Adam Osborne began talking up a new machine, helping to push the company into bankruptcy." That was one of his mistakes; there were many more.

As a columnist Osborne had criticized others for their financial irresponsibility, premature product announcement, raising instead of lowering prices, product incompatibility, and more. As a failed entrepreneur he blamed Jaunich for the company's demise, noting that at the time he was not an officer at the company.

Not willing to admit his own shortcomings, Osborne told the press he was not finished as a player in the field. There would be an attempt to bring out the Vixen and the organization of Paperback Software, an operation he meant to act as a marketing cooperative for small software writers. "I was right about the computer business," said an unrepentant Adam Osborne, "and I know I'm right about the software business." Not really. Some of the products were strikingly similar to those already on the market, which led to a lawsuit filed by Lotus that complicated his life.

While it might appear Adam Osborne was not fit for the tasks of management, it should be noted that such usually is the case with new industries, which by their very nature are populated by young people who are writing new chapters in the history of business. Consider that roster of automobile companies with which this chapter began. Most of them met the same fate as did Osborne, and for similar reasons. Then consider that at the time of the Osborne failure the likes of Texas Instruments, Atari, and Mattel were reporting huge losses on their personal computer businesses. KayPro, Osborne's major competitor, failed to convert to the IBM standard fast enough, came out with some products that did not meet with favorable reception, and it, too, failed. IBM was to have a disaster with its PCJr., and Coleco with its Adam. Within a year of the Osborne failure there were some 60 different portable computers from which to select, and most of these companies would fail as the pace of technological change, the need for financing, and inadequate management brought them down by the score. Vector Graphic, Morrow, Otrana, Escort, Teleram, Fortune, Intertec Data Systems, Grid, Coleco, Chameleon, Zorba, Televideo, Eagle—the list goes on and on. Adam Osborne had the right idea. He just didn't know where to go with it. The difference between Osborne and the other failures was that he had soared so high before crashing. Even at the end, the company was perceived as more substantial than it really was. On September 14, the day of the company's bankruptcy filing, *The San Francisco Examiner* headlined the story, "Major Computer Firm Fails." It says something about the nature of the industry in this period that Osborne was considered a "major" firm. So it was, but more accurately, it was a pioneer firm in its niche. As Andrew Carnegie once remarked, "Pioneering doesn't pay." Perhaps not, but Carnegie was a pioneer himself. The aphorism might be altered to "Pioneering doesn't pay, if you suffer from serious flaws."

When big companies in established industries make mistakes, they usually manage to survive. Coca-Cola, IBM, General Motors, RJR Nabisco, Federated Department Stores—the list is endless—all overcame errors of judgment. Montgomery Ward lasted for decades after it lost its way. Not so small companies in new industries. There the casualty count is high, and survivorship is dependent as much on simple good fortune as on errors of competitors, intelligence, skills, and superb leadership, products, and services. The success of Compaq and the failure of Osborne indicate as much.

E. J. KORVETTE:
THE BLUNDER OF HUBRIS

I n his essay, *The Hedgehog and the Fox*, Isaiah Berlin quoted the Greek poet Archilochus as writing, "The fox knows many things, but the hedgehog knows one big thing." Foxes—those entrepreneurs and managers who can move easily from one business or product to another—are often found in corporate America. More common until fairly recently, however, are the hedgehogs, who devote a lifetime to one industry. The same is true of corporations themselves. Now and then a product or service appears that fills a niche perfectly. The hedgehog companies remain devoted to it, concentrating on refining and honing it and seeking new markets. As will be seen, for most of his career David Sarnoff, a hedgehog, grew RCA from radio-receiver manufacture to radio stations to networks, phonographs and then records, motion-picture theaters and a studio, talent agencies, and so on. Almost everything he was interested in, however, had some relationship to entertainment and electronics. Even so, there was a touch of the fox in him as well, such as his foray into refrigerators and air conditioners. Many businesspeople combine elements of both.

Minnesota Mining & Manufacturing is one of those hybrids that fashioned its success out of extensions of existing talents and capabilities, but also was willing to stretch a bit. It began with a mine from which the founders hoped to extract corundum, a mineral used in grinding wheels. They did not find corundum, but rather anorthosite, which was not nearly as hard. Anorthosite could be used in sandpaper manufacture, and so those founders made do with what they had. Sandpaper required adhesives to bind the sand to the paper, and the company developed them. Out of that came a cloth abrasive known as

Three-M-Ite, and then the company purchased the rights to a water-proof sandpaper, Wetordry, which had a huge market in the automobile industry in the painting of cars. Of course, there were losers, such as a new automobile wax, which, however, brought the company into a yet closer relationship with the automobile industry.

3M learned the auto manufacturers needed masking tape for use in two-tone paint jobs, and so it developed such a product, and it was a short hop to the famous Scotch Tape. The step from there to Thermo-Fax and Post-it notes was both logical and clear. But there were more losers, such as "Mmm! What a Tan!" suntan lotion. That came from adhesives—the lotion was advertised as remaining on the skin longer than products turned out by competitors. Such are the ways of hedgehogs who at times become foxy.

In contrast, foxes are rarely content with past and present achievements. Encouraged by accomplishments in one field, managements attempt to extend operations into unchartered areas in the hope that horizontal or vertical expansion will enable them to repeat successes in others. As will be seen, the conglomerateurs that proliferated during the 1960s were the archetypical foxes, and none was foxier than James Ling, to whom a chapter is devoted. Foxes rarely attempt to behave like hedgehogs, since it isn't in their nature. When, due to business opportunities, hedgehogs play the role of foxes they invariably fail. Talents and proclivities suited to one product, service, or industry usually are inappropriate for others.

Berlin might have classified the young Eugene Ferkauf as a hedgehog, since originally he had one central organizing revelation that made him the undisputed king of discount marketing. Had he stopped there, or expanded upon his base more logically, he might have gone on to successes not only in the United States, but throughout the world. Instead, he attempted to expand upon that base, as did 3M so successfully, and fashioned a merchandising empire that at one time encompassed 58 department stores and earned him a place, alongside Rowland Macy, A. T. Stewart, Bernard Gimbel, Frank Woolworth, and Aaron Montgomery Ward, on *Fortune*'s roster of great merchants. What happened to the creations of these men is one of the sadder tales in American business history. Montgomery Ward is a dwindling, minor force, to which a chapter of this book will be devoted. Macy's fell into bankruptcy in 1991. Woolworth closed in

1998. Stewart and Gimbel are only memories. So are the stores Ferkauf managed, known as E. J. Korvette, which were shuttered on Christmas Eve, 1980. The flair Ferkauf demonstrated in discounting home appliances and the like couldn't be transferred to clothing and merchandise that sold on the basis of style.

Gene Ferkauf came to retailing naturally. His father, Harry, ran two luggage stores, known as Rex Luggage, in midtown Manhattan, one on Fifth Avenue, the other on Lexington. These were reasonably successful. In a highly competitive business, with a dozen other luggage stores within walking distance, Harry maintained a large selection of goods, prided himself on excellent service, and offered competitive prices. But then, so did the other stores that survived during the Great Depression. Harry assumed Gene would inherit them one day.

To prepare for his own career, Gene took a year of accounting courses at City College of New York, whereupon he became a salesman at one of the stores. Service in the Army during World War II followed, and upon discharge in 1945 he was to return to Rex.

Gene indeed was interested in retailing, but had larger ambitions than could be realized in his father's stores. He had heard of a luggage wholesaler named Charles Wolf who operated in lower Manhattan— an area in which the cognoscenti knew bargains were to be found. Wolf sold luggage to retailers at the usual markup, but also distributed his business cards, which contained a message offering a discount when presented at his storage depot. Without knowing it, this unknown wholesaler had originated discounting. He was not a retailer, however, an important point at this time, for had he acted as he did from such a location, he would have been in violation of a law that had passed during the tail end of the New Deal.

This legislation arose from the Great Depression. One of the earliest and most ambitious programs of the early New Deal had been the National Recovery Administration. Under the leadership of General Hugh Johnson, the NRA was charged with drawing up codes of fair competition for most American industries, from brooms to automobiles. The idea was to shape working hours, wages, trade practices, and all else affecting business behavior. It was the most ambitious attempt to regulate the economy ever made during peacetime, which supporters believed would eliminate some of the anomalies of capitalism and opponents called the coming of American fascism.

Among those business practices to be controlled was pricing. Prices were to be fixed; competitors could not undercut each other in the marketplace. This seemed reasonable enough at the time. Unemployment was at 25 percent, and the economy was in shambles. Competitors would do almost anything to win customers, including harsh price cutting. In addition, the large retailers could club the small ones into dissolution by vigorous predatory pricing. This led to lower wages and profits, more business failures, and more unemployment.

The NRA was declared unconstitutional in 1935, and with this the experiment with fixed prices came to an end, but not the rationale that supported them. Some states passed fair-trade laws, and in 1937 Congress passed and President Roosevelt signed the Robinson-Patman Act, the centerpiece of which was a new fair-trade provision that obliged retailers to charge prices fixed by the manufacturer. The purpose of the measure was to deny chain stores and other large retailers advantages they might obtain from discounts resulting from quantity purchases. In this way, mom-and-pop operations would be able to survive competition from Woolworth's, Macy's, and other large retailers that might cut prices in order to increase market share. The law extended to such products as electric razors, fountain pens, radios, and the like, but not to foodstuffs and clothing, where there either was little attempt to enforce the law or differentiation was so great as to make comparisons impossible. By the end of World War II, however, the law was pretty much a dead letter, because extensive and aggressive price cutting on branded items rarely if ever took place. Price wars on such items, as is seen today, did not occur, although there was plenty of competitive pricing.

Competitive pricing was hardly new; Harry Ferkauf practiced it at his small shops, and Macy's and Gimbel's usually tried to do the same from their opposite sides of 34th Street. Just about everyone who purchased a car prior to the war haggled with salespeople. This wasn't difficult to do with cars, clothing, and furniture, but it was another matter with heavily advertised branded items such as the aforementioned shavers and fountain pens. Retailers who attempted to charge less than "manufacturer's suggested prices" for such merchandise could and did face legal penalties, not from government directly, but from the larger operations that filed complaints. Some, including a retailer called "The Pep Boys, Mannie, Moe & Jack," which sold automotive parts and supplies, took the matter to the Supreme Court and lost. In 1948 the subject seemed settled: Branded merchandise could not be sold below what the manufacturer wanted it to be sold for.

Such was the situation Gene Ferkauf faced during the postwar period. He knew of the Robinson-Patman Act, but also that now-forgotten luggage salesman who eluded the law during the late 1930s. Perhaps he could do the same.

Move up to the summer of 1948. The economy was booming, as the anticipated post-World War II recession had failed to materialize. The housing shortage was far from being overcome in New York City, and apartment houses were sprouting in Queens, the Bronx, and Brooklyn, while Levittown and other major projects were underway on Long Island. The baby boom was in full swing, and owners and renters were installing washers and dryers, upgrading their other household appliances, and even considering the purchase of their first television set. Young people born in the early 1930s were entering high schools and colleges, while millions of former servicepeople financed by the G.I. Bill of Rights, were hitting the books. The market for "white goods" such as large home appliances was larger than ever. So was that for stationery supplies. Other branded products, from jewelry to watches to luggage to cigarette lighters were doing fine. Ferkauf observed all of this and acted upon his instincts and knowledge.

In June 1948, Ferkauf opened his first E. J. Korvette store on 46th Street, not far from Fifth Avenue and Rockefeller Center, where rents were low. It was a small operation, on the second floor, and the entrance was difficult to locate. There was no window display, no large sign. It didn't look like a retail store, and Ferkauf didn't say it was one. Rather, it was a "membership store," which was Ferkauf's way around the fair-trade laws.

In those early days Korvette was staffed by the guys from Brooklyn with whom Ferkauf had grown up and trusted. As teenagers they had played stickball in the streets, gone to the movies together, and did all the other things Brooklyn teenagers from middle-class homes did in those days. Most of the original staff of 38 had graduated from Samuel J. Tilden or Erasmus Hall high school and hadn't gone to college. They were known, collectively, as "the boys." Others who came in soon after did so through marriage or friendship. In addition to Joe Zwillenberg there was Murray Beilenson, whose father owned the local luncheonette and learned how to handle consumer products in the Army

Quartermaster Corp. David Thorne, Ferkauf's brother-in-law, entered the company; George Yellen, who was Zwillenberg's brother-in-law, was another recruit. Abe Goldstein, also from Brooklyn, ran into Ferkauf during the war, when both were stationed in Camp Crowder, Missouri. Mel Friedman, another friend, convinced William Willensky, a fire department lieutenant, who later became president of E. J. Korvette, to come over. Friedman, who was to become executive vice president, told an interviewer, "I knew Gene from Brooklyn. He lived on Rockaway Boulevard and Church Avenue and I lived at Rockaway Boulevard and Willmohr." Leo Cohen told how it was done: "I was in the men's clothing business for three years and had no thought of joining Korvette. Then I met Mel Friedman, whom I had known from the old neighborhood. I knew Ferkauf, too, and he painted a great picture. I joined. I had a variety of jobs the first few years, selling jewelry, managing the photography department, and then I became an assistant manager of the small Hempstead store where Bill Willensky was manager." They were a genial, somewhat rough bunch, who worked hard, had penchants for big cigars, married their childhood sweethearts, and gobbled fast dinners at the closest greasy spoon.

Soon word of E. J. Korvette spread. What did the name stand for? people wondered. Later it would be asserted it was named by the founder as a short way of saying "Eight Korean War Veterans," which clearly wasn't the case, since the Korean War was two years away. Rather, the E. was for Eugene, the J. for Joe Zwillenberg, and Korvette was a different way of spelling Corvette, which was a Canadian fighting ship of World War II vintage. Ferkauf thought it sounded classy.

Ferkauf's approach was simplicity itself. The staff consisted of those friends, who now were salesmen, stockboys, and did anything else that required doing. They would arrive at work around 7:30 A.M., fill in inventories of fountain pens, watches, shavers, lighters, jewelry, juicers, and all else. They would be at their posts for the 8:30 opening. Some of the salesmen would station themselves outside the store to hand out flyers listing the recommended selling price of selected items, along with Korvette's price, which was around a third lower than what was charged at the department and jewelry stores. Individuals taking the flyers were told E. J. Korvette was open only to members. The hawker then would hand a membership card to the questioner, who now was authorized to enter Korvette.

Once inside, shoppers would proceed to one or another of the display cases that lined the walls, behind each of which was a salesman. The customer would point to, say, an electric razor, and note the list price was $24.98. When asked the Korvette price the salesman either would announce it from memory or look at a small sticker, which might have read "846613." The customer might have thought this a stock code, but the salesman knew otherwise. He would drop the first and last numbers, then reverse the others, and tell the customer it would cost him or her $16.64 plus sales tax.

Korvette did not offer credit; all sales were for cash, though the customer could return most purchases for a full refund in a set time, usually a week. Korvette would not make deliveries on larger items such as television sets, and there might be only one of each offered on the floor. The customer would be told this was so because the store had limited storage space.

Korvette would order major appliances from the manufacturer and let the distributor hold the stock and make deliveries, with the customer paying on delivery. Some critics charged Korvette with buying on consignment, in effect taking orders for merchandise it didn't actually have on hand. Korvette conceded its suppliers often would make refunds on unsold merchandise.

After a while the leaflet suppliers outside the store would switch places with the salesmen inside. So it would go into the night. When the store closed at around 6:00 P.M. all would sweep up, lock up, walk to the subway, and return to their Brooklyn homes. For this they would receive around $80 a week plus a generous year-end bonus. This was more than the pay of salespeople at Manhattan department stores, but they worked harder—six days a week, or 48 hours, versus the 40 hours at the conventional retailers. The hole-in-the-wall operation was always packed. During Christmas rush the salesmen would work through the night, sleeping on the floor. In that first year Korvette did close to a million dollars in sales, which worked out to $2,500 per square foot. Inventory turned over an astonishing 30 times a year.

One of Ferkauf's more difficult problems was with customers who felt something must be wrong with the products if they were priced so low. Although there was no policy decision on this issue, the pace of business resolved it for Ferkauf. The salesmen were so busy they couldn't spend much time with individual customers and also tended to be brusque, though not discourteous. The first time Ferkauf learned a salesman had been rude, he would be warned, and the next time, fired. "I know why things cost so much more at Macy's" one customer was heard to say. "There they treat you like human beings. They don't at E. J. Korvette." She figured a warm smile and patience wasn't worth the 30 percent higher price at Macy's. She shopped at Korvette.

In 1951 Korvette opened a second store, this one on the ground floor, on 42nd Street near Third Avenue, across the street from a Horn & Hardardt Automat restaurant, within a few steps of the elevated train, and a short walk from United Nations headquarters. Ferkauf figured the closeness to transportation and the 42nd Street crowds would bring in one kind of clientele, while UN workers would mob the place during lunch hours to get appliances and other wares to send home to consumer-products-hungry relatives and friends overseas. It worked. There were long lines outside the store from 11:00 A.M. to 2:00 P.M., and foreign workers would buy a dozen Remington shavers or a gross of Parker 51 and 21 fountain pens at a clip. The salesmen weren't surprised. They would descend into the basement and bring up cartons of merchandise every ten minutes or so.

Ferkauf opened new stores whenever a promising site eventuated. A third store was opened on 48th Street in 1954, soon followed by the fourth in a storefront in suburban White Plains; the fifth was opposite the Rockefeller Center skating rink, the sixth an abandoned supermarket in Hempstead, New York. All were discount operations; all sold the same kind of merchandise as in that first store.

And all the while Ferkauf had running battles with the department stores and in some cases manufacturers the more conventional retailers had prodded into action. In this period Korvette did no advertising; none was necessary. The New York newspapers carried stories of legal actions brought against Korvette by Macy's and other stores due to Ferkauf's low-price policy; readers learned of the store and rushed to buy. Temporary restraining orders were regular affairs, but Ferkauf was learning how to deal with them. Once Parker Pen managed to have a judge issue one forbidding Korvette from selling the pens at a discount. Ferkauf responded by giving away a Parker pencil with each pen. When that was blocked, he would give away cigarette lighters or some other non-Parker product.

By 1956 there had been 35 fair trade lawsuits filed against Korvette. Most either were dismissed or dropped. In one of the Parker cases the judge found for Korvette, and after that there were few complaints, since the manufacturers and retailers were learning that the publicity was hurting them. In time the Robinson-Patman Act was repealed. By then discounting had become a way of life; we now know the main thrust of the Ferkauf revolution was over, but it didn't appear so in the second half of the 1950s.

E. J. Korvette grew exponentially. For 1950, the first year for which accurate figures are available, revenues came to $2 million, while profits were $27,000. For 1954 revenues came to $17.8 million, and profits were $353,000.

By then some quite conventional problems associated with rapid growth surfaced. One of these was the matter of personnel. In 1954 Ferkauf started hiring part-time salespeople, and soon after was taking on full-time workers as well. These new people lacked the dedication of the old timers, and many found it difficult to stand the pace. Then, too, Ferkauf's reliance upon personal relationships proved troublesome. "He runs Korvette as if it were a high-school fraternity," said a former executive. "If you are a friend, you can get away with anything, even incompetence. But it's almost impossible to be a friend unless you were with him before the tenth store. If you came later, it doesn't matter how strong or loyal you are." In personnel, this is a recipe for disaster, as both the old and new hires resented one another, creating divisions and inviting bitterness and charges of favoritism.

Hiring remained on a haphazard basis. For example, a part-time salesman, a New York University graduate student who attended classes at night and worked the 11:00 A.M to 3:00 P.M. shift at the store, told Willensky in 1956 he would soon be leaving to seek a position as a university professor. "Forget about quitting," Willensky replied. "Go back to school and take some courses in accounting. You have a future at Korvette." The salesman had no interest in accounting, but Willensky persisted. "We're going to be the biggest retailer in America. We'll need accountants." It hardly was the usual way of recruiting personnel. The young man left anyway. Not only did he have no interest in this kind of career, but like so many others who had learned of Ferkauf's plans to rival Macy's, thought that this was not likely to take place.

Then there was the matter of financing. The rapid expansion strained the treasury. In opening his 48th Street store Ferkauf came up short, so he asked his salesmen to invest in the operation. So they did, raising $150,000. It paid off, and in the first year his investors earned 30 percent on their money.

At this point Ferkauf decided the next step was to expand into new and unfamiliar lines of merchandise, an attempt to transform E. J. Korvette into a "promotional department-store" chain. This was not a novel idea. John Wanamaker, who had started out in men's clothing, had opened the Grand Depot, the first true department store, in 1876, having done so after a long period of study, preparation, and consultation. "All but one solitary man thought I was going to fail," Wanamaker said, "that one being myself." Ferkauf was equally convinced that he would succeed, but he went ahead without making the required kind of preparations.

While possessing a fine intuition, Ferkauf was unorganized and unfocused. He conducted business on the run, didn't have an office or secretary, and told reporters he never wrote or dictated letters, preferring the telephone or face-to-face contacts. This was not a major obstacle when it came to those small discount stores, where he could direct his old friends and their old friends from the field. But that was about to change.

In late 1955 Ferkauf erected his first department store. He had selected his site carefully. It was at an open field in Carle Place, Long Island, not far from the Roosevelt Field Mall where Macy's was thinking about putting up a store. He needed at least $500,000 for the effort, a large sum in the mid-1950s, more than had been required for all the other stores combined. Of this $300,000 would go for fixtures and the rest for working capital. Ferkauf chipped in $100,000, the boys another $200,000, the builders, Kane & Schwartz, took a $100,000 share, and other friends came up with the last $100,000. To stock the store Ferkauf took in $1.7 million in merchandise on credit.

The work on the store had to be rushed, since Ferkauf hoped to open in time for the Christmas season. Staffing was a problem; some of the veterans were transferred from the discount stores, but hundreds of new hires were made. Ferkauf was dazzled by the prospects, but worried about personnel, financing, site location, and the scores of other problems large retailers faced.

There were signs of strain in all of these areas, but the early returns were promising. The store was a huge success. On its first day the area was hit with traffic jams that caused lateness in nearby businesses and as far away as Hofstra College in Hempstead. There were lines outside the store starting at around 7:00 A.M., with customers hoping to pick up bargains advertised in *The Long Island Press* and *Newsday*.

Those who had shopped the Korvette discount houses found this new promotional department store was quite different from either the old discount operations and the familiar Sears, Montgomery Ward, and Macy's stores. To be sure, there was that barebones appearance, and it was obvious by cracks that already had appeared where walls met ceilings the building had been constructed rapidly and rather cheaply. But they also found clothing, linen, and other "soft goods" that hadn't been available at the discount houses. There even would be a food market, run at a loss, to attract customers. Korvette used to be compared with Masters, Vim, and other discounters that had appeared during the previous years. Now it was being likened to Klein's, a cut-rate clothing store that had a branch in nearby Hempstead.

Yet it was different. Put aside those cheap fixtures and the voice that came in over the loudspeaker every 15 minutes or so to announce specials and you had Macy's, Gimbel's, Abraham & Strauss, or any other department store—with lower prices, but the same familiar personnel. If one looked carefully he or she might spot a rather rugged-looking character in a dark suit, his white shirt seeming too tight at the collar, the patent leather shoes a trifle gaudy. Those with long memories would place him as one of Ferkauf's Brooklyn pals, John Duddy, a clerk who sold electric razors and fountain pens in the 42nd Street store. He was now a manager.

"Korvette City" as it was called, was a huge success, the first of several in 1955. That was the year Korvette sold its initial stock issue, with Loeb, Rhoades placing 1.2 million shares at $10 a share. Now Ferkauf had additional funds for expansion. Within a year the stock stood at 22. Ferkauf was a millionaire at a time when that meant something. The boys weren't there yet, but they seemed on their way.

There also was talk of a merger between Korvette and J. W. May, Alexander's, or Ohrbach's, respected veterans whose stress was on soft goods. It seemed a natural. Ferkauf had no experience with soft goods, which the other three could supply, while through Korvette they could participate in the most exciting development in retailing of the post-World War II period. It didn't work out due to personal frictions, but Korvette did the next best thing; it purchased 42 percent of privately owned Alexander's for $9.7 million.

Ferkauf continued his practice of visiting at least one of his stores a day. As he always had, he refused to spend a single evening away from home. He wore the familiar sports shirts, rejected suggestions he have an office or at least a desk, and the telephone receptionist took his calls. But now he prowled the countryside seeking new sites for stores. He found them in New Jersey, Connecticut, and Pennsylvania. Quietly those six small discount stores were closed; Korvette was wholly in the department-store business.

Ferkauf opened new stores at a rapid pace—one every other month for a while—and the personnel was stretched thin. Profits were high, but margins were slipping. Ferkauf was learning that he could make far more money on easy-to-sell branded items such as TV sets than he could on clothing. Korvette's dresses and suits weren't as stylish as they might have been, indicating a weakness in purchasing. It was one thing to take dozens of RCA television sets, something else to try to purchase ties, underwear, and the like.

Revenues rose from $17.8 million in 1954 to $54.8 million in 1956 and then went over $100 million in 1958, by which time Korvette had 12 stores. In 1956 *Fortune* noted that Korvette's total sales had gone up an astonishing 2,650 percent over what they had been six years earlier. But strains were showing in higher costs of doing business, and the chain's expenses were skyrocketing.

Ferkauf recognized his weaknesses, and in the late 1950s and early 1960s actively sought a merger partner from among retailers with management depth. None appeared. Even so, Ferkauf was able to hire executives from other bargain department stores such as Klein's, Ohrbach's, and Alexander's. In time they might be able to do for apparel what he himself had done for television sets and refrigerators.

In 1961 Ferkauf announced that Jack Schwadron, the manager of Alexander's fashion business, would join Korvette. Schwadron became a director and general merchandise manager, and three years later he was named president and chief operating officer. With this move, Ferkauf signaled his recognition that the boys who had performed so well in the discount houses were out of their depth when it came to running what soon would be a $200 million company. In addition, he indicated that the time would soon arrive for him to leave the company. Running a major retail enterprise had its moments, but Ferkauf appeared to have enjoyed himself more in those small discount stores, where life was simpler. Increasingly, he turned command over to Schwadron, who relished the authority given him. "Our major task is to see that our profit margins move along with our volume," Schwadron told a reporter. "Our profitability has been hampered by the rapidity with which we have opened new stores. But we have finally been able to build the kind of base from which we can develop profitably into a nationwide company."

Schwadron had still more ambitious ideas. While at Alexander's he had attempted to win approval for a move into high fashion that would lead the company into competition with the best Fifth Avenue stores. He had failed to convince management there of the potential of such a move. Now Schwadron painted the picture for Ferkauf. Korvette could be the kind of store that sold jeans to students, but also fur coats to society matrons. Would they buy? If you could sell $10 jeans for $6 and draw them in, why wouldn't $2,000 coats for $1,200 do the same?

This was the chimera that would ultimately destroy Korvette.

Meanwhile the store openings continued, with Korvette taking positions in the Chicago and Baltimore markets, but the most important developments were in Manhattan. In 1962 Korvette opened a store on 47th Street and Fifth Avenue, within walking distance of some of the world's most upscale stores. Imagine. Brooks Brothers, Tiffany, Lord & Taylor—and now, E. J. Korvette! Years later, when sidewalk peddlers invaded Fifth Avenue, the old-time patricians would sniff that it all began with Korvette.

Even so, the Fifth Avenue store did well. It sold upscale items at discount prices, and this led to the same kinds of problems Ferkauf had encountered when he started out. Just as Parker and Remington protested when he sold pens and shavers at discounted prices, so manufacturers of fashionable sweaters and suits tried to keep their products out of Korvette. Ferkauf responded by cutting the names off labels. If the buyer wanted the sweater and the label, she could pay $60. But if she were willing to take the sweater alone, the price would be $40. The manufacturers settled. The Fifth Avenue store was a success, and Korvette stock responded. Adjusted for a 3–1 split in late 1961, it sold for close to 170 in the summer of 1962.

When asked whether Korvette might develop a form of corporate schizophrenia, given the mix of Fifth Avenue and Carle Place, Murray Beilenson responded: "If you stand on Fifth Avenue and watch the taxis stop and watch the customers walk in with Bonwit Teller, Lord & Taylor, or Henri Bendel bags, you begin to understand it isn't schizophrenia; it's the fact that everyone loves a bargain. We have Cadillacs that pull up to the store, and women get out and enjoy, as everybody enjoys, being able to buy something a little bit cheaper than they normally would."

Even so, familiar problems soon developed at the new store. Ferkauf treated it as though it wasn't much different from Carle Place. The merchandise might be more upscale, but the place itself soon became shabby. Within a few years the carpets were stained, the paint faded, the elevators creaky. By 1965 those Cadillacs no longer stopped at the door, and suburban customers and those from the outer boroughs didn't trek to Manhattan to get bargains they might find locally.

Not only did Korvette have the Fifth Avenue store, but Ferkauf, who had developed a taste for fine art, opened an art gallery in Douglaston, Queens, where paintings selling for more than $50,000 were displayed. Some change from those shavers and pens! Like so many Ferkauf sallies, this was a hobby and diversion and never made money.

Ferkauf had been a visionary, and he remained one. There were plans for making a big splash in California and taking the Korvette idea to the United Kingdom and new kinds of specialty stores. Ferkauf had demonstrated an ability to manage discount stores and even those first department stores. He was ambitious. "All I want for this company is that it should do all the merchandising business in the United States," he once remarked.

There remained nagging problems regarding performance. Revenues were rising steadily—they would be over $500 million in 1965, but profits were meager—$17 million. What was the use of being big if you couldn't be profitable? The food business was a loser, and Ferkauf didn't know what to do about it. Soft goods now accounted for 40 percent of sales, and clothing most of that. Schwadron hadn't been able to work miracles there. Ferkauf still didn't have anyone who knew how to wring profits out of that business. His furniture lessee, H. L. Klion, went belly-up, and this forced

Ferkauf into another business he knew little about. Impulsively, he purchased Federal Carpet, yet another unfamiliar area.

Finally sensing that Schwadron was moving too fast to create a new image, and not at all certain his policy made sense, Ferkauf moved boldly to solve that problem and the ones related to the losses in food. In February 1965 Korvette purchased Hill's Supermarkets, a Long Island-based operation. Three months later its CEO, Hilliard J. Coan, became chairman, with Schwadron moving to the presidency and Ferkauf to the chairmanship of the executive committee. With this, Ferkauf ceased exercising day-to-day control of Korvette.

Coan brought a sense of order to Korvette, plugging losses, computerizing operations, and attempting to rein in some of Ferkauf's expansion plans. He failed in this last effort. On June 4, 1965, Ferkauf announced he would take over the troubled Saks-34th Street store, next to Macy's and Gimbel's. Schwadron put on a brave front, while displaying his growing schizophrenic outlook toward the business. "We'll continue to keep our prices below our competitors and yet give good service. And we hope to bring Fifth Avenue high style to 34th Street." Korvette closed it down, started pouring funds into the shabby store, and remodeled the facade. All of this took more than a year—and much more money than Schwadron had anticipated spending. In the end the facade and interior of the new Korvette made for a flamboyant, cheap-looking building. It attracted crowds of bargain hunters the first few weeks, but then activity slowed down. The store was profitable, but Macy's and Gimbel's had little to fear from their new neighbor.

Schwadron wasn't around to see the opening. A week after the announcement he "resigned" from Korvette, signaling that Coan's star was on the rise. Winning increasing support from the board, Coan was able to block Ferkauf's attempts to invade the California market.

Ferkauf seemed eager to share power. Sales were expanding, and it appeared reasonable to expect Korvette to be a billion-dollar corporation by the end of the 1960s. The chain had grown to 45 stores in nine metropolitan areas. "When a business is small, you can put your arms around it," said Ferkauf plaintively. "When it gets big, it needs other arms, too."

Statements such as this could not mask what was becoming increasingly evident. Ferkauf was tired of operating a company that for reasons of temperament and inclination he could not control. He was still quite young—in his early forties—and could move on to something else. But he didn't want to be supplanted by Coan, whom he had grown to resent. By the end of the year there was talk of Coan, too, resigning, to take a position at Sears Roebuck.

There was another way out. In 1966 Ferkauf met Charles Bassine, an apparel manufacturer who also operated Spartan Industries, which among other holdings had Spartan-Atlantic discount stores. Bassine's son, David, and Ferkauf's daughter, Barbara, were engaged. Maybe something could be worked out with the Bassines, with the business remaining in the families.

Meanwhile, Coan planned to take all authority. In May there was a showdown, with Coan asking Ferkauf to step down. Ferkauf's response came shortly thereafter. He initiated merger talks with Bassine, and in September Korvette was folded into Spartan, whereupon Coan left the company. Ferkauf joined the Spartan board, but he had no managerial authority at the stores he had founded. "My attitude today is one of relief. I feel that I have finally found the man to run the Korvette operation after many years." Bassine was characteristically optimistic. "Korvette had a sound merchandising policy, but it lacked a system of controls on knowing how much goods to buy," he said, indicating a lack of understanding of the problem. "Now it has that system."

Bassine brought tighter management to Korvette, but never solved the problem of image. He closed the supermarkets, sold off other units, as well as the stake in Alexander's. During the next few years the out-of-town stores faltered. Bassine moved farther from the discount image and clearly was trying to compete with Macy's and other conventional retailers. Prices were hiked, to the point that they were practically the same as Macy's and Gimbel's. With no reason to shop Korvette, bargain hunters went to those stores, or more likely, to other discounters, which now proliferated.

Troubled by business and domestic problems, in 1970 Bassine merged with Arlen Realty & Development, a firm that had constructed some of the Korvette stores. Arlen was controlled by Bassine's son-in-law, Arthur Cohen, who had no background in retailing. Cohen closed the furniture departments, instituted further economies, but through his tenure seemed far more interested in erecting shopping centers than in running the chain. In time he brought in a new president, Leonard Blackman, who was replaced soon after by David Brous, a seven-year Korvette veteran. Such rotation in office usually is a sign that the corporation involved was foundering. This pretty well describes Korvette in this period.

One by one "the boys" resigned or retired. Ferkauf now devoted himself to charities and a new specialty store, Bazar, which failed. Along the way he sold most of his Korvette shares. By the mid-1970s E. J. Korvette no longer had any of the attributes of that small, successful 46th Street store. More departments were closed—furniture and carpets went in 1972. Profits continued to decline. In 1973, on sales of $606 million, profits were a mere $8 million. But at least there were profits. Not for long, however; Arlen lost $22 million in 1974, and $60 million the following year.

By then it seemed clear Korvette was dying. In desperation, management asked outside agencies to study the company and come up with recommendations. Their findings were not surprising. There was no typical Korvette customer. Upscale buyers went there for low-price branded merchandise, but purchased clothing elsewhere. Poorer customers went to Korvette for bargains, and to other discounters for branded products. Attempting to come up with an answer, Arlen instituted a program called "The Other Korvette," implying there were two distinct kinds of stores. It bombed.

In 1977 Korvette reported revenues of $590 million and a loss of $4 million. Arlen's losses continued. Cohen was shopping Korvette to potential buyers. In April 1979 the French firm of Agache-Willot, which operated department stores and clothing factories, purchased 51 percent of Korvette for $31 million. Agache-Willot instituted a program of cost cutting, slashing employment to the bone. Sales fell. Losses continued. The company closed its stores for the last time in December 1980, after a disappointing holiday season.

The reason for Korvette's failure certainly wasn't Ferkauf's lack of vision, but rather his inability to integrate all of his ideas into a cohesive strategy. Other reasons were mismanagement, weak personnel and financial policies, haphazard expansion, and an inability to control costs. None of these had been a problem when Korvette was a discount chain. The company hadn't been able to make the switch to department-store status because its leaders, from Ferkauf on, could not decide what it wanted to be.

Recall Willensky's statement to that departing salesman in 1966. Like Ferkauf, he had ambitions for Korvette that included being the biggest retailer in America. Had Ferkauf stuck to discounting hard goods and had then expanded into specialty shops, he might have made the grade. Ferkauf admitted as much. After it was all over he ruefully remarked that the Carle Place store had a separate 10,000-square-foot toy store. "Why didn't we go into a separate chain like Toys R Us?" he asked. Had Korvette done this, he suggested, it would have performed superbly. But the company did have separate furniture stores and supermarkets, and these did poorly.

Barely noted in all of this was an action taken by Professor Malcolm McNair of the Harvard Graduate School of Business. Considered one of the major experts on retailing, some dozen or so years earlier McNair had published a list of the greatest merchants in American history. Gene Ferkauf was the only one still alive. Now McNair removed him from the list.

To consider how highly Ferkauf was appraised at the height of his celebrity, one only has to regard the others on the McNair roster. There was Frank Woolworth, who developed the variety store, and J. C. Penney, founder of the chain department stores. General Robert E. Wood, who as will be seen transformed Sears Roebuck from a mail order house to the world's largest retailer, was on the list. So was Michael Cullen, who thought up the idea of supermarkets and organized the first one, King Kullen. Finally, John Wanamaker was on the honor roll. Wanamaker did it right.

Regard the case of another company that did it right. Kresge became a discounter in 1962, the year Korvette opened the Fifth Avenue store that marked its change of direction. As noted, there were many store chains imitating the Korvette approach, and the new company, renamed Kmart, didn't appear more promising than most. Kmart also expanded rapidly, but its focus was always clear, its strategies carefully worked out, and its financing in place. There was an excellent trainee program, whereby Kresge managers were recycled and inculcated with the concepts required for success in discount department stores. At first cameras, sporting goods, jewelry, and men's clothing were leased, so Kmart personnel could watch and learn. Finally, Kmart had an additional advantage: It could learn from Korvette's blunders. Recall that Andrew Carnegie remark, "Pioneering doesn't pay." Perhaps so. Often the followers succeed by avoiding pitfalls uncovered by the trailblazer. And Korvette certainly hit all of the potholes when it became a department-store chain.

KAISER-FRAZER: THE BLUNDER OF IGNORANCE

N ew industries are populated by amateurs and mature ones by professionals. How could it be otherwise? While in their youths, the first railroaders did not know the shape, size, and configuration of a locomotive. The Wright brothers had to figure out for themselves what airplanes should look like and how they were to be powered. Adam Osborne was daring in making his foray into territory IBM and others avoided, and he had to imagine the shape and purpose of the first transportable computer. Gene Ferkauf had to make a leap of imagination to develop the discount store. The succeeding generations, of course, had models to follow. They would experiment and innovate, but at least they had a clear idea of what the product or service looked like. It was their object to develop and produce a superior version of something that existed, at a competitive price.

Those who attempt to enter established industries face multiple problems and hazards to overcome, not the least of which is having to develop their products and services for a market already commanded by other, experienced companies led by people who know the territory. This is why new industries attract entrepreneurs and older ones managers. Of course, there are always exceptions, but these are rare.

Such was the difficulty faced by Henry J. Kaiser when, after World War II, he decided to manufacture and sell automobiles. He was not successful, primarily because he was woefully ignorant of the industry and sublimely confident of his own abilities to do practically anything. As far as he was concerned, automobiles was just another business to conquer. He had done it in other fields. Why not this one? There was a simple answer, if he had only asked the right people or thought it through more carefully than he did. Kaiser had to contend with the veterans of an industry who were well-seasoned. By the time he arrived on the scene the pioneers were gone, and a new generation, which had grown to maturity under their aegis, was in charge. They knew the territory; Kaiser did not, and was unwilling to accept guidance from those in his organization who knew what they were doing. For a while, however, it appeared he might pull it off.

All but forgotten today, Henry Kaiser was a wonder-worker to that generation of Americans. As the population ages, and those who recall the dazzling reputation he earned during the period between the World Wars and during World War II apply for Social Security benefits, memories are bound to fade and perhaps disappear. For younger people, let it be noted that at the peak of his power, Kaiser was considered a visionary builder-businessman who epitomized the best of American business during a time of economic troubles and then in World War II. There were many entities bearing his name, among them Kaiser Steel, Kaiser Aluminum, and Kaiser Ventures. The Kaiser Foundation Health Plan, more commonly known as Kaiser Permanente, was founded in 1945 as a way to keep his employees at his Permanente cement plant healthy. It is one of the country's oldest, largest, and most successful health-maintenance organizations. It is the most visible Kaiser entity. Yet most of those who use its services probably don't know who he was. Once there were 32 Kaiser companies and 50 affiliated ones, and Henry Kaiser was the most renowned American businessman, deemed the model of what such individuals should be. Those companies are largely gone, and while Kaiser's monuments survive, his reputation does not.

His was a typical American success story. Kaiser was born in upstate New York, the child of German immigrants. His father was a mechanic, his mother a practical nurse. In 1895, toward the end of the worst depression to that time, the 12-year-old boy left school to become a $1.50-a-week clerk at a nearby dry-goods store.

Kaiser bounced from job to job, winding up in 1912 as a salesman and manager for the Hawkeye Fuel Company of Spokane, Washington, a gravel and cement firm involved in road construction. He enjoyed the work, which paid enough so that he could purchase a Model T Ford. Between the job and the car, Kaiser perceived the future of automobiles and the roads needed to serve them. Two years later he left Hawkeye and formed the Henry J. Kaiser Company, capitalized at $20,000, and started bidding on highway contracts across the border in British Columbia.

Kaiser was too impetuous and ambitious to tarry long at any single undertaking. His experience thus far had convinced him there was no subject or task he couldn't master. His motto at the time was, "Find a need, and fill it." If anything, he was an opportunist of the first order. Then in his early thirties, Kaiser demonstrated that unique combination of boundless stamina and enthusiasm that would continue into his seventies. Already pudgy and balding, he had an infectious, toothy grin and a craving for challenges, united with an eagerness to take risks.

For the time being Kaiser concentrated on construction, starting by paving streets in Vancouver and Victoria. He learned through experience how to bid on contracts and work with politicians, borrow funds, hire and fire workers, purchase materials and equipment, and improvise. Kaiser paid his workers well, but insisted on results. He invariably brought projects in on time and usually on or below budget. This assured him a steady flow of work, which in turn enabled him to keep his work crews together in an industry in which layoffs were common. As a result, by the mid-1920s Kaiser had attracted some of the ablest individuals in the industry to his company.

Kaiser did well enough to cast about into other markets, among them northern California. He relocated to Oakland in 1921, which remained his headquarters for the rest of his life. This marked the beginning of a quarter of a century of Kaiser accomplishments unmatched by any other building tycoon in scale and scope. Robert Moses comes to mind, but Moses was limited to New York State, while Kaiser constructed his projects in several states and foreign countries, and he was to have a role during World War II Moses did not match.

Kaiser won major contracts in Cuba, where he constructed a 300-mile, 200-bridge road across that country's swamps. He constructed levees on the Mississippi River and pipelines in the South. In 1931 Kaiser became instrumental in the construction of the Hoover Dam, one of the greatest engineering feats in history. In the process he erected Boulder City to house the 5,000 workers on the project. While he was engaged at the dam, another Kaiser company led the way in the construction of the San Francisco-Oakland Bay Bridge and the Bonneville and Grand

Coulee dams. When the New Deal arrived Kaiser became expert at extracting contracts for FDR's many projects, becoming quite chummy with Reconstruction Finance Corporation (RFC) chief Jesse Jones and others at the agency. By the eve of World War II, Kaiser was involved with more than 1,000 projects totaling $383 million.

During the summer of 1942, with war raging in Europe, North Africa, and the Pacific, Kaiser went to Washington with a bold offer. At a time when Axis submarines were sinking American shipping in alarming numbers, he offered to construct a fleet of 5,000 cargo planes, which would lessen the reliance on cargo ships. What did Kaiser know about airplane design and construction? Nothing, but matters such as this never deterred him. The plan was rejected, so Kaiser entered the shipbuilding business instead, backed by the RFC. Not knowing much about ship construction either, he formed an alliance with John David Reilly, president of Todd Shipyards, who gave him a tutorial on the ins and outs of the business. Eventually Kaiser managed seven shipyards that produced close to 1,400 vessels, which was one third of America's production. Included were hundreds of "liberty ships," constructed in five days by substituting welds for more time-consuming rivets. Reilly had told him that the welds wouldn't hold; there was a good reason why the industry used rivets. He was right. After the war those ships had an unfortunate tendency to fall apart. Kaiser knew this would happen, but he also realized that by then they would no longer be needed. The professionals may know a thing or two, he probably thought, but his vision was clearer.

In 1942, with more funds borrowed from the RFC, Kaiser constructed the first complete steel plant in California, which produced over one million tons of ingot steel during the war and later became the largest steel producer west of the Mississippi. The following year he purchased Fleetwood Aircraft and with it entered the warplane business. In 1944 he added gypsum and magnesium to the mix. He also dabbled in helicopters, ferrosilicon, and insurance. Kaiser planned to produce a five-passenger, 140-mph airplane that was spin proof and stall proof, along with at least 1,000 new airports. He wanted to manufacturer a "jet-propelled dishwasher" that did not require electricity but rather was powered by running water from a kitchen tap.

Throughout the war Kaiser played with an idea he had turned around in his mind for a decade: automobiles. In 1935 he had seen a three-wheeled model at the Berlin International Automobile Show. That design fascinated Kaiser; in 1942 he hired famed architect R. Buckminster Fuller to create another three-wheeler called the "Dymaxion." Nothing came of this, but Kaiser continued urging industry leaders to plan for the postwar markets, harping on the need for an inexpensive, spartan vehicle that would sell for around $400. If they wouldn't accept his ideas, Kaiser suggested, he might enter the field himself.

Where did he get such notions? From reading biographies of Henry Ford, who by then was well past his prime but still nominally at the helm of Ford Motors. Kaiser knew that with the fabled Model T, Ford had created a car for the masses. Now Kaiser wanted to do no less than create a new version of the T. It was a common ambition in this period. Adolf Hitler, too, was entranced by Ford, and out of his dreams came the Volkswagen. All of this, of course, was to be undertaken after the war.

Kaiser was so much of a war hero that he was talked of as a possible presidential contender in 1944, and that year FDR considered him as a vice-presidential running mate. After the victory in Europe, which came on May 8, 1945, General Eisenhower invited Kaiser to tour Europe to let the troops see the man who had done so much to help win the war.

Kaiser cared little about politics, but rather turned his attention to the needs of postwar America, in which he was convinced there would be an economic boom. He liked to point to the $43 billion invested in war bonds. "That's not debt. That $43 billion is pure venture capital." He meant to tap into it. Toward the end of the war Kaiser considered becoming a home builder and entering the appliance and paper industries. He juggled half a dozen other possibilities. This wasn't unusual for the man, or the era. As it happened, most of his time in this period was devoted to those automobiles. He thought to become possibly the next Henry Ford, or at least the new Walter Chrysler, who had been the last person to create a major automobile company, having done so in the late 1920s. He was neither. Instead, automobiles were Kaiser's first significant failure.

According to one often repeated account, in the spring of 1955 Kaiser called a press conference to announce the end of his foray into automobiles. He supposedly told reporters, "We expected to toss $50 million into the automobile pond, but we didn't expect it to disappear without a ripple," to which one seasoned industry veteran replied, "Mr. Kaiser, in automobiles, $50 million will buy you one white chip."

So wound down the last domestic attempt to crack the ranks of the automotive Big Three—GM, Ford, and Chrysler. As the reporters left that press conference, they must have considered the established structure in automobiles invincible. If Henry Kaiser hadn't been able to carry it off, no one could.

The trouble with this rendering is that it probably never happened, and Kaiser's company didn't lose $50 million; by the time it built its last car in June, the net reported loss came to $78,341,369. Adding other expenditures, it was more on the order of $150 million, which would make it around half a billion dollars in today's currency. Moreover, Kaiser's company didn't collapse with an abrupt announcement, but rather wasted away, under the rubric of Kaiser Motors and then as part of Kaiser Industries, which controlled automobile operations in its last stages.

So much for the myth, one of several dealing with the auto industry of the period, when half a dozen businesspeople thought they could make a pass at the Big Three. The most famous was Preston Tucker and the Tucker Torpedo, but Tucker was small potatoes compared with Kaiser. From the first those within the industry knew that Tucker—and Playboy, Crosley, and a few others who got into the business after World War II—hadn't a chance of success. They were underfinanced, led by lightweights, and couldn't realize the economies of scale necessary to make a go of it in the capital-hungry auto field.

Kaiser-Frazer was another matter entirely. It, too, was aiming for the stars. Kaiser would have it no other way. His sidekick, Joseph Frazer, who knew the industry, was convinced it had to be all or nothing. "If you want to die a slow death," he told reporters on several occasions, "be a small independent in the auto industry." Given a few breaks, millions of Americans might be driving Kaisers and Frazers today. But in an industry in which a big company can take many blows and still survive, small ones can't afford mistakes, and Kaiser-Frazer made several that could not be overcome.

In the spring of 1945 no one could know when the Pacific war would end, but even so, post-war thinking was on in earnest in Detroit. Learning of Kaiser's ambitions in automobiles and hoping to provide jobs for workers dismissed from war-related industries, Rolland

Thomas of the United Auto Workers wrote to him. If Kaiser were truly serious about entering the auto business, he might consider making a bid for the huge Willow Run plant just outside Detroit, which was owned by the government and at the time operated by Ford to produce B-24 warplanes. Ford wouldn't need the facility after the war, which might easily be converted to auto production. Kaiser indeed was interested, sent for Thomas, and the two men met to talk about cars. By the time they were finished, Kaiser was eager to see Willow Run.

Of course, while he refused to admit it, Kaiser still knew little about automobile production and distribution. What Kaiser needed even more than a plant was an automotive equivalent of Todd Shipyard's John David Reilly, and he found his man in the aforementioned Joseph Frazer.

From the start Frazer was the unknown half of the Kaiser-Frazer team. Even when it appeared K-F might make the grade, few outside the industry knew much about him, so powerful was the Kaiser personality. Yet Joe Frazer was no cipher, but a well-respected and shrewd automobile pioneer who had served at several companies in a wide variety of posts, but never in production.

Frazer was born in Nashville, Tennessee. His mother was a descendant of George Washington, whose family before the Civil War owned the world's largest tobacco plantation. Frazer's father was a judge whose family arrived from Scotland before the American Revolution.

Unlike most auto men of his generation, Frazer was not a Midwestern mechanic or even a tinkerer. After attending the Nashville Day School, he was sent to the Hotchkiss Academy and then on to the Sheffield Scientific School at Yale, from which he graduated in 1911. Frazer then sought a position as a mechanic's helper at Packard, for which his brother was a dealer. While he liked the shop floor, he clearly was suited for other things. Almost from the first he gravitated toward sales and found such a position at Packard's New York agency. He then transferred to his brother's Nashville dealership, and by the time World War I had ended, had his own Saxon Motor dealership in Cleveland.

A troubled General Motors, sorely in need of executive talent, was Frazer's next stop. He arrived there in 1919 and remained until 1923, serving first in sales and then moving on to other posts, ultimately serving as treasurer of General Motors Export Division, where he helped organize General Motors Acceptance Corporation. That same year GM "loaned" Frazer to Pierce-Arrow, in order to establish a credit agency for that auto company.

Walter Chrysler, then resurrecting Maxwell-Chalmers, hired Frazer to head Maxwell sales, and he remained there when Chrysler transformed the company into Chrysler Motors. As vice president of Chrysler Sales and vice president of the Plymouth Division, Frazer became one of the industry's most prominent executives.

In 1939 Frazer resigned to become president and general manager of the troubled Willys-Overland, where he staved off bankruptcy, increasing sales by 60 percent his first year. When World War II erupted, Willys entered the competition to produce a general-utility vehicle for the Army. Another company, Bantam, won the contest, but Ford and Willys also built the vehicle. It was the famous Jeep, which took sales, and it boosted Willys revenues from $9 million to $170 million.

Frazer left Willys in 1944 to become president of the newly organized Warren City Manufacturing, which turned out tanks and boilers, but he quickly realized he wasn't interested in this line of business. Warren City's predecessor company was a subsidiary of motor-car company Graham-Paige. Through an exchange of stock, Frazer and his associates became majority owners of Graham-Paige, and now Frazer became its chairman and president. It was a nothing kind of company. In 1941, the last full year of American production, Graham-Paige had produced 544 cars out of an industry total of 3,779,600. Nonetheless, along with other industry executives, Frazer had plans for the postwar market, including a new car that he wanted to call the Frazer.

In early July, while Kaiser was still considering Willow Run, Frazer arranged a meeting with A. P. Giannini of the Bank of America, the most powerful West Coast banker. By then Kaiser had started several companies in California, and now Giannini visualized an automobile industry in that state, financed by the Bank of America and headed by Kaiser.

Frazer took with him plans for his automobile, a sleek affair with plenty of glass, quite different from the prewar offerings, which he hoped would interest Giannini sufficiently for him to provide financing. The car had been designed by Howard "Dutch" Darrin, one of the most respected figures in the industry. Darrin had worked for the likes of Packard, Duesenberg, and even Rolls-Royce, as well as Graham-Paige, General Motors, and Dodge. So Frazer had reason to hope for success.

They discussed the matter of financing, and toward the conclusion of the talk, Giannini remarked, "You're a salesman. But what about the production side? Why don't you see H. J.?" Frazer demurred, but the desire to expand caused him to change his mind.

Frazer had first encountered Kaiser three years earlier, and the two men didn't get along at all. Frazer had publicly ridiculed as "half-baked" Kaiser's notion to produce that $400 car, and for his part, Kaiser thought Frazer arrogant and boorish. But the differences derived more from personality and background than from ideology. Kaiser fairly bubbled with enthusiasm and was willing to try anything. Although Frazer was a natural salesman, he was more reserved and conventional. Both men were built like fire plugs, but Kaiser was habitually disheveled, while Frazer had a bandbox appearance, and was known within the industry as "Gentleman Joe"; which is to say, they were quite different kinds of men, each a success, both somewhat imperious and unwilling to play second fiddle to anyone. One could hardly expect them to work well together, and they didn't. Indeed, they knew there would be trouble even before they were the objects of Giannini's matchmaking.

Kaiser and Frazer conferred reluctantly on July 17, 1945, and soon realized each had something the other wanted. Graham-Paige was strapped for cash, and Kaiser needed the help of people like Frazer and Darrin who understood the industry. *Life* magazine described the meeting as "love at first sight," but all who knew about the two men realized nothing could be further from the truth. Nonetheless, on August 9, Kaiser-Frazer was incorporated, to be jointly owned by the Henry J. Kaiser Company and Graham-Paige, which started with $5 million in capital, half contributed by each parent. The Kaiser would be produced somewhere on the West Coast, while the Frazer would come out of the Graham-Paige Detroit operation. There was no mention in the press of Willow Run.

The public received the news enthusiastically. It was another example of the American "can-do" spirit.

Frazer organized a dinner to introduce Kaiser to the Detroit moguls. Kaiser came with a group of managers brought to K-F from his other ventures. After dinner he rose to outline his ideas for new cars, which to the audience must have seemed rather naive and simplistic. But the man was so animated and sincere. "In the Frazer there is—the heart—of Joe Frazer—and in the Kaiser—you will find the soul—of Henry Kaiser." Kaiser's California associates cheered. The Frazer men were glumly silent.

That there were problems ahead was manifest. The Detroit Establishment promptly labeled Kaiser and his colleagues "The Sunshine Boys." Soon the Frazer contingent was spreading jokes about the orange juicers. One of these involved a Westerner, all of whose previous experience had been with ships. When he saw a Kaiser Traveller, a hybrid model that carried its spare tire inside on the left, he indignantly told Kaiser, "That's all wrong. You've got the life preserver on the port instead of the starboard side."

The Californians would never be accepted by the motor-city aristocrats. Or by Frazer and his associates. "The Kaisers brought a lot of people—they were nice young fellows," said Frazer when it was all over. "But they had no previous experience in the automobile business and did not do a good job at all. The people I brought in were all automobile people—most had experience at Chrysler and Willys-Overland as I did."

Nonetheless they had reason to expect success. In 1945 there were 25.8 million cars on the American roads, half of which were more than ten years old and most of these well beyond their useful life. "Every week," wrote *Fortune*, "literally thousands of cars will drop dead somewhere in the United States. This is the golden vision that lures Henry and Joe."

No cars for the civilian market had been assembled since 1942, and the arithmetic was compelling. Detroit figured there was a market for 12 to 14 million cars annually. In no year before the war had more than 4.5 million been produced, and that was in 1929, the last of the boom decade. In 1941 3.9 million had been made, and the factories that churned them out would now have to be converted from military production. The conventional wisdom of the time was that every car produced during the next three to six years would be snapped up by eager buyers. This seemed to indicate that K-F would be able to count on strong sales at least till 1948, by which time both founders thought they would be well-established, entrenched, and profitable. As it happened, this analysis was both right and wrong.

K-F would have to go against some stiff competition, not only from the Big Three—GM, Ford, and Chrysler—which before the war had 90 percent of sales, but also the independents, such as Studebaker,

Nash, Packard, and Hudson, which had loyal followings of their own. All of these companies had plans for the postwar market, and uniformly they agreed the public wanted pretty much what they had had before the war—inexpensive, small cars for the multitudes, ponderous large ones for the affluent. There would be no pioneering, no flash and dash, but rather safe and sensible sedans and coupes. In fact, most models would be produced from dies used in the 1941 and 1942 models and then put into storage.

Frazer's strategy was to come to market as rapidly as he could with a genuine postwar car, not the revamped prewar models Detroit was planning. In military terms, Frazer would be able to solidify a beachhead from which K-F might expand rapidly. The company would be led by executives who Frazer knew from his Chrysler days, with Kaiser's son, Edgar, serving as production chief. Together they made plans for the new cars, the facilities at which they would be produced, and the distribution network to take them to potential buyers.

The work initially proceeded smoothly, due in part to a stroke of good fortune. The UAW had called a strike at General Motors, which meant not only that the leading auto company's cars would come late to market, but that an army of unemployed GM engineers would be available to work for K-F for the duration of the walkout.

At first Kaiser wanted to have three different models, the 444, the 555, and the 666. The 444 stood for 44 horsepower, 444 pounds curb weight, and a $444 price tag, and the others followed the pattern. His intent was to price the cars lower that those offered by the others and so dominate the low end of the market. Frazer knew the numbers were sheer fantasy, and he devoted a good deal of time to trying to talk Kaiser out of such notions.

In the end it was decided to have two cars with a family resemblance. Darrin's plans for the Frazer would now be expanded to provide a prototype for the Kaiser. The Kaiser was originally to be a low-priced alternative to the Chevy, Ford, and Plymouth, while the Frazer would go against Buick, DeSoto, and Mercury.

Kaiser had become convinced Willow Run was close to ideal for his purposes. Giannini would be disappointed in not getting his California auto plant, but perhaps something could be done later to make things right. With Reconstruction Finance Corporation help and cooperation from the UAW, the company purchased the huge installation, which was to be transformed into the world's largest automobile works. The new company received sweetheart terms from the RFC. K-F would pay rent of $500,000 for the first year, $850,000 the second, and $1.25 million thereafter. To sweeten the deal, the RFC agreed to rent part of the Graham-Paige plant for two years at $500,000. This meant K-F would pay no rent the first year and only $350,000 the second. The strategy was to have the Kaisers produced at Willow Run, and for the more expensive Frazers to come out of what remained of the old Graham-Paige facility.

For all of the hoopla about the freshness of the company, at first K-F seemed a larger version of Graham-Paige. The leadership re-enforced this, since there were four Graham-Paige nominees on the board and three from Kaiser. Kaiser would be chairman and Frazer the president, in charge of day-to-day operations. Under Frazer's direction many of the Graham-Paige plans and concepts were reworked for the new company, while Kaiser arranged financing and acted as company spokesman. Giannini promised a $10 million line of credit, and Kaiser and Frazer agreed to issue 2.2 million shares of common stock at $10 a share. Each would take 250,000 shares, and the remaining 1.7 million would be sold to the public to raise $17 million.

This all happened in 1945, when the public still was wary of common stock and memories of the Great Depression were fresh in everyone's mind. On the day Kaiser and Frazer prepared to announce the organization of their company the Dow closed at 165 on volume of 700,000 shares. At that time a $17 million initial public offering seemed awfully risky to the district's timid bankers. In addition, Kaiser had often inveighed against Wall Street and New York, and so could not expect a warm reception there. Frazer knew this, but he made the rounds of banks anyway and, as expected, had no luck.

Then Kaiser turned to Cyrus Eaton, who headed Otis & Co., a Cleveland bank. Eaton, too, had his differences with the New York financial establishment that had shut out bankers from the provinces, and this was compounded by his friendly attitude toward communism. Eaton agreed to underwrite the issue, which was taken public in September. To the surprise of all involved, the stock was oversubscribed by a factor of six, and immediately jumped to $11.75. At the time it seemed an indication of better times ahead for the securities markets.

Emboldened by the success of the initial public offering, Kaiser and Frazer considered a secondary offering to raise additional funds. Ever the optimist, Kaiser wanted to use the money to buy a surplus Douglas Aviation plant in California to produce cars for the West Coast and make good on pledges made to Giannini. There was talk of a Canadian subsidiary as well. Frazer thought this was too much too soon, but reluctantly agreed to support the plan. In early January they went ahead with a secondary of 1.8 million shares, due out on January 23. At the time K-F common was selling at around $15.

Three days prior to the offering a crowd estimated at 156,000 shuttled in and out of showrooms at New York's Waldorf-Astoria at K-F's preview. What they saw were midsized prototypes, a green Kaiser and a red Frazer, spare on chrome, and somewhat sleeker than what Detroit's Big Three were showing. As expected, their offerings were rehashes of the prewar cars. The Kaiser and Frazer were lower-slung than the ones most Americans had known and quite wide—K-F claimed four adults could sit comfortably in the rear. They also differed from the Darrin-designed cars that Giannini had been shown. The original design was sleek and rounded. Now the fenders were slablike. Darrin had wanted a one-piece windshield. The new windshield was the more familiar two-piece variety and was smaller than that in the original design. The changes were made for the sake of economy. Darrin was displeased, but the public took no notice of such matters.

The viewers were not permitted to sit in the cars or even touch them, but performance reports were optimistic. According to *Mechanix Illustrated*'s Tom McCahill, the Kaiser was an easy-steering, fairly well-powered, and roomy car. The transmission was somewhat noisy, he thought, but the engineers promised to rectify the situation on production models. The cars did not have automatic shifting; GM refused to sell K-F its hydromatic drives.

Had the company permitted McCahill and those visitors to peer under the hood and crawl under the chassis they would have realized many of the components had been purchased from suppliers and that the Frazer's six-cylinder engine was underpowered, designed for the smaller Graham. The handling McCahill so admired was due to torsion-bar suspension, the first for an American production car. The Kaiser prototype was a front-wheel-drive vehicle, an unusual touch that was soon abandoned as being too revolutionary.

K-F did not announce prices, but this didn't matter. Nearly 9,000 visitors plunked down deposits, not knowing either the cost or the delivery date.

The company was flooded with letters from well-wishers. "I enclose a $100 contribution to your business," read one. "God bless you and keep up the good work." This, before a machine tool arrived, much less the first car appeared. Potential dealers wrote for interviews—one letter was from John F. "Honey Fitz" Fitzgerald, the grandfather of John F. Kennedy, the future president. An initial 800 dealers were selected, and many of them were at the Waldorf to admire the cars and dream of floods of sales once the fabled Henry Kaiser got into gear at Willow Run.

The show boosted the price of K-F stock to $17 and soon after to $24, a sign of confidence the two men could pull it off. The secondary went at $20.25, bringing in another $34 million after commissions. Once again, the offering was oversubscribed. "It was our big mistake," Kaiser wailed later on. "We should have raised $150 million or $200 million."

K-F next started advertising its cars. The company stressed these were no warmed-over models, but new from wheels up, "combining a greater number of design and major engineering developments than any other new auto in production history," and promised to produce them at a rate of 300,000 cars in 1948 and much more thereafter. Kaiser went on the road, speaking to dealer conferences, and found them dazzled to meet the man who had become a legend and now would lead them to the financial promised land. Kaiser seemed delighted by this celebrity and became increasingly hyperbolic in his pronouncements. "They tell me I'm going way out on a limb," he told one dinner meeting. "Well, that's where I like to be—way out on a limb. We're out to service the nation, the whole world. We're out to produce 13 million cars."

Orders continued to roll in. By early April customers had put down deposits for close to 400,000 Kaisers and 270,000 Frazers, and still not a single car had left the factories. Not till June did the Kaisers make their appearances in the showrooms. Seven cars were produced that month, but then the pace quickened, so that the company turned out 11,763 for all of 1946.

Los Angeles-based "Mad Man" Muntz, who was to become K-F's most renowned dealer, received the first cars. Muntz summed up the reasons for success in his radio jingle, in which he indicated—falsely—that the cars would soon be in the showrooms:

> Kaiser-Frazer, yours at once.
> Direct from Mad Man Muntz.

The initial New York shipment arrived on June 29, provoking a mob scene at Regional Auto Sales in Manhattan. Frazer told the audience that the company had orders for 900,000 cars, which would be produced as rapidly as possible. Mayor William O'Dwyer was there and asked when he could get the car he ordered. All Frazer could say was, "Mr. Mayor, I'll do the best I can."

The basic Kaiser listed for $1,898, which meant it was priced above the Chevy-Ford-Plymouth class Kaiser originally had hoped to target—a deluxe four-door Chevy or Ford went for $1,325. Instead the Kaiser would be pitted against Pontiac-Mercury-Dodge. The Frazer, at $2,053, competed with the likes of Oldsmobile and Chrysler—rather heady neighborhoods for autos that Kaiser had said would be for the frugal.

Those higher prices were caused by deals Kaiser had to strike with suppliers, who knew K-F had to take what it could get and so extracted premium prices while they could. K-F got some of its steel from Kaiser Steel on the West Coast, but transport charges from the mill to Willow Run made this an expensive proposition. According to one estimate, K-F paid a 40 percent premium for the rest of the hard-to-get steel it purchased in those years. Such costs plagued the company during its entire existence.

Those prices troubled Frazer, who had hoped to overcome whatever sales resistance existed by offering the cars in several "special" models, a throwback to the time of custom-made autos. The Manhattan, for example, was a $3,000 car meant to appeal to Cadillac types who couldn't obtain the scarce Caddies. Frazer needn't have bothered, yet. The order books were full in 1946 and into 1947, and the public purchased whatever it could get. Kaiser, who by nature was an optimist, took this as a sign of future triumphs. And there were successes to celebrate. The Kaisers and Frazers performed as promised; no serious mechanical glitches appeared. Some owners complained the cars were underpowered, but this didn't seem a major problem.

On September 25, 1947, K-F rolled out its one-hundred-thousandth automobile. Production that year came to 144,000 vehicles, far below Chrysler and Ford, and one tenth the figure for industry-leader GM. K-F was now the industry's fourth largest factor, ahead of Studebaker, Nash, Hudson, and Packard. Amazingly, K-F showed a profit of $19 million for the year, matching the losses due to start-up expenses in 1946. That the company did so well so quickly was considered another industrial miracle from the workshop of Henry Kaiser.

For the time being, then, the gamble appeared to have paid off handsomely. Kaiser celebrated by approaching a Packard board member with an offer to purchase a large block of that company's stock. He made no secret of his hope to buy the entire company, add it to K-F, become a full-line manufacturer, and go head-to-head with the Big Three. The bid went to the Packard board, where it was rejected after a brief discussion. "The proposed Kaiser merger question didn't take much time," one member recalled, "because we all knew Kaiser didn't have the expertise to become a strong competitor in our industry."

By then Frazer had taken on 4,000 dealers, many of whom were prospering. More were added; eventually there were 4,600 of them. While sales were humming along, there were few complaints from Willow Run about dealers. After all, Frazer had made his reputation in sales, and the industry thought he must have put together a fine team.

As it happened, the dealer organization was decidedly second rate, something that should have been recognized early in the game. The other companies had spent decades creating their distribution structures, learning from mistakes, developing strategies and tactics, winnowing the poorly performing agencies, rewarding the better ones, and developing training programs. During the war the dealerships declined, having to concentrate on servicing existing cars and buying and selling old ones. Many dealers went into the Armed Forces, but the basic structure remained and after the war was resurrected.

K-F had none of these advantages. Some of its dealers were opportunists out to make a quick buck and then leave the business, while more were eager but ignorant, unable to offer the kind of service customers demanded and, in general, inadequate to the task of convincing the public a K-F product was on par with those of the older companies. This was not realized in 1946–1948, but became apparent in 1949, when the shortage of cars ended and those K-F dealers, who initially were mere order-takers, had to engage in selling, a task at which they proved inadequate.

By then, too, Detroit had retooled, and the older companies were offering models that were at least as fresh and technologically advanced as the Kaisers and Frazers, and in some cases, even more so. Studebaker came first, in 1947, with its low-slung, "futuristic" Raymond Loewy-designed line. Hudson followed in 1948 with its longer, lower, sleeker cars. That was also the year of the Cadillac tailfins. In 1949 Ford offered its radically redesigned cars, and Nash came out with something that looked like a garish bathtub. Chrysler arrived late to the game, but it, too, was shucking the prewar designs.

The K-F engines remained a problem. They still were underpowered and more important, the company didn't have an eight-cylinder engine at a time when these were becoming increasingly popular, going from 20 percent of the market in 1947 to close to 30 percent in 1951. K-F was finally able to purchase automatic transmissions from GM, but they came too late to do much good for sales.

In 1948 the company produced 181,000 cars. Then, as shortages of cars vanished and the problems at the dealerships surfaced, the partners started to squabble. This was no surprise; the two men had never really meshed, and the same was true for their staffs. There were Kaiser men and Frazer men, but few were true K-F devotees. Kaiser lost confidence in Frazer when sales started to decline, telling cohorts that it appeared Frazer's reputation as a supersalesman was inflated, while Frazer pointed out Kaiser's deficiencies. In this period there were a series of wildcat strikes at Willow Run. Those workers who had been so eager to get jobs at Kaiser due to fears of depression now realized prosperity was here to stay, and their demands accelerated while their production declined. For this, Frazer blamed Kaiser, since labor was supposed to be his bailiwick.

The situation came to a head in late 1948, when K-F attempted another stock offering, this time 1.5 million shares at $13.50. Rumors of dissension at the company kept investors away, and Kaiser and Frazer entered into a three-way shouting match with Cyrus Eaton. The underwriting was received badly, at below the target price, whereupon tensions between Kaiser and Eaton resulted in a series of lawsuits.

Kaiser and Frazer fought over the company's relations with the RFC. Kaiser wanted to borrow $40 million from the agency to use in the creation of new models, while Frazer wanted to hunker down. In the end Frazer stepped down as president to be succeeded by Edgar Kaiser. With this, the Frazer people started to leave, though Frazer himself remained on the board, as a very silent member.

Now out of work at the age of 62, Frazer spent most of his remaining years as a consultant. He also became interested in aeronautics and attempted to develop and import the Allard Palm Beach roadster. He retired to Newport in the early 1960s and became an avid sportsman and sailor. His death there in 1971 was barely noticed.

In 1949 Kaiser cut prices and introduced new models—stationwagon sedans, hardtop convertibles, and four-door convertibles among others—but these were poorly received. The 1946 look remained, and although there were attempts to freshen it, nothing seemed to work. Production that year came to 58,000, and there was talk of insolvency. Perhaps this would have been the best way to go, but Kaiser brushed aside the suggestion. For one thing, the failure of any Kaiser company would hurt the others, especially Kaiser Steel and Kaiser Aluminum, both of which were in need of financing. Also, Kaiser had never failed at anything he attempted, and pride would not permit him to throw in the towel at K-F. At least not yet.

Since he was in full control, Kaiser decided to revive his old idea to produce a mass car at a low price. At the same time he accelerated work on a complete refashioning of the Kaisers.

Today Kaiser's new car would have been called a compact. This is not to say Kaiser was a pioneer who was ahead of the industry. Other companies, including Nash and Willys, were experimenting with compacts, and there were some imports, particularly British and French, in the field. Crosley had a subcompact that had been introduced in 1939, which survived until 1952. But Kaiser's car, the Henry J., made the greatest impact in this category. Ironically, when Kaiser spoke of it to Frazer and they talked of a name, Frazer suggested "Mustang."

The Henry J. was a barebones affair, without a trunk or glove compartment and with shoddy upholstery. Powered by a 68-horsepower engine, it got 25 miles per gallon in traffic. The Henry J. was introduced in February 1950, with a price tag of $1,299, only $50 less than the most inexpensive Chevy, and so was not a bargain. Nonetheless it received good reviews, and dealers booked 30,000 orders in the next three months. Then interest and orders faded. Casting about to goose sales,

Kaiser entered into a deal with Sears Roebuck, under which the Henry J. would be sold in Sears stores as the Allstate. It was a bad move; Sears was able to sell only 2,600 vehicles, and the concept backfired in lost Henry J. sales, as customers rejected the experiment.

By then the dealerships had dwindled from 4,600 to around 2,000, which turned out to be one of the positive elements in the company's outlook. Gone were those marginal agencies who never should have been taken on in the first place. What remained was a core of financially sound and now experienced K-F people, who had managed to survive during the poor years of the late 1940s.

The newly designed Kaiser was another plus. To many aficionados, it remains one of the most elegant cars in all of American automotive history. With its large, widow's-peak windshield, low beltline, and clean lines, it immediately caught the public's attention. Kaiser added vinyl roofs on some models, a cosmetic change that proved popular then and was copied by the other automakers. On top of all of this, the car received generally good reviews from the enthusiast magazines and *Consumer's Union*. Sales picked up sharply, due largely to the initial sales of the Henry J. and the good reception for the new Kaiser. Emboldened, Edgar Kaiser took on another 700 dealers.

Then came the reality check. The new Kaiser, for all its charms, was priced at around $2,200, slightly higher than the Buick Special, the Hudson Pacemaker, and the Studebaker Commander, more luxurious cars and all with eight-cylinder engines.

Even more ominous was the profits picture. Simply stated, there were none. For 1950, the second-best year, when 151,000 cars were sold, K-F lost $13 million. Hudson sold 144,000 cars, for a profit of $12 million. Later on there would be apologists who argued that K-F's problems were largely due to an inability to realize the kinds of economies of scale available to the Big Three. But this ignores the Hudson experience. A more likely explanation was that while the orange juicers were fine at dams and ships, they couldn't hack it with automobiles.

The entire industry suffered from a cyclical decline in 1951 and 1952. Cars were harder to sell and prices had to be cut. K-F continued to lose money. The industry as a whole recovered in 1953, but not Willow Run, where the talk once more was of bankruptcy. What now was renamed Kaiser Motors was desperately in need of financing, and given the status of the company at the time, this was impossible.

Throughout this period, Edgar Kaiser consulted regularly with GM CEO Charles Wilson, who was generous with advice and assistance. The reason for this help wasn't difficult to understand. GM wanted K-F to succeed, if only to forestall threatened antitrust prosecution against the industry giant, which was being charged with monopoly practices.

In April 1953, Kaiser Motors surprised just about everyone with the announcement that it would purchase Frazer's old company, Toledo-based Willys-Overland, for $60.8 million. How could this be, since K-F was close to insolvency? It turned out the money would come from other Kaiser companies plus a stock purchase by Transamerica Corp.

The merger was made for accounting and tax reasons, and not automobile considerations. Because Willys had earned $6.1 million in 1962, Kaiser would be able to offset its own losses against these gains and through other financial gimmicks get Willys at a bargain price. Then, in November, a fire demolished GM's Livonia transmission plant and Kaiser took the opportunity to sell that company the Willow Run facility, for $26 million, and moved the Kaiser operation to the Willys plant. Kaiser tried to put a brave face on the move, but he knew, as did most in the industry, that Kaiser Motors was doomed.

The reasons for failure were clear. In addition to the management and labor problems, the company was underfinanced and still hadn't develop an eight-cylinder engine when this was what the public demanded. The car cost too much to make and was priced too high for the market it had originally targeted. Kaiser gave in too often to the unions, and his work force was not as productive as it should have been. The company still lacked the superb dealerships a new car needed, a problem resolved too late to do much good.

Only 17,000 Kaisers and Willys were produced at the Toledo plant in 1954, and in 1955, a record year for the industry, production for the two models came to under 6,000. Then it was over—but not altogether. What now was called Kaiser Industries continued turning out cars overseas from the Kaiser dies, and some in the United States as well, only these were produced by the Willys unit. Kaiser never got over his infatuation with automobiles. In 1954 he flirted with the idea of purchasing the near-moribund Studebaker-Packard, but nothing came of this. By the time of his death in 1967 he was all but forgotten.

CHAPTER FOUR

RCA: THE BLUNDER OF NEPOTISM

There are failures in business—as in other areas—of children pressured into competing with the real or imagined accomplishments of their parents. Most offspring faced with such circumstances are doomed to misfortune or obscurity. Adolph Zukor founded Paramount and Albert Einstein was arguably the greatest scientific mind of this century. Their sons, Eugene Zukor and Hans Einstein, won't be found in the history books. John Patterson founded National Cash Register and dominated his firm, the industry—and his son, Frederick. When John Patterson died Frederick had to make the kinds of decisions that would enable NCR to retain its lead in business machines, and this was beyond his abilities. He was incapable of action, as though fearful of disappointing the ghost of his departed father.

This wasn't unusual; few sons of major businessmen have become significant in their own rights. Most were adequate, intelligent enough people, simply unable to compete with a legend. Some were miserable flops and blunderers, largely because of attempts to duplicate or surpass their parents.

Such was the problem posed to Bobby Sarnoff. In 1965, when he was named president of the Radio Corporation of America, *Fortune* magazine ran a brief profile of the little-known 47-year-old executive. "Robert Sarnoff has had to shoulder the burden of being the son of a man who is both great and controversial. No one can do that easily."

As it turned out, he did *not* do it easily. Bobby Sarnoff stumbled badly and repeatedly, as he tried manfully to fill the extremely large pair of shoes he been bequeathed. From his father, David, he had inherited a vital company with strong positions in broadcasting, manufacturing, and recording, among other things, and a major new foray into computers. That project was doing badly when he took over, but, Bobby mismanaged it further and then sold what remained at an absurdly low price. More important, he managed to transform a superb electronics concern into a slapdash conglomerate, while playing a key role in handing over an important American industry to its Japanese competitors, a process, to be fair, that also had been started under his father. He did all this in less than a decade. Indeed, so complete was his botch that the fact that RCA no longer exists can be considered part of his legacy.

Still, as with so many disasters, this one has mitigating circumstances. With a different father, Bobby might have had a decent but undistinguished career. This wasn't to be for the son of David Sarnoff. Given this, Bobby Sarnoff was programmed for failure almost from the start, by a parent who, as in so many cases, seemed to have had the best of intentions. The trouble was that RCA was David's true son. David once shooed his son's dog out of the living room, and the boy remarked, "I'll bet you wouldn't mind the dog if you could talk television to him."

David realized his errors as a parent and mentor when he was an old man, but by then it was too late to change these relationships. He didn't know how to be a father to his children, alternately coddling and intimidating Bobby while pushing him into positions he either didn't want or for which he was unprepared.

Throughout a good deal of his early career at RCA Bobby (it usually was the diminutive, which may tell you something right there) had to carry the burden of that surname, and all there knew he had come to his position more as a matter of inheritance than of demonstrated abilities. His father, the fabled David (no one called him Davy) Sarnoff, was a business genius, one of the 15 original members of the *Fortune Business Hall of Fame*, and an egomaniac and bully. Like many such individuals, he created many problems for his children.

Sarnoff's arrogance was legendary. The story is told of how, after breaking his leg, Sarnoff hobbled onto an elevator where he encountered former President Harry Truman. "Well, General," Truman cracked, "I guess now for a while you'll have to kick people in the ass with the other leg, won't you?"

Unwilling to permit others to create a niche for him in business history, David fashioned his own. Elmer Bucher, himself a telecommunications trailblazer, tagged after Sarnoff, taking down his every word. In 1941 Bucher started a 21-year career writing a hagiographic biography of the Leader. There are 56 volumes in all, comprising 388 chapters, concluding with a 393-page *Tribute to David Sarnoff.* After going through a roll of giants in the business field—John D. Rockefeller, James Hill, Theodore Vail, Henry Clay Frick, Andrew Carnegie, among others—Bucher concluded: "Historians of the future will properly add David Sarnoff's name to the roster of America's industrial pioneers, acknowledging his far-seeing leadership in radio, television, and other developments born out of radio invention."

Were this not enough, Sarnoff commissioned Eugene Lyons, his journalist cousin, to write *Sarnoff: An American Success,* which was released in 1968. On the first page, Lyons stated that "he has probably affected the patterns of the daily lives of more Americans than anyone since Thomas Edison." The General must have liked that. In fact, he even might have dictated the words.

Several years ago, visitors to the David Sarnoff Library and the David Sarnoff Research Center in Princeton would be given paperback copies of the Lyons book and might peruse the Bucher manuscript under the watchful eye of a large portrait of the founder in a properly heroic stance. After RCA was folded into General Electric in 1985, the Research Center was sold to SRI International,

As they would with so many consummate perfectionists, psychologists might have had a field day with David Sarnoff. He was what a later generation would call an overachiever, what some scholars would observe could be said of the vast majority of distinguished individuals. Sarnoff arrived in America as a poor immigrant boy, a Russian Jew, whose family settled on the lower East Side of New York. He left school to earn a living for his family. Like most with his background, the ambitious Sarnoff, whose debt to his adopted country never left his mind, had a mania to succeed.

Were it not for Sarnoff's vision and drive, Radio Corporation of America would not have become the innovative, exciting company it was in the 1920s and afterwards but in the beginning there was the legend. Sarnoff achieved fame as the telegrapher who broadcast news of the *Titanic* sinking. The only trouble with this tale is that he forwarded the *Titanic* news from a telegrapher at sea and didn't originate it as his public-relations teams liked to claim. Nor was he the founder of RCA, as is generally believed. That these self-serving myths persist is unfortunate, since there was in the Sarnoff story a good deal of material from which one could conclude that he was *the* major player in the early days of radio and television. David Sarnoff may have been vain, arrogant, and a bully, but he also was a farsighted businessman, a superb manager, and a clever tactician.

As early as 1915, as an assistant traffic manager for the Marconi Wireless Telegraph Company of America, Sarnoff pushed for the development, production, and mass marketing of what he called the "radio music box." In a prescient memo to his superiors, he wrote: "I have in mind a plan of development that would make radio a household utility in the same sense as a piano or phonograph," and he predicted sales would eventually reach $75 million. Marconi's management wasn't impressed by the plan, but when the company was reorganized as RCA, David jockeyed himself into a position from which he might put his ideas into action.

Originally jointly owned by General Electric, A.T.&T., Westinghouse, and United Fruit, RCA was supposed to become the American entry in the international struggle to dominate wireless communication. It was Sarnoff who led it into other, more fruitful, paths. He got RCA into the broadcasting industry in a big way through National Broadcasting Network (NBC), which had two networks, the Red and the Blue. In time he would negotiate the company's independence from its owners, and take RCA into phonographs and records, motion pictures, talent agencies, and a host of related businesses. By the 1930s RCA had become the giant of the entertainment industry, the class company in a glamorous and profitable new industry with the largest profits and greatest promise. What Bill Gates and Microsoft have been to the late 1990s, David Sarnoff and RCA were to the early 1930s. Sarnoff even made RCA a force in home appliances, through control of Whirlpool Corp.

At the 1939 New York World's Fair RCA personnel set up and operated demonstrations of a new medium, television. At the dedication Bobby, recently graduated from college, was at his father's side. Television had to wait while the United States participated in World War II, however. David Sarnoff obtained a commission. Most of his military service was in public relations and procurement. During the war he continued to manage affairs at RCA and to obtain contracts for the company. For the rest of his life he liked to be addressed as "General," but that rank was earned in the reserves, not on active duty. Sarnoff encouraged the press to write of him as though he had been a war hero who was at General Eisenhower's side.

After the war the General's formidable investments in television started paying off, and despite some early setbacks, RCA quickly became a leader in both receiver manufacturer and broadcasting. Sarnoff entered into a competition with Columbia Broadcasting for domination of color TV, and when Columbia's system seemed superior, employed his wile and guile to delay acceptance until RCA caught up. Columbia was crippled, and today's TV system is what Sarnoff wanted it to be.

On September 27, 1951, Sarnoff asked for three presents for his fiftieth anniversary in radio, which was to be five years later: a device that would record programs from television; inexpensive tape on which the records would be made; and a lightweight air conditioner. He got the first two; RCA became a pioneer in videotape technology. As for the third, that year RCA entered into an arrangement with Fedders-Quigan to produce electronic air conditioners. At the time Sarnoff thought his reinvented air conditioners might be hung on walls like pictures, eliminating the plumbing and electrical complications of existing models. It didn't work and was quickly dropped. There were other failures. Earlier Sarnoff had pioneered FM radio, only to cut back sharply in order to devote RCA's resources to television. He left it to others to develop this medium. RCA's 45-rpm phonograph players and records proved duds and were abandoned as the nation took to Columbia's 33 ⅓ version. There were other failures and dead ends, none of which seriously hurt RCA, but indeed, were tributes to the company's attempts to pioneer with new products.

In 1955 RCA's revenues topped $1 billion, almost twice those of IBM and three times those of arch-rival CBS. By the late 1950s the General was at the peak of his powers, while RCA was one of the nation's most admired corporations. Its stock was one of the stars of the bull market. It was then that the General, now 64 years old, may have overreached, with two switches in corporate strategy with scopes as ambitious as the move into television. If successful these would have altered RCA considerably, transforming the existing businesses into cash cows that would finance the new ones. RCA would have been larger even than General Electric, and in fact would have resembled what that company became in the 1980s.

The more important of the General's two-pronged strategy was the foray into computers. Given RCA's resources and history, such a move was natural and sensible. In the 1950s computers were seen as accumulations of electronic gear, and RCA had become a premier electronics concern, with magnificent research capabilities. While still wedded to vacuum tubes, Sarnoff had built upon expertise garnered during the war to take the company into transistors, so that the company could claim to be "the leading domestic supplier of solid-state semiconductor devices for consumer products." The RCA Research Center was a showplace and one of the top technological centers in the world, more prestigious than its IBM equivalent and the equal of the Bell Laboratories.

RCA started in computers in a big way, organizing the Computer Systems Division (CSD), which proclaimed itself the future leader in the field. During the early 1950s RCA committed more than $10 million, a large amount in those days, to computer development, telling the press of plans to sell the machines to the government and then to private corporations and others. In September 1956 more than one thousand people gathered in the Great Ballroom of the Waldorf-Astoria Hotel in New York to celebrate Sarnoff's 50 years in the industry. The General took advantage of the occasion to predict the "fruition" of computers in the next two decades. Later in the year he announced the release of the BIZMAC computer, which was advertised as having military capabilities as well as civilian uses. At the time it seemed that while IBM might come to dominate the civilian markets, RCA had a leg up in the military area. Even then it was inevitable these two companies would clash.

There was a personal element to the struggle that fascinated the business press. The IBM-RCA conflict would pit the two leading families in electronics against each other. IBM's Tom Watson, Sr., and David Sarnoff shared several of the attributes often found in founders of major businesses. While without the megalomaniacal tendencies Sarnoff often displayed, Tom, Sr., too, had a colossal ego, which was occasionally displayed in his attitude toward his sons. Born in humble circumstances and raised in a small town in upper New York State,

eager to succeed and a workaholic, like Sarnoff, Watson, too, had little time for his children.

Arthur "Dick" Watson usually bowed to his father's will, and
while he had an impressive career, was always under the shadow of his
elder brother Tom, Jr., and often seemed incapable of independent
action. Young Tom, on the other hand, was a rebel, who while growing up regularly defied Tom, Sr. By the time he took over, Tom, Jr.,
had confronted his father in a well-publicized struggle over IBM's
future. The older man was wary of computers, but Tom, Jr., wanted
to stake the company on this new technology, and in the end the
father bowed. He also accepted Tom, Jr.'s, advice on settling a major
antitrust suit.

The two Watsons respected each other, perhaps because Tom,
Jr., regularly demonstrated love and esteem along with independence. One might easily imagine the stubborn father fighting his son
to the end, secretly hoping Tom, Jr., would triumph and so display
those qualities so evident in his own actions as a young man. As will
be seen, the same kind of relationship existed between Gussie and
August Busch at Anheuser Busch. It is not unusual when fathers and
sons are at the top at the same company. Joseph and Peter Grace of
W. R. Grace had no real conflict, because while his father was alive,
Peter didn't indicate any desire to move into a leadership role, and
the person he strove to surpass was his dead grandfather, not his ami-
able father.

The Watsons were able to end whatever animosities existed, and
in May 1956 Tom, Sr., stepped down in favor of his son. Only 42 years
old at the time, Tom, Jr., nonetheless was considered by then a seasoned and capable leader, well prepared for a face-off with the aging
but still active General Sarnoff.

Bobby Sarnoff, who observed the beginning of the confrontation from the sidelines, couldn't help comparing himself to Tom, Jr.
"One of my problems was convincing people outside NBC that I was
running things on my own," he once remarked. "I guess Tom Watson
went through the same thing." Yes and no. Only four years younger
than Tom, Jr., Bobby was nowhere near IBM's leader in stature and
demonstrated abilities. Neither man could have made it up the ladder
as rapidly as he did were it not for his father's patronage. Tom, Jr.,
could joke about this, knowing he had the abilities to have become

successful even without that magic name. Perhaps this was why he was so close to John F. Kennedy, who had the same attitude toward his father.

Life would have been difficult for anyone who followed David Sarnoff, but Bobby, bearing the magic surname, suffered that additional liability. What is more, he knew it. In the 1980s a RCA executive who knew both men told a reporter that when someone said Sarnoff was on his way to the office, "I half-expected to see the General burst through the door." That wasn't a problem at IBM.

At first blush Bobby's résumé seemed quite impressive. As befitted a youth of his time and class, he boarded at a prestigious private school, Andover, and entered Harvard in 1935, where he majored in government and philosophy. Recognizing he could never match David's achievements in radio, Bobby initially sought a different kind of career. Personable and uninterested in science, he briefly considered becoming a public-relations man, but David nixed the plan. "When I suggested advertising, he suggested law," Bobby told a reporter in 1952. "He would have liked one of his sons to be a lawyer and another an engineer," suggesting that David was guiding his sons' lives in somewhat the same fashion Joe Kennedy was doing for his heirs. Bobby wasn't pleased with the idea. "As for myself, I had my doubts. I honestly doubted that I would be a good lawyer, but I agreed to try it." He dutifully attended Columbia Law School for a year, but then left for naval duty during World War II.

After his discharge Bobby tried mightily to break away from the General, working for a while as an advertising man and then assistant to Gardner Cowles, publisher of the *Des Moines Register* and president of Cowles Broadcasting. David's fine hand could be seen in this; he got him both the job and the promotion, wanting Bobby to have some broadcasting experience. Bobby returned to New York in 1946 as an executive for *Look* magazine, and two years later he was summoned to Rockefeller Center to become an account executive at NBC. As Eugene Lyons tells it, Bobby discussed his prospects at the network, "not with his father but with his friend Frank Mullen then the executive vice-president of NBC. . . . Though the elder Sarnoff had expressed some misgivings, he raised no objection" to his son's hiring.

Not quite. The General had engineered the whole thing. He would do the same for his other two sons. The middle one, Edward, ran an RCA franchise before quitting to start a messenger service, and the youngest, Thomas, worked for a competitor, American Broadcasting, and then moved on to NBC's West Coast operation.

Bobby didn't make much of an impression at the network. Below average height, he was somewhat pudgy, unimaginative, and awkward. He strained to appear decisive, but instead came off as inept.

During the next few years Bobby moved up the ladder at NBC, training under a series of executives, each of whom must have realized he was grooming the person who was destined to take his place. By 1953 he was an executive vice president under Sylvester ("Pat") Weaver, then the network's fair-haired boy. Two years later, when Weaver was elevated to the chairmanship, Bobby became president of NBC. Soon Weaver was out, and Bobby became chairman of the network. "I knew I was just warming up the seat for Bobby," said Weaver to the press.

This wasn't unusual. Tom, Jr., too, had a series of mentors whom he replaced, but there were differences. For one thing, IBM was more a meritocracy than RCA, and Tom had to perform or stagnate at a subordinate level. Then, too, Tom, Sr., was a stern man, but meticulously fair, refusing to play favorites, while the General ruled through a combination of fear and rewards. Significantly, Tom, Jr., worked at IBM itself—the center of power—while Bobby was at the network, receiving orders from headquarters, and so had no practical experience in running the parent company.

Bobby knew that during the 1920s David had been offered leadership at NBC, but opted to remain in a lower position at RCA in the hope of eventually achieving power there. He wasn't giving Bobby the opportunity he had insisted upon for himself, and the young man must have realized this. Even if he didn't, RCA veterans knew what was happening: The General didn't seem to think his son was up to the demands in the central executive suites.

Meanwhile David was deeply involved in his new challenges. Going against IBM in the nascent computer industry was a contest fit for the likes of General Sarnoff. This was a new product area in which the General could mobilize his forces for a series of set battles, and for a while this was what he did.

Not so his second new area of opportunity, which was conglomeration, at the time more commonly known as "diversification into nonrelated areas." If computers represented a more or less logical extension of RCA's business, conglomeration implied something new, more like RCA's earlier venture into home appliances with Whirlpool. It was a concept practitioners had difficulty in rationalizing. ITT's Harold Geneen said conglomeration enabled that corporation to weather economic storms by balancing cyclical against growth holdings, marrying cash cows with capital-short companies, foreign and domestic businesses, service and manufacturing, and so on. While some business-school professors liked the notion and others being floated at the time, within the industry conglomeration was known to be little more than opportunism, the search for profits in any areas where they might be found.

Toward the end of his life, when conglomeration was still in vogue, Sarnoff claimed to have made RCA an "entertainment conglomerate," but this was not truly so—there was synergy between the networks, the receiver manufacturing arm, the phonograph company, and much of the rest. But in the last year of his stewardship at RCA, he took the corporation further afield than before.

The General nibbled at Random House, which under Bennett Cerf had become one of the nation's premier publishers. Cerf, was a panelist on the TV program *What's My Line?* (broadcast on CBS), a nationally recognized figure and one of the shrewdest CEOs in the publishing business. The price he was asking for his company was pretty high—$40 million in stock, for assets valued at $10 million—but given Random House's intangibles, the deal might be justified. During the negotiations, Sarnoff glowered and said, "You may not realize it, Bennett, but you are dealing with a very arrogant and egotistical man," to which Cerf replied, "General, I'm just as arrogant and egotistical as you are." So he was.

When it was learned Sarnoff was going after Random House, acolytes at the Rockefeller Center headquarters spoke of the synergy between the companies—Random House novels could be turned into scripts for NBC productions, for example. It wasn't necessarily a new venture, then, but like computers, a sensible extension of RCA's already powerful capabilities. But no one took this very seriously.

The negotiations were conducted without major input from Bobby. Even while elderly and ailing, the General could do what he wished at headquarters and displayed remarkable insensitivity toward his eldest son.

David finally stepped down as RCA CEO in January 1966 and was succeeded by the owlish Elmer Engstrom, who had joined RCA as a young engineer in 1923. He was a key figure in the development of television and had served as vice chairman, chairman of the executive committee, and chief operating officer since 1961. Engstrom had many credentials, not least being he had always been close to the General, worked well with him, could be counted on to take orders, and entertained no ambitions to remain CEO for any longer than it took to prepare Bobby for the job. He had a five-year contract, but he was out in two, with Bobby taking his place as everyone knew he would. The General, now 75 years old, would remain as chairman of the board, while Bobby became RCA's CEO. According to the press release, this promotion was Engstrom's idea, as a reward for the fine job Bobby had done at NBC. "NBC enjoyed its most successful years in terms of service, prestige, and profits. He demonstrated at NBC, as well as in many other important assignments for RCA, those qualities of business and administration judgement and leadership that make him thoroughly qualified to administer the operations of RCA." Within the firm, however, it was generally believed most of the credit for that showing should have been given to Robert Kintner, the NBC president.

Bobby's actions during those first years as the company's CEO were those of a person eager to make his impact but uncertain regarding just what he should do. He seemed in a hurry to go somewhere, but ambivalent as to his destination, wanting independence but at the same time yearning for the security that came from following his father's approach. It could be seen in some of his initial moves, which were cosmetic and symbolic rather than substantive.

For starters, the new leader insisted on being called "Bob" rather than "Bobby," which evoked snickers rather than enhanced respect. He sold the marine-radio operation, which was a minor part of the corporation. This had been RCA's original business, so Bob indicated he was cutting that tie to the David Sarnoff era. Ventures into medical technology and electronic microscopy that had intrigued the General were dropped. Several months later Bob had his office redecorated in the modern decor his father hated.

These and other symbolic changes rankled the General, who made no secret of his distaste for such evidence of rebellion. The ailing man tried to make the best of this change. "Well," he mused, "Even an old girl can appreciate a new dress," but he preferred the old girl the way he left her.

Other symbols were to go. RCA took on a new public-relations firm and mandated it to come up with a modern image. Gone was the art-deco logo featuring a bolt of lightning that had served the corporation since the 1920s. Nipper the Dog, RCA's most familiar symbol, was played down and in time discarded, and the motto, "His Master's Voice" eliminated. The company's name was changed from Radio Corporation of America simply to, RCA. "Radios are a tiny part of our business, and we sell 12,000 different products and services nearly everywhere in the world," Bob explained.

This last move was more than the General could bear. He threatened a special meeting of the board and a confrontation unless the order were rescinded. Bob permitted the full name to appear in the annual report that year, but it vanished once the General was gone from the scene.

Under Bob's direction, in 1967 RCA purchased Arnold Palmer Enterprises, which turned out golf equipment and sports clothes. Bob overpaid for an unpromising business. The financial analysts speculated about the reason. "Perhaps someone at the network thought it would be a good idea to have Palmer on board in some capacity," said one executive years later, trying to justify the move. "Or it might have been they wanted to play golf with him. Also, Arnold Palmer was a hell of a better symbol than Nipper the Dog for the 1960s."

Besides the superb corporate reputation, the General had bequeathed his son a handsome legacy. The TV business and the network were throwing off large amounts of cash, as were several of the ancillary businesses. The other consumer electronics products were doing well. Random House wasn't delivering as promised, but at least it was profitable.

Yet there also were weaknesses unrecognized at the time. In order to boost profits and cut debt, the General had slashed research and development. At the same time, RCA's peerless reputation in television was such that the government decreed that the company had to license its technology, but could not charge domestic competitors fees for this proprietary material. The consent decree did not apply to foreign companies, however. So RCA started selling technology patents to foreign companies, especially the Japanese. These were for old products and processes. The General hardly would sell the crown jewels. Even so, he might have asked himself what the Japanese companies found so valuable in those patents. That they were important could not be doubted, at least by the Japanese companies and government. In 1960, while on a visit to Japan, the General had been awarded the Order of the Rising Sun for the aid he had given that country's electronics industry. Would RCA have made these sales had the United States Justice Department not punished it for earlier successes? Who can say, but in retrospect, the sales were a major blunder.

For the most part, Bob was content to manage his inheritance, and except for those surface changes and Arnold Palmer Enterprises, going along the same paths his father had set down. The trouble with this was that the General had always been able to turn around to meet changing conditions, while Bob seemed incapable of recognizing these shifts in the business climate.

The General had known the computer business would be diffi-cult to crack and that the company had to expect a string of deficits before turning profits. Such had been the experience of others in the field, but more important, it had been the same with color television, one of RCA's greatest triumphs. After a decade of red ink, color TV finally went into the black and went on to become one of RCA's major profit centers. Bob knew that if computers flourished the General would get the credit for having placed RCA into that business, but he hoped that he would receive at least some recognition for the success. So he plowed ahead, even as losses mounted and warnings of mis-management reached his ears.

Conglomeration was even more intriguing, partly because Bob could claim originality here and not be accused of following his father's footsteps. Deciding to start big, while the General was still at the firm but ailing, Bob went after a giant, Hertz, the leading firm in car rentals. This was no Random House. For one thing, it was much bigger, and for another, there could be no assertions of synergy with Hertz. This was true diversification, paid for with stock worth more than $200 million.

Andre Meyer, the legendary leader at Lazard Freres, had tried without success to interest the General in Hertz. David said he didn't know anything about car rentals and intended sticking to electronics. Now Meyer wooed Bob. He sketched for the young man fanciful images of how RCA might become another ITT, which was then one of America's most admired companies and for which Meyer was banker. Bob was dazzled. Meyer would make him an industrial statesman. Or so it seemed.

In the end Bob succumbed, taking on a fine company that, unfortunately, needed large capital infusions at a time when RCA was pumping funds into computers. After Hertz, Meyer thought he could sell Bob anything. "Andre always looked upon him as the General's son," thought Felix Rohatyn, Meyer's close associate in the deals. "Even when he was chief executive, I don't think Andre ever took him seriously."

In 1968 Bob went after St. Regis Paper, a $721 million cash-short giant. Why St. Regis? Some at headquarters opined that this would catapult RCA into the ranks of the top-ten American corporations in terms of size and would provide Bob with instant status of a kind. St. Regis was a troubled company. Fortunately for RCA, this one fell through.

Undeterred, Bob purchased F. M. Stamper, a leading packager of frozen foods, for $141 million in common stock. He changed the name to Banquet and told reporters it would become the leader in a growing industry. He then obtained Cushman & Wakefield, a New York-based real-estate company.

Bob next made a pass at Loews, which was a huge conglomerate based on hotels, tobacco, and real estate, which he intended buying for stock. Why did Loews CEO Larry Tisch turn down the merger? "We couldn't see that much in the deal for our stockholders," he said, flashing a sign that he thought Bob would run RCA into the ground and didn't want to be stuck with that company's shares.

Bob had decided to meet IBM across the board with a complete array of computers, this to make CSD second in the industry prior to an assault on "Big Blue" itself. Industry observers knew this was foolish. Even then it was evident that only those companies that sought special niches had a chance against the leader. Control Data was managing it in huge mainframes and Digital Equipment was in micros, while others concentrated on different markets. Strong, experienced firms such as Honeywell, Sperry Rand, Burroughs, NCR, and even

GE were reporting large losses with little promise of a turnaround. How could RCA hope to do better?

In 1969 CSD shipped more than a quarter of a billion dollars worth of mainframes, many of them purchased by the parent company for leasing, but this was enough only to make it the fifth-largest company in the industry. The company claimed to have posted its first profit in 1968 and promised more to come.

The raw statistics masked a major corporate disaster in the making. Later it would be learned RCA hadn't a clue as to the profit situation. Lease records were kept on a haphazard basis. The auditors were screaming. Executives came and went. The company had no way of knowing whether any particular machine was actually making money. "I hadn't seen what was happening," conceded Edward Donegan, who had come in from IBM to handle sales. "The group financial staff hadn't seen it. The outside accountants who were in our skivvies hadn't seen it."

By 1970 the division was spinning out of control "Perhaps only an individual with engineering knowledge could have developed a strategy for CSD," reflected one veteran, who admitted the division was foundering. "The General wouldn't have made those basic errors," they said. RCA executives hunkered down, each protecting his own turf. RCA was no longer a centrally controlled corporation, but rather a confederacy of divisions with little relationship to one another or knowledge of what was happening elsewhere in the firm. Bob's reputation at CSD fell to zero, and the gloom there spread. In 1970 RCA's net income slid from $161.2 million to $91.3 million, while its debt rose to $973 million, more than triple what it had been in 1966. In 1967 RCA common had sold for 65; it was below 20 in the summer of 1970. Then the stock started to rise—on rumors that CSD would be sold. Bob indicated it just might happen. "We'd still like to be number two in the computer business," he told the 1971 stockholders' meeting, adding, "We're more interested in profitability." But profits, too, were a chimera.

Bob had transformed RCA into a foundering giant and hadn't a clue where to turn next. That year he purchased Coronet Industries, a large carpet manufacturer, for six million shares of RCA common, which made Coronet's CEO Martin Seretean RCA's largest noninstitutional shareholder. Seretean received a seat on the board, from which he soon became one of Bob's major critics, urging Bob to get rid of CSD and then trying to oust him as chairman.

Moving quickly, without seeming to know exactly what he was doing, Bob put CSD on the block. Only months earlier Honeywell had purchased GE's computer business, causing GE to suffer a public-relations disaster. Bob might have reasoned a sale by RCA wouldn't seem so humbling in the face GE's humiliation.

There were plenty of potential buyers: Xerox, Memorex, Mohawk Data, and Sperry Rand were among the obvious candidates. In the end Bob opted for Sperry Rand and sold for a price that left the industry gasping: $127 million. Sperry's UNIVAC division would take over a customer base of 500 companies and government agencies that by itself was worth more than the price Sperry paid for CSD. UNIVAC also received more than 1,000 RCA computers on lease, which had cost more than $900 million. Most important, it obtained a fine technological team. "You could never go out in the open market and get so many people with that kind of talent," said a pleased UNIVAC executive. "It's like taking the Eastern Division of the National Football League and saying you can take the top ten guys from each team."

Perhaps this was overdone, but within the industry it seemed obvious Bob had botched the deal, and those hundreds of RCA engineers and executives now with UNIVAC soon spread horrific tales of mismanagement at the CSD division.

To make matters worse for Bob, the General died during the negotiations, and his obituaries told the tale of how an immigrant boy had gone on to such great successes. This was in unspoken contrast to Bob's failure. Bob didn't do himself any good when telling reporters "A hell of a lot of people disagreed with my father going ahead with color. It took a certain amount of courage and guts and he stayed with it. There is a kind of parallel in a way. It took courage to get out of computers." This convoluted reasoning was hardly impressive.

RCA took a half-billion dollar writeoff in 1971, and everyone realized just how costly the foray into data processing had been; this reduced the company's net worth by a quarter. RCA was in its worst financial shape since the mid-1930s. Even so, Wall Street didn't believe the figures. Bob Sarnoff had lost all credibility. Rumor had it the losses were closer to half a billion and that RCA was close to illiquidity.

Equally important, the botch caused RCA's leaders to lose their nerve. Under the General the company spoke airily of serving the national interest and taking command in all markets. Now such talk was no longer heard. Instead, there was a growing nostalgia for the old days and dissatisfaction with Bob's regime.

Just as the earlier optimism had been overdone, so this gloom exaggerated RCA's problems. There were some bright spots. Hertz was doing well, as was broadcasting. But consumer electronics, once the company's biggest moneymaker, was sliding badly. The General had left Bob a fine inheritance there and a peerless reputation. These were squandered mindlessly. It was perhaps inevitable that rivals would cut into RCA's market share in the lucrative color-TV market. By 1974 profits from this sector had declined to $11.1 million from the $53.7 million of 1971. Now RCA was earning more from Hertz than from consumer products. It was an amazing change.

Bob hoped to reverse this trend with new products: videotapes and recorders. But he had to do it on the cheap, stinting on R&D expenditures, which in the end doomed the move to failure. John Jamison, RCA's head of marketing, knew what had happened. "There was considerably less willingness to make massive investments that will pay out way off in the future. Now the emphasis is on getting into a new business for as little as possible and making a buck as fast as you can."

Had the General behaved this way, RCA would never have gone into broadcasting or television. Indeed, there might never have been an RCA. But Bob and those around him were now mesmerized by fears of failure. "The computer venture cost $2 billion pretax," explained William Webster of the Princeton Laboratory, "and it took away RCA's courage to take on major new projects." Instead, Bob's RCA would make many "half a dollar bets," acquiring small companies, hoarding cash, and trying for short-term income enhancements. Like selling technology. The worst was yet to come: the continued squandering of RCA's patent rights.

American manufacturers had owned the consumer electronics industry in the 1960s. Magnavox, Zenith, Motorola, and of course, RCA, were the names of TV and radio receivers, phonograph players, and the new tape recorders. Today this industry is almost completely owned by foreigners, the Japanese in particular. Bob Sarnoff wasn't the only American responsible for this, and once more, the problems were started by the General, but RCA was one of the more important contributors to the debacle.

The beginning of this collapse might have been in 1962, when Sony started selling fully transistorized monochrome TV sets for a third less than the same-sized RCA models. These were poorly received, since "Made in Japan" still signified inferior products. Then, the following year, the General committed a major blunder, born of arrogance and ignorance and perhaps old age and illness—he was 73 at the time.

RCA had long enjoyed a harmonious relationship with Sears Roebuck, whereby RCA produced household appliances and consumer-electronic products to be sold under the Sears nameplate. Now Sears wanted to do the same with color TVs. David Sarnoff refused, insisting these be offered under the RCA logo. This wasn't as daring as might appear. Zenith and other American firms had taken the same position. The demand for color sets was such they thought they could dictate terms to Sears and other large buyers.

Such was the situation Bob inherited in 1965. He did nothing to change it. Sanyo was prepared to sell Sears as many sets as it wanted and to do so at a lower price and to the American retailers' specifications. Sears accepted, and from 1963 to 1977 purchased 6.5 million Japanese receivers from Sanyo and later Toshiba worth more than $700 million. These two companies came to dominate the private-label market for both monochrome and with other Japanese producers, color as well, without significant opposition from RCA.

Where did the Japanese companies obtain the technology for such a major foray? It wasn't from their laboratories; as late as 1965 they spent less than 6 percent as much as the American companies on consumer electronics research. Simply stated, the Japanese started out by purchasing the technology from American firms, led by RCA. At one point, RCA earned almost as much from licenses as from product sales. "Japan was dependent on foreign sources for virtually all of the technology employed even to the stage of color television" concluded James Abegglen, the leading authority on the subject. "RCA licenses made Japanese color television possible." Nor was the licensing limited to television; of the 236 agreements concluded in 1970, 89 were in tape recorders, players, and related gear and a like amount in semi-conductors, tubes, and components related to consumer products.

The statistics told the story. In 1963 imports accounted for 7 percent of consumer-electronics purchases; 11 years later the Japanese had 40 percent of the markets, and the leading company in the field was Matsushita, not RCA. Even in color TV, a category it once owned, RCA declined. By 1974 its market share had fallen to 20 percent, due in large part to Japanese competition; the Japanese companies between them had slightly more than that amount of the market. And it wasn't only the Japanese who caused this falloff. Humiliatingly, RCA couldn't compete with American firms either. Zenith had passed RCA with a 24 percent share. Why? In part because Bob insisted on trying to market large console-type sets at a time when the public seemed to prefer smaller tabletop models. Also, RCA's quality declined while Zenith's rose. Bob tried to reverse this situation, but accomplished little. With unseeming haste, RCA departed the market, selling sets manufactured by others by slapping on the RCA logo, a practice that would become increasingly popular, as will be seen in the chapter on Schwinn.

As a graphic sign of its humiliation, RCA had become a licensee—to Matsushita. Today one can't buy a TV manufactured by an American-owned and -based company. The Japanese victory in consumer electronics was more complete and startling than that in automobiles, and RCA played a major role in this.

Crushed by criticism and struggles for power within the company, Bob became increasingly moody and withdrawn. He had health problems as well. Bob had divorced his first wife and married opera star Anna Moffo, which caused bitter clashes with David, and became concerned with her career. He had started out as a PR man, and now reverted to that role, which he found more comfortable than that of an RCA CEO.

In late October 1975, while Bob was away with his wife on a tour of the Far East, the RCA board met to discuss his future with the company. A majority decided he had to go. Bob lacked the ability to lead so large and complicated a concern. "Bob Sarnoff had an attention span that was fully 90 seconds long," complained an unnamed associate—leaks like this were now commonplace. "He would take great intuitive leaps from an unwarranted assumption to a foregone conclusion."

Bob accepted the board's verdict without a fight. The announcement of his resignation "to pursue other interests of a personal nature" was made on November 5, 1975, to take effect at the end of the year. He was to be replaced by Anthony Conrad, an RCA veteran known as a good detail man. The press thought Conrad was there to clean up the mess Bob had left, after which he would retire to make way for a more visionary, charismatic type of leader. By then it seemed RCA had become accident-prone. Soon after, Conrad admitted to tax irregularities and stepped down voluntarily.

In 1982 *Fortune* selected RCA as one of America's least admired companies. As noted, seven years earlier the magazine's board had named David Sarnoff as one of the original members of its Hall of Fame.

Into RCA came Edgar Griffiths, a dynamic type who expanded RCA's conglomerating efforts. Revenues and profits rose, but the golden days could not be recaptured. Under Griffiths RCA introduced the videodisc product known as SelectaVision, a technology by which motion pictures and other presentations were recorded on what seemed at first glance a long-playing phonograph record. The disc program had been initiated by Bob Sarnoff, who was quite enthusiastic about its prospects. By the time it came out, however, the public knew of videocassettes, which were less expensive, accepted by the studios and the public, and most important, enabled the owner to record programs as well as play them, something the videodisc could not offer. SelectaVision was a major disaster, costing the company upward of half a billion dollars. While Bob Sarnoff was correctly seen as the father of SelectaVision, he could not be said to have caused this blunder. Rather, delays in introduction brought it down. Had SelectaVision arrived a few years earlier, it might well have succeeded, providing some luster to the Bob Sarnoff image.

Griffiths lasted until late 1981, when it was becoming apparent SelectaVision would be a major failure. He left under generally amicable circumstances, however, making way for Thornton Bradshaw, the smooth, well-connected former CEO of Atlantic Richfield and an RCA board member. There was no secret regarding Bradshaw's intentions, which were to sell RCA to a high bidder. This turned out to be General Electric, which purchased RCA for $6.3 billion in 1986. And with this, RCA passed from the scene.

Bob rarely spoke to reporters after leaving RCA. Even then he was on his way toward obscurity, but they sought him out when the deal with GE was announced. "One of America's greatest and best-known international companies, whose pioneering efforts in communications and electronics over six decades have contributed so much to our country and the world, will cease to exist," he said in a prepared statement. "I think it's a tragedy." So it was. The reporters were too polite to ask who or what caused that catastrophe.

In 1986 Kenneth Bilby, who had been associated with the General and RCA for more than 20 years, wrote the first important biography of the Great Man since the Lyons work. It was properly deferential, and Bilby went out of his way to be kind to Bob. But he criticized the conglomeration program and the way the computer business was handled. Bilby strongly implied that given another decade of leadership, the General would never have permitted the Japanese to succeed in consumer electronics as they had managed. Had the merger taken place, he wrote, RCA, not GE, would have been the surviving company. "Like Agamemnon sailing against Troy in the Hellenic wars, he would offer any sacrifice to ensure the sempiternity of RCA." One can almost hear drum rolls in the background: "The surviving company must be RCA—*the* RCA, as he always labeled it—the golden Radio of his youth, the RCA of monochrome and color, the RCA that cheered the nation with broadcast sound, the RCA that pursued the electron wherever it led. And, as always, the mission would be to innovate, to inspire, to create new wealth and new values where none existed before."

What might Bob's role be in this kind of myth? Bilby is silent on this matter, but clearly he would afford him no place next to such a paragon, except perhaps as a spear carrier. Still, Bob will be remembered because of his role in the David Sarnoff epic rather than because of what he failed to accomplish at RCA. Such often is the fate of sons of the celebrated.

Toward the close of his life, in 1968, the General had appeared at Bob's fiftieth birthday party and reflected upon their relations. "There always was and there always will be a difference between the generations, and there is no formula to meet it," he began, as though to explain his earlier lapses. All present knew the two men had frequently clashed and that the General more often than not had bullied Bob into submission. Now, too late, the General wanted to make amends.

> I know it's sometimes claimed that it's a cinch to be the boss's son. All you have to do is be born and the rest is made for you. Well, neither the father or son would agree to that formula. It isn't easy for either one, but it's probably more difficult for the son than the father. The father has caught the trolley car, but the son still feels that he has to run after it and sometimes the shadow of the father obscures the son—never intentionally, but sometimes unwittingly.

Bob's dismissal and the disappearance of RCA a decade later provided a special irony and poignancy to the way the General concluded this tribute to his son, a remark that negated the message of much of his talk and revealed, certainly unwittingly, at least part of the reason for Bob's utter failure. "I cannot separate RCA and Bob and David Sarnoff. The fortunes of one are the fortunes of all of us. Any hurt to one is a hurt to all." Which was the problem from the start. With the best of intentions, as has been noted, the General considered RCA, not Bob, to be his oldest and most favored offspring.

W. R. GRACE:
THE BLUNDER OF
NONSTRATEGIC EXPANSION

N ovelist F. Scott Fitzgerald didn't think there were second acts in American lives, implying that many people burn out while relatively young. This may be a snappy phrase, but the thought is not borne out by impartial observation. History is replete with examples of individuals who run full tilt till death or late retirement and perform well throughout their careers.

Are there second acts in American business? Sure. Many corporations have proven capable of regeneration and reform, of mutating into a new form to meet new challenges. One need only consider the likes of General Electric, 3M, du Pont, and IBM to realize this is so. Indeed, most companies that have lasted through the century have had to adjust to changing circumstances in the economy and marketplace.

The need to embrace change has been contemplated and investigated by scores of business consultants and analysts until it has become a cliché. They celebrate CEOs who entered new areas of opportunity when the existing ones turned sour. Nonetheless, few have proven capable of switching from one industry to another successfully. The canal builders and managers in the second quarter of the nineteenth century did not become railroaders. Nor did the steamship entrepreneurs, with the exception of Cornelius Vanderbilt. Only one important automobile tycoon came out of railroading, and Walter Chrysler had been a railroad mechanic, not the head of a major line. Some auto companies thought to enter aviation, and all failed. Likewise, none of the vaudeville impresarios or theater moguls did anything significant in motion pictures, which as Neil Gabler has observed, was an industry dominated by Polish Jews born within a relatively few miles of Warsaw, who came out of the clothing, junk, and other nonartistic venues. The consensus judgement of the conglomerate movement of the 1960s is that it demonstrated that contrary to assertions at the time, a good manager could not switch easily from one industry to another.

Even so, there are dramatic examples of companies that successfully accomplished major changes. The most recent was the swift and dramatic transformation that occurred at Westinghouse Electric in the three years from 1994 to 1997, when that old-line manufacturer of a wide variety of electric equipment sold off close to $10 billion of its companies and purchased $15 billion worth of media operations, including CBS, whereupon it took that company's name. Media was the future, thought CEO Michael Jordan, and manufactured equipment the past—at least for Westinghouse. Realism won over nostalgia, and Jordan moved the headquarters from Pittsburgh, its historic home since Westinghouse's founding in 1886, to New York. Even so, as has been noted, Westinghouse was one of the companies that participated in the creation of Radio Corporation of America, and its Westinghouse Broadcasting Co., which owned and operated television and radio stations, was in operation long before Jordan had arrived, so communications weren't altogether alien to the company.

An even more dramatic change occurred at W. R. Grace under the leadership of Peter Grace. Not only did Grace divest *all* of the empire he inherited and purchase an entirely new one, but did so in the face of a family tradition one might think would have militated against such action, a tradition stronger even than that which Bobby Sarnoff faced at RCA. Then he faltered. W. R. Grace was to have its second act under his leadership, but Peter Grace failed to have a third, since after that splendid remaking of the company he meandered over the business landscape without evidencing the strategic vision he once had shown.

Peter Grace was one of the most fascinating of the conglomerateurs. Unlike some of the others—Tex Thornton, Royal Little, Charles Bluhdorn, and James Ling, for example—he did not come out of the provinces to found an enterprise. He was more akin to Harold Geneen, who took over at ITT, and after attempting to revamp it, transformed the company into a conglomerate. Even while he dominated ITT, however, Geneen lacked the cachet Grace enjoyed. As Peter Grace liked to observe, his name was on the company and on its New York's 42nd Street headquarters building.

W. R. Grace had been founded by Peter's grandfather, William Russell Grace, who was succeeded by Peter's father, after whom came Peter. At first he was compared to his predecessors, and unfavorably at that, but unlike Bobby Sarnoff, he did not have his father on the scene to remind him of *his* successes. Rather, there was the ghost of his grandfather, the founder, to reckon with.

W. R. Grace was not a particularly large company in W. R.'s day, but it was well-known and highly respected, with an unusual, exotic history. Without an appreciation of that history and an awareness of the importance of tradition there, one cannot fully gauge the magnitude of Peter Grace's accomplishment, for because of this, in the view of veterans there, what he did to W. R. Grace amounted to sacrilege.

William Russell Grace's tale is the quintessential American success story, only it wasn't exclusively American and had more to do with the South American west coast. Grace had left Ireland during the potato famine of the 1840s and had bounced around the world as a sailor. In 1851 he shipped out to Calleo, Peru, then in the midst of a boom in the guano trade, and after a brief apprenticeship W. R. entered that business.

The harvesting and sale of bird droppings for fertilizer was only one of his many interests. W. R. was bold in vision and daring in the execution. He would go wherever profits were to be had, purchasing or founding projects and then discarding them when they lost their glow. In 1854, when it suited his needs, he organized W. R. Grace & Co. as the vehicle through which most of his efforts would be channeled.

W. R.'s activities expanded at what for the time was a breakneck pace. Conglomerateurs of the 1960s might have recognized in his various operations a nineteenth-century version of what they were doing. So might the sedentary merchants of the eighteenth century, who from their perches in counting houses invested in a wide variety of enterprises. But W. R. was rarely sedentary. He owned and ran Peruvian textile mills and sugar estates, a rubber industry in a Brazilian jungle, and a nitrate business in the Chilean desert. There were Grace-constructed railroads in the Andes. W. R. introduced American agricultural and electrical equipment to the west coast of South America. He was even involved in a scheme to dig a canal across Nicaragua that preceded the Panama Canal. When Peruvian finances were in shambles, W. R. and his brother, Michael, were asked to help reorganize them and put the country back on its feet.

W. R. was concerned with politics on three continents. Even while deeply involved in South America, he pursued holdings in other parts of the globe. He founded Grace Brothers & Co. of London and then went on to the Orient. Within two decades, W. R. had accumulated trading interests that stretched from Peru to Tokyo and from the Baring Sea to the Straits of Magellan.

One of the keys to his success—in addition to his intelligence, perception, and ability to work astonishingly long hours—was W. R.'s uncanny talent for selecting and training good managers. In a period when communications were poor, managers had to have great leeway in making decisions. W. R. didn't give them independence until they had proven themselves under experienced, trusted veterans. The executives he trained were to take the company to new heights after he passed from the scene.

W. R. relocated to New York in 1865, where he became the first Catholic mayor of the city, leading a reform campaign and leaving office with a solid record of accomplishment. Afterwards he returned to business and started some companies in the United States, among them a machinery concern that later became one of the components of Ingersoll Rand.

In 1898 W. R. suffered a stroke, and he hurt himself in a fall two years later. By then he had prepared the way for the change in command. Michael Grace and nephew Edward Eyre had been trained to take over, and Eyre became president. Behind them were W. R.'s son, Joseph Grace, and D. Stewart Iglehart, his right-hand man. W. R. died in 1904, but the succession went smoothly, and his stamp remained on the company three decades later.

Such was the legacy of William Russell Grace. It was a story Peter Grace and all at headquarters and in the company knew well.

In 1936, W. R. Grace was still synonymous with the South America trade and, as in W. R.'s day, was involved in a wide variety of businesses. It owned and operated sugar plantations in Peru, along with refineries, a paper plant, and a facility that produced caustic soda, chlorine, and muriatic acid. The company made rum from molasses at Cartavio in Peru. There were tin, wolfram, lead, and zinc mines, to go with textile mills in Colombia, Peru, and Chile. An oilseed operation. A coffee plantation in Guatemala. A trading business in East Indian coffee and cocoa. The ship agency operations in 30 or so ports. Cotton mills. Woolen mills. And much more.

The Grace Bank, which handled the company's business, was known as the savviest financial institution in its special niche. The Grace Line was one of America's most renowned carriers, taking cargoes and passengers to and from the United States to ports along the west coast of Latin America. Panagra, a joint venture with Pan American, was the major air carrier from the United States to points south and will be discussed in more detail in the chapter dealing with that airline. A popular radio program of the time, *Nights in Latin America*, spun visions of the exotic southern continent, along with playing native music.

Hanover Square, where W. R. moved his New York headquarters in 1885, is located just off Old William Slip near Pearl and Water Streets. In 1936 there were several coffee roasters near the Square, which provided the district with an aroma old-timers at Grace never forgot. W. R.'s ghost seemed to hover over Hanover Square. Even today, it seems more a slice of late nineteenth-century America than a neighborhood just blocks from the Wall Street financial center.

The Grace headquarters of that period was a stately old gray building. On the first floor was the Grace Bank, with offices in the back. At the end of the row of marble columns hung a painting of the clipper ship "W. R. Grace," with signal flags unfurled to "Report Me All Well."

The Grace offices were populated by men more familiar with the Cordillera de Andes than the Rockies, who would be lost in Chicago but knew their ways around Lima. Almost all had served for many years in one or more of the Grace *casas* in Peru, Ecuador, Chile, and Bolivia. Conversations over lunch in the nearby India House often were conducted in Spanish. They would still stop there half a century after W. R.'s death and, for luck, rub the fat belly of a wooden Buddha in the vestibule.

As was the case with all new hires, after graduating from Yale, where he spent far more time playing polo, hockey, and baseball than cracking the books, Peter began in the mail room. He considered this a matter of no great consequence. At the time he cared little for business, not even for W. R. Grace. In fact, he was a singularly limited young man, with no discernible intellectual curiosity. Simply put, Peter was a jock, who often tried to slip away from the mail room to perform as practice goalie with the New York Rangers.

Joseph Grace was the W. R. Grace CEO in 1936. He was a competent leader, who kept the many Grace heirs happy by paying fat dividends. In the course of time, Peter might have expected to inherit the mantle. But not necessarily. Scores of Graces and other relatives depended upon the company for their incomes, and they weren't about to permit Peter—who at the time seemed more interested in a position on the American Olympic polo team than in learning the business—to botch their inheritance.

His behavior soon changed. As he continued to work at the company, Peter Grace was obliged to follow that rigorous training regimen, moving from one division to another, from New York to Peru, Chile, and beyond. In an old Grace tradition he became a generalist and developed the same commitment to business that he had previously displayed for sports, devouring piles of reports and putting in the 80-hour weeks for which he later became famous. "The only way we can know the details and be ready to make decisions on any aspect of a business as diversified as ours is to work harder than other businessmen," he said. Though he found time to marry, he gave up some of his athletic pursuits and paid less attention to his wardrobe. In fact, one reporter later observed, he had a "generally linty appearance," as if he had "just come out of a pillow fight." Ever aware of his limitations, throughout his life Grace sought and usually found mentors, older men whose guidance he followed. One of the first of these counselors was Raul Simon, who headed the company's Chilean operations. Before then, Simon had served in government, worked as a journalist, and authored several books. He was one of the very few Grace executives who could be considered an intellectual, and this intrigued Peter, who had little exposure to such people.

In 1940 Grace traveled to Chile, and there he and Simon had a series of conversations that started him thinking about the company's future. Simon predicted the United States would enter the European war then raging. Latin American countries would sell a great deal of raw materials to the United States and come out of war quite prosperous, which would prove their undoing.

Simon believed demagogues would come to power throughout Latin America, promising the people endless prosperity. In time all foreign investments would be taken over, while inflation would destroy values. Simon convinced Grace that the company would have to leave South America before this happened.

At that time Peter Grace was involved with the company's burgeoning South American trade, and as Simon had predicted, the countries to the south were sending increasing amounts of raw materials to the United States. These activities were enormously profitable. In 1938, the last full prewar year, W. R. Grace had revenues of $1.7 million; three years later they came to $9.1 million and reached just under $12 million in 1945.

That year his father died, and after a brief struggle, Peter became president of W. R. Grace. At first his powers were limited. At the time the board was comprised of W. R. Grace's elder statesmen and conservative Grace family members. The most sobering influence was that of William Grace Holloway, Peter's much older cousin, who served as board chairman. All there monitored him warily. Many of the Graces and older timers at Hanover Square had watched Peter grow up and still thought of him as a playboy sportsman. Peter was determined to change their minds on this score and worked harder than ever. "It is evident that the third era of Grace will have a character all of its own," wrote Freeman Lincoln in *Fortune* soon after the change at the helm. "The new Grace won't look too much like the old Grace, and it will be Peter's Grace."

During the war Grace had pondered Simon's prophecy and saw much of what he had predicted come true. By then he had developed a three-part plan. In addition to taking the company out of South America, he would have to unearth other businesses for it to enter. W. R. Grace could either start companies or purchase them, and under the circumstances, purchases made more sense. The firm lacked the requisite expertise and knowledge to operate anything but those Latin American enterprises and would need managers and technicians from the acquired companies.

The third part of the strategy was to transform W. R. Grace into a public company, in this way easing the task of raising funds. In addition

Peter could then use stock options to keep and attract the kind of talent he would need to operate the acquired businesses. These new managers would be specialists, not generalists like the Grace veterans, and this, along with the other changes, was bound to cause friction.

All of this had to be done with a board that still didn't take him seriously and a family that considered him a menace to their dividend payments and was accustomed to viewing W. R. Grace as the family preserve. Now the young, untested president wanted to let strangers through the door. Given this, the program had to be carried out slowly and deliberately so as not to upset the existing operations. As board members retired or died, Peter would replace them with new people who agreed with his vision for the company. It was an uphill climb.

While Peter was able to update the company's antiquated accounting systems and hire and promote new executives, he had less success convincing the board of the need to adopt his three-pronged strategy. "In 1952, just before the diversification started and we were in the depths of everything, I got into an automobile accident and spent three months in the hospital," he later told a *Forbes* reporter. "That's when they tried to fire me. My Number Two man went after me. He didn't want to do the diversification, and neither did some of the directors. If I'd been well, that son-of-a-bitch would never have tried anything." That would be Andrew Shea, one of the Latin American hands, who felt that he had to save the old company. Peter survived this challenge, and reluctantly the board agreed to a public stock offering by just one vote. W. R. Grace was listed on the New York Stock Exchange in early 1953, by which time Grace had perfected his plans for diversification.

With the aid of his staff Peter had narrowed the field to three possible areas: petroleum, chemicals, and electronics, all of which were promising. It didn't take long to erase petroleum from the list. Exploration was too risky, refining too costly, and marketing out of the question. Electronics was exciting and fresh, but evolving too rapidly, and no one at the company knew how to evaluate personnel or companies.

Chemicals were a large, diffuse field, with many players and a large number of niches, some of which resembled several of W. R. Grace's old businesses, such as caustic soda, muriatic acid, and chlorine. It was a purely opportunistic decision, arrived at after applying a rigorous calculus of profit and losses. Grace didn't know much about chemicals and had little interest in learning more, but he applied himself to the tasks ahead.

Grace used his connections to acquire the proper talent. Into the company came retired General Electric CEO Charles Wilson, Ben Oehlert from Coca-Cola, and Robert Haslam from Standard Oil of New Jersey, and they were followed by more executives and scientists, including some contentious ones, like Otto Ambros, who worked with Wernher von Braun on rocket fuels and during World War II became known as "the Devil's Chemist." There were few prominent executives with much experience in chemicals, and the ones Grace wanted couldn't be lured into the new venture. Instead, Grace took on a group of bright younger men who had to learn about chemicals on the run.

When Peter was ready to start acquiring new companies, Haslam, who was to serve as his mentor in chemicals, led him to Davison Chemical, whose fertilizer and insecticide businesses complemented W. R. Grace's capabilities in these areas in South America and also had a strong position in the catalytic field. Davison could provide W. R. Grace with an entry into petrochemicals, an area Peter and Haslam considered most promising. Davison had twelve plants, most quite modern, and a triple superphosphate plant in the planning stage in Florida. The stock seemed underpriced, and Peter loved bargains. This was a hostile takeover, which boosted the price somewhat, but by late 1953 W. R. Grace had a 63 percent interest in the company and soon after acquired the rest of the stock.

Without pausing, Peter approached another chemical company, Dewey & Almy, at the urging of Haslam, who was on the board. Haslam told Peter of a product D&A had called cryovac, which first appeared in 1949. Cryovac met with indifferent success and was used primarily for bagging turkeys, but in 1953 it was taking off for other uses. In addition, D&A pioneered in the vacuum packing of coffee and packaging beverages in metal containers. The company also did some interesting work on insulators. At the time D&A had two cryovac plants running full blast and undergoing expansion, while a third was being erected. Wall Street perceived D&A as a respectable company, turning out many specialty items, but no more than that. In W. R. Grace's favor was that all of this expansion took money, which D&A

lacked. Peter borrowed heavily and acquired the company. Barely pausing, he went on the prowl for more deals in chemicals.

All of this activity in chemicals troubled W. R. Grace's South American hands. They knew Peru and Chile and the rest of Latin America. Peter Grace, Haslam, and others were talking about super-phosphates and plasticizers. In the Latin Americans' time, W. R. Grace had been an exciting, romantic company, with the ships, Panagra, and the bank. Latin American mines and factories were a lot more interesting than urea plants. Peter could understand and sympa-thize with that perception. He, too, knew more about paper mills than urea. For him, chemicals remained an obscure area. Some years later, when trying to win over several recalcitrant directors to a new project, Peter stumbled over the word, "hydrofluosilic," prompting one direc-tor to retort, "I'll be damned if I'll vote for a chemical project that Peter can't even pronounce."

Yet chemicals were the tomorrow of W. R. Grace, and South America the yesterday. Peter knew that. So did the old-timers. Peter invested more than $250 million in chemicals during those first ten years. In 1950 the chemical business represented 3 percent of the company's assets; by 1957 the figure had grown to 55 percent, and W. R. Grace was one of the ten largest chemical companies in America. In the same period revenues rose from $265 million to $460 million and earnings from $8.5 million to $15.5 million.

In 1957 recessions struck in both the United States and much of South America. Peter was able to fight off critics who wanted him ousted, and with the economic recovery, W. R. Grace prospered once again. This experience would be repeated several times, as W. R. Grace became a company whose businesses were quite cyclical.

Since the wartime boom in South America continued into the 1950s, Peter was prepared to invest in that part of the world as well. By the mid-1950s, however, the companies there suffered under the weight of currency fluctuations and political instability. Peter awoke every day wondering what was happening.

It was in the early 1960s that Peter seemed to start to lose his sense of direction. His natural impatience had gotten more pro-nounced. One W. R. Grace executive said that his attention span was about three months, after which he would become bored with a busi-ness and look for something new. Another problem was that by then he had accumulated sufficient power to do anything he wanted to do. The old-timers had been weeded from the board, which was then made up of personal friends and consultants, and his own staff was populated largely by yes men.

There were exceptions. Shea was permitted to survive his attempt at a coup, because his expertise and connections were needed and he had the support of Grace family members. After Shea retired, his role as chief Peter Grace gadfly was taken by Felix Larkin, who often opposed Peter's actions and ideas. Why did he keep on board a man he so disliked? One reason was that Peter had a constitutional incapacity to fire people: Shea had taken care of that duty, and now Larkin filled the role. In addition, Peter was aware of his flaws and knew he had to have at least one person around who could be blunt and direct with him, even though his advice would not be accepted. Larkin was that man.

And the flaws increasingly were coming into view. In addition to that notoriously short attention span, Peter rarely gave a manager free reign. Unlike his father and grandfather, he attempted to microman-age, displaying a compulsive concern with data. He would inundate the board members with information, most of it in statistical form. Before most monthly meetings each member would get a report run-ning around 400 pages, crammed with accordion-pleated spread-sheets, some of which ran to more than 100 columns. Once a board member dropped one of the books and the spreadsheet spilled out for what seemed to be yards. He said, "Peter, I'm going to buy International Paper. I want to own stocks in some paper companies."

While it was true that Peter Grace was obsessed with statistics, there was another reason for this behavior. Those large volumes put the board members in awe and in fear of looking foolish. Imagine the poor board member who asked a question only to be told the answer was on page 365? It was like a schoolboy who wanted the answer to a question, and the teacher responded sharply that the answer was in last night's assignment. This would prove he hadn't done the work. Also, the board assumed anyone who went into so much detail must know just about everything there was to know.

Such methods made Peter a sucker for businesses with good past financial performances that were not necessarily an indication of future prospects. "He lacks marketing instincts," said one of his colleagues. "Many times the figures will tell you that a company is going to make a good return on your investment. Then two years later you suddenly have to inject a couple more million dollars because your product is becoming obsolete."

Once Peter had taken a fix on an idea, there was no talking him out of it. This was so in Latin America, where he started putting businesses on the block, and also in the American-based firms involved with Latin America, including the Grace Bank, the interest in Panagra, and the Grace Line. The Bank was sold to Marine Midland in 1965, and Panagra to Braniff two years later. "We thought we had a deal to sell our half interest in Panagra to Pan Am for $15 million," Peter recalled, "but that one fell through. We got even in 1967. Troy Post had bought Braniff from Tom Braniff's estate and wanted Panagra to give him a lock on the region. We sold him our half, and [Pan Am's Juan] Trippe had to sell him his share. So Panagra went to Braniff. Our take was $15 million. Part of our history was no more."

The Grace Line, once the company's most visible and popular symbol in the United States, was sold to Admiralty Enterprises in 1969 for $44.5 million, of which $42 million was in cash. Peter felt unhappy about this sale. The Grace Line was much more fascinating than a plant making can sealants.

That was the year a Peruvian military junta started expropriating foreign properties, among them some of the W. R. Grace holdings, with a payment much smaller than Peter thought equitable. Disgusted, in a fit of temper he ordered the wholesale divestiture of all South American companies, which was completed in a few years, often at prices below what they should have fetched.

By then Peter was off and running into several new areas of opportunity. W. R. Grace had not been doing as well as he thought it should. Specialty chemicals had performed well and had become the backbone of the new W. R. Grace. But the commodity-chemicals business was highly cyclical, and earnings dipped again in early 1962, and so Peter started looking for new industries in which to invest. Now that he was more secure, he was prepared to act boldly and to purchase companies in industries he found interesting. With this, his career entered a new phase.

In December 1962, W. R. Grace acquired a majority interest in one of the world's leading chocolate manufacturers, the Dutch firm of

C. J. Van Houton & Zoon. At the time this was not perceived as any-thing novel for W. R. Grace, especially in that era of conglomerates. For a number of years the company had been a leading manufacturer of chocolates and other food products in Chile and Peru, so it seemed a continuation of the tradition. This was a consequential action. Peter thought that if he could do with foods what he had accomplished in specialty chemicals, W. R. Grace would have another string to its bow.

Why chocolate? Peter was a chocoholic, and this was one field into which he could pour himself with zeal. He also felt that he could understand food much more easily than he might chemicals. To be sure, there would be further acquisitions in chemicals, along with divestitures, but nothing like the pace in foods, which now took most of his attention. In rapid order W. R. Grace acquired Cacaofabrick de Zaan in Holland; Hughes Brothers, an Irish ice-cream company; and Urney Chocolates, another Irish company.

What did these businesses have in common? Clearly all were European, all peripheral factors in their industries, and all had been purchased for what Peter considered discounts from their true values. They would form the basis for The Food Group, out of which was to evolve what he liked to call "The General Foods of Europe," the cap-ital for which coming from loans and the sale of those South American interests.

The basic strategy was to buy small companies run by families, both in Europe and the United States, and unite them into a consumer-products enterprise. The idea sounded plausible, but as in so many other Peter Grace projects, wasn't implemented well. Peter and oth-ers involved didn't seem to realize that once they sold their companies, the old managers at family businesses had no desire to remain and work for someone else. Thus, the very people who made the enter-prise prosper were no longer there, replaced by newcomers, some of whom had to learn the business from the ground up.

The Food Group made many purchases in the late 1960s. There were Fanny Farmer Candy Shops; Nalley's Fine Foods, a West Coast producer of potato and corn chips; SeaPak, one of the nation's leading suppliers of frozen shrimp and other fish products; and chewing-gum manufacturer Leaf Brands. Barilla, Italy's leading pasta, became a W. R. Grace company. Ice-cream companies, more candy, groceries—you name it. W. R. Grace companies were selling chewing gum to

Germans, dairy products to Spaniards, jam to the French, and snack foods and pickles to customers in the United Kingdom. The names of some of the companies were unfamiliar to most outside the businesses or their locales. Tamara. Person. Wayne Candies. H. B. Ice Cream. Raak Nederland. The executives at the Food Group purchased some fine companies, but they were better at buying businesses than at getting executives who could grow them, develop the product lines, and make moves into new markets.

One of the most interesting purchases was a stake in Miller Brewing, obtained in 1966. Miller performed in a mediocre fashion, and when Peter was unable to purchase the rest of the shares, in 1968 he sold his holdings to Philip Morris for $130 million. Under Philip Morris's control, Miller became the country's second-largest brewer. Grace was disarmingly frank in assessing why Philip Morris had succeeded. The reasons by then were familiar: "They had a talent we lacked."

Almost all traces of the original W. R. Grace were gone by the early 1970s—except for the Hanover Square offices, and these would go in 1973, when the company relocated to the new W. R. Grace Building, a modern skyscraper on the east corner of 42nd Street and the Avenue of the Americas. Peter said the move had been necessary because the company needed more space, and the new locale was more convenient for commuters from Long Island and Westchester County. Perhaps so, but nonetheless the symbolism couldn't be missed. W. R. Grace was *his* company, and no longer W. R.'s. As he told a reporter toward the end of the decade, "My grandfather didn't found any of the things we have now. He didn't found this company. I did." Just as Bobby Sarnoff labored in the shadow of his more famous father, so Peter Grace was driven to surpass his legendary grandfather.

By then, too, Peter had gone from foods to restaurants, a logical enough move and one quite typical for him. While considering the sale of Miller he had breakfast at a coffee shop called Coco's and thought the milk shake was "fantastic," a word he often used. The manager told him Coco's was owned by Far West Services, which also had a group of restaurants that operated under the names of Plank House, Reuben's, and Sunday's, among others. So in 1970, after pursuing it for two years, he bought Far Western. Charles Macintosh, who had founded and managed the company, left, along with many of his crew.

After learning about the restaurant business by observing the many Far Western outlets, Peter went on a tear. He now considered America ready for several Mexican operations, so in late 1976 he purchased El Torito-La Fiesta, a highly successful 23-unit dinner-house chain in southern California. The following year, he formed the Del Taco Corp., 80 percent owned by W. R. Grace, the other 20 percent by Del Taco Inc. In came Gilbert/Robinson, a Kansas City-based company that had 30 full-service restaurants, the best known being Houlihan's Old Place, which was something like TGIF, a hangout for young people. But Joe Gilbert, the founder, departed, and the business went nowhere without him.

Peter kept on buying. There was Jojo's, which operated 110 coffee shops in 15 states. Sam Wilson's, Annie's Santa Fe, Fred P. Ott's, Capt'n Jeremiah Tuttle's, and Plaza III. El Torito opened Who-Song & Larry's Cantina, which featured singing waiters, and Rosa Corona, where every night was a fiesta. It also had Tequila Willie's, and Chubasco, along with five other specialty restaurants that were Peter's bid for the upscale market. One of the El Toritos was given the appropriate name of "Que Pasa," which means "What's happening?" All were forgettable.

Peter Grace seemed out of control, relying more on whim than on any carefully thought-out strategy. He then made W. R. Grace a major force in specialty department stores, his mentor in this area being David Yunich, the former head of Macy's and one of the most respected figures in retailing. With Yunich's help, Peter purchased Herman's, Sheplers, Channel, Pic 'n' Pay, and other stores and chains. Few people remember Elmex or Handy Dan, but with better management they might have bested Toys R Us and Home Depot, since they were in the businesses before those two successful operations made it big.

In addition, W. R. Grace made a foray into petroleum. By acquiring many small firms, it had become one of the 30 or so largest independent producers in the country. Peter purchased several drilling companies, all of which required heavy capital expenditures, which mandated borrowing. This seemed worthwhile. The company performed spectacularly during the energy crisis of the 1970s, when specialty chemical prices also were strong. In 1981, on revenues of $6.5 billion, the company had earnings of $361 million, both records.

A severe recession, combined with the energy bust, took 1986 revenues and earnings down to $3.7 billion, while write-downs associated with divestitures and a poor situation in chemicals and energy caused W. R. Grace to report a loss of $375 million.

Another, different crisis hit W. R. Grace at this time. In 1978 the Flick Group, a large German firm, had purchased 7.3 million W. R. Grace shares. Peter Grace was pleased, since this would place a major stake in friendly hands. In 1985 the Flicks had to sell their shares, at a time when W. R. Grace was experiencing hard times and the stock's price was low. Peter felt certain the shares would fall into the hands of a corporate raider, who would try to take control of the company and carve it up. To prevent this, W. R. Grace would have to purchase the shares itself. Peter scrambled to borrow close to a billion dollars, which he did, and used. As recently as 1975 the corporation's long-term debt had been $667 million; at the end of 1985 it came to $1.6 billion. The need to cut back on the debt, combined with the obvious failures of several aspects of the new W. R. Grace, provided Peter with the means to exit from the failed ventures smoothly.

Peter had learned the hard way that specialty retailers and restaurants were not the kind of growth vehicle he thought they would be. At least, not for him. He let it be known that they were for sale at the proper price. In the mid- to late 1980s, in a replay of the exit from South America, Grace sold off the restaurants and the retailers, but this time he was able to repay profits from the sales. The stake in Herman's that had cost $6.7 million went to Dee's, a large British retailer, for $227 million. Channel and some other home-supply stores—201 in all—were sold to an insider group and fetched $250 million. Almost all the restaurants, except Del Taco and a few others, went for $536 million for the 690 units. Del Taco was finally sold in 1991, to PepsiCo, which had succeeded in an area where W. R. Grace had failed; its Taco Bell's became highly popular, and the Del Tacos were transformed into Taco Bells. In his defense, Peter asserted that in his time, W. R., too, would sell off holdings when they soured, but there was no true comparison.

While now 73 years old, Peter Grace had no intention to retire, or for that matter, give up on entering new fields. This time it was to be health care. He rationalized that there were some synergies between health care and specialty chemicals. For example, cryovac was being used for ostomy pouches. More important, however, was his constant need for new challenges.

As had become his practice, Peter entered the field slowly, trying to learn as he looked over potential takeovers. Also as before, his strategy seemed to be to acquire the best companies he could find at reasonable prices, use the expertise generated by managements in those companies, and then locate others, purchase them, and just keep going.

In 1983 he acquired Amicon, which manufactured filtration materials used in the biotechnology and health-care industries. Other small units followed. Then, in 1984 W. R. Grace took a 49.99 percent interest in National Medical for $360 million, increased its holdings in the years that followed, and in time acquired the entire company. National Medical, which was led by the mercurial Constantine Hampers, was the largest supplier of outpatient kidney-dialysis services from more than 200 centers in the United States and Canada. The fit with Amicon was obvious.

National Medical provided the foundation for what was to be W. R. Grace Health Care, into which came the usual Peter Grace variety of companies—Infusioncare, Symbion, and more. American Homecare Equipment, a leading force in its area, was purchased for $129 million, and Home Nutritional Services cost $110 million. Meanwhile, the newly formed Grace Ventures made a series of investments in small high-tech companies, such as Access Medical Systems, Gen-Prove, and Oral Research Laboratories.

In 1990 Grace discovered he had cancer of the hip, which a year and a half later had spread to his lungs. Reluctantly, he named his successor, who was to be J. P. Bolduc, who became president and chief operating officer, while Peter remained as chairman and chief executive officer.

Peter Grace had eight children, some of whom worked at the company, but none were considered qualified at the time for the CEO or COO posts. So it was to be Bolduc, the first non-Grace to reach so exalted a position.

Peter had met Bolduc while engaged in work on the Grace Commission, a body named by President Reagan to look into government waste. A former consultant with Booz Allen, Bolduc impressed Peter with his intelligence, energy, and toughness. Soon after, the company relocated to Boca Raton, but Peter remained in New York, working from his old offices at the Grace Building and going to his doctors for radiation therapy. Meanwhile Bolduc restructured the company, sold off additional properties, and was giving W. R. Grace a more focused appearance than it had before.

The next step in the succession came in January 1993, when Bolduc replaced Peter as CEO. Grace continued as chairman, but at the time it appeared the company was Bolduc's alone. With this, Peter's business career seemed about over. This was not so. There remained one final messy act before the curtain came down.

By late 1994, Bolduc and Hampers were clashing over National Medical's future, and for that matter, the prospects of W. R. Grace itself. Under certain circumstances, Bolduc indicated, he might be willing to break up W. R. Grace into its components to enhance shareholder values, and Hampers wanted to buy National Medical.

It was against this backdrop that Bolduc abruptly resigned on March 2, 1995, citing differences with the board as the reason. Immediately, Hampers announced his intention to contest for the CEO post. At month's end, allegations surfaced that Bolduc had sexually harassed five female employees, and this was supposed to be the real reason for his departure.

The fur flew at the Boca headquarters, and repercussions were felt in New York. Peter now came in for criticism for having held onto his perquisites too long and for charging personal expenditures to the company. Large institutional shareholders, stunned by the revelations, concluded that Peter had put his own needs before those of the company. Finally the unthinkable happened: the board—Peter Grace's board—asked him to step down as chairman.

On April 6, 1995, Peter rose from his hospital bed to attend his final board meeting. Too weak to complete his speech, he let his wife deliver the final line. "I have spent my life serving this company." He died on April 19, days before the annual meeting at which he was to have stepped down as chairman. It was an ignoble end to a colorful career.

In his time Peter Grace came in for much criticism for his *modus operandi*, which did seem erratic, serendipitous, and downright quirky, but his legacy at W. R. Grace, expressed in the numbers he cared so much about, was hardly shabby. Then, too, never before or since has a major company undergone such a radical transformation. It is as though IBM opted to become a restaurant chain, or General Motors a textile operation. But with all of this, so powerful was the image of the company Peter had inherited that even now, many people believe W. R. Grace is a major force in Latin America.

Peter really had several careers at W. R. Grace. In the first he had a clear strategy and the wisdom to seek out assistance from experts in order to implement it. In the process he created, within the framework of a company devoted to activities on the west coast of South America, a North American chemical complex that became a leader in its segment of the industry. Once it became clear that the Latin American companies were not as viable as they had once been, he initiated a program to eliminate them from the company. This was not done in an organized fashion, and in time some of the companies Peter dumped performed outstandingly, but this might have been expected given the scope of his tasks.

Then Peter embarked on a series of diversifications that while sensible enough on the surface were poorly implemented. The concept of a General Foods of Europe did not take account of business conditions there. The diversification into restaurants and retailing was done in a haphazard, almost accidental, fashion. Peter would have lunch in a restaurant, like the food, and buy the chain. He would wander through a mall, enter a retail establishment, smile approvingly, and it would be added to his portfolio of unrelated stores. Then he started purchasing health care companies, on the hunch that this was to become a large industry and W. R. Grace might as well have representation in it.

Conglomerateurs were known for their interests in varied industries, but most of them were not as wildly opportunistic as Peter Grace, who confused statistics with concepts and appeared to wander through the variegated garden of American business, picking those flowers that he found attractive, keeping those that flourished under his care, and discarding others that wilted. Toward the end of his life he ably defended his record, noting quite accurately that had he not taken the company out of Latin America when he did, there would be no W. R. Grace. He was able to point to successes in chemicals and show visitors a list of companies he had purchased and then sold. It made for impressive reading. Missing from the list, however, were those companies that had failed to make the grade, and there were more of the latter than the former. True, Peter Grace hit some home runs, but he struck out more often. Moreover, it showed up in the numbers he loved to accumulate. In 1993, when he turned the company over to Bolduc, W. R. Grace had revenues of $4.4 billion and earnings of $26 million. In 1984 on revenues of $6.7 billion the company earned $196 million.

CHAPTER SIX

PACKARD: THE BLUNDER OF DOWNWARD BRAND EXTENSION

Some companies and products have names that are synonymous with quality, class, and exclusivity. Tiffany . . . Mont Blanc . . . Rolex . . . Chanel . . . Fendi. There are more, but not many. It is an exclusive club.

This isn't to suggest other jewelry stores, fountain pens, wristwatches, perfumes, and handbags are inferior. Parker produces a fine fountain pen and Seiko a perfectly acceptable wristwatch, but they aren't targeted by "knockoffs," as are Mont Blanc and Rolex. The reason isn't difficult to find. Rolex and Fendi deemed in special categories because of their *craftsmanship*. Parker and Seiko are considered *mass produced*.

Managements of companies producing fine products face strong temptations to put out popular-priced versions. Not content to merely maintain tradition and image, some seek to expand in order to capitalize on fame and to reap a larger volume of trade and profits. Almost always they fail. What would happen if Chanel put out a low-priced line of perfumes? Or Fendi sold a $20 handbag? Who then would buy the $200 perfume, the $400 handbag? A firm that acted in such a manner would soon lose its buyers who prize craftsmanship and probably wouldn't gain enough customers on the lower end to make up for the difference. Kmart can operate a discount operation. For Cartier it would prove suicidal. Once the magic associated with the marque is gone, the aura of distinction evaporates. The product becomes common and in some cases vanishes altogether.

Perhaps the most striking example of how this works occurred during the 1930s, when after nibbling at the edges for a decade,

Packard entered the midpriced segment of the auto market, posted excellent sales there, and for a while also managed to retain the loyalties of its blue-blood clientele. Management congratulated itself on what seemed a major success. What hadn't been taken into account was that this was during the Great Depression, when the market for expensive cars melted or, to be more precise, when customers who earlier wouldn't settle for anything but the best were willing to compromise. Purchasing a midrange Packard under those circumstances provided them with a cachet that was exclusive at the more modest price. Also, in those years brand loyalty was much stronger than it would be later on. Camel smokers were wedded to them for life, as were Coke drinkers. So it was with Packard drivers. The company's management counted on this in making their calculations.

Lincoln, one of Packard's prime competitors, refused to offer downscale models and suffered sales declines. Earlier Cadillac experimented with a lower-priced car but gave it up. Losses from these cars could be endured, since they were parts of the huge Ford and General Motors operations; the red ink posted by Lincoln and Cadillac were compensated for by profits on Fords and Chevrolets.

As a result, the other high-end cars soon caught up to and then passed Packard in their market segment. Packard's leaders seemed not to realize what had happened. Nor were they equipped to battle it out with Buick and Chrysler in the midrange market. Packard slid into obscurity and finally, in July 1958, rolled out its last car. It is a classic tale of marketing failure caused in part by loss of image.

In its time, Packard was known as "The American Rolls-Royce." It is forgotten today except by hobbyists and collectors and a handful of individuals over the age of 70 who recall a different era. At the turn of the century there were thousands of automobile producers. If one counted as a manufacturer every individual who in his barn cobbled together what at the time passed for an automobile, there were thousands of them. The situation in autos then was much as it was to be in personal computers, and there was more than a passing resemblance between the auto enthusiasts of the 1900s and the hackers of the 1970s. In 1901 approximately 7,000 automobiles were produced by more than 100 companies recognized as "manufacturers" rather than tinkerers. That year 1,500 Locomobiles, 700 Wintons, 425 Oldsmobiles, 193 Whites, 140 Autocars, 105 Knoxes, 81 Packards, and 80 Stanleys were turned out. Among the new manufacturers that appeared in 1902 were Apperson, Baldner, Binney & Burnham Steam, Blomstrom, Brazier, Bristol, Centaur, Cloughley, Covert, Davenport Steam, Decker, Flint Steam, Franklin, Fredonia, Gaethmobile, General, Graham Motorette, Holsman, Ideal, Kunz, Model, Murray, Northern, Pomeroy, Rambler, Reber, Rockaway, Sandusky, Santos-Dumont, Studebaker Electric, Toledo, Tourist, Union, Upton, Walter (also known as American Chocolate), Wick, Wildman, and Yale. Of course, some stood out almost from the start, and several of these survived and became significant if not prominent companies— Studebaker lasted until after World War II—but most of them hung on for a few seasons and then folded.

Almost all of these pioneers were tinkerers and interested amateurs. They manufactured and sold their cars to a market comprised of affluent trendsetters. Those early automobile purchasers were invariably wealthy with a curiosity regarding the "buggyauts." In the first decade of the century those who stared at cars on the roads simply assumed their drivers were wealthy. Who else could afford such a conceit? Governor—and later President—Woodrow Wilson perceived in the auto a vehicle that would lead to social frictions. Owners of cars, wealthy and arrogant, would inflame class distinctions and engender revolutionary impulses. Not until Henry Ford came along did the vision change, and the car became the symbol not of wealth, but the triumph of the common man over time and distance. It wasn't that way in the beginning, however, and certainly not with Packard.

As with the Dodges, Lelands, Duesenbergs, Duryeas, Appersons, Studebakers, and Fishers, brothers all, James and William Packard, who had developed an interest in automobiles, founded the company that bore their name. In 1893 William Packard, who with James owned a successful electrical equipment business, contracted auto fever and began tinkering with them. Two years later William purchased a De Dion-Bouton buggy. Not to be outdone, in 1898 James acquired his first car, a Winton. It proved a lemon, and James, who was the mechanic in the family, traveled from his home in Warren, Ohio, to Cleveland to complain to Alexander Winton, a dour Scot who then manufactured cars in a shed behind his bicycle company and three years later would be the second largest American manufacturer. Not a particularly tolerant man, Winton fired back something to the effect that if Packard thought he could do better, he should try assembling his own car. James took this literally, told William what had transpired, and had no difficulty convincing his brother it was a good idea.

At the dawn of the auto age founding a company took little more than a generalized interest in the product, a bit of capital, and a place where parts purchased from suppliers might be assembled. The Packard's company was organized in this way with the help of a former Winton employee, George Weiss, whom James had wooed to Warren. Packard & Weiss was created in late 1899, with James chipping in with $6,000 and Weiss, $3,000. Their first car, called the Ohio, and designed and built by Weiss and another former Winton worker, W. A. Hatcher, rolled out of the shed that was the Packards' factory late that year, whereupon the company's name was changed to Ohio Automobile Company.

That first car was powered by an eight-horsepower one-cylinder engine and was known as the "Model A." Three more, called the "Model B," were produced in 1900 and were quite innovative, sporting the first steering wheels and gas pedals. Five were assembled in 1901, by which time the company's name was changed to Packard.

It was then that James made what would be his most significant contribution to Packard Motor Car Company: its slogan. His secretary had given him a letter written by a potential customer, who wanted the company's brochure. "Tell him we have no literature—we aren't that big yet. But if he wants to know how good an automobile the Packard is, tell him to ask the man who owns one." At the time such a person would have been difficult to find, even in the small town of Warren.

The Packards never intended this company to be more than a pastime, but those first cars captured the imagination of two rather important individuals. One was William Rockefeller, who purchased three of the 1901 cars after seeing them at an auto show. The other was Henry B. Joy, an ebullient Detroit railroad tycoon and real-estate speculator, whose interests extended to wildlife conservation, skeet shooting, and later, radio broadcasting. Joy had purchased a Packard and was delighted by the one-cylinder beauty. He went to see the brothers and offered to buy a share in the company. The Packards were surprised but pleased. Together with several friends, Joy purchased a majority interest and moved Packard to Detroit.

In 1904, the first full year in Detroit, Packard turned out 250 cars, making it America's eighth-largest car company and transforming Joy into an automobile tycoon. If there were any justice, the car would have been named for him, for during the next decade and a half Joy almost singlehandedly fashioned Packard into one of the industry's leaders. He replaced the Packard's feeble one-cylinder engine with a four-cylinder powerhouse, helped design a massive radiator that became the Packard trademark, started advertising, and created a distribution network.

That last accomplishment was important. Packard dealers were carefully selected, monitored, and inculcated with Joy's vision. Unlike some companies, Packard refused to permit its dealers to sell other brands. More often than not they were college graduates at a time when with few exceptions only the wealthy attended college. The showplaces where Packards were displayed demonstrated the company's esprit. Some were designed by leading architects; America's aristocrats shopped there as they might at an art gallery.

The company did all it could to encourage buyers to have their cars serviced by dealers, to the point of refusing to sell parts at wholesale to independent shops and offering discounts and even free service at the dealerships. Customers were greeted by name, and their cars were serviced by uniformed master mechanics whose shops were meticulously clean. A few years later the company described its product as "a car built for gentlemen by gentlemen."

Profits were high and sales not particularly difficult, since at the time Packard stood at the pinnacle of the luxury class, the preferred car for the old-money crowd. This was the period of the "three Ps," standing for Packard, Peerless, and Pierce Arrow, which were vying for the lead in the luxury market. Packard dealers smilingly suggested that the other two "Ps", along with Lincoln and Cadillac, were for the parvenu.

Customers were invited to consult on the design of their cars, and many were custom fashioned by such renowned coachmakers as Dietrich, LeBaron, and Rollston. Packard proclaimed its models with slick brochures said to have cost $35 a copy to produce, but given free to selected clients.

Under Joy's leadership Packard manufactured a distinctive line of high-priced cars. In 1907 the huge Model U, which sold for

$4,200, was the talk of the industry. Packard produced 1,403 cars that year and earned more than a million dollars. In 1911 Packard's cadre of superb engineers fashioned a 525-cubic-inch six-cylinder engine that went from a standing start to 60 miles per hour in 30 seconds and had a reputation of being the most reliable in the market. It was placed in the Packard 48, which sold for $5,450, and at that price there was a waiting list for them. With the 48, Packard went to the head of the class.

In 1910 Joy hired a new general manager, Alvan Macauley, a former patent attorney who had worked at National Cash Register and Burroughs. The two made a fine team. Joy was imaginative and innovative, while Macauley was dour and conservative, concerned primarily with the bottom line and dedicated to preserving the Packard image. They shared a penchant for quality and wanted a product of which they would be proud, which is to say, would be finely turned out with less regard for price than for distinction.

Unlike Henry Ford, Joy and Macauley had no ambitions to reach the average American family. While others were striving to mechanize most operations involved in production, Packard prided itself on handmade parts and custom tooling. At a time when Ford was pioneering in mass production, Packards were fashioned lovingly, one at a time. It showed in the numbers. During the 1913 model year, Packard's 4,525 workers manufactured 2,984 cars, which worked out to two cars for every three workers *per year*.

In the 1915–1916 model year Macauley and Jesse Vincent, his chief of design and technology, produced a 12-cylinder 424-cubic-inch engine—the "twin six"—which, together with a new chassis, enabled sales to approach the 9,000 mark. This car sold for $2,000 less than the 48, which still placed it in the high-priced market. The new engine was but one example of its technological leadership. Out of the Packard works came the first automatic spark advance, the soon-to-be-familiar H-shaped shift, thermostatically monitored radiators, radiators, torsional vibration dampers, and a host of other improvements, including factory training for dealers and employees, which continued until the end of the company's life. In 1914 most auto companies entered into a cross-licensing agreement to prevent duplication and to share information. Packard did not join. Macauley felt Packard would not gain much from such an arrangement.

With Packard's reputation as a leading manufacturer and innovator secure, Joy thought the time ripe for the original owners to cash out. The board disagreed. Hoping to stir some activity, Joy threatened to resign. To his surprise the board accepted his letter of resignation and turned the company over to Macauley.

During World War I Packard produced Liberty aircraft engines as well as its twin-six cars, giving it experience in mass production that would prove beneficial in the 1920s and beyond. Packard sales dipped after the war, due largely to a short but severe depression, but they soon rebounded, and the twin six led the way.

This was the beginning of Packard's golden age. In 1921, for the first time, an incoming president rode to his inauguration in a car. Warren Harding arrived at the reviewing stand in the back seat of a Packard twin six, and during the presidency of his successor, Calvin Coolidge, there were seven Packards in the White House garage. Packard was the preferred car for Supreme Court justices and affluent legislators. It was the official royal automobile in Belgium, Egypt, India, Japan, Norway, Rumania, Saudi Arabia, Spain, Sweden, and Yugoslavia, and in the republics of Chile, El Salvador, and Mexico. The Maharajah of Gawilor rode in Packards during his tiger hunts. In New York, Packards were driven by Arthur Hayes Sulzberger, John Astor, Henry Luce, and other movers and shakers. George M. Cohan had a custom-made Packard, as did Al Jolson and Rudolph Valentino, Tom Mix, and Cecil B. DeMille. Gloria Swanson tooled around in a $2,785 Packard sportscar that weighed a ton and a half and also had a two-ton limousine that cost $2,885. All were custom-made. When a Packard rolled by, bystanders wondered who was in the car and dreamed of being in one too.

In 1921 Macauley had his staff produce a six-cylinder engine, which was placed in a somewhat smaller car. As it happened, the entire industry was going in this direction, as sleeker models, which nonetheless were as plush as those of the prewar period, were coming into vogue. Moreover, due to major design improvements, the new six was almost as powerful as the twin six. The company's plan was to market the six as an off-the-floor luxury car, while the eights would be customized. Its success prompted Macauley to drop the twin six. Packard six-cylinder cars performed well; during the 1925–1926 model year they outsold the eights ten to one.

Even so, Macauley was troubled by this success. By then mid-priced cars such as the Buick, Franklin, and Dodge were offering six-cylinder models for $800 to $1,000 less than the cost of a Packard six. Did Packard truly want to produce cars that were considered to have less status than the eights? The answer was "no," and in 1928 the sixes were discontinued. Two years later the company came out with a new eight-cylinder engine, more powerful and efficient than the twin six. In the Annual Report Macauley wrote:

> The Eight in its standard form is equipped with every luxury and embellishment the markets of the world afford. It is the most powerful and usefully active car in the market. Its riding qualities are unsurpassed, due to its long wheelbase, its long, flexible springs, and to its scientific weight distribution. The broadcloths, silks, and fabrics with which the body is trimmed are the finest obtainable. In order to cater to the wishes of an exacting clientele which often desires bodies built to respond to some unusual personal preferences, we offer a complete line of custom bodies. We have not sought quantity production in connection with the Eight. We think it best to keep them on a plane where they will always be in demand and where in normal times the demand will be somewhat greater than the supply.

There was a definite Packard style during the 1920s, which would not be compromised. Nor would Packard go in for regular styling changes, as General Motors was to do. In 1924 a Packard advertisement proclaimed, "The Packard you buy today will not look out of date in 1934," and there were only minor cosmetic changes in 1928 and 1929.

The stress on status paid off. In 1929, 43,318 Packards were manufactured (out of a national total of 4,445,100), at the company's 80-acre facility. Profits came to $25 million, or $577 per car. That year Ford produced 1,507,132 cars, with a profit margin of less than $50 per car. There were two reasons for these showings. The first and more obvious was that higher priced items usually have higher profit margins than the lower priced ones. In addition, during the 1920s car prices fell steadily, as prices of new products generally do. Not so the Packard, whose prices declined only slightly.

Most new companies in new industries concentrate on one or two products designed for a single market segment. In time, however, comes the desire to expand into other parts of the market. General Motors, headed first by William Durant and then by Alfred Sloan, was the innovator in this stage. Durant accumulated marques without much of a plan. GM produced a wide variety of cars each with its own market and character, with many overlaps. Sloan rationalized this collection of marques a strategy summarized with the motto: "A car for every purse and purpose." As a *Fortune* writer put it in 1938, "Chevrolet for the *hoi polloi*, Oakland (later Pontiac) for the poor but proud, Oldsmobile for the comfortable but discreet, Buick for the striving, Cadillac for the rich." While each car in the family looked different, they shared parts and even bodies, and so were able to realize enormous economies of scale. As a stand-alone company, Chevrolet would have been successful, but Cadillac might have had major profitability problems. As much as anything else, this was the key to GM's success.

Ford would do the same, with the Ford going against the Chevy, the Lincoln against the Caddy. Chrysler would also make the effort, but while Plymouth could compete with Ford and Chevy, the Chrysler never achieved the status of the Lincoln and Cadillac.

The other car companies fell in between. In the 1920s these were Studebaker, Willys-Overland, Maxwell, Stutz, Hudson, Chalmers, Nash, Hupmobile, Reo, Rambler, Franklin, and several other niche players. In time all would disappear, in part because each had difficulties in defining its market, their sales would not permit the economies made possible by mass production, and the marketing power of the Big Three was too much to overcome.

For the time being Packard's leaders were content to be one of those niche players, slightly larger than Cadillac, smaller than Hupmobile and Graham-Page, and more profitable than all combined, with that all-important reputation for craftsmanship. After 1924 Packard outsold Cadillac, Pierce-Arrow, and Lincoln almost every year for the rest of the decade, and in 1929 its sales were three times those of Cadillac.

The Great Depression that followed caused American car sales to plummet. Packard's sales declined to 28,177 in 1930, 13,123 in 1931, and then to 8,018 in 1932. The company reported losses for 1931 and 1932. Sales collapsed to 7,670 in 1933, but there was a small profit—$89,000.

During this time Macauley had to decide where the Packard market—and future—would hinge. What image did he intend Packard to project? He yearned for the majestic years of the 1920s, when the wealthy and famous settled for nothing less than Packards. There weren't enough of such people during the Great Depression. That suggested the future rested in the midrange part of the market, where there were more sales, but lower prestige and profit margins.

One obvious alternative was to come out with a different kind of car with a name and dealership arrangement of its own—the way GM had Chevies and Cadillacs, each with its own constituency. But Packard lacked the resources for such an approach, and in any case, to do so would be to relinquish the advantage of the Packard name, which was the company's greatest asset.

When the Depression began, Packard had three lines of cars: the Eight ($2,350–$3,285); the Super Eight ($2,950–$3,800); and the Twelve ($3,820–$4,750); in addition to its custom business, these costing upward of $6,000. Obviously the runs were quite small; the company was selling cars at the rate of only 21 a day. The bottom came in 1934, when 6,071 units were produced, and Packard posted a record loss of $8.5 million.

By then the market for luxury cars had all but disappeared. In 1933 the industry turned out 20,000 of them, against 150,000 in 1928–1929. Packard had 40 percent of the sales in this category, and still couldn't show a profit. Clearly there were too many players in this field for any to be profitable, and within four years such prestigious marques as Duesenberg, Franklin, Marmon, Peerless, and Pierce-Arrow disappeared.

So did the insistence on craftsmanship. In retrospect it seems obvious the time of the finely crafted car would have ended even without the Depression. Those lovingly handcrafted automobiles belonged to a different age, one in which multimillionaires had "cottages" in Newport, wore tails to the opera, and owned racing stables. The new era that dawned after World War I was one in which middle-class families lived in suburbs or apartment houses in cities, went to the movies, and listened to radios. They demanded inexpensive, reliable cars, such as those provided by GM and Ford. Middle-class Americans might admire those Duesenbergs, Franklins, and Pierce-Arrows, just as they might envy the wealthy denizens of Park Avenue.

But they also seemed to know that the path they were taking was the one that would prevail and that the handcrafted cars would soon no longer be produced.

would Seeing his market melt away, Macauley changed course. Packard would have to look elsewhere for sales if it were to avoid the fates of companies that had failed to survive. "We have an Episcopal reputation," Macauley said succinctly. "We want to do business with the Methodists." In 1933 he told his dealers, "I believe we must concede that there is not the quality, style, performance, or prestige differential between the low-priced car of today and a Packard that there was in 1925."

Even before the Depression struck, Vincent had sketched plans for a lower-priced car. In 1935 Packard brought out the 120, the designation indicating the wheelbase, smaller than the other Packard sedans, and at $1,060, far less expensive as well. It weighed 3,510 pounds, against the full-sized Packard's 4,935 pounds.

Macauley felt he had no choice, since sales of his luxury models had declined and Packard was posting losses. Besides, he was infatuated with the idea of product extensions; like all of the independents, he harbored dreams of challenging the likes of GM, Ford, and Chrysler. Faced with this situation Macauley, now in his late sixties, decided to invade the middle range of the market. He would attempt to imitate at least part of the GM-Ford-Chrysler approach.

Had he gone all the way and come up with a different car with a new name, Macauley might have succeeded. Certainly at a time when Packard was synonymous with automotive quality, it made sense, at least in the short run, to sell Packards rather than, say, Macauleys. Imagine, if you will, being given the opportunity today to purchase a BMW for $18,000. Surely many would jump at the chance to purchase such a car at the price of a Plymouth, but what would this do to the existing BMW owners' perception of their cars. Such was the situation in 1935. It was so much less adventuresome to use the Packard marque, which Macauley did, to the company's short-term success and long-term failure.

In 1927 GM had been faced with a similar problem, filling the price gap between Buick and Cadillac. At the time the temptation to produce a less expensive Cadillac might have presented itself, but Alfred Sloan, GM's CEO, opted instead for a new nameplate, La

Salle. More recently this was the thought that motivated GM to name its new compact car the Saturn. It was hardly likely that without a new name, introduced as an extension to the Chevrolet line, the company could have lured American compact car buyers from the Hondas, Nissans, and Toyotas. In contrast, when GM, in trying to meet the Japanese challenge, introduced the small four-cylinder Cimmeron it did so under the Cadillac nameplate, hoping as did Macauley the name would sell the car. The Cimmeron bombed, and Cadillac lost status.

In order to produce the 120, Macauley and Vincent had to move from craft to mass production, and they did so by raiding GM, by then the leader in this technique. Into Packard came scores of GM technicians, machinists, accountants, and managers. Corners were cut and efficiencies introduced, as even during the Depression auto buyers looked forward to the introduction of the 120.

The car was an enormous success; 10,000 were sold sight unseen. From January through October 1935, Packard produced 24,995 of them, out of a company total of 31,889, a more than 800 percent increase over the previous period. In 1937 the price would rise to $1,235, still quite low for a Packard. Macauley knew the customer could buy a Buick with most of the 120's features for around $1,000, but he thought the Packard name was worth $200. It was. Production rose to 80,699 in 1936. Macauley seemed to have hit upon a strategy that worked.

That Packard performed so well was due to Macauley's success in convincing middle-class drivers that they were getting a true Packard. The 120s *looked* like the Packards of old. They were simply smaller versions of the $3,500 twelve-cylinder luxury cars. Also, the reputation for craftsmanship remained years after the company had bowed to the dictates of mass production. In 1937, when the smaller Packards were making so great a splash, a *Fortune* writer would say:

> Next to Ford, Packard is perhaps the most valuable *name* in the industry. For a generation its luxurious cars had never carried less folks than rich invalids to their airings, diplomats to embassies, gangsters to funerals, stars to the studios, war lords through Chinese dust, heroes through ticker tape, heiresses across Long Island and Grosse Point.

In 1937, as the nation suffered through a steep economic slide that ended the Roosevelt recovery, total U.S. car sales were 3,929,200. That year Chevrolet led the pack with 868,250 sales, down from the previous year's 975,238. Packard production was a record 109,518. Justifiably believing he had found the formula for success, Macauley took the next step. In addition to the 120, Packard now had the 115G, soon renamed the 110, with an even smaller wheelbase and a six-cylinder engine. At around $800, it sold quite well.

Between them, the 110 and 120 accounted for all but 7,093 Packard sales. The 110 and 120 cars were well made, but not with the kind of care lavished on the upscale models. For example, the average worker on the 110s and 120s produced 21 cars per year, while across the street, where the eight-cylinder beauties were turned out, workers still averaged slightly more than two cars per year. All the other single-nameplate-crafted cars had vanished from the scene, leaving Packard, which now had managed to appeal successfully to upper-middle-class buyers.

Something significant was happening in the market, however. When the owner of the $5,000 Packard Super Eight realized that individuals with less status than he could buy a car with the same nameplate for less than $1,000, he looked elsewhere for his next purchase. Cadillac sold more high-priced luxury cars than the Packard Super Eight and Twelve. Undaunted, Macauley ordered a discontinuance of custom bodies and the upper end of the line and transferred facilities to the production of the 110 and 120. The twelve-cylinder giants were dropped in 1939, just before the coming of World War II.

Packard produced a total of 66,906 cars in 1940, against Cadillac's 40,245, with most of the sales derived from the 110 and 120, which outsold the larger Packards, the 160 and 180, by a ratio of eleven to one. Cadillac sold more of the expensive cars than did Packard and showed signs of taking an ever larger market share in the future. If Macauley couldn't decide where to go with the company, the market would decide for him.

By then, Packard in fact was essentially a manufacturer of mid-priced cars. Macauley knew the importance of that upper-class reputation, however, and so the ads placed in upscale magazines featured the big Packards in front of stately homes, while the smaller cars were advertised in the mass magazines in the same vein as were Buicks and

Oldsmobiles. But the Packard salesrooms indicated just what the company had become. Gone were those aristocratic salesmen in their refined outlets and in came salesmen virtually identical to those who attempted to sell Dodge, Mercury, and Pontiac offerings.

Had the game been worth the candle? Owen Goodrich, an executive who was there when all of this happened, later related his belief that "the people brought in to build the 120 ruined the firm." Yet had the company not entered the midmarket, it might have suffered the fates of the Peerless and the Pierce Arrow. It might be argued that without the 120, Packard would have died in the 1930s. Even so, to reiterate, while one might argue the decision was necessary, it was not necessary to call the car a Packard.

In 1938, at the age of 66, Macauley stepped down as CEO, but remained as chairman. In his place came Max Gilman, who had been a pilot during World War I, had put in 20 years at Packard in various administrative capacities, and was best known as the man who had led the 120 program. At the age of 50, Gilman not only represented the new generation, but the new company as well. He was a backslapper, somewhat crude and boisterous, and quite different from the patrician Macauley.

One of Gilman's more important moves was to invite Howard "Dutch" Darrin, the man who later would design the Kaisers and Frazers, to design a car for the company. From this came a car that broke with that Packard tradition of featuring a massive look with imposing grills. The Darrin Packard, which was called the Clipper, had a modified Packard grill, front fenders whose line swept into the front doors, and a roof that went into the trunk in a broad swing. It was low and wide, sleek and expensive looking. The Clipper was priced at $1,400, between the $1,200 120 and the $1,800 160. Offered in April 1941, it was well-received.

Due to the advent of World War II Gilman was able to delay making other decisions in the automotive area. For the 1941 model year Packard produced 72,855 cars, of which 16,600 were Clippers. Then, in the spring of 1942 car production ground to a halt. Packard produced 6,085 cars that year. There would be no new Packards until 1945.

As had been the case in World War I, Packard now was asked to produce military gear. In 1940 it received a contract to produce 9,000

Rolls-Royce engines for the British and 3,000 for the U.S. Air Corps, the total value of which exceeded $165 million. The first of these were delivered the following year. Packard prospered during the war, as sales—virtually all of them to the military—topped $460 million in 1944 and earnings came in at $24 million. By the time the war had ended Packard's balance sheet, in parlous state in 1940, was strong, with $41 million in current assets against $12 million in current liabilities.

In this period there was a sudden and important change in the executive suites. In August 1940, Gilman was seriously injured in an automobile accident, but even more damaging was the revelation that his passenger was Ruth Adams, the young wife of another Packard executive. Rumors flew, and they reached Macauley, who demanded Gilman's resignation, which was submitted. Gilman received a generous settlement, promised never to discuss the incident, and was replaced by George Christopher.

With Gilman at the helm the old devotion to quality might have remained, since he would not have been named to the post by Macauley had he not given at least lip service to craftsmanship. Not so with Christopher, who had worked at Pontiac until 1934, when he abruptly retired to become a farmer. Within two months of his buying a farm, Gilman came up with the offer for him to supervise the 110s and 120s, which he accepted.

Christopher not only had Methodist tastes—he *was* a Methodist, who loved the assembly line, where he chatted with the line workers. On Tuesday nights he bowled in the company league and literally wanted to be considered "one of the boys."

Christopher was as tight-fisted as Macauley (behind his back he was known as "Pinchpenny George"), but where Macauley recalled the glory era and yearned for its return, Christopher had no such memories and ambitions. He presided over the erosion of the Packard image.

Given intelligent and farsighted leadership, Packard might have been one of the success stories of the postwar period. The company did not lack assets. It had a considerable military backlog of the kind that would not be cut. Packard had become a leader in the development of jet engines, a high priority for the Air Force. The country was hungry for new cars after a decade of depression and the wartime years of sacrifice and had paid off debts and saved during the early 1940s. Packard's prospects hadn't been so bright since 1937.

Christopher was unsuited by temperament and inclination to capitalize upon opportunities, but he also had some bad breaks. Macauley remained on as chairman and with age—he was 73 years old when the war ended—had lost much of his vigor and keen appreciation of possibilities. He reveled in being called "The last of the pioneers" and blocked the efforts of younger, more imaginative men. It was one of those instances of a once fine leader who overstayed his usefulness to the company. Macauley finally retired in 1948, by which time he might have recognized the scope of his errors in judgment.

The postwar Packards, featuring the Clipper, arrived in 1946. They were pretty much the same as the 1941–1942 models, which wasn't a problem. Not only was this the situation at rival companies, but the Packard prewar designs were considered so advanced that they were quite popular. There was one series of six and four of eight-cylinder cars, two of which were geared to the higher-priced end of the market. The models met with mixed reception. Some praised their classic lines, the massive, solid bodies for which Packard had been famous. During that car-hungry period Packard could have sold every unit it produced with little difficulty, but it had trouble converting its factories back to cars, and in 1945 turned out only 2,722 of them. Christopher promised to produce 100,000 in 1946, but for much of the first three months of the year Packard workers were on strike, and there were shortages of just about all the materials that went into making cars. Thus, Christopher was able to deliver only 42,102 automobiles.

After the prosperous war years, Packard lost more than $8 million in 1945–1947. Seeking a solution to the problem, Christopher ordered style changes for 1948 and got a car that seemed to many to resemble an inverted bathtub. Old loyalists turned to Cadillac, which that year came out with a sleek model that featured the first "fins," a design change that met with public approval and was soon imitated by others. Even so, the Packards cars sold well—anything that moved on wheels sold in the car-hungry postwar period.

That year, the first without production problems, Packard turned out 98,897 cars, and Christopher promised 200,000 for 1949. The company had the capacity to turn out that many, but the dealers couldn't sell them, arguing that the styling wasn't as tolerable as it had been, and the prices were out of line. Packard was able to sell its surplus engines to other manufacturers who were enjoying booming sales. It was another sign of decline.

Traumatized by the postwar losses, Christopher had become more dedicated than ever to the bottom line. Government sales, which accounted for 35 percent of revenues, were profitable, but Packard was losing money on the cars. Christopher responded with across-the-board cutbacks. He rejected design changes, insisted upon the use of cheaper upholstery and fittings, and even refused to approve the repainting of the women's rest room at company headquarters. Only when chief designer William Graves threatened to quit did Christopher reluctantly give the go-ahead for design changes, which wouldn't be ready until 1951.

Far more problematic was the Packard pricing policy. During the 1920s the car was geared for those for whom price was no problem. With the Clippers of 1941 the company discovered that a midpriced luxury car would sell. In 1948 Christopher also came out with the Standard Eight, a luxury model that sold for $500 less than the least expensive Cadillacs, on par in terms of price with the Oldsmobile 98, the Hudson Super Six, the Studebaker Land Cruiser, and the new Frazer. This was correctly seen as yet another move out of the luxury market. Packard had a range of offerings running from $1,000 to $5,000, but four out of five were for less than $2,000. Young people no longer thought of Packard as a manufacturer of status-enhancing cars. In 1946 and 1948 Packard outsold Cadillac, but Cadillac sold far more cars to high-priced customers.

For 1949 production came to 105,000, half of what Christopher had forecast. With this he resigned. "I'm going back to the farm," he told reporters. "Farming is a damn sight easier than the auto business. You don't have so many bosses on the farm." Former treasurer Hugh Ferry now became CEO, a position he hadn't sought and didn't relish. "I just wasn't fit for the job," he later conceded, "and I knew it."

Ferry approved the long-delayed new models designed to recoup Packard's reputation. What emerged in 1951 were large, massive, ungainly cars with poor suspension and old-fashioned straight-eight cylinder engines. Gone were the trademark grilles, replaced by monstrosities that looked like the gaping jaws of a shark. In came two-tone paint jobs that appealed to the midrange buyers, but not to the classy individuals whose trade Packard had once owned. One industry insider thought they looked like an old lady with garish makeup.

From the first Ferry considered his major task the naming of a successor. All of Packard's executives were old, timid, and dispirited, so Ferry looked outside the company for an heir. In June 1952 the board gave the job to 51-year-old James Nance. The first outlander to head the company, Nance was a salesman who had sold office equipment for National Cash Register, refrigerators for General Motors, and electrical equipment for General Electric. He had no experience in the automobile business, or for that matter, in any form of manufacturing.

In naming Nance, the Packard board was signaling its belief there was nothing wrong with its cars. Rather, the company's problems rested in matters of image and marketing. After a three-week tour of the facilities the salesman in Nance perceived Packard's major problem. He told the board something the members must have known for quite a while: The once premier American car that had made a successful foray into the midmarket before the war had lost its former customers to Lincoln and Cadillac and was unable to convince middle-class customers Packard was their kind of car. Privately, Nance said Packard was dead in the water. "The company has been just successful enough to be lulled asleep. It will have to be shaken out of its lethargy and made to realize that you can't stand still." Packard's top-of-the-line cars still were competing against Cadillac and the bigger Buicks, and had only 3.5 percent of that market. "If we are going to make a quality car, then let's get in the race; and if we are going to abandon the field, then let's do it with honor, and not default." In other words, he was proposing that Packard abandon the top of the line entirely and concentrate on the midmarket.

Nance's analysis was sound, but he didn't carry through. He established three classes. The Packard Patrician 400, to sell for around $4,000, was Packard's bid for reentry into the super-luxury end of the market. The others were the Packard Cavalier, a $3,000 "touring sedan," and the Packard Clipper, a $2,500 car. Nance intended to alter the name of the latter to just Clipper once the car was established, a symbolic move that would have made sense in 1939, but came too late to accomplish anything in 1952.

There was a major flaw in the design. While there was little similarity between the Cadillac and the Buick, the Patricians and Clippers bore strong family resemblances. In other words, the Patricians simply weren't distinctive enough. Packard, which had lost some of the luxury market in the mid-1930s, lost what remained in the early 1950s and was unable to make up for the loss with its entry in the midrange market. It could be seen in the sales. Of the 89,730 Packard registrations in 1953, Patricians accounted for 7,631.

So Nance floated a different idea. Why not merge with another auto company to produce a giant that might transform the Big Three (GM, Ford, and Chrysler) into the Big Four? Any of the other three specialty companies—Studebaker, Nash, and Hudson—might do the trick. In addition, there was that feeler from Kaiser-Frazer to consider.

In 1954, a year during which Packard produced 27,600 cars, the lowest total in two decades, it united with Studebaker to form Studebaker-Packard. Nance became chairman, proclaiming that S-P was "now the fourth full-line company." Nominally Packard had acquired Studebaker. The reality was that the Studebaker executives took command. Nance spoke bravely about a line of cars than ran from the Studebaker Champion, which sold for around $1,500, to the Patrician at $5,000, with the Cavaliers becoming gussied-up versions of the Clippers. But S-P fizzled, though not before Packard was finally destroyed.

In 1955 S-P turned out its new line of Packards. They had new engines, suspensions, and what perhaps was the best automatic drive in the industry. They couldn't match the GM rivals in speed and acceleration, however, and soon after introduction the engines developed problems. Packard, once the symbol of integrity and superb engineering, was known as a lemon. There were 55,517 Packard registrations that year, a decided improvement, but in the wake of these sales were thousands of dissatisfied customers.

In 1957 the Studebaker people all but scrapped Packard and put the nameplate on the largest Studebakers, which were promptly nicknamed, "Studepackards." "When they put my Clipper taillights on the rear of that tired '58 Studebaker," said one of the last loyalists, "it was enough to make a maggot vomit." Packard registrations were now 4,809.

The last Studepackard rolled out of the old Studebaker South Bend, Indiana, facility in July 1958. Its passing was barely noticed.

The lesson of the Packard failure was not that there was no room for an elite luxury car in the American automobile market, but that once lost, image and cachet cannot be regained. Packard is no longer with us. The reason was adumbrated in 1952 by CEO Nance. "You can always downgrade a name. That's easy in merchandising, to take a high-priced product and bring it down the price scale." He noted, "In my judgement as a marketing man, they just turned the luxury car business over to Cadillac on a silver platter." He added:

> To the man in his forties or over, Packard stands for quality—he still thinks of it as a quality car, an impression he got as a young man. But to the younger person, say thirty-five, *Packard doesn't stand for anything*. Now you ask the man in the street today, whether he is twenty-five, fifty, or seventy-five, what Buick stands for and you'll get a pretty universal answer. It's a good solid automobile in the upper middle-price class. You ask what Cadillac stands for and every kid on the curbstone will tell you, "That's the best, mister."

CHAPTER SEVEN

SCHLITZ AND PABST: THE BLUNDER OF CUTTING CORNERS

When David Leiderman organized David's Cookies to sell his version of America's chocolate-chip favorite, he noted that the average American rarely had the opportunity to have the best of anything. In the 1920s he certainly could not aspire to a Packard. His automobile, his home, his clothing—virtually everything he owned and used—was not premium. Leiderman intended to do something about this. "For one dollar he can have the best chocolate-chip cookie available."

Leiderman went on to short-run fame and became more than modestly wealthy. He did so by following that simple dictum that has performed as promised for other entrepreneurs. The perception of quality in everyday, inexpensive products can enable their producers to raise prices and enjoy greater-than-standard profit margins. It is why Marlboro and Camel outsell generic cigarettes, Coke and Pepsi do better than store brands, and why the national brands of gasoline do much better than the off brands that charge a nickel or a dime less per gallon.

It certainly is the case with beer. Today the big three of brewing are Anheuser-Busch, whose flagship brand, Budweiser, is far and away the national leader, followed by Miller, which made its big splash with Lite, and Coors, whose Colorado origins has provided it with a special cachet. Much of the time they sell at approximately the same price. Above them in status and price are the super premiums and the imports. Beneath them are the economy brands, such as Stroh, Erlanger, Goebel, Schmidt, Blatz, Pabst, and Schlitz.

Consider what these names have in common. All are German. Consider, too, that once those economy brands were local and regional powerhouses with loyal followings, and some were more than that. A century ago Anheuser-Busch was one of the big three, but the other two were Pabst and Schlitz, and often these two outsold Budweiser.

There are few major industries in which one ethnic group predominates, as is the case with brewing. German-American families who founded breweries in the mid-nineteenth century, rose to be dominant forces when German lager beer became popular, and every town seemed to have its own brewery. Large cities often had more than a dozen of them, where customers could go, "growler" (bucket) in hand, and purchase beer. Some breweries had gardens in the rear, where families would come on weekends to enjoy a brewer-sponsored picnic, complete with oompah band and other festive touches. All of this is gone, of course, although quite a few microbreweries have attempted to revive the practice in modern form, and the Busch Gardens were the attempts of family patriarch, August "Gussie" Busch, to reinvent the entertainment aspect of beer that was so relished a century ago.

Anheuser-Busch, Miller, and Coors honor their German-American founders. Members of the Busch and Coors families are still in charge at those firms, but the Millers are long gone from Miller, now a part of the Philip Morris empire. The Busch and Coors clans compete intensely with each other, but there is a mutual respect and feeling of comradeship between them that does not extend to those at Miller, which is run, in their parlance, by "the tobacco people."

The breweries remained family affairs until the end of World War II. Among the Anheuser-Busch directors were a collection of cousins—Eberhard and W. Fred Anheuser, Liechester Busch Faust, Adelbert Von Gontard, Edward Magnus, Percy J. Orthwein, and Walter Reisinger. Anheuser and a Von Gontard were vice presidents, and together with Gussie Busch, comprised the Executive Committee that ran the firm. There were many Griesediecks at Falstaff, and as late as 1961, of the thirteen members of the Schlitz board, eight were Uihleins and the other five were sons of mothers whose maiden names had been Uihlein. In most cases the eldest son of the CEO would take over when his father stepped down, but there were exceptions. In the absence of a qualified son, a son-in-law could assume leadership. Thus Frederick Pabst succeeded Phillip Best, Adam Gettleman was the son-in-law of George Schweikart (Gettleman Brewing), Otto Lodemann was the son-in-law of Joseph Uhrig (Uhrig Brewing), and Adolphus Busch was Eberhart Anheuser's son-in-law.

In 1961 only four of the nation's ten largest breweries (Anheuser-Busch, Schlitz, Falstaff, and Pabst) were publicly owned. The others— Ballantine, Carling, Hamm, Liebmann, Schaefer, and Miller—were in the hands of families or business interests divorced from public pressures, with penchants for privacy and the preference for close control, even when selling stock would have made financial sense. This was not unusual; we have seen the process in action at W. R. Grace.

Family ties and parochial outlooks were more common than professionalized management in the boardrooms. For the most part these beer companies were conservative, with boards more interested in preserving what they had while extracting large dividends from the firms than attempting to expand aggressively. Opportunities to do so were there, but not many managers showed interest in them.

Prohibition brought an end to all of this, but some breweries survived by seeking other businesses. Anheuser-Busch turned to yeast, ice cream, vehicular bodies, soft drinks, and a variety of other interests, while Pabst produced and marketed malt syrups. Coors entered ceramics, near beer, and malted milk. With the end of Prohibition came the renewal of brewing and new leaders to quest for new markets.

Local brewers would continue strong so long as their customers remained loyal. So it was that Milwaukee remained devoted to Schlitz, Pabst, and Blatz; New York to Ruppert and Schaefer; Philadelphia to Schmidt; and St. Louis to Budweiser and Falstaff. In 1938 Goetz (34-thousand barrels) was popular in Kansas City, Missouri; Effinger (8 thousand barrels) in Baraboo, Wisconsin; Dixie (50 thousand barrels) in New Orleans; and Red Bluff (5 thousand barrels) in Red Bluff, California.

Challenging the local brew was difficult, but attempts were made. At first some of the Midwestern brewers shipped barrels of refrigerated beer to nearby eastern and southern markets. With the coming of pasteurization and efficient bottling the beer was sent even farther, but discerning drinkers asserted the taste wasn't the same and remained loyal to the locals. Convincing drinkers that the bottled (and later canned) beer was as good as the unpasteurized version obtainable from taps and the brewery was a major challenge for those brewers who hoped to go regional.

The growing popularity of containerized beer in the late 1930s accelerated the earlier movement to expand into new markets and brought strong competitive pressures to the industry. Since beer, a high-bulk low-priced product that was more than 90 percent water, could not be shipped economically from, say, St. Louis and Milwaukee to New York or San Francisco and hope to compete on a price basis with local brews, relatively little of these beers reached distant markets. Even so, some of the breweries did send their beers out of their marketing areas, knowing that the prices charged would have to be higher. The brewers rejected outright the notion of establishing branch breweries. Accustomed as they were to local markets and local tastes, and bound by tradition, they feared their beers could not be successfully replicated elsewhere.

Pabst was the first to venture into unexplored territory. In order to augment its malting operations, in 1932 the company acquired the Premier Malt Products Co. of Peoria Heights, Illinois, which prior to Prohibition had been Decatur Brewing Co. Two years later that facility was relicensed as a brewery and turned out Pabst Blue Ribbon beer. Pabst had difficulties convincing wholesalers that the Blue Ribbon brewed in Peoria Heights was the same as that from the Milwaukee facility, but in the end accomplished this goal, making the task easier for those brewers who followed.

Along with Premier came its president, Harris Perlstein, who in the absence of a suitable male heir was elevated to become Pabst's CEO. A man of vaulting ambition who spoke expansively of creating a giant corporation with breweries in all parts of the nation, Perlstein had to put his plans on hold when war broke out, but among the minor results of that conflict was the creation of a potential national market for beer.

Ten million young American males, many of them already beer drinkers and most of the others soon to take to the brew had been sent far from their homes and had had experiences that otherwise would have been denied them. In the process they came into contact with different brands of beer. When the war broke out New Englanders seemed to favor brews with a "hoppier" flavor than did residents of the mountain states. Pittsburgh's popular Iron City was quite different from Coors, preferred in Montana. Olympia led in Idaho, Pearl in Texas, Associated in Indiana, Falls City in Kentucky, Hamm in Iowa,

National in Maryland, and Grain Belt in Nebraska. Few were known outside their area, and each had only one brewery. None were among the top 10, and some didn't make the top 20 industry leaders.

During the war most of the leading domestic brewers—Anheuser-Busch, Schlitz, and Pabst in the vanguard—vied for government contracts. The locals lacked such facilities. This meant that a soldier from Detroit, where the beers tended to be dark, and a sailor from Harrisburg, where strong, bitter brews were preferred, now would spend a few years drinking and becoming accustomed to the lighter brands produced in St. Louis and Milwaukee.

There were some who would not return willingly to their old beers; they would seek out Budweiser, Schlitz, and Pabst, creating a demand to be filled by taverns and restaurants, the retailers, the wholesalers, and ultimately, the breweries. This tendency, together with the growth of packaged beer and new forms of advertising and promotion, would revolutionize the industry. These changes affected virtually all of the companies, and certainly those with national aspirations.

It was not surprising that given its tradition, Pabst was the first to make the move. Perlstein started out in 1945 by entering the New York market through the purchase of the Hoffman Beverage Co. Hoffman was a local company that originated as a brewery, which in 1920 switched to soft drinks. Perlstein reconverted part of the facility to the production of Blue Ribbon, but only after assuring himself that the water and other ingredients were such as to enable him to replicate the Pabst taste. He managed this successfully; most beer drinkers found the Pabst brewed in New York indistinguishable from that from the Milwaukee facility. With this success, Pabst turned to the West Coast, purchasing Los Angeles Brewing in 1948. Los Angeles Brewing's brand, Eastside, was popular on its own, having sold 600,000 barrels the previous year. Now Pabst announced it would continue turning out Eastside and would also construct a brewery for Blue Ribbon. The $15 million installation, with a capacity of one million barrels, was ready for business in late 1953. This made Pabst a major factor in the Pacific Coast market and indicated to other brewers that the time was ripe for a major move to that part of the country and that satellite breweries could produce acceptable beers. Schlitz, which was the most popular non-California beer in the state with around 25 percent of the "import" business, was one of the first to seriously investigate erecting a brewery in California. But as significant as California was to become, for the time being New York was more important.

At the time the large New York beer market was dominated by locals, who were prepared for challenges, not only from Schlitz, but from Anheuser-Busch as well. The leaders of these two historic rivals monitored each other's actions carefully, each intent on not permitting the other to gain an advantage.

Gussie Busch was an irascible, shrewd, and flamboyant businessman with a penchant for grand gestures, in which regard he resembled his grandfather, Adolphus, who had created the brewery and made it the leader it became before World War I. Gussie succeeded his brother at the helm and was absorbed in the task of making Anheuser-Busch the powerhouse of brewing. He tended to rely upon instinct in making his decisions. Erwin Uihlein, who headed Schlitz in this period, had as much pride in his heritage as had any of the Busches, and he certainly was one of the most distinguished and learned American brewers. Uihlein had studied economics at Cornell, brewing at the Wahl-Henius Institute in Chicago, and then took additional courses at Copenhagen's famed Carlsberg Laboratories, after which he returned to Cornell to obtain a law degree. "My father's great goal," he said, "was to make us observant, to notice everything that was going on around us, and not to neglect the slightest detail." He didn't; Schlitz was nothing if not efficient.

Not that Anheuser-Busch was less capable, but with a difference. Schlitz's top management was devoted to the goal of making its brewery the most modern and economical in the industry, while Anheuser-Busch was as concerned with maintaining the integrity of its beers, which for that company had a higher priority than efficiency. This was the essential difference between the two. It was the classic confrontation of science and art.

As early as 1945, Gussie Busch started looking at a possible site for a new brewery in Newark, New Jersey, on U.S. Highway 1, across the road from Newark International Airport. Location there would ease communication between the home office and a new brewery, and access from the brewery to markets would be uncomplicated and inexpensive. The locale was close to the Pennsylvania markets, so

Budweiser might consider challenges to the likes of Schmidt in Philadelphia, Duquesne in Pittsburgh, and Stegmaier in Wilkes-Barre as well as Ruppert, Schaeffer, and Ballantine in New York. Budweiser brewed there could service the entire East Coast and even the Gulf states by means of coastwide freighters, whose charges were lower than those of truckers and railroads.

That expansion was necessary was evident. While Schlitz and Pabst modernized and expanded operations and experimented with less expensive ingredients, Anheuser-Busch held back, and in the immediate postwar period could not turn out enough beer to satisfy retailers, who on occasion were put on allotment. Busch argued that without expansion the company would decline, and so it did. In 1947 it was the third largest brewer, behind Schlitz and Ballantine, the latter sold mostly in the New York area, an indication of the importance of that market, while Pabst was in ninth place. The following year Pabst displaced Anheuser-Busch, which was now the fourth largest brewer.

Busch had turned out all of its beer from the one St. Louis brewery, but during the war, in 1943, it had purchased the small ABC Brewery in St. Louis. That was a local affair, however, and not considered true expansion, since all that was wanted was the land, and not the facility itself. Now Busch was suggesting setting up a new brewery in New Jersey almost a thousand miles from home, presumably to be run by individuals recruited from the home operation, who could not be overseen on a day-to-day basis. Given the distances involved, it seemed to some on the board that this would necessitate a loss of control over quality and expenses. Busch could point to the Pabst experience in New York, which indicated it could be done successfully. While economics dictated a Newark brewery, tradition was against it, and tradition counted for a great deal at Anheuser-Busch. Busch had his way. Ground was broken for a one-million-barrel facility in Newark in March 1950. Running at capacity, it would increase Anheuser-Busch's sales by 20 percent and give it the lead in the industry. Newark proved a major success and was followed by other breweries.

Gussie Busch then made a series of on target moves. When in 1953 it appeared the St. Louis Cardinals would be sold to Milwaukee interests, he purchased the team, keeping it in the city. At the time

Falstaff was the city's leading beer. No more. Grateful St. Louis beer drinkers, horrified that the team would depart and doubly troubled that its new home would be the place where Schlitz and Pabst were brewed, switched to Budweiser. Also, St. Louis was the major-league city that was the furthest south and west, and was avidly followed on radio by fans in these parts of the country, who also rallied to Budweiser and its sister brands. Pabst and Schlitz also had important sports connections. Schlitz started broadcasting the games of the nearby Kansas City Athletics, while Pabst continued its coverage of "Blue Ribbon" boxing programs. Neither had the impact of the Cardinals purchase.

Busch loved animals and dreamed up the idea of creating theme parks, which he did, starting in 1959. Entertainment was not new at the breweries, many of which had guided tours for the public capped with a visit to an on-site pub where free beer was served. Gussie Busch took it one step further, with the opening of Busch Gardens in Tampa, on a 15-acre tract close to the company's brewery. In time Anheuser Busch would become the second-largest theme park operator, behind Walt Disney.

While Anheuser-Busch experienced major growth in the late 1950s and early 1960s, Schlitz stagnated. That brewery experienced an important management change in 1961, when 44-year-old Robert Uihlein took over from his uncle Erwin. Erwin had been superbly fitted for the tasks of brewing beer and had made Schlitz one of the most efficient factors in the industry while preserving its quality. He lacked marketing skills, however, and had the misfortune to control the company when Gussie Busch, who was a master at selling, was at the helm at Anheuser-Busch.

Unlike Erwin, Robert did not have a strong background in brewing. Rather, after graduating from Harvard, he attended the University of Wisconsin Law School and upon obtaining his degree entered the company through the sales department. Almost all of his career had been in sales, and so his stress on this area was not unexpected. Given the company's tradition, neither was Uihlein's continued efforts at streamlining operations. This was to be the cornerstone of his strategy: Schlitz would produce beer at lower prices than Anheuser-Busch and use the profits to continue modernizing the breweries and aggressively promoting its beer in new markets. Robert

Uihlein meant to continue the Schlitz tradition while changing some aspects of marketing to bring the company up to Anheuser-Busch's level, at the same time introducing a few new wrinkles of his own.

One of Uihlein's first moves had come in 1959, when he convinced his uncle to reintroduce Old Milwaukee to give the firm an entry in the popular-priced market segment. It was a debacle. The new beer, like the old, was dark, and Uihlein did not take into account changing customer preferences toward lighter brews. Old Milwaukee was revamped, repackaged, and then reintroduced, with a new set of slogans, among them "Roll Out the Burgie," and "America's Light Beer . . . Brewed for That Wonderful World of Leisure." It was provided with a redesigned white label that stressed lightness. Advertisements claiming Old Milwaukee combined premium taste with a popular price were placed in all of the media. Sales picked up sharply thereafter, with much of the credit given to the analysis and programs developed by Uilhein's new marketing vice president, Fred Haviland, who altered the marketing operations in a way to resemble those of other consumer-goods companies rather than breweries.

Haviland provided each of the Schlitz beers with its own brand manager, who was responsible for all phases of operations, from brewing to wholesaler relations. With the power went responsibility, and the managers knew that while good performance would be rewarded, a poor showing would not be tolerated. It was that way at Bristol Myers and Colgate-Palmolive, but not so at Anheuser-Busch and other major breweries, where top management still had important say in all decisions. Furthermore, Haviland pioneered in market research at a time when Gussie Busch still relied upon his instincts. "We research, and out of research develop specific things, develop the best programs we can, carry them out, and then do an evaluation," said Haviland. "Our objective is to find out what makes the beer drinker tick, and how to get to him—on his terms, rather than the brewer's. Beer to us is a product to be marketed—like soap, corn flakes, or facial tissues." This was quite revolutionary for an industry so steeped in tradition. "It's the Procter & Gamble way," Haviland exuded, leaving no doubt as to the source of his inspiration. "We're the Procter & Gamble of the beer business!"

While transforming Old Milwaukee, Uihlein and Haviland were attempting the same kind of change with Schlitz. New promotions were utilized, and Schlitz expanded upon its sponsorship of local festivals and celebrations. The old slogan, "The Beer That Made Milwaukee Famous," was one of the better known in the industry and served well in earlier years, but not so in the age of scientific advertising. The Leo Burnett agency provided Uihlein with a new ad and image—Schlitz was now the beer that provided "gusto," as in "Real Gusto in a Great Light Beer," and the pictorial advertisements, featuring strong men drinking the beer and obviously enjoying themselves, underlined the gusto theme. As Haviland put it, "You imbibe the image along with the brew."

One of the more important changes had come in packaging, and this would continue in the next decade, with Schlitz accounting for several of the pioneering efforts. Customers were being presented with beer in a variety of sizes of cans and bottles, and to complicate matters, Schlitz's 1963 introduction of the flip-top lid, quickly taken up by others, meant that each can size might have two lines.

All the brewers were intrigued by several interesting new technologies developed in the 1960s, and while they were studied intensively, only a few were adopted. Phillips Petroleum and Union Carbide developed a method of producing beer concentrate that, had it been perfected, might have revolutionized the industry. The new process was geared to removing most of the water, enabling brewers to ship concentrate to bottling plants, where water and carbonation would be added. Tremendous economies might have been realized if this technique had been successful. Most of those new breweries that had been constructed since the end of the war need not have been undertaken, but instead "superbreweries" might have been erected, from which the entire nation could be supplied.

There even was talk of packaging the concentrate for home sale—each drinker could become his or her own bottler, using beer concentrate as he or she might frozen juice concentrate or instant coffee. Reconstitution caused something of a stir in the early 1960s, but never amounted to anything. Rather, it indicated that modern science was being employed to create economies in brewing as it was doing in other areas. Was this a sensible path? In America 20 percent of the population drank 80 percent of the beer, and much of that 20 percent had strong notions regarding just what constituted an acceptable brew. They liked what they were drinking. Would they equally enjoy a scientifically designed beverage?

Of more interest was continuous brewing, which involved the automation and restructuring of the brewing process. Beer had always been brewed in batches; those involved with continuous brewing talked of a steady stream of beer being produced in a network of pipes, each performing a different step in the process. All of those huge copper vats would be scrapped, as would those five-story-high brew houses required to support them. Much of the labor force would be eliminated, and in their place would be a single individual, at a control panel, monitoring the process as might an engineer at a petroleum refinery.

Robert Uihlein monitored both developments but accepted neither. Rather, his new breweries would utilize automation, but only in more conventional and proven operations. Schlitz's breweries were to be large affairs—there would be three with capacities of four million barrels in the 1970s—that employed fewer workers than facilities a fraction that size. Where one of the antiquated Old Milwaukee breweries employed 24 men on a brewhouse shift, the newer ones got by with two. This gave Schlitz an edge over Anheuser-Busch. Gussie's new facilities were equally efficient, but the giant St. Louis plant, which remained its largest, was not one of these. Of the company's 11.6-million-barrel capacity at the beginning of 1965, 7.3 million was in St. Louis. Moreover, due to different and more costly brewing methods, labor costs at the St. Louis plant ran three to five times higher than elsewhere.

Uihlein was convinced that success in the economic area and marketing would combine to give him the industry lead. This led him to take steps that seemed drastic to traditionalists. The production of beer in the 1950s was pretty much what it had been earlier, which is to say that the operations would not have surprised Adolphus Busch or Colonel Jacob Ruppert. Yet there were significant differences in the way each brewer functioned. Schlitz did not age its beers as long as Anheuser-Busch did Budweiser and Michelob. Busch continued to insist upon using a mix of imported and domestic hops in Budweiser; Schlitz used the less expensive domestic variety and then went over to hop extracts and then to the even more economical hop pellets. So as to maintain quality control, Anheuser-Busch produced more than four fifths of its own malt, against Schlitz's one third. As before, Anheuser-Busch employed rice as a grain adjunct in Budweiser and Michelob, as well as aging the beers with beechwood chips. In the early 1960s Schlitz used a combination of corn grits and rice, and quickly shifted entirely to the less expensive corn, and then to corn syrup. Gussie Busch railed against what he called "inferior beers," and like his predecessors, refused to brew the "corn juice" turned out by rivals. None of this was secret to those within the industry, but the changes resulted in a different beer. As one Arthur D. Little scientist observed, "Today's Schlitz isn't the same product as yesterday's," inferring that Budweiser was. For the time being at least customers didn't seem to mind. Later on, one analyst remarked, "Schlitz, in the process of rapid expansion, had become a discount producer, while Anheuser continued expansion in a normal way and maintained its quality image."

At first these changes at Schlitz appeared to work. Robert Uihlein had reinvigorated the company. From 1968 to 1973, Schlitz sales increased at an annual rate of 13 percent, placing severe pressures on Anheuser-Busch. In the former year Anheuser-Busch had 16 percent of industry sales while Schlitz had slightly more than 10 percent. By 1973 Anheuser-Busch's market share had risen to 21 percent, but Schlitz's stood at 15 percent.

This rapid rise of a formidable competitor led by a man whose new approach to brewing and invigorated marketing caused consternation in St. Louis. There were some at Anheuser-Busch who hinted that it might be well to make changes, but Gussie refused to budge when it came to brewing methods, ingredients, and promotion. He insisted on maintaining the traditional procedures insofar as raw materials, aging, and processing were concerned, while Schlitz continued to seek technological shortcuts. As a result, Anheuser-Busch's new breweries were more expensive to build and operate than those erected by Schlitz. According to one estimate, in the 1960s Schlitz spent around $25 in capital costs to obtain an additional barrel of capacity, while Anheuser-Busch had to spend between $35 and $40 a barrel.

Consider the situation in Texas, a major beer market. Anheuser-Busch's new Houston brewery cost approximately $35 million, while a larger Schlitz facility in Longview came in at $20 million. As one St. Louis executive later complained, "We use five times as much labor as Schlitz does. We've got to import and store hops. We require larger aging facilities. I would say their product is less than $20 per bbl., and

ours about $30." From 1961 to 1965 Anheuser-Busch spent nearly
$130 million on new plant and equipment, with almost all of the
money coming from retained earnings. In the same period Schlitz earmarked close to $50 million for that purpose. Schlitz got more capac-
ity for its dollar, while Anheuser-Busch was spending more than two
and a half dollars for every one of Schlitz's in this category.

As for promotion, even his critics conceded that Gussie Busch
was the grand showman of the industry and had diversified brilliantly.
In contrast, Robert Uihlein met with failure when he ventured from
brewing. In addition to seeking the number-one slot for Schlitz,
Uihlein planned to transform the company into an international conglomerate, doing so with a buying spree that cost approximately $100
million. Among the acquisitions made in this period were breweries in
Turkey, Puerto Rico, Spain, and Belgium. There were Chilean fish-
meal plants and a fishing fleet, along with a glass factory and citrus
concentrate facility in Pakistan. None was profitable, prompting the
hiring of a new financial vice president in 1969 whose major task was
to dispose of these ventures.

These failures didn't deter Uihlein, who continued seeking new
areas of opportunity. The wine business was growing and bore some
similarities to beer, so Uihlein went after the Paul Masson and
Charles Krug wineries in California, and Nicholas, the largest winery
in the world; he failed in all these attempts. Uihlein tried to buy
Lawry's Foods and several other specialty operations, only to be
rebuffed. He finally succeeded in obtaining Geyser Peak Winery and
Murphy Products, the latter a Wisconsin grain company. Then there
was C & D Foods, a duck farm, which Uihlein thought would make
a fine fit with Schlitz, since it would be a near-perfect market for
spent brewery grain to be used as feed. All miscarried and went on the
market to be sold at losses.

The apparent drift at corporate headquarters resulted in the
departure of key executives. President Roy Stachell left in 1973, and
Uihlein, whose strong point was strategic thinking, not management,
was obliged to assume his post as well as continuing to fill that of
chairman. This might have been sustained were it not for disaster at
the breweries.

In 1974 the company reformulated Schlitz once again, using a
number of additives to enhance appearance and shelf life. While Uihlein

was roundly criticized by some in the industry for these changes, the new Schlitz was being well received by customers. Gussie Busch, of course, considered them only a cut above criminal and was vocal in his criticisms.

Schlitz had introduced a new brewing process at its Milwaukee facility. Known as Accelerated Batch Fermentation, it cut the process from 12 days to less than 4, which promised additional economies. By using lower-cost ingredients and such new techniques, Schlitz was able to reduce the cost of producing a barrel of beer by 50 cents, which in 1974 translated into $9 million in earnings. In all of this, cost considerations were paramount.

Next, Uihlein shifted pricing strategy. Prices to wholesalers were increased, as Uihlein tried to convince them they would be able to pass on the boost to retailers and consumers. They could not. Sales fell from the torrid pace enjoyed earlier, with the growth rate slowing to 6 percent. In 1975 Schlitz's market share came in at more than 15 percent, only fractionally higher than it had been in 1973, while Anheuser-Busch rolled on to 23 percent. It seemed Schlitz was doomed to be perennial runner-up. Even so, the company was profitable, solvent, and secure. Ford had long been second to General Motors and had turned in excellent profits and was well regarded. In Milwaukee it seemed Schlitz might have to settle for just that.

For years the Food and Drug Administration had talked of obliging brewers to list ingredients on their cans and bottles, and in late 1975 it seemed such would soon be required. Gussie Busch had strongly supported the idea, which would enable him to focus on his more expensive ingredients, while Robert Uihlein adamantly opposed it. By then Uihlein had become convinced labeling would come. Accordingly, on January 1, 1976, he sent word to his Milwaukee, Memphis, and Winston-Salem breweries to replace a silica gel containing enzymes used in brewing with a substitute called Chill-garde. Supposedly Chill-garde did the same job as the silica gel, which was to prolong shelf life and stabilize the beer. This might provide Schlitz with an advertising gambit to counter beechwood aging and the use of rice and expensive hops. Chill-garde would be removed before the beer was containerized, and so would not have appeared as an ingredient on labels should these be required. If Uihlein thought its use would assure beer drinkers of Schlitz's forward-looking approach to brewing, he couldn't have been more mistaken.

As it turned out, Chill-garde reacted with another ingredient Schlitz utilized, a foam stabilizer called Kelcoloid, which resulted in the coagulation of protein particles. These appeared in the beer as tiny flakes, giving it a milky appearance. They did not alter the taste and were not dangerous, but would hardly be welcomed by drinkers.

The Milwaukee plant manager noted the change and reported it to headquarters, but surprisingly, nothing was done. Then, in late February came angry complaints from wholesalers, who were getting returns from their retailers. This prompted a major recall effort—more than 10 million cans and bottles of beer—that Schlitz tried unsuccessfully to conceal. The total cost was over $1.4 million, but more important than the financial loss was that in reputation and morale. Wholesaler discontent mounted, and relations with headquarters deteriorated badly.

There followed a management shakeup at headquarters. Four top executives resigned that summer, as paranoia ruled in Milwaukee and the field. The problems mounted; Uihlein seemed incapable of turning the situation around. To further complicate matters, in this period Schlitz was the subject of several government investigations alleging violations of postal, income tax, and antitrust laws. It also faced accusations of having given kickbacks to retailers for offering Schlitz rather than competitors' brands.

Then, in October, Uihlein learned he had leukemia, and two weeks later he was dead, leaving no designated and prepared successor. Schlitz was a sinking company and brand. Not only had it been unable to displace Anheuser-Busch as industry leader, but now it was slipping behind other, more aggressive firms. Sales declined by almost 10 percent in 1977, as Schlitz fell to third place in the industry, with a less than 14 percent market share.

By then new executives and two new players had entered the big leagues of beer. In 1975 Gussie Busch was confronted by his son, August III, who won a majority of the board to support his challenge. August quickly proved as capable as his father if not as imaginative and colorful. Some thought him more modern than Gussie and willing to sacrifice tradition for earnings. They were soon disabused of this notion. When asked about this he replied, "Never, never! You have to have the best. Sooner or later the customer will recognize quality." So the old ways in brewing would remain in place.

As for the new players, Miller, now under Philip Morris control, underwent a rebirth largely due to its success with Lite Beer. Knowing that most surveys indicated that "real men" didn't like diet foods and that women who did were not great beer drinkers, Miller CEO John Murphy opted to leave the Miller name off the beer and present it as a new offering. If it failed, Miller's reputation would not suffer; if Lite succeeded, Miller would have a fine stablemate. Succeed it did, but in time other brewers came out with their versions. Anheuser-Busch nibbled at the market with Natural Lite and Michelob Lite before taking the plunge with "Bud Lite," which capitalized on the Budweiser imprimatur. It was too late to change Lite to Miller Lite, and Lite's market share declined.

The other player was Coors. With its single brewery in Colorado and its low advertising budget, Coors broke the two cardinal rules of brewing and got away with it. The beer became popular by word of mouth and enjoyed great success, rising rapidly in sales and profits. But there was a problem with this success. By the 1980s Coors wanted breweries elsewhere, but that would mean the loss of the value given the beer by having been made from Rocky Mountain water. Coors was never a challenge to Anheuser-Busch's position in the industry, and in time Miller would settle down in the comfortable number-two position that once seemed certain to be filled by Schlitz.

By then many of those brands familiar to Americans over the age of 40 either were no longer brewed, or if they had survived, were turned out in modest amounts by consolidated companies. Such was the fate of once-proud labels as Ruppert, Ballantine, Schmidt, Hamm, Rheingold, Blatz, Griesedieck, and Eichler. Liebmann (Rheingold) was part of Schmidt, Schaefer had been taken over by Stroh, Blatz was a unit of the failing Pabst, and Lucky Lager had been transformed into General, which brewed less than 400,000 barrels a year.

In the process the industry's geography had been sharply altered. New breweries were established by the major firms in prime marketing areas. There were five of them in Portland, Oregon, and three in Los Angeles. Yet the Anheuser-Busch facility was the only one remaining in the entire state of Missouri. New York City, once the home of many of the industry's top brewers, did not have a single brewery after Rheingold closed its plant.

Schlitz was easily the biggest prize in the takeover contest. Still reeling from the Chill-garde fiasco, in 1977, after a brief interlude during which the company was headed by interim CEO Eugene Peters, the board passed over David Uihlein, Robert's cousin who had brewing experience, and turned instead to Daniel (Jack) McKeithan, a geologist by education. McKeithan had headed an oil-exploration company and became a member of the Schlitz board in 1973, getting there through his marriage to Gillian Uihlein, the daughter of one of the Schlitz directors. They divorced in 1974, but nonetheless the other Uilheins on the board thought he had the drive and imagination to do the job. McKeithan promptly raided Anheuser-Busch to hire Frank Sellinger, who by then had become one of Busch's top lieutenants. At any other company Sellinger would have been a near-ideal choice for CEO, but he knew he could not hope for the top position in St. Louis and took the Schlitz position with August's blessings.

Realizing he had to retrench before attempting a comeback, Sellinger obtained approval to shutter the landmark Milwaukee brewery, which by then was inefficient and underutilized. It came as a shock to the industry and the city. "The Beer That Made Milwaukee Famous" was no longer being brewed there.

This was followed by another surprising move: the three-year-old Baldwinsville facility was sold to Anheuser-Busch for $100 million. Busch needed the extra capacity, as Budweiser sales were rising rapidly. It was a transaction that benefited both companies, one in dire trouble, the other concerned with fortifying its already dominant industry position. Of course, Anheuser-Busch could not use the existing plant without extensive alterations, since its brewing methods were so different from those of Schlitz. These changes would cost the company an additional $100 million. Sellinger took other steps to cut costs and bring Schlitz under control. With some reluctance and delay the board agreed to eliminate the dividend, and capital spending was slashed to the bone.

In 1981 Sellinger attempted to resolve some problems by using a large portion of his treasury surplus to buy Stroh, which could use his excess capacity. The merger would create a much larger concern with a veritable supermarket of brands, which might compete with Anheuser-Busch and Miller on several fronts. Nothing came of this. Instead, Schlitz found itself pursued by its old rival, Pabst, whose offer of $588 million for the company was rejected. Even so, by then it was apparent that if the Justice Department did not rule the merger a violation of antitrust laws, Schlitz would be acquired. This was what the Uihleins wanted and what they intended to have happen.

Several firms outside the industry evinced interest in Schlitz. One was R. J. Reynolds, the large cigarette company, which perhaps thought in terms of emulating Philip Morris and Miller. Others rumored to be interested included Norton Simon and Coca-Cola. In late 1981 it seemed Schlitz would go to either Heileman or Stroh, which were following similar strategies of expansion through acquisition. By then its market share had fallen to under 8 percent and was headed downward. Heileman was stymied by Justice Department opposition, but Stroh persisted and in 1982 won the prize, acquiring the company that once had tried to acquire it. The disappearance of Schlitz into Stroh after the unsuccessful Heileman takeover bid and the sale of Pabst came long after these two brands had ceased being industry leaders.

Pabst's error was quite common. It had difficulties maintaining market share and attempted to reverse the situation through increased advertising, meeting with mixed results. In 1955 the company sold 3.2 million barrels; two years later the figure was 2.9 million. There was a stream of losses from 1956 through 1958.

Hoping to reverse this situation by broadening its offerings, Pabst acquired Blatz in 1958, enabling it to realize important economies of scale. Just prior to the acquisition, Blatz had lowered the price of its beer, transforming it from a premium to a popular-priced brand, and sales had risen. Now Pabst did the same for Blue Ribbon, with the same result. For a while sales expanded, as Blue Ribbon temporarily retained its premium luster while being promoted at prices lower than Schlitz and Budweiser. There was an impressive recovery into the 1960s, but the experience seemed to indicate that even so well-known a brand as Blue Ribbon would have difficulties competing in the intense competitive environment of the period.

Pabst's sales and profits did not decline rapidly. Rather, they slid gently. Old loyalists remained, but when the brewery tried to realize economies by changing the brewing mix they deserted as well. The next generation would be attracted to Bud, Coors, and Miller. Today Pabst is a marginal brand, after having been sold in 1985 to S&P, which also owned Falstaff, another of those fallen leaders.

This is not to suggest that what is known as "repositioning" need fail. Miller did this successfully with Miller High Life, which once was known as "the champagne of bottled beer," sold in a clear bottle to those willing to pay a premium price for the product. The trouble with that image was that people who wanted champagne did not usually want beer, which is a more plebeian drink that appeals to the eponymous "Joe Six Pack." Miller's John Murphy changed the packaging and mounted a massive TV advertising campaign aimed at that blue-collar market. He hit all the right notes. "Our ads identify with the American work ethic. We see work and workers of America as heroes and that's how we present them in our TV advertising." Murphy also kept the premium price, and his reformulation of the beer was more, not less, costly. He instituted better quality control and came up with such novelties as a seven-ounce bottle, realizing that during hot summer days, the larger bottles tended to get warm toward the end of the drink.

For all of Murphy's imaginative leadership, he was not able to overcome Anheuser-Busch's lead within the industry. Miller, rather than Schlitz, was to be the runner-up in an industry that had been drastically altered during the past three and a half decades. Of the top five brewers in 1950, only one, Anheuser-Busch, remained, and it had become the industry's leader by far. In 1950 there had been more than 400 breweries in operation; by 1985 the number was down to 105, but actually there were far more than that, because the figure does not take into account the emergence of microbreweries.

LARGEST AMERICAN BREWERS, 1950 AND 1985

Brewery	1950	Rank	(millions of barrels) 1985	
Schlitz	5.1	(1)	Anheuser-Busch	72.3
Anheuser-Busch	4.9	(2)	Miller	38.7
Ballantine	4.4	(3)	Stroh	22.8
Pabst	3.1	(4)	Heileman	16.1
Liebmann	2.7	(5)	Coors	15.2

Source: United States Brewing Institute

Microbreweries, where amateur or semiprofessional brewers prepared what might be called "boutique beers" for an even more select group of devotees, was a phenomenon that became most visible in the 1980s. While accounting for less than 1 percent of the nation's consumption, these minuscule operations nonetheless were the fastest growing segment in the mid-1980s, rising from 10 million barrels of sales in 1983 to 110 million in 1986. Among the more important were Samuel Adams in Boston, Manhattan Gold Lager in New York, and San Francisco's Anchor Steam, whose high-priced products placed them in competition in their market areas with the likes of Michelob and Lowenbrau.

By the 1990s some of the microbreweries added restaurants. It was a reprise of the situation in the 1850s, when local breweries sold beer to saloons within a few miles of the plant. These breweries were often led by owners who pledged themselves to providing brews with "old-time flavor." It was the kind of approach that at one time informed the approach and actions of Schlitz and Pabst, whose experiments that involved abandoning such thoughts has resulted in their declines.

JAMES LING: THE BLUNDER OF FIGHTING THE GOVERNMENT

T here are times when the downfall of a company is speeded by a government agency that attempts to come to the aid of other businesses it threatens. This often happens when the economy undergoes major secular change, resulting in the appearance of a new crop of industries and tycoons that challenge the existing ones, who then appeal to political forces for help. Today it can be seen in government attempts to prevent Microsoft from achieving what some fear might be a monopoly position in its corner of the software market. Government also is trying to control cloning, even while not knowing the implications of this procedure.

Such efforts are not unusual; they have happened before. They occurred at the turn of the twentieth century, when leaders of new national and international corporations made possible by the widening of marketing areas and invention inspired fear and admiration, depending on how one was affected. The rise of the industrial corporation was both swift and breathtaking, as business creation expanded sharply. Firms that had been local or regional now aspired to larger horizons. This could be seen in many areas—consumer products sold throughout the country, for example—and in such subtle ways as the beginning of usage of four terms in corporate names "American" (as in American Bridge Company), "National" (National Steel), and "United States" (United States Rubber), and even "Continental" (Continental Tobacco) in place of state, local, regional, and family names.

Those smaller firms weren't pleased by this development, and who can blame them, since the economies of scale the large corporations enjoyed threatened to put them on the historical scrap heap?

Besides, in those days, when there was little or no regulation, predatory capitalism was not unusual. The result was the antitrust movement, an alliance of old business and enlarged government attempting to reign in the industrial corporations.

The next time such an alliance formed was after World War II, when the conglomerate movement was remaking the industrial scene, threatening old established firms with takeovers. There were several reasons for conglomeration. Among the more important was a confident belief that a good manager could direct many different kinds of business. Another was pessimistic, the thought that diversification would lessen risks that came from having only one string to a company's bow. Then there was the desire to grow rapidly, which could come with a plenitude of opportunistic mergers and acquisitions.

Within the conglomerate community fears were palpable of a renewal of what had been widely believed was the New Deal's antibusiness viewpoint. In the late 1930s the Temporary National Economic Commission all but blamed big business for the persistence of the Depression and recommended measures that businessmen took to be socialistic. Passage of the Celler-Kefauver Act of 1950, which placed prior restraints on mergers that might lessen competition, was perceived as the beginning of this new phase of the movement. Putting all of this together, some businessmen concluded that growth through mergers of nonrelated businesses would not—and possibly could not—be considered a violation of law or make the companies that engaged in such practices subject to antitrust prosecution.

Finally, the ebullient financial markets made it possible for conglomerateurs to utilize their securities to purchase ongoing enterprises. So they did. In spades.

Among the more famous conglomerateurs were Harold Geneen (ITT), Tex Thornton (Litton), Charles Bluhdorn (Gulf + Western), and Royal Little (Textron). All were new men from the provinces, and except for Geneen lacked widespread experience. Most of the conglomerateurs were founders of their enterprises. All had legal problems, which they overcame.

Not so Jimmy Ling, whose brashness, arrogance, colorful antics, but most of all, the threats he seemed to be posing to the Establishment, brought him down with a crash, thus precipitating the climax of one phase of the conglomerate movement. In a period with so many entrancing conglomerateurs, Ling stood out as an American original. His rise was spectacular. Ling soared like a rocket and then fell like a rock, when in a weakening market one of his daring schemes did not work out. Moreover, as one of the prime symbols of the conglomerate movement, he was the victim of a vendetta inspired by those interests the conglomerate movement threatened, who brought him down as a notice to the others.

How fast did Ling rise? In 1965 his company, Ling-Temco-Vought (later known as LTV), was number 168 on the *Fortune 500* roster. Four years later it was fourteenth, and seemed on its way to spring ahead of a surging ITT. How far did Ling intend going? The flashy, rugged tycoon responded with an aphorism familiar to his fellow Texans. "I don't want all the land in the world. I just want that next to mine." Hubris such as he displayed has resulted in the downfall of men from Icarus to the present. Flying too close to the sun can result in disaster, but it also has proven the formula for successes. One must keep in mind the old saying that a cat that is burned on a hot stove will not sit on one again, but also will avoid cold stoves. Even so, a string of successes can lead a CEO to believe he or she can accomplish anything he or she sets out to do, and for a while that CEO might. Then comes the all-but-inevitable plunge. Such was Ling's fate.

A classic outsider, Ling was born in 1922 in the small town of Hugo, Oklahoma, not far from the Texas-Oklahoma state line. His father, Henry, was a Bavarian immigrant and his mother, Mary, came from a family long resident in the area. Riled by anti-German and anti-Catholic taunts, Henry killed one of his tormentors, was acquitted of murder charges on grounds of self-defense, but after a few years, plagued by guilt, he abandoned his family and entered a Carmelite monastery in San Antonio. Mary died in 1933, and the family scattered. Restless and disinterested in school, Jimmy dropped out in 1935 and became a hobo. He wound up in Dallas, where he worked as an electrician's apprentice, married, and started a family. During World War II Ling served in the Navy, where he earned the designation of master electrician. Mustered out in 1946, he returned to Dallas hoping to become an electrical subcontractor.

Ling was 24 years old by then, a tall, muscular man who bore a resemblance to tough-guy writer Mickey Spillane. In time he would wear conservative business suits, and eyeglasses softened his broad, spadelike face. In the immediate post-war period, however, Ling looked just like what he was—a former hobo turned budding businessman, who was keenly ambitious and aware of his educational shortcomings.

As it turned out, Ling was superbly qualified to enter the business world of that period. Intelligent, hard working, and resourceful, he did not hew to the old ways of business that were rapidly becoming outmoded in the new environment, if only because he didn't know what they were, and so was free to innovate.

Recognizing there would be a building boom after the war, in 1947 Ling opened an electric shop in Dallas. The time and place were right; Ling was a superb salesman, and the company flourished. Ling Electric grossed $70,000 in 1947. The following year revenues advanced to $200,000, and in 1949 it became a $400,000 company. By the early 1950s Ling Electric was bidding for contracts throughout the region and had construction units in New Orleans and San Diego. Requiring funds for expansion, Ling decided to sell shares in his company. In 1955 he reorganized it as Ling Electric, Inc., and sold 450,000 shares at $2.25 each, most of them from a booth at state fairs.

By then those changes in the business scene were becoming more evident. Television, electronics, computers, and a host of other new industries were aborning. Old, aggressive companies such as IBM and RCA were thriving, while newer ones—Xerox, Polaroid, Control Data, and Texas Instruments, among others—were capturing the public's imagination. Charles Merrill had created "People's Capitalism," urging middle-class Americans to "own their share of America," while NYSE Chairman Keith Funston suggested that by owning common stock Americans would signal their support of their country and hatred of communism.

On November 30, 1953, the Dow-Jones Industrial Average surpassed the old 1929 high of 381 for the first time. Volume that day was less than 2 million shares. Within a few years four-million-share days would be commonplace. In the late 1960s 10-million-share days would be routine, and it also appeared the 1,000 mark on the Dow would soon be surpassed. In between, the nation enjoyed a new great bull market. The public was yearning for common stock. And where there's a demand, Wall Street creates a supply.

Ling was quick to grasp this simple truth. It was the first lesson he was to learn in his self-tutored program that would lead to unusual and innovative financial gymnastics of the kind that wouldn't be seen again until the 1980s.

In 1956 Ling made his first acquisition, L. M. Electronics, a California firm that turned out a line of testing equipment. Ling paid for L. M. with $200,000 in cash and securities, renamed it Ling Electronics, and took it in as a wholly owned subsidiary of Ling Electric. The company was profitable, Ling Electric's earnings rose to reflect this, and the stock started to move.

Having learned how an acquisition can boost earnings, Ling purchased another company, a bankrupt fabricator called Electronic Wire & Cable, for which he paid $50,000. He merged this and a start-up of his own, Electron Corp., which manufactured parts for the newly emerging TV cable industry. This helped sales, but temporarily flattened earnings. As a result, Ling Electric common barely budged, which both interested and troubled Ling. Perhaps the best way to grow, both the company and the stock, would be through acquisitions, but there was much about this he had to learn. Ling engaged in a self-study program regarding securities and quickly recognized that he could purchase desirable companies with the freshly printed stock the public seemed to crave.

Up to then all Ling did was fairly conventional. This was soon to change. Ling made a public offering of 1.3 million of Ling Electronics stock and convertible debentures, most of which was offered to and subscribed to by Ling Electric shareholders. Next, he formed a new company, Ling Industries, which exchanged shares with Ling Electronics and to which he transferred all of his contracting business in return for additional shares. "Industries" then sold the contracting operations to "Electric" in return for all of its stock. The result was that Ling Industries became a pure holding company, owning all the stock of Ling Electric and most of that of Ling Electronics.

Other regroupings followed, along with acquisitions. One of these was Altec, an important manufacturer of audio equipment purchased for 335,000 shares of Ling Electronics, after which Ling renamed his company Ling-Altec. He then went after Texas Engineering and Manufacturing (TEMCO), which in 1959 was twice the size of Ling-Altec. The following year Ling bought it for more shares, renaming the company Ling-Temco Electronics, a $148 million operation.

Next Ling approached Chance-Vought, a troubled manufacturer of military aircraft. After a contested tender offer (this was one of the period's first unfriendly takeovers) Ling acquired C-V and promptly renamed the company Ling-Temco-Vought (LTV).

This operation required cash, which Ling borrowed from local banks and insurance companies. In the process LTV became top-heavy with debt. Ling sold some C-V subsidiaries to raise cash, and while earnings collapsed as did the price of the common, Ling seemed capable of transforming his holdings into a respectable electronics and military supplies firm. At this point this seemed the limit of his ambitions.

Not for long. Military procurement complications led to losses at the C-V operation, causing Ling to reflect on the problems posed by overreliance upon the military. He switched strategies, vowing to transform LTV from a military-electronics supplier into a conglomerate. Ling reflected on this change several years later.

> I made a vow that never again would any company for which I was responsible be dependent upon any one market, any one product, or any one technology. Our concept would be that we would continually and on a sustained basis seek diversification. We are a diversified company today, as the result of some rather unique experiences some six years ago.

Ling not only would become a conglomerateur, but one with a difference, which was to have echoes in the efforts of some takeover barons of the 1980s. His intention was to go after large, ailing concerns that after acquisition could be dismembered and sold for more than their purchase price. T. Boone Pickens, Carl Icahn, and others would later do the same using junk bonds. Ling generally used equity, the preferred "currency" of the period. Or if the target so desired, he would swap bonds for assets. If this didn't suffice, Ling would borrow money from banks and pay in cash and then restructure the new holding in such a way as to enable him to repay the loans.

These techniques created problems. One problem was that the issuance of bonds and bank borrowings would require significant cash flows to service them. Another, more serious problem when it came to takeovers was that the expansion of the equity base could result in lower per-share earnings. Given the markets of the time, this would translate into lower prices for the stock, which would make it less desirable to potential takeover candidates. So one of Ling's paramount responsibilities was to enhance the price of his stock, which he intended doing through manipulating earnings, repurchase programs, and other forms of financial razzle-dazzle.

Ling knew (as did others) that there were two paths to increasing per-share earnings: either report higher earnings with the same amount of shares outstanding or maintain earnings while the number of shares declined. He would attempt to do both.

Ling's first effort to shrink capitalization began in 1964 and was quite conventional. He offered to exchange one share of a new convertible preferred stock that paid $3 in dividends plus $15 in cash for three shares of common. It was an attractive proposition, since the common then paid 50 cents and the preferred could be converted into 1.25 shares of common at the option of the owner. Those who accepted would have the cash, twice the dividend income, and still have a stake in LTV common through the conversion process.

What would Ling gain from all of this? He would slash the equity base, thus boosting the per-share earnings. It worked. LTV was able to decrease its capitalization from 2.8 million shares to 1.9 million. The effect was dramatic. LTV's 1963 net income was $6.2 million, which worked out to $2.12 per share. Income for 1964 actually declined to $4.9 million, but since the capitalization was so much lower, per-share earnings came to $2.32. As Ling anticipated, LTV stock responded by staging a respectable advance. Everyone seemed to have won in this, the first of Ling's machinations.

In late 1964 Ling announced what he called "Project Redeployment," which had everything to do with enhancing the stock price.

The initial step was to establish three wholly owned subsidiaries, LTV Aerospace, LTV Ling Altec, and LTV Electrosystems. These were "shell" companies; none had any assets other than their common stock. Then Ling divided LTV itself into three unequal portions and exchanged the appropriate ones for all the common shares of each of the three new entities. LTV Aerospace received most of Chance Vought and a substantial part of Temco, LTV Ling Altec obtained Altec and some miscellaneous properties, while whatever was left over went into LTV Electrosystems. Now LTV's only assets were furniture, an office lease, and three bundles of securities.

The next step came in April 1965, when LTV offered one half share of each of these three companies, plus $9 in cash, for each share of LTV common tendered to the parent company. Ling hoped that as many as 800,000 shares would be offered. This time some stockholders, sensing they would be better off with their equity, held back. Another reason was that many of them, in common with most Wall Street analysts, had difficulty figuring out whether or not it was a good deal, a problem that would plague Ling throughout his career. But enough shareholders accepted to enable the parent company's capitalization to be reduced to 1.8 million shares.

The three entities now had public shareholders, greater visibility, and eventually, listings on the American Stock Exchange. As it turned out, those who accepted Ling's offer did quite well for themselves. The book value of the three companies at the time of Project Redeployment was $7.9 million. The market values of the shares a year later came to $35 million. In a way, 1 + 1 + 1 worked out to around 13.

Ling took pains to explain that all three companies were autonomous, even while they shared common parentage, "Each is its own technological center. Each has its own profit centers. Each has its own separate markets. And, most importantly, each is its own management motivation center, and has individual access to public and private financial markets."

How might each of these three companies be considered autonomous when LTV owned a majority of its stock and so dictated the choice of officers and members of the board and had an effective veto over long-term plans? How might true independence be achieved when the officers of the three firms held posts at the parent, even though these were nominal? Finally, if the firms were truly independent, why did Ling continually refer to them as "subsidiaries"? While pondering these questions, Wall Street analysts thought about the nature of the company. What was it—a holding company, a conglomerate, or a closed end trust? It had elements of all three, but it was most certainly not an operating company.

Ling didn't bother with such questions, but rather plunged ahead. In October 1965, he acquired Okonite, a major manufacturer of copper wire and cable, for $31.7 million in cash. Then followed a typical Ling redeployment. LTV began by raising $20 million from a consortium of banks, putting up as collateral $73 million worth of its own securities, mostly the equity of the three subsidiaries, and paid off part of the loan. Then, as their share prices advanced, Ling sold additional stock in all three, with LTV borrowing the money from them to pay off more of the loans. Last, he sold 17 percent of Okonite, the money then used to retire the rest of the loans. Okonite common reacted by advancing.

In this way Ling furnished LTV with a fourth subsidiary, supplied Okonite with a market valuation, and secured more than sufficient funds to pay for the purchase. Once again the rising stock market had enabled him to expand. In effect, LTV had 83 percent of Okonite at virtually no cost other than Ling's time and effort, and approximately $3 million in market value of subsidiary stock. Okonite was able to contribute immediately to LTV's earnings, which made its common stock seem more appealing than ever.

In 1965 LTV reported a modest net-sales increase to $336.2 million from the prior year's $332.9 million. Earnings were up sharply to $6 million from $4.9 million, due to the Okonite contribution, while per-share earnings went from $2.32 to $2.82. Without the Okonite deal, LTV's figures would have declined along the line. As it was, investors responded by pushing the price of LTV common from 17 to 58.

The next step was yet more audacious. In 1966 Ling fixed his gaze on Wilson & Co., the nation's third-largest meat packer, which had sales of more than $1 billion. Since the stock was selling for around 50 and there were 2.4 million shares outstanding, this famous company was being valued by the market at less than $125 million.

The market saw a sluggish giant; Ling saw the opportunity for a replay of Project Redeployment. In addition to meat-packing operations, Wilson was a major manufacturer of sports equipment (from hides and skins came footballs and basketballs). Wilson Sporting Goods was the largest entity in its field, producing equipment for most sports. Then there was the pet-foods operation, which got its raw materials from meat unfit for human consumption. From the fats came soap. Finally, Wilson had developed a small but rapidly growing unit in pharmaceuticals derived from animal organs. From this staid company might be carved three, four, or even five units.

And that was Ling's intention, as he embarked on what he called "Operation Touchdown." With only $24 million in the LTV treasury, he began raising money through a two-year Eurodollar loan and a three-year domestic dollar loan via Lehman Brothers. He "borrowed" $10 million from Okonite. More money arrived through a secured loan from the LTV pension fund.

Ling struck in December 1966, offering $62.50 in cash for each of 750,000 shares of Wilson common, which would give him 30 percent of the outstanding shares. Management objected, embroiling Ling in another unfriendly takeover.

In those days before poison pills and golden parachutes, Wilson's management fought back with advertisements imploring shareholders to demonstrate loyalty and attacking Ling as unfamiliar with the industry and a raider, to no avail. The offer was oversubscribed. Ling purchased additional shares on the open market and within days had half of Wilson's stock at a cost of slightly less than $82 million. Then he exchanged $115 million worth of $5 preferred stock for the remainder of the shares.

This deal transformed LTV into a $1.8 billion corporation and was completed with no dilution of equity, though the senior capital and short-term debt had been substantially enlarged. Not for long. As those who by then knew his method of operation, it was apparent that Ling was planning another redeployment.

First LTV stripped Wilson of its cash and set aside four packing plants to be leased to a new Wilson & Co. at fat fees. Ling also transferred $50 million in European loans from LTV to Wilson. When this was finished LTV's total cash investment in the old Wilson had been reduced to only $6 million.

Ling then organized three new shell companies: Wilson & Co., Wilson Sporting Goods, and Wilson Pharmaceutical & Chemical. In exchange for their shares, LTV provided each with the relevant segments of the old Wilson & Co. It wasn't long before Wall Street dubbed these new firms "Meatball," "Golfball," and "Goofball."

Ling sold 18 percent of the new Wilson & Co. to the public, realizing $21.8 million. A quarter of the shares of Sporting Goods added another $17 million, while 23 percent of Pharmaceutical & Chemical fetched almost $6 million. In all, LTV had more than $44 million from the sales, which came close to offsetting the rest of the borrowings.

Sporting Goods and Pharmaceutical & Chemical became semi-glamour stocks in the great bull market of the time. By autumn LTV's equity in these three companies had a market value of approximately $250 million, on an investment of less than $200 million in cash and securities. This is not the way Ling calculated the cost, however, which in his view came to around $6 million in short-term debt and the $5.7 million annually to service the $5 preferred issue.

At the time Ling was being hailed in the business press as the greatest American financier since J. P. Morgan, a flattering comparison. These bromides usually are uttered during periods of great corporate restructuring and often are a sign the movement is about to come to an end.

In 1967 Ling made a pass at Allis-Chalmers, considered going after ABC Paramount and Sperry Rand, and failed in all three. He did take over some smaller companies, but by then only billion-dollar enterprises capable of being sliced into segments interested him.

The following year Ling fixed his gaze on Greatamerica Corp., which was controlled by a friend, Troy Post. Greatamerica was an umbrella for a wide variety of companies, most of them financially oriented. These included Franklin Life, American Amicable Life, Gulf Life, Stonewall Life, and First Western Bank & Trust. Greatamerica also had a controlling interest in Braniff Airlines and was in the process of acquiring National Car Rental. With Post's support, Ling made a tender offer for Greatamerica common, then selling in the low twenties. For every 100 shares he would exchange $3,000 in LTV 5-percent debentures maturing in 1988 plus a warrant to buy ten shares of LTV common at 115.

The offer seemed appealing, and in the past going along with Ling had provided investors with profits. News of the tender caused LTV common to rise to 125. The takeover was soon completed, whereupon Ling arranged for sales to raise funds to repay the debt. Stonewall was sold for $15 million, First Western for $62.5 million, and American Amicable for $18 million. Ling received funds equal to 20 percent of the debentures and still had most of Braniff, all of National Car Rental, and a grab-bag of small insurance companies.

As a result of all of this activity, LTV's total long-term debt had ballooned to $1.2 billion, and his equity base to 4.7 million shares. As recently as 1965 the debt had been $43 million, and the company had 1.8 million shares outstanding. Learning that a top Wall Street analyst had questioned his balance sheet, Ling asked him to come to his office for a talk. On seeing the man had a touch of gray at his temples, Ling snorted, "What could I expect from someone over 40?" Yet he also realized something had to be done to cut back on that debt and reduce the shares outstanding, which explains his next, most audacious move. Aided by his bankers, Goldman Sachs and Lehman Brothers, in October 1968 Ling put together a "unit" comprised of:

One share of Braniff Class A stock

0.6 shares of National Car Rental common

One share of National Car Rental Class A

1.1 LTV warrants exercisable at 103.35 expiring in 1978

One third of a share of Computer Technology (a small entity Ling had recently put together, and now would become a public company)

Then Ling sprang his plan. He offered:

1.1 units for 1 share of LTV common

9.75 units for $1,000 of LTV 6.5 percent notes

10 units for $1,000 of LTV 6.75 percent debentures

6.7 units for $1,000 of LTV's 5 percent debentures

9.5 units for $1,000 of LTV's 5.57 percent debentures

The impact of the offer was electric. Owners of LTV paper called their brokers to have the deal explained and ask for advice, and the brokers simply didn't know how to answer. Was it or was it not a good deal? No one quite knew, but all agreed that if successful, LTV would have a much lower debt and perhaps significantly less equity, while retaining important blocks of Braniff, National Car Rental, and the new Computer Technology.

Was Ling a charlatan or a genius?

As this was going on, Ling set about attempting to locate his next target. There was talk it would be Westinghouse, Bendix, North American Aviation, one of several medium sized petroleum and natural gas companies, or Youngstown Sheet & Tube. The last was closest to the mark. The victim would be Jones & Laughlin Steel.

Few could understand why Ling wanted the company. J&L wouldn't lend itself as easily to divestitures as, say, Wilson, and it certainly wasn't glamorous. But J&L common was selling for around $50, while the shares had a book value of $85, which also appeared understated. J&L had recently completed a $400 million capital improvement program, which worked out to another $50 a share.

What did Ling see in J&L? Like meat packing, steel was an aged, cyclical industry that combined high capital requirements with low returns on investment, but that was about the only similarities between them. J&L didn't have anything remotely as glamorous as the kinds of properties that might be made into analogues of Pharmaceutical & Chemical and Sporting Goods.

Ling met with J&L chairman Charles Beeghly to discuss a deal. It was an uneven contest. Ling had become a master of finance, but Beeghly knew steel, and more specifically, the strengths and weaknesses of J&L. Beeghly agreed to recommend a sale if the price were right. After some discussion they settled on $85 a share in cash. Ling said he wanted 63 percent of the stock to start with, which would require $425 million for financing. When it was all over Ling admitted that he had made a mistake with J&L. "There were more unknowns in the potential redeployment of a steel company than there are in other companies we had acquired," he told a reporter, adding, "and there were alternative methods of investing $425 million."

The money raised through the sale of Greatamerica assets went into the war chest Ling was creating for the J&L takeover. He also sold 600,000 shares of LTV common at around 100, bringing in another $60 million. Then $200 million was raised through the placement of short-term notes in Europe as well as in the United States. And of course that unit exchange was geared to sop up part of the debt in preparation for the final absorption of J&L.

All of this came together at the end of 1968—and the beginning of the end of the great bull market. The topping out in 1968 coincided with Ling's complex exchange offer and the attempted purchase of J&L.

Ling's luck had turned. It began when an insufficient number of bond and stock holders tendered their debt for those units, and so the offer failed. Ling found himself strapped for cash to pay interest on the debt amassed for the takeover. Now he was obliged to liquidate holdings to raise money.

The clearance began in February 1969 with the sale of two million shares of Braniff and continued throughout the year. LTV's remaining shares of Computer Technology went in April and were followed by the sale of National Car Rental. By December the three Wilson companies were selling assets and remitting funds to the parent. One of them, Wilson & Co., conducted its own version of Project Redeployment, organizing four subsidiaries: Wilson Beef & Lamb, Wilson Certified Foods, Wilson Laurel Farms, and Wilson-Sinclair, to be followed by Wilson Agri-Business Enterprises. Pieces of all were sold, but the offerings were not well received in a bear market. Nor could Ling sell additional LTV shares to raise funds.

The J&L situation went from promising to disastrous. It turned out that Ling had made the purchase at the top of the steel cycle. He had expected J&L to earn $38 million in 1969, and he would be able to send most of it on as a special dividend to help repay debt. Earnings came to a mere $22 million, adding to his distress. There were problems at Braniff, too, which earned a disappointing $6.2 million, of which LTV's portion came to $3.5 million. Other units were also in trouble.

Ling was attacked on another front. During this period reformers in Congress sought methods of halting the seemingly inexorable march of the conglomerates, which was wreaking havoc on the business scene. Attempts were made to prosecute the conglomerateurs under the antitrust statutes, but there they ran into problems. Conglomerates such as LTV and ITT did not dominate any single industry. Indeed, one of the reasons for conglomerates was attempts to evade prosecution under the statutes. Donald Turner, who headed the Antitrust Division during the Lyndon Johnson Administration, thought nothing could be done absent new legislation. "I do not believe Congress has given the courts and the FTC a mandate to campaign against 'superconcentration' in the absence of any evidence of harm to competition," he wrote.

Attempting to frame such legislation, Representative Emanuel Celler (D, NY) scheduled hearings on the matter for February 1969, shortly after the inauguration of President Richard Nixon. Five conglomerates were called to give testimony, one of which was LTV. Ling acquitted himself well, and it soon appeared the Celler Committee would fail to come up with the needed legislation. Nonetheless, a new attack was soon mounted by President Nixon's selection to replace Donald Turner. Richard McLaren, a Chicago lawyer, had spent most of the past 20 years defending corporate clients against the Justice Department and was a close friend of the new attorney general, John Mitchell. McLaren announced he disagreed with the Turner view on conglomerates. Echoing this view, Mitchell said that conglomeration "discourages competition among large firms and establishes a tone in the marketplace for more and more mergers," which he considered harmful to the economy.

That Richard Nixon would use the antitrust weapon after Lyndon Johnson refused to do so puzzled liberals. This seemed a bizarre reversal of positions. Such was not the case, however. Nixon, Mitchell, and McLaren represented the Establishment, which the likes of Ling and the others were threatening. No one seemed to notice that several of the companies menaced with takeovers were also clients of the law firm of Nixon Mudge Rose Guthrie Alexander, headed by John Mitchell until he went to Washington.

Not waiting for the Celler Committee to act, on March 22, 1969, McLaren informed LTV that he intended to file an antitrust brief to prevent the J&L takeover. So he did. On April 14 the government alleged that the combination would lessen competition in the steel industry. How might this be, since LTV didn't have a steel company? McLaren never responded, but later said the merger would involve reciprocity violations. How this could be proven prior to the takeover wasn't made clear.

The sensible LTV response would have been to abandon the merger, which by April didn't look as good as it had in 1968. Ling certainly had an out, which not only would be to LTV's benefit, but could be accepted without a loss of reputation. Yet he stubbornly pressed on. "I think I can beat McLaren if I stick with it," he said in June, adding, "but that would be just to satisfy my ego. He asked, rhetorically, "Is it—trying to look at it from a historic point of view like in Vietnam— a matter of getting so engaged in it to win my point that I might hurt other people, when there is really no other point in staying in the fight?" He must have known the answer, but he wouldn't budge.

Ling twisted and turned in his attempts to raise funds. He came up with a scheme whereby owners of the 5 percent debentures, now badly depreciated, might swap them for lesser amounts of 6.5 percent debentures and warrants, calculating to eliminate $400,000 of long-term debt and $11,000 in interest payments for every million-dollars worth of debentures tendered. There was a bizarre scheme to sell control of Braniff to Howard Hughes. He wanted Hughes to make a tender for two million shares of LTV at 50, while at the same time Ling would announce Hughes was granted an option to purchase his Braniff holdings for around $230 million.

In his typically baroque fashion, Ling fashioned "Project Home Run" for the deal. The first step (or base) would be the exchange of those two million shares plus around $100 in cash for LTV's interest in Braniff, which would halve LTV's capitalization and provide it with funds to repay most of its short-term debt. This would have the effect of doubling LTV's earnings (second base) and eliminate Braniff's meager contribution to the bottom line (third base). The home run would be completed when the public bid up the price of LTV common on seeing the quantum leap in earnings. Hughes was intrigued by the idea, but ultimately rejected it, forcing Ling into other ploys.

Next came "Master Game Plan." Ling would purchase all of the Okonite shares in the hands of the public and then divide the now-private company into two segments, one that owned all intangible assets (trademarks, patents, and the name) and the other with the physical plant and a new name. Then Ling would try to find buyers for each, on the assumption once more that 1 + 1 would equal much more than 2. Master Game Plan was not put into effect due to lack of time. Instead Ling raised some money by selling his shares in Wilson Sporting Goods to Pepsico ($63 million), and tried and failed to sell Braniff to Norton Simon or Gulf + Western.

In March 1970, after a year-old struggle, an exhausted Jimmy Ling agreed to terms of a settlement with the Justice Department. LTV acquiesced to either divest itself of both Braniff and Okonite or its shares of J&L. In addition the company pledged not to acquire a company with assets of more than $100 million during the next ten years. Stubborn to the end, Ling announced he would sell Okonite and Braniff and buy J&L.

The terms dictated by the government were outlandish. LTV didn't have to be prevented from acquiring companies. Rather, it was a takeover candidate itself with Chapter 11 bankruptcy a definite possibility. Revenues for 1969 came to $3.8 billion, up by $1 billion as a result of the J&L acquisition, but LTV posted a loss of $38.3 million as against 1968's profits of $29.4 million. At the time of the announcement, LTV common was selling for 12. The company had an empty treasury. Its 5 percent bonds were going for 25, to yield 20 percent. By May LTV common was under 10 and those 5 percent bonds were being offered at 15.

On May 17, 1970, LTV's outside directors asked Ling to step down as chairman and continue on as president, which he did. Six weeks later he quit the company completely.

Now came the necessary restructuring, which was handled badly. In 1971 LTV sold its stake in Braniff and Okonite as part of the antitrust settlement. It purchased Lykes, a manufacturer of petroleum equipment, and Youngstown Steel in 1977. Wilson was sold in 1981, leaving the company with its steel operations, Lykes, LTV Aerospace & Defense, and LTV Energy Products. In 1984, with the steel business ailing and low-priced foreign steel pouring into the American markets, it purchased Republic Steel for $770 million. On the ropes financially, LTV sold most of its nonsteel operations.

Ling's path from obscurity to renown and back need not have ended as it had. Of course, anyone swinging from one business trapeze to another can slip and be dashed to the ground. Ling took big risks for big rewards. Throughout his career he was more a deal maker and hustler than a businessman. He had never shown any ability at or interest in management, preferring instead "creative financing." Such a stance was possible in the 1960s, the age of the conglomerates, as it would be in the 1980s, the era of the leveraged buyouts. By 1970 conglomeration was over. In 1968, the peak year for the movement, there had been 207 mergers accounting for more than $13 billion in aggregate assets. In 1972 only 70 mergers were reported, involving $2 billion in assets. Some credited (or blamed) McLaren for having stopped the conglomerate movement, and he was quick to accept whatever applause came his way, especially for having halted LTV. Others thought the stock market's decline after 1968 was more important in ending the movement. Several analysts suggested that the major conglomerates would have had to slow down under the best of political and economic circumstances, if only to digest the takeovers of the late 1960s. Whatever the reason, it was over, and so was Ling's career on center stage.

Yet it needn't have been so. LTV did not collapse of its own weight, but rather, had to be shoved. The company and its leader had earned the ire of government, which considered Ling disruptive. So he had to go. This is not to suggest that a conspiracy existed between political leaders and old business, but rather that neither have any use for those who disturb the way business is conducted in any major fashion. Government did not so much push Ling and his company down the tube, but rather placed a banana peel in a strategic location.

CHAPTER NINE

DREXEL BURNHAM LAMBERT: THE BLUNDER OF ISOLATION

T hat capitalism requires competition in order to function efficiently is an axiom discussed in every economics class and textbook. Likewise, some of those texts and the professors who assign them inform students that there is no such thing as an absolute monopoly, since there are substitutes for virtually all products and services for which the supplier attempts to charge a monopoly price. Of course, there are some exceptions, such as a life preserver for a drowning person, but not many.

This is one of the more difficult lessons for former communist populations to learn. With freedom comes restraint. Unbridled capitalism can lead to a jungle environment in which none are safe and simple survival, not progress, is a matter of concern. So it is that American firms compete intensively with one another, but do so in the light of morality, tradition, and law. Transgressors often are turned upon by their fellows and the government. Correctly so, for if they are not put on guard, others may be encouraged to do the same, and then the fabric of society would start unraveling. When deviance is common, it ceases to be deviance and becomes the rule, and from there the path to anarchy is open.

Often those who fall behind in the competition accuse successful companies and individuals of having achieved their positions through devious and unfair methods. The winners, not the also-rans, are the targets. In the late 1960s the government went after IBM and AT&T, not Burroughs and General Telephone, and 30 years later it was Microsoft's turn, not Novell or Corel.

We already have seen how this worked out during the conglomerate era, when the new breed of businessman threatened the existence of many large and midsize companies and their leaders. During that period government strove to find the legislative means to block takeovers, which in a few years had created such giants at ITT, Gulf + Western, and especially James Ling's LTV. These and others were subjected to governmental actions geared to curb their activities, and in the case of LTV, it ended with that company's bankruptcy and James Ling's removal from the business scene.

This move was not unprecedented; a similar situation at the turn of the century resulted in the antitrust movement and the prosecutions of big business during the administrations of Theodore Roosevelt, William Howard Taft, and Woodrow Wilson. Their chief target then was the "money trust," which reformers believed made the others possible. Behind the predatory businessmen were the bankers, led by J. P. Morgan, Kuhn Loeb, and lesser lights.

It happened again in the 1980s, when a new breed of takeover artist threatened the existence of many large companies, both old-line firms and newer conglomerates. Once again targeted companies demanded legislation and instituted legal actions. At the climax of the takeover age, the focus was on the investment banking firm of Drexel Burnham Lambert and its chief asset, Michael Milken, who were harassed by government figures charging them with criminal violations. Were this not enough, Drexel had a problem with other investment banks, which by its actions it had alienated, and so couldn't turn to them for assistance.

While it did not become a major player on modern Wall Street until the 1980s, Drexel had one of the longest and most distinguished lineages in American investment banking. Its roots can be traced to the arrival in Philadelphia in 1817 of Austrian emigré, Francis Martin Drexel. Drexel became a portrait painter, who traveled to South America in search of commissions, and as he went from country to country, he learned a few things about money changing. Drexel returned to Philadelphia in 1831, where he participated in a brewery. This didn't last for long. Four years later he formed F. M. Drexel & Co., which dealt in bank bills. One of Drexel's sons, Anthony, would gather the bills from the interior and then bring them to the issuing bank for redemption, in the process making contacts and learning about the country and the business.

Francis took Anthony and his two brothers, Francis and Joseph, into the firm in 1847, whereupon it became Drexel & Co. At the time it was a small player in an increasingly large pond, but Drexel did help finance the Mexican War by selling government bonds to its long list of customers. By the time of the Civil War, Anthony Drexel was considered one of the leading bankers in the city, acclaimed for his placement power. It was said that he could market more than $10 million worth of bonds a week to investors who relied upon him for secure paper. Working in tandem with Jay Cooke, Drexel became one of the more important banks in financing the Union efforts in the Civil War.

In 1867 Anthony sent his brother Joseph to Paris to help organize Drexel Harjes & Co., which placed the firm in the international sphere. On a trip to Europe in early 1871, Anthony went to London, where he visited Junius Spencer Morgan to inquire about a possible alliance with that banker, which would give the American firm greater influence in that city. The elder Morgan said this was not possible, but that some kind of arrangement might be made with his son, John Pierpont.

Upon his return to Philadelphia, Drexel contacted the 34-year-old Morgan, inviting him to his office for a talk, which led to the formation of Drexel Morgan & Co. J. P. Morgan returned to Wall Street where he became the nation's leading banker, while Drexel remained in Philadelphia as the senior member of the alliance. At the time, Drexel Morgan and Jay Cooke & Co., both centered in Philadelphia, were the nation's two most powerful investment banks. Moreover, they were full members of the community, which gladly accepted their leadership.

As it turned out, the rivalry between the two cities was even then being settled in favor of New York. Drexel remained powerful, however, because of its leader's placement power and reputation. Even so, the bank became known as "the Philadelphia end of Morgan."

Anthony died in 1893, leaving a fortune of $30 million. Two years later, to indicate the passing of power, Drexel Morgan became J. P. Morgan & Co., and the reconstituted Drexel & Co. went off on its own. Under Anthony Drexel's successors the company did well enough, but its power and prestige increasingly came from the connection with the Morgan bank. It did not prosper as much as the New York banks did during the 1920s, but was in on some of the larger underwritings and was still deemed a consequential force.

This changed during the 1930s, as the banking business dried up. When the New Deal forced the separation of investment and commercial banking, Drexel abandoned investment banking and became a commercial bank, although some of the partners reconstituted the investment bank later on. In 1950 it was only the seventeenth-largest syndicator, underwriting $20 million in securities, while the leader, Halsey Stuart, did $723 million of business. Yet when the Justice Department filed an antitrust suit against Wall Street banks—the so called "Club Seventeen," Drexel was included. This was taken by Judge Harold Medina, before whom the case was heard, as a sign of the frivolous nature of the action. "I just can't figure it out," he said two and a half years into the trial. Drexel had underwritten less than one percent of the offerings brought out during the 15-year period the government had studied.

Limping along, in 1965 Drexel merged with Harriman Ripley, another firm with a fine pedigree that also had left investment banking and then returned, with the thought that the combined assets of the two companies might lead to better times. It didn't. Drexel Harriman Ripley was eighteenth in underwritings in the 1960s, sandwiched between Lazard Freres and Paine Webber. By 1970 Drexel had only ten *Fortune 500* clients, which put it in the same league as the stagnant Dillon Read and the smallish Hornblower & Weeks. Moreover, it was badly in need of capital and was obliged to trade a 25 percent interest in itself for $6 million from Firestone Tire & Rubber, which was interested in a foray into banking. Now the firm's name changed again, to Drexel Firestone.

Salvation was already there, though few at the firm had any inkling of this. In 1969 one of his professors at the Wharton School of the University of Pennsylvania found Michael Milken a summer job at Drexel Firestone, and he continued on as a part-time trainee when he returned to school. Upon completing all the requirements for the M.B.A. except the thesis, which was completed afterward, Milken came to work on a full-time basis. He went to the firm's New York headquarters as director of research for "low-grade bonds" at a salary of $25,000 a year.

Although a product of what was considered the finest graduate program in finance, Milken was not particularly impressive. He had been born into a middle-class family, attended local public schools, and then went to Berkeley, which at the time was in the middle of political turmoil. Milken was not interested in such matters, instead taking a job at the accounting firm of Touche Ross, and marrying his childhood sweetheart. He decided to attend Wharton not so much out of ambition, but rather because that school was willing to grant credits for some exams he intended taking. He was a good student, but so were some of the others considered by their professors superstars of the future. Milken, with his shy grin, incapacity for small talk, and interest only in work and family, did not seem the kind of person intended for greatness. His professors did not mark him for outstanding success. Wharton's superstars went to firms such as Goldman Sachs, Merrill Lynch, and Morgan Stanley, not to Drexel Firestone.

Despite the title Milken was given, the job wasn't considered a plum assignment. The action in finance was still in equities. Bonds, which were declining in price and attraction in the inflationary atmosphere of the time, were perceived as unpromising and dull. So Milken was a bond man while it appeared the play was still in stocks. This did not seem to bother him. Indeed, there was reason to be pleased with this situation, since it might mean he was coming in at the bottom of the bond-market cycle. The timing was right, as was the venue.

Milken had a keen mind and an extraordinary capacity for work. As it turned out, he also was a convincing salesman, with a message that was both simple and plausible, and in addition was an echo of one that was central to Wall Street debate at the end of the nineteenth century. In the late 1890s critics of Wall Street had spoken of "watered stock," shares sold to the public at less than their net-asset value. So it might be that a steel company had assets on its books of $40 a share and be offered to the public at $60. These critics claimed that in such case, $20 of the price was "water." The underwriters might reply that market share, reputation, leadership, patents, and more assets that were not represented on the balance sheet were assets as well, but to suspicious critics, this was simply smoke and mirrors.

In his time, Milken thought investors had an inaccurate concept of what constituted risk and how it had to be reflected in securities prices. A Wall Street axiom in the 1950s was "the greater the risk, the greater must be the reward." This meant that common stocks, which had a lower claim on the company than its bonds, should provide investors with a higher yield than did bonds, and such indeed was the case. In 1949, when government bonds yielded an average 2.3 percent, high-grade corporate bonds, 2.7 percent, and preferred stock, 4 percent, the Moody's composite index of common stocks returned 6.6 percent.

New issues underwritten by young companies, which paid no dividends at all and whose earnings were meager, had difficulties being sold. In 1955 Martin Mayer, then a newcomer to Wall Street, wrote that while it might be possible to place such securities with friends and relations, "without such friends a corporation will find that the price for 'venture capital' is high as a gallows." In a popular college finance textbook of the period, *Investments* (1953), Professor Julius Grodinsky told a generation of students that "the investors in common stocks are the genuine risk bearers in the system of capitalism and free enterprise," and risk was not sought by investors of the early 1950s.

This axiom was challenged with the coming of the bull market in the mid-1950s, when gradually, owners of common shares learned to obtain their rewards from an increase in the prices of their stocks, not from dividends. This remained the case when Milken appeared in New York. He perceived something such as this insight was needed for bonds as well.

Milken believed the rating agencies—Standard & Poor's and Moody's—were correctly concerned with balance sheets and related data, but assigned such matters far too much importance. How about the management talents, works in progress, research and development, and the like, that advocates of common stock discussed in the late nineteenth century? Didn't these count for anything? He felt this was particularly true for the knowledge companies then coming into being, young or restructured firms long on intangibles but short on tangibles. The assets of these rested more on the abilities of managers and researchers than on the production of factories. Steve Ross, CEO of Warner Communications, then an entertainment conglomerate that became one of Milken's clients, once told an audience that every weekday, in the late afternoon, he would look out of his office window and see his inventory drive away. Ross said he hoped they would return the following day, since without them, he had no business. Because such intangibles could not be quantified, the rating agencies would assign low ratings to the bonds sold for such companies, and these bonds became known as "junk" and had to be sold on the basis of their high yields. This was the area at Drexel Firestone where Milken found his niche.

In 1973 Drexel Firestone became Drexel Burnham, upon receiving an infusion of cash from Burnham & Co., a small, generally conservative brokerage that I. W. "Tubby" Burnham had founded in the difficult year of 1935. Burnham very much wanted his name on an investment bank, and by investing in Drexel, he received just that. He became the firm's president, but retired soon after to be succeeded by Mark Kaplan. Shortly thereafter Drexel Burnham acquired Lambert Brussels Witter, a Belgian company that specialized in research, whereupon it became Drexel Burnham Lambert.

The petroleum crisis of 1973 caused a flow of red ink at many banks and brokerages, and soon mergers and dissolutions became epidemic. Not so at Drexel, for by then Milken's unit had started generating striking profits, and his remuneration went to $52,000 plus a portion of the profits his unit generated. Armed with impressive academic research, Milken took three major steps that catapulted him to national attention and astounding wealth, and ultimately to his incarceration and the collapse of Drexel.

The first step was selling his ideas—and the bonds upon which they were based—to customers. When these invariably wealthy people wanted to know whether the bonds were risky, Milken would reply that every investment carried some degree of risk, but these bonds were not as hazardous as was commonly believed. In the mid-1970s he told a buyer that the bonds of MCI, then seen as an improbable competitor for AT&T, were safer than government bonds issued by Argentina. "How could this be so?" he was asked. "You can seize MCI for failing to pay interest," Milken replied. "You can't seize Argentina." Moreover, while the stocks of companies that failed often went to zero, bonds did not, since in the reorganization the bondholders often received shares in the now reconstituted company. Finally, Milken told the buyers and others that these bonds were not to be viewed as long-term investments, but rather were to be purchased for capital gains. And just as J. P. Morgan had assured his customers a century earlier that he was both literally and figuratively underwriting the bonds he offered—that he knew the merchandise and would monitor the situations carefully—so Milken convinced his expanding circle of wealthy investors and eventually mutual funds, pension funds, insurance companies, and thrift institutions that he knew the securities very well indeed and would notify them if and when they should be sold.

Once he had a large band of investors, Milken was in a position to take the second step, that of underwriting the bonds of those young, previously unrated companies in need of financing, which found the traditional methods closed to them. It is problematical whether the companies that used Milken's services could have found funding elsewhere. Of course, they had to pay high interest rates, and Milken insisted on safeguards to protect his customers; these are the fundamentals of investment banking.

Milken moved into this area cautiously. The first underwriting, for Texas International, an oil-drilling company, was a disaster. In 1977 Milken raised $30 million for the company in exchange for its 11.5 percent bonds, which he then placed with customers. Texas International fizzled, and went bankrupt in 1987. Then there was Flight Transportation, for which Drexel sold $25.6 million in stocks and debentures, which proved a scam involved with smuggling gems on Caribbean flights. When this was discovered, Milken insisted on returning capital to his customers, including interest. Drexel backed American Communications to the tune of $14 million, and soon after it fell into bankruptcy. Likewise Grant Broadcasting.

These proved the exceptions. From 1977 to 1984, the period when Milken concentrated on the young and restructured companies, Drexel underwrote 166 junk-bond issues, five of which wound up in bankruptcy. Some proved outstanding, and these included Turner Broadcasting, MCI, McCaw Cellular, Viacom, Cablevision, Duracell, Barnes & Noble, Calvin Klein, and many of the new casinos in Las Vegas. He was able to raise money for Chrysler when, after that company barely escaped bankruptcy, it couldn't obtain financing elsewhere. Based on his success, Milken, who never felt comfortable in New York, in 1979 was able to move his operations to Beverly Hills. There were several reasons for this beside his desire to leave Wall Street and return home. He could arrive for work at 5:00 A.M. or so and be there at his desk when business began in New York, and he could continue until late at night in California, when New York had closed down.

Drexel's rise from previous underwriting obscurity was rapid. In 1978 the firm accounted for one third of all junk financing, and it led the field every year but one from then until 1989, and in many of them with more than half the market.

Milken and his team were well remunerated for their efforts. Under the terms of his original deal with Drexel, Milken was permitted to retain one dollar of every three he earned for the firm. He was given that amount to distribute among his unit. Always Milken set aside the largest portion for himself. Accordingly, he made $46 million in 1983, $124 million in 1984, $135 million in 1985, and $295 million in 1986. In 1987, Milken's bonus pool came to $700 million, of which he awarded himself $550 million. As the newspapers of the time liked to remark, Milken made more in remuneration than the total profits of most firms on the *Fortune 500* list. In addition to this, he earned substantial amounts from ancillary ventures.

By the mid-1980s not only was Milken one of the nation's better known financiers, but several of his customers were making names for themselves in their fields. Fred Carr, a flashy fund manager during the 1960s, took over at First Executive Corp., which owned First Executive Life Insurance. By 1984 First Executive had a $4.8 billion junk portfolio, which was performing so well that First Executive was able to sell insurance policies at lower premium rates as well as offering attractive annuities. Other insurance companies followed his lead. Prudential, CNA, Reliance, and Presidential Life held large junk portfolios.

Although it was later thought junk was present in many if not most thrift-institution portfolios, such was not the case; the thrifts invested far more capital in real-estate schemes. Tom Speigel's Columbia Savings & Loan had $6.4 billion in junk by 1984, however, which enabled it to pay depositors high interest on their accounts, and there were others, including Charles Keating, whose Lincoln Savings & Loan was later involved in criminal practices revolving around land deals.

Milken would later claim that the financing of small and mid-sized companies was the most pleasurable aspect of his work. It was calculated that from 1980 to 1986, firms employing junk bonds accounted for more than 80 percent of all job creation at public corporations. Had he stopped with that, he might perhaps be applauded today as one of the men most responsible for the reinvigoration of the American economy. In the late 1980s he was hailed on Wall Street as the greatest banker since J. P. Morgan, which seemed plausible at the time, although his lineage might better be traded to A. P. Giannini, the founder of what became the Bank of America, who opened credit and deposits to the multitudes. But most of the plaudits he received were not for these financings, but rather for the actions taken in the third step in his career, the one that made him a billionaire, but also destroyed both him and Drexel.

The opportunities presented in that period derived from an anomaly in the way the stock market valued the assets of some large corporations as a result of the great inflation of the 1970s. Not since the 1930s had prices been so out of line with their net underlying assets. Never before or since, as long as reliable records have been kept, had consumer and producer prices risen so much and for so long. The Consumer Price Index more than doubled from 1970 to 1980, while the stock market gyrated and wound up in 1980 close to where it had been a decade earlier, with the price/earnings ratio for the Dow Jones Industrials slightly higher than 7. This meant that the breakup value of companies that at the beginning of the period had had large amounts of fixed assets and had obtained more along the way, had risen sharply, while the stocks of these companies were very low by historic standards. This was particularly true for the petroleum companies. The price of a barrel of Arabian light crude, which had been around $3 a barrel in 1973 before the Organization of Petroleum Exporting Companies imposed an embargo, was in the mid-$30 range at the end of the decade. Yet the stocks of the major petroleum companies did not reflect this tenfold increase in the value of their reserves.

It didn't take too much imagination to realize that many were selling for below the value of their petroleum reserves. As one observer noted, the cheapest place to find oil was on the floor of the New York Stock Exchange. In the summer of 1981 Getty, which had assets of $250 a share, was selling in the low seventies. Marathon had $210 in assets and was in the high sixties. Cities Service had $130 a share in reserves alone, and was in the midfifties. In 1983 the engineering firm of John Herold estimated that the shares of giant petroleum firms were selling for about 40 percent of their net worths. All would be gone by the end of the decade, the victims of raiders.

These were the fundamentals behind the hostile-takeover movement of the 1980s, during which fully one third of the companies on the *Fortune 500* roster vanished into mergers, liquidations, acquisitions, or simply fell by the wayside. In the process, enormous amounts of money were made; according to one calculation, stockholders' gains from restructurings and takeovers came to more than $650 billion. And of course, the profits for the banks that handled these deals were immense.

Fred Joseph, who had arrived at Drexel in 1974 to head the corporate-finance department and rose to become the bank's CEO, had close relations with Milken. He understood the situation and wanted the company to capitalize upon it. He thought Drexel might help finance some of the raiders who were going after those underpriced companies. The method was simplicity itself. Take a company whose breakup value was estimated at, say, $100 a share, whose stock was selling for $40. The raider would offer the shareholders $60. Management would protest that it was worth far more than that, and the raider would shoot back that if this truly were so, then management was admitting it had been doing a poor job. At the end of the day the raider might obtain control of the company by using borrowed funds to pay the shareholders. While doing this he would have engaged the services of an investment bank, often Drexel, but there were others, to arrange for permanent financing. Milken and his team would then design a junk bond that would appeal to Drexel's long list of customers, often selling more bonds than were needed, the idea being that the extra money would be used to purchase bonds of other Drexel deals. In the end the client would control a large company with a very large debt. Assets might then be sold and the money thus obtained used to repurchase the bonds, with substantial amounts left over for the client.

In 1983 Drexel underwrote its first billion-dollar deal for MCI Communications. Joseph initiated contacts with the company during the late 1970s, and in 1981 Milken was able to place $125 million of the company's bonds. This was followed by a 1983 $1.1 billion placement of subordinated notes and warrants, which was the largest corporate underwriting till then.

The following year Drexel handled a complex leveraged buyout of Metromedia by CEO John Kluge. Metromedia was one of those conglomerates cobbled together in which the components were not dependent upon each other, and so might easily be detached and sold. It owned television and radio stations, outdoor advertising, and other nonrelated businesses such as Ice Capades and the Harlem Globetrotters. Kluge had purchased depreciation rights to $100 million of New York City buses and subway cars, invested $300 million in the nascent mobile-telephone industry, and expended $400 million in a stock-repurchase program. He had borrowed heavily to accomplish all of this—Metromedia had $550 million in long-term bonds outstanding—and as a result its debt-to-equity ratio in the spring of 1984 was 3:1.

Drexel's bankers put together a plan whereby Kluge's 26 percent stake in the company would become 75.5 percent through the replacement of equity by additional debt, much of the money coming from Prudential Insurance, which would receive short-term rates plus a fee for initiation. He accepted the plan, and Drexel's bankers proceeded with the first stage, which was an offer of $30 a share in cash and debentures with a face value of $22.50 but an actual value more on the order of $10, for each share of stock tendered. When this offer was protested, Drexel added a half-warrant to purchase another debenture plus a 19-cents-per-share dividend prior to the buyout, which brought the total to around $41 per share. The shareholders accepted the deal on June 20, and with this, Moody's lowered the company's credit rating. "Metromedia's existing business remain sound and are strong cash-flow generators," it said. But "over the next few years, protection for fixed [interest] charges will be significantly reduced by the magnitude of new debt and associated interest expenses."

The next step was for Milken to arrange permanent financing. This was a key and questionable part of the deal. Metromedia's prior-year cash flow would not cover interest on the debt, and its net worth of debt was negligible. But Milken and Joseph knew the company's intangibles were quite valuable and could be disposed of easily for high prices.

The financing would come in the form of a $1.9 billion debt offering, quite complex and the largest for a nonfinancial corporation at the time. There would be $960 million in six tranches of zero-coupon bonds maturing from 1988 to 1993, $335 million in senior exchangeable variable-rate debentures due in 1996, $225 million of 15 5/8 percent senior subordinated debentures of 1999, and $400 million adjustable-rate participating subordinated debentures of 2002 offered at a discount, with interest payments to rise starting in 1988 should there be a specified amount of earnings from the radio and TV stations. It was an imaginative, bold, and somewhat puzzling offering. The entire underwriting was cohandled by Drexel Burnham and Bear Stearns on November 29. Almost all of the buyers were lined up by the Milken team prior to the offering, which sold out in less than two hours.

Critics of the deal predicted that Metromedia would fall into bankruptcy within a year. But in May 1985, Kluge sold the company's TV stations to Rupert Murdoch for $2 billion plus $650 million in debt. Other sales followed, and by early 1987 Metromedia had raised close to $6 billion through asset sales. Kluge made more than $3 billion and became one of the nation's wealthiest men, and the Drexel-Milken reputation was burnished.

Metromedia demonstrated the power of Drexel as well as its imagination and boldness. Wall Street quickly perceived that what the bank had done in a perfectly friendly fashion for Metromedia could be done in a hostile fashion as well. Such indeed was about to happen on a large scale, but there had been hostile takeovers well before then.

The first truly hostile takeover of the modern era came in 1974, when International Nickel acquired ESB, formerly known as Electric Storage Battery, with the aid of Morgan Stanley. Other banks then entered the business. In fact, almost all who could did so, because the profits from such deals were so attractive. In the process the banks developed sharp elbows and still sharper tempers. The gentlemanly nature of investment banking, which had existed when the business was highly regulated and the rules of behavior relatively clear, was giving way to a jungle-like atmosphere where practically anything went. In 1981, for example, Drexel and Merrill Lynch were jointly underwriting an issue for Volt Information Services, and Drexel was handling the travel arrangements for the "road show" to meet with investors. Drexel booked its bankers and the Volt people first class while the Merrill Lynch crew traveled coach. Drexel changed the site of a meeting with Chicago investors and did not inform Merrill Lynch, which missed the meeting. Joseph later apologized, but such activities continued, and Drexel's reputation on Wall Street suffered. In 1985 M. William Benedetto of Dean Witter told a reporter, "Drexel's relationships with the Street leaves a lot to be desired."

Likewise the reputation with clients. One Milken associate, James Dahl, approached Staley Continental's CEO Robert Hoffman to suggest a leveraged buyout, indicating that if he did not agree to the plan, Dahl would find someone else and do the buyout, hinting that Hoffman would then be out of a job. Staley later charged Drexel with extortion. A similar situation developed with CPC International. At Green Tree Acceptance, Dahl double-crossed the client to get better terms for the customers, who had purchased a large block of Green Tree stock. Fearing a hostile takeover, Green Tree repurchased the shares at $12 above their market price, providing a windfall for the customers, and Drexel.

Felix Rohatyn, a veteran banker of the old school, was thinking of Drexel when he said, "A cancer is spreading in our industry. Too much money is coming together with too many young people who have little or no institutional memory, or sense of tradition, and who are under enormous economic pressure to perform in the glare of Hollywood-like publicity. The combination makes for speculative excesses at best, illegality at worst."

Meanwhile the differences between stock prices and underlying values prompted a series of well-publicized takeover attempts. One of the more spectacular of these was T. Boone Pickens's failed 1983 run on Gulf, which wound up being taken over by Chevron at $80 a share. Pickens's shares, purchased for an average in the low fifties, had made his company, Mesa Petroleum, a profit of $500 million, and other owners of Gulf shares did quite well. As for Drexel, which handled the deal for Pickens, it not only earned a large fee, but Milken, who raised $1.7 billion from his customers in a few days, was now seen as one of the most powerful figures in finance. Pickens became a celebrity and would go on to more forays, as would other raiders. In the seven years from Pickens's gulf war to that of George Bush, 657 American petroleum and natural gas companies would be either acquired or merged.

The oil companies were not the only ones raiders sought. With the help of Drexel and other banks that followed it into the takeover game, Ron Perelman, Carl Icahn, Saul Steinberg, Irwin Jacobs, Nelson Peltz, Victor Posner, and Carl Lindner went after the likes of Revlon, TWA, ITT, and a host of other bloated, underpriced, or simply troubled companies. "From a purely mechanical point of view, we could do any size acquisition," opined David Kay, who headed Drexel's mergers-and-acquisition department. So it appeared. When Icahn sought Milken's aid in his quest for Phillips Petroleum, $1.5 billion was raised in two days.

Not surprisingly, the CEOs of targeted companies or of companies thought of as becoming targets reacted and did so on three fronts: through lobbying, working with friendly congressmen to pass legislation curbing takeovers, and on the publicity front. The key player in this effort was the Business Roundtable, which had been created in 1972 with the help of such government figures as Secretary of the Treasury John Connally and Federal Reserve Chairman Arthur Burns. The Roundtable was composed of the CEOs of 200 of the largest American companies, which together accounted for half the nation's GDP. As might have been expected, such individuals considered hostile takeovers the equivalent of business warfare, and there was no doubt as to their stand. The chairman at the time was Champion International's CEO Andrew Sigler, who had some experience in this area, having fought off three takeover attempts.

Prompted by the Roundtable, in 1984 several congressional committees investigated takeovers and considered framing legislation to curb them. Those in Congress with long memories might have thought this exercise familiar: This was the way critics of the conglomerates had tried to bring an end to their activities. Senator J. Bennett Johnson of Louisiana, an oil state, proposed a ban of mergers and restructuring of the top 50 petroleum companies, which was applauded by the CEOs of major petroleum companies, including Unocal, Phillips, Ashland, and Sun, all considered prime candidates for takeovers. Others came up with similar plans, and so it appeared the takeovers might be ended through congressional action.

Democratic Senator William Proxmire was one of those liberal legislators who was wary of the hostile takeovers. "In theory, hostile takeovers are supposed to increase efficiency by ousting inept corporate managers," he said on one occasion. "In reality, they serve little purpose but to make millions for professional raiders, their lawyers, and investment bankers." Proxmire thought there were three ways to bring an end to the movement: Congress could eliminate the deductibility of interest paid on bonds used in such takeovers; it could ask bank regulators to discourage banks and other financial institutions from making unfriendly takeover loans; and finally, it might amend the Williams Act, which had been passed in 1968 to bring an end to conglomerate mergers, which initially required those that accumulated 10 percent of a company's stock to disclose sources of funds and other information to targets and not be permitted to purchase additional shares unless it were done through a tender offer open to all shareholders. Later the threshold was lowered to 5 percent—Proxmire wanted it upped to 15 percent instead. If approved, the Proxmire recommendations might have brought an end to hostile takeovers, permitting Milken and his people to return to the earlier business of financing smaller companies with their junk bonds.

Other senators had plans of their own. In the summer of 1985 Timothy Wirth of Colorado prepared legislation requiring raiders to have financing in place before making their offers and would restrict financial involvement by federally insured lending institutions. Massachusetts Senator Edward Kennedy was thought to be preparing even more stringent legislation. Nothing happened on the legislative front, however. In 1984–1985, 31 measures were introduced to limit takeovers. None passed, but pressures continued. Troubled, Milken met with Joseph and others at the firm and recommended Drexel stop financing hostile takeovers, but his colleagues disagreed.

Fred Hartley, CEO of Unocal, another of the companies Pickens threatened, emerged as the raiders' most vociferous and clever adversary. Together with others in the Business Roundtable and the American Petroleum Institute, he put together the kind of alliance of political liberals and economic conservatives that had smashed Ling a generation earlier. To this mix he added representatives of the old Wall Street such as Dillon Read CEO and future secretary of the treasury, Nicholas Brady, whose firm refused to engage in hostile takeovers and would defend companies against them. "Busting up corporations for the sake of a few extra dollars for shareholders is a very short-term view," he said. "We ought to be a little careful in allowing a system that dismembers corporations." Unsurprisingly, Dillon Read became Unocal's banker in the defense against Pickens. Before congressional hearings on hostile takeovers, it often was Brady and Joseph, appearing on opposite sides of the issue. Discussing Drexel, Brady said, "They were just junk people buying junk bonds."

As part of its assault, the Business Roundtable placed advertisements decrying raiders who plundered companies, leaving behind wrecked communities and companies crippled by debts incurred by having to raise immense sums to finance stock buybacks. CEOs appeared on television news programs criticizing the "predators," and motion pictures and plays on the subject became topics of discussion. It was difficult to sympathize with a raider who made hundreds of millions of dollars on a single deal, or with Milken, "the $550 million man," and easy to do so for a worker in a town who was fired due to financial stringencies caused by takeover activities. There was much noise and shouting, but nothing came of any of this. The critics were discouraged, but then hopes were revived by an unexpected event.

On May 12, 1986, while several antitakeover measures were before Congress, Drexel banker Dennis Levine was arrested on charges of insider trading in 54 stocks. This was for Drexel the equivalent of what the discovery of the Watergate break-in was for the Nixon Administration.

Levine was not quite the prototypical "yuppie" banker of this period, but he came close. He did not have the Ivy League background, the veneer of breeding, or the circle of celebrity friends. But he was a demon trader and considered a rising star at Drexel, where he had been placed by a headhunter who received a fee of $250,000 for his find. Levine was on his way to wealth and perhaps fame as well, but it wasn't coming fast enough. Besides, the temptations to cross the line were tempting. So between 1980 and 1985 he made more than $11 million on his illicit trades. Then he was found out and arrested.

The Security and Exchange Commission's chief of enforcement, Gary Lynch, and U.S. attorney Rudolph Giuliani offered Levine a plea bargain if he would cooperate with them in unearthing his accomplices. Levine accepted and fingered several individuals, among them Ivan Boesky, a well-known plunger, who in return for acceptance of his plea bargain also named names. One of these was Martin Siegel, a well-known expert in takeover defenses who, like Levine, had joined Drexel. When confronted, Siegel admitted to having engaged in insider trading with Boesky while at Kidder Peabody, and he, too, agreed to cooperate. In short order Levine, Boesky, and Siegel were imprisoned, receiving light sentences for having talked. Siegel fingered several other bankers, among them Robert Freeman of Goldman Sachs, who also went to prison. Boyd Jefferies, who headed his own securities firm, had assisted Boesky; he was fined $250,000 and given probation.

Wall Street's glamorous bankers were falling like a stack of cards, and at the center of it all were prominent Drexel figures. By 1987 and early 1988 the atmosphere in New York and at Milken's Beverly Hills office was steeped in paranoia, while in Washington Representative John Dingell was scheduling hearings on "Securities Markets Oversight and Drexel Burnham Lambert."

As part of his plea bargain, Boesky had told Giuliani of his dealings with Milken. Armed with the Racketeer Influenced and Corrupt Organizations Act (RICO), which had been passed as a weapon against organized crime but had been used against businesspeople as well, Giuliani went after Drexel. Under terms of the act penalties were harsh, and the need for convincing evidence to obtain indictments was minimal.

True to the agreement, Boesky accused Milken of crimes, and in September, 1988 the SEC charged Drexel of 21 violations of the securities laws, of which two involved insider trading. In late November the government initiated the filing of RICO charges against Drexel and Milken. As had the others before them, several Drexel bankers agreed to testify with promises of immunity and plea bargains. There were leaks to the press and rumors galore, as Giuliani closed in on his target.

All this occurred before an indictment or trial. With RICO, Giuliani felt he had the power to destroy Drexel without a trial.

In mid-December, 1988, Giuliani told Joseph he was prepared to bring forth indictments on RICO charges unless Drexel agreed to a settlement on his terms. As one Drexel banker characterized the meeting, "Giuliani put the gun on the table and said to us, 'Either you will pick it up and use it on yourself, or I will.'" It was clear by then, even without the leaks, that Milken and Drexel were Giuliani's prime targets. All the while the Business Roundtable and the congressional critics looked on, well aware that Giuliani was doing what they had intended to do, and in a swifter and more effective fashion.

The Drexel high command was divided in its reaction. Some of the leaders, especially the bankers involved with the junk-bond business, wanted to fight, while others, management-oriented, advocated making a deal that would deliver Milken to Giuliani while preserving the company. In the end, the 22-member board elected to cooperate with the government.

On December 21 Drexel agreed not to contest six charges of malfeasance and pay $650 million in fines and damages. That these admissions would result in further civil suits seemed obvious. The firm also agreed to add three outside directors, including John Shad, who became chairman of the board. Shad, formerly a banker and then head of the SEC, had been highly critical of the use of junk bonds. "The more leveraged takeovers and buyouts today, the more bankruptcies tomorrow," he had remarked. "The levering-up of American enterprise will magnify the adverse consequences of the next recession, or significantly raise interest rates."

Finally, Drexel agreed to place Milken on a leave of absence, and no one at the firm would be permitted to remain in contact with him. Part of his earnings, $200 million, was to be held in an escrow account, and the company was to cooperate in the government's investigations. Of course, all of this took place without Milken's being charged with crimes, not to say being convicted of any wrongdoing.

These unprecedented moves, while cheered by some on Wall Street who resented Drexel's command of the junk market, unnerved others. Markets had been edgy since the October 19, 1987, crash, when on heavy volume the Dow Jones Industrials fell by 508 points, and while the market had made it up, fears of another steep decline remained. How might Giuliani's actions affect the junk-bond market? Milken had developed a tight circle of clients and customers. Would anyone at Drexel—or some other bank or banks—be able to fill the gap he left?

Milken's isolation took place when a struggle for control of RJR Nabisco was beginning, with Drexel committed to raising funds for Kohlberg Kravis Roberts, a leading leveraged-buyout firm, with Merrill Lynch the comanager. How would this deal fly without access to Milken's customers? Joseph attempted to assure all involved that the deal would go through as planned and that Drexel could handle clients and customers as Milken. John Kissick, who had arrived from Shearson in 1975 and had worked closely with Milken, became the head of the high-yield department and was well-known to Drexel's customers. For a while, everything seemed to fall into place, but selling began in the junk market, and prices started to decline, not so much due to financial problems at the issuers, but fears of liquidity and additional action by the Justice Department and Congress that would further unsettle the markets.

A time of testing arrived in June, 1989, when Drexel's bankers were unable to roll over $40 million of commercial paper for a client, Integrated Resources. In the past Milken had rescued clients in such circumstances, if only to maintain the bank's reputation for supporting them and preventing a meltdown. One of those rescues had been for Integrated Resources. But not this time. Declaring itself illiquid, on June 15 the company defaulted on $1 billion of debt, most of it owned by Drexel customers, some of whom had guarantees on it from the bank. The default jarred Drexel's clients and customers alike.

Two months later Congress passed the Financial Institutions Reform, Recovery, and Enforcement Act (FIRREA), which required thrift institutions to mark their junk bonds to market, which is to say, carry them at market prices rather than face value, meaning that some would show large losses due to the selloff. In addition, they would have to dispose of their junk portfolios by June 1994. Finally, they were prohibited from purchasing additional junk bonds. Drexel spokespeople were quick to note that except for credit cards, thrift institutions had made more on junk bonds than on any other investment. Moreover, only a few had sizable holdings. Of the approximately $200 million in junk bonds outstanding, only $12 billion was held by thrifts, and more than half of that was held by four institutions. At the time, the thrifts were suffering from horrendous losses, but most of these came from failed real-estate deals, not from junk bonds. FIRREA caused a loss of confidence in thrifts, which hemorrhaged deposits, even though most were covered by federal insurance. In 1988 there had been 223 failures; the following year, when FIRREA was in effect, there were 328 of them. Yet none of these failed because of their junk portfolios. In 1990, when there were 217 failures, a *Fortune* writer estimated that only four, and possibly five, had been caused by a junk-selling panic.

Other legislation was being considered, and this too unnerved the market. The junk network was crumbling. On July 14, 1989, Southmark filed for bankruptcy. Then Seaman's Furniture missed a debt payment. Ramada scrapped a $400 million offering. Resorts International defaulted on $325 million in debt in August. Each time news of such happenings hit the press more people and institutions sold their junk.

Nicholas Brady, who became secretary of the treasury in September 1988, did what Congress had not been able to do: eliminate junk as a tool in corporate takeovers. In conjunction with the Federal Reserve and the Comptroller of the Currency, the Treasury notified commercial banks that loan criteria would be watched more closely in the future. In January 1990, the Fed noted that more than 70 percent of the banks had tightened their standards, which translated into saying that the temporary financing for raiders was being ended.

There was more to come. New York declared state pension funds could not invest in junk, and California announced its pension funds would sell $530 million face value of its junk. Other states followed, as did insurance companies.

The economy was then entering a recession, and collapses of those companies that had issued junk increased. Junk failures, which had averaged slightly less than 2 percent in the 1977–1988 period, rose to more than 4 percent in 1989 and to 8.7 percent in 1990. Milken's defenders blamed FERREA and the wholesale dumping of junk, together with what they considered to have been a government vendetta against new junk, while critics charged that it was those failures that caused owners to lose confidence in the paper. Whatever the reason, the desires of those embattled CEOs to rid themselves of raiders had been realized. Without bankers and customers, their major tool, junk, could not be used to finance the deals.

The movement would not come to an end before it claimed two more victims: Drexel and Milken. The bank was stuck with a junk portfolio of more than $1 billion that could not be marketed. Joseph had to take $400 million out of its securities subsidiaries, which caused reserves there to fall below capital requirements. In early February 1990, he was informed that creditors of Drexel's Belgian parent company had refused to extend its credit line for commercial paper. Drexel had $1 billion in its broker-dealer subsidiary, which ordinarily would have been available to the parent, but now the SEC ruled that the company had to raise money on its own. Joseph and other top executives spent the weekend of February 10–11 trying to raise more than $300 million, and failed.

Joseph hoped for a rescue of the type earlier afforded Chrysler and New York City. In 1987 E. F. Hutton had been in distress, and on that occasion, with Washington's approval, other banks pitched into help until a suitor could be found. Drexel was a huge bank, much larger than Hutton, and its failure could demoralize the district and perhaps cause a major financial panic. Joseph informed Fed Chairman Alan Greenspan and the head of the New York Fed, E. Gerald Corrigan, of Drexel's plight. They offered no help. Neither did SEC Chairman Richard Breeden, who had often criticized the bank. Secretary Brady took a telephone call from Joseph, who must have known there would be nothing forthcoming from that quarter either.

Now Drexel's rivals on the Street, which might have mounted a rescue campaign of their own, got into the act. Salomon Brothers, a major competitor in the junk market, announced it no longer would transact business with Drexel. Others followed, led by Merrill Lynch. NYSE Chairman John Phelan said the Exchange had no responsibilities in this situation. Everyone who might have helped refused to do so. Joseph knew he was licked, and why. "There are constituencies out there that have reason to dislike what Drexel has been able to achieve," he told a reporter. "We have found ways to finance medium-sized, growing companies. That has taken business away from the banks." Then he struck the right chord. "There are clearly companies that have been attacked in the takeover game that feel very bitter about us." "We were tough on the way up," added another Drexel officer in a moment of candor. "We never made friends. We stole business from other firms. We made the banks look silly. This was payback time. The Establishment finally got us."

In the late evening of February 12, Joseph was told by the Fed and the Treasury that Drexel either had to file for bankruptcy or accept a government-led liquidation. It was a reprise of the Giuliani offer. Drexel would shoot itself, or the government would do it for the bank. The next morning the board voted for bankruptcy.

There was no panic, but much joy at other banks, which were quite happy to hire Drexel bankers and support staff. Smith Barney purchased its brokerage business. Salomon made a bid for and won its database, which included customer holdings, and this enabled that bank to take a lead in the junk-bond business. Employees other than professionals would have a more difficult time of it. Drexel was gone, and its 7,000 employees had to seek work elsewhere. In the midst of all of this, *The Wall Street Journal* made a crucial statement: "Now someone from the Justice Department needs to explain what it was that Milken allegedly did to justify the punishment being inflicted on the capital markets."

The pressure was on the government to demonstrate just that. If Milken were not guilty of major crimes, Giuliani and the other attackers would have to answer for their destruction of Drexel and the unsettling effect this action had on Wall Street. On the other hand, were he guilty, then the demise of Drexel might be justified as the elimination of a criminal element from American finance.

Giuliani was not around for the end game, having announced his resignation on January 18, 1989. He was replaced by Benito Romano, who on March 29, a month and a half after Drexel's failure, finally brought a 98-count indictment against Milken, including 54 for mail fraud, 33 for securities fraud, 5 for false filing of income-tax returns, 2 for RICO-related crimes, and 1 for assisting in the preparation of bogus income-tax returns. If found guilty, Milken could be stripped of all he had and incarcerated for up to 520 years.

When the prosecution began, Milken's lead attorney was Edward Bennett Williams, who indicated he would file a plea of not guilty. But Williams was dying of cancer, and Arthur Liman, who favored some kind of deal with the prosecution, took his place. In the end, on Liman's advice, Milken agreed to plead guilty to six felony counts, which involved parking securities, the differential in charges to a mutual fund, and assisting a banker in generating tax losses to lower his payments to the government. The last was so trivial that the banker was not charged with any wrongdoing. None concerned insider trading, or any of the lurid stories that had appeared during the previous few years. Liman had thought that since the charges were so minor, Milken might get off without having to serve time in prison. He was wrong. Milken was sentenced to ten years, plus 1,800 hours of community service a year for three years, and was fined $200 million, which came on top of $400 million he already had paid into a restitution fund. Later there would be an additional $500 million. Six years of the ten had been for assisting Boesky; Boesky had received a fine of $100 million plus three years in prison.

In the minds of many, the guilty plea and the sentence served to validate the destruction of Drexel Burnham Lambert. Except for the company itself, and a handful of students of the matter who understood what had happened, few had sympathy for Drexel or Milken.

In the aftermath of the Drexel collapse and Milken incarceration were other scandals at investment banks. In one of the more important of these, Salomon banker Paul Mozer was found to have violated Treasury rules by bidding for more than 35 percent of securities offered in an auction, a rule that existed to prevent any single firm from cornering the market. Mozer bid for Salomon's 35 percent, but also submitted other bids for customers without telling them of it, and then transferred the securities to Salomon's account. It was quite effective. In May 1991 Salomon controlled 86 percent of a $12.26 billion offering. Those banks that had to deliver securities to customers, and others that had shorted the issue, had to pay the prices Salomon asked.

When in April Mozer thought he was about to be found out, he told his supervisor, John Meriwether, what he had done. Meriwether spoke of it to Tom Strauss, his superior, and Strauss took the matter to the firm's CEO, John Gutfreund. Meriwether, Strauss, and Gutfruend then met with one of the firm's attorneys, Donald Feurstein, to determine the next step. Feurstein told them that the act was probably criminal in nature and that the New York Fed had to be informed of what had happened.

Nothing was done for close to four months. Not until August 8 did Salomon notify regulators and its board of Mozer's actions. Gerald Corrrigan, still head of the New York Fed as he had been when Drexel fell, was irate at this behavior, but was willing to discuss a salvage operation. In six trading sessions Salomon's common stock, which had been at $36, collapsed to $28. Amid talk of stiff fines and possible bankruptcy, Gutfreund and Strauss resigned. When Secretary Brady announced that Salomon would not be permitted to participate in future auctions, the price went under $24, and bankruptcy seemed quite plausible. With this Brady relented and changed the ban to making bids for its own account, meaning that Salomon could make purchases for customers.

Mozer pleaded guilty to having lied to the Fed and spent four months in prison. Salomon paid a fine of $190 million. That was it. Salomon survived and in 1997 was taken over by Travelers Group for $9 billion. Had not Brady relented, Salomon might easily have fallen. But then, Gutfruend had not antagonized the Street as had the Drexel brigades, and his replacement at Salomon, Warren Buffett, is one of America's most popular businesspeople.

There is a moral in all of this: Don't anger Uncle Sam, or your business rivals.

CHAPTER TEN

THE PENN CENTRAL: THE BLUNDER OF THE MISMATCH

F riendly mergers, the corporate equivalent of arranged mar-
riages, often are plagued with unanticipated problems. What
may appear a sensible match in the abstract often turns out to
be a nightmare when actually undertaken. There are problems of
melding different corporate cultures, eliminating redundancies, and
perhaps satisfying the government regarding matters of competition
and regulation. Some of the most important hurdles are human: who
gets what under the new dispensation, who reports to whom, and even
the location of the headquarters.

Usually the acquirer is the company whose traditions are continued, while the acquired has to adjust to a new environment. That can
cause troubles. Sensitivity is required from all involved, and often this
is lacking. In addition to economists, lawyers, accountants, and others
involved with mergers, it might be wise to employ the services of a few
psychologists during the transitional phase.

Executives experienced in takeovers know this. ITT's Harold
Geneen, who engineered scores of them, used to arrange meetings of
leaders of even the smallest acquired companies with the top brass at
headquarters and would seat them in prominent places at corporate
dinners and other occasions. Dover Corporation went so far as to
commission its history and provides it to executives at firms it hopes
to acquire so they could understand just what kind of a company it
was. Textron's Royal Little made it a rule never to enter into an
unfriendly acquisition; he wanted to talk with companies that came to
him wanting to be acquired, and there were no contested takeovers in
his time. Not all executives and companies are that sensitive.

The classic case of a mismatch was the coming together of the Pennsylvania and New York Central Railroads in 1968. Little care was taken to orchestrate the marriage and harmonize matters. To compound the difficulties, even before the merger executives at both companies made no secret of the fact they considered it a mistake. The two companies had long been rivals, contesting for business in the Midwest. Neither brought to the table anything the other needed. The promised economies never materialized. Top managements scorned each other. While it was true that technologies and markets dictated mergers in the railroad industry, and some of them worked out well, this one did not. Finally, government intruded in ways to make success even more unlikely.

The role of government in the railroad industry might be the best place to start. To understand this, one has to go back more than a century, for it was then the seeds of the Penn Central collapse were planted, by people who had praiseworthy motives, to be sure, but an uncertain understanding of railroad economics.

Government regulation of railroads seemed both reasonable and necessary at the time, which was 1887. The railroads, the first national businesses, often dominated the regions through which they passed. Farmers hoping to get their produce to market had little choice but to accept their terms. Coal miners the same. Ditto travelers. Even the government, when transporting soldiers to fight the Indian Wars in the West, had to accept railroad rates, though these were lower than for civilian traffic due to the terms of the land grants that made some of the western roads possible.

The railroads had entered into pools and rate-fixing agreements to boost freight and passenger rates in areas where demand was relatively inelastic, but these did not work when there were alternatives. The Pennsylvania had little competition in Pittsburgh, but had to face the New York Central and the Erie for traffic between Chicago and New York. As a result, freight charges from Chicago to Pittsburgh were higher than the much longer haul between Chicago and New York. The railroads competed with ships for the business of bulk transporters, and so transcontinental shipment charges from New York and Philadelphia to San Francisco and other West Coast cities were lower than from the East to Denver, Salt Lake City, and other interior locations. There were rebates for favored customers and extra charges for others. When the railroads balked at cutting back rates for John D. Rockefeller, he threatened to erect a pipeline to carry his petroleum to markets. Rockefeller got his rebates. In a time and place where marketing was crucial, the railroads had the power to make or break customers, but it could not do so in all places and at all times.

The railroad industry and some of those who worked for the companies were romanticized. This was a period when engineers and telegraphers were looked upon as adventuresome. Not so for the other workers, however, for most of the lines had what now would seem harsh and even cruel labor policies, which prompted the formation of labor unions. Railroad strikes were chronic and sometimes violent. In one of the most severe of the strikes, workers on the Union Pacific and Missouri Pacific went out for three months in mid-1886 and were finally subdued by strikebreakers hired by Jay Gould, who controlled both lines.

Gould had more than 10,000 miles of railroad in his grasp and dominated other companies, including Western Union. He was in command of New York City's elevated railways. He owned and dictated editorial policies for several newspapers, which lambasted the unions. Gould epitomized the emerging business class that appeared destined to control the country through their businesses and the work of political frontmen. He didn't like unions and wouldn't abide them. Few railroad tycoons would.

While public opinion did not favor the railroaders, they, too, had grievances and explanations for those seemingly high rates. The railroads observed that they had heavy fixed costs and had to pay interest on the bonds issued to raise needed capital. The "granger" railroads that carried grain to markets added that they had little traffic much of the year and had to make money by raising rates when farmers shipped their crops.

Neither side believed or trusted the other. In this period there were demands from the railroads' customers for regulations to keep them in line. Several states passed laws obliging the railroads to cease what they considered unfair practices, but there seemed no hope for the same on the national level, since railroad lobbyists were powerful and legislators susceptible to accepting bribes. In 1878 the House of Representatives passed the Reagan Bill (named after Texas Senator John Reagan), which would have introduced the principle of regulation, but it was defeated by the railroad senators. Then, in 1886, a year of many strikes, two events in Washington changed matters. The Supreme Court handed down its decision in *Wabash, St. Louis & Pacific Railroad Co. versus Illinois*, a case that involved the validity of an Illinois statute prohibiting short-haul rate discrimination. A majority of the Court held that the statute was a constitutional violation of the commerce powers of the federal government. This meant that all the state laws regulating railroads were unconstitutional and that the states didn't have the power to regulate the lines.

The second development took place in the Senate, where a special committee was meeting to consider federal railroad regulation. Out of this came a 1887 law that would forbid rebates, rate discrimination, and pooling and would be administered by an Interstate Commerce Commission (ICC). The law called for "reasonable and just" rates, but did not indicate what these were. The ICC was empowered to look into company books, hold hearings, and issue cease-and-desist orders.

There had never been anything quite like the ICC, which was to be included in the executive branch, but would have quasi-judicial and quasi-legislative powers. In time other regulatory agencies would be created, and for the most part, after a few years of feeling their oats, they would become captives of the industries they were established to govern. Not so the ICC. Indeed, for most of its history it was hostile to the railroads.

Until fairly recently the railroaders had a hard time of it with journalists and historians, who considered their leaders predatory and cruel. This view has been moderated. Recent scholarship has indicated that rates at the time were quite reasonable. But even if one concedes the need for regulation a century ago, times change, industries evolve, and then new approaches are appropriate. For example, in 1887 it might be plausible to argue that a railroad had a monopoly in its area unless there was a competing line nearby. For all practical purposes, in the early twentieth century the New York Central and the Pennsylvania Railroads had a duopoly on passenger travel between New York and Chicago. It could even be argued that there was such a thing as a railroad industry. Today, when one can travel between the two cities by automobile, bus, or airplane—on several airlines—there is no such concept as a railroad monopoly or even of a railroad industry, but rather a transportation industry with a great deal of competition. That this would develop might have been forecast as early as the 1920s, certainly by the late 1930s. That was the time to think about eliminating the ICC, or at least changing its policies. It was also possible then for the industry to be unified, and there were plans to nationalize the systems, and that too would have spared the railroads and the country a great deal of grief and pain. There even were precedents that might have been evoked—some states, such as Michigan and Pennsylvania, had erected railroads through state commissions.

Harsh regulation continued long after it was needed. There would be no unified railroad system. These were the first blunders in the Penn Central disaster.

In the years that followed passage of the law, the ICC was granted additional responsibilities. In 1903 Congress passed and President Theodore Roosevelt signed the Elkins Act, which contained a strong antirebate clause. Under the terms of the Hepburn Act of 1906, the ICC was empowered to fix rates, hear complaints from shippers and act on them, and regulate express and terminal companies as well as the railroads. This was followed by the Mann-Elkins Act of 1910, the strongest railroad legislation yet signed into law. In the past the ICC could investigate rate changes after they were in effect; now the Commission could suspend proposed changes for 120 days while holding inquiries and could then ask for an additional six months of delay if the time were needed. The ICC could also initiate rate changes on its own volition and was given control over freight classification.

The motivation behind this legislation was the continued desire to punish the railroads for their arrogant behavior and curb their awesome economic powers. In succeeding periods in American history different businessmen come to symbolize rapacity and ruthlessness for critics of business. Most of the time the bankers bear the brunt of criticism. Bankers were the targets of the Jacksonian reformers and Wall Street for the post-Civil War critics. During the Great Depression of the 1930s bankers again were attacked, and so they were in the age of conglomerates and that of hostile takeovers. They came in for criticism in the late nineteenth and early twentieth centuries, but then, in the view of populists and progressives, bankers were merely the servants of the "interests," which to reformers of this period meant the railroads. Press lords and reformers considered Gould, E. H. Harriman, Leland Stanford, and James J. Hill despots. True enough, J. P. Morgan was deemed the most powerful business figure of his era, in part because he had helped cobble together railroad consolidations, but in the countryside, where farmers and manufacturers came into more contact with the railroaders, they were the villains.

The railroaders tried to educate Congress and the public on the economics of their industry, without much success. They appeared regularly before the ICC and congressional committees to ask for rate relief, claiming that without higher rates their properties would be subjected to hardships and the nation as a whole would suffer as a consequence. Their opponents questioned their sincerity and statistics. One of the more striking encounters came in late 1910, when William Brown, president of the New York Central, observed that the ICC had been established in a period of declining prices. This ended in 1897, when due to worldwide gold discoveries and a strong economy, prices started to rise, advancing 44 percent between then and 1907. In this period rates remained unmoved. He wanted the ICC to approve adjustments, without which the railroads would fall into the red.

Brown offered impressive evidence to support his case, most of it provided by impartial academics. The price of coal had risen by 66 percent in this span. The wages of engineers had risen 24 percent and those for firemen, 30 percent. Interest rates had gone up too, from 3.9 percent in 1897 to 4.6 percent in 1907, making it difficult for the railroads to borrow. The customers knew they were getting bargains; freight haulage had increased by more than 150 percent. Brown observed that the Central paid an average dividend of 4.7 percent on the par value of its stock, and was putting one quarter of its profits into improvements. To lower the dividend would damage the line's credit on Wall Street and make it difficult to raise funds at low rates. To cut back on improvements would make it uncompetitive. Something had to give, he concluded. Brown asked for rates on a level that would enable the Central to at least get back to the return on capital of the late nineteenth century.

Louis Brandeis, who represented the ICC, charged that a recent dividend increase was proof the railroad was in good shape and did not need higher rates. "We raised the dividend to the rate which a person could get on a first-class mortgage," Brown responded, to which

Brandeis countered that if the railroad had been run efficiently, it would not need rate relief. In the end, the Central did not get its rate increase.

A pattern had been set. The railroads would complain that they couldn't maintain their lines without rate increases, while their critics would deny this and claim mismanagement and gouging were taking place.

Acting in unison, the railroads came to Washington to ask for rate relief in 1911 and again in 1912, which was denied on both occasions, even though the statistics generally favored their case. Without additional earnings, they said, there was no way they could modernize their lines. In 1913 the Pennsylvania Railroad's chief counsel, laid it out before the Commission.

> The Pennsylvania system in three years has invested $207 million, [yet] finds its net $11 million less. . . . In 10 years from 1903 to 1913 they invested $530 million upon which there was a munificent return of 2 1/4 percent. And mark you, this was not in speculative enterprises . . . not in buying the stocks of other companies . . . not for building any lines into a new country. It was expended in the intensive development of the richest traffic-producing sections in the world.

The Commission rejected the petition. Instead of a rate increase, the Pennsylvania was notified it and other lines would be investigated. Just before he left office, President Taft, a critic of the railroads, signed authorization for the ICC to make a comprehensive study of the lines, and some reformers again spoke of the need to nationalize them.

What was not obvious to the reformers of the period was that the railroads were sorely in need of both rate relief and consolidation, the former to pay for upgrades, the latter to eliminate needless duplication. One key statistic in the industry was the expense-to-revenues ratio, which measured the railroads' expenditures in relation to the money taken in. In 1902, when railroads indeed were powerful and in good shape in part due to J. P. Morgan's restructurings, the ratio was 64.6 percent. By 1908 it had risen to more than 70 percent and remained there. World War I resulted in a boom for the lines, especially in the industrial heartland of the Midwest and Northeast. Yet in 1916, when industry revenues and profits were $3.7 billion and $735 million respectively, the ratio was 65.7 percent.

Railroading was a mature industry. In 1915 only 933 miles of track were set down. In the midst of seeming prosperity, the Central and the Pennsylvania could not finance orders for new rolling stock from earnings. More and more lines filed for bankruptcy; that year railroads with 37,000 miles of track—one in ten for the nation—were in receivership. Pennsylvania President Samuel Rea warned the ICC that "the condition of the railroads today presents a menace to the country."

Those who knew the industry best argued for rate relief. Even former President Taft, who while in office had castigated the railroads, admitted he was mistaken. "The inadequacy of our railroad system is startling," he said. "We have had many warnings from railroad men as to what would occur . . . their warnings are now being vindicated."

When the United States entered World War I in 1917 there not only were freight and passenger line shortages, but breakdowns had assumed record proportions. American railroads arguably were in the worst shape of any in the industrialized world. In the light of the emergency the railroads petitioned for a 15 percent rate increase, observing that for the first nine months of the year revenues rose by $123 million but profits fell $57 million. President Woodrow Wilson set up a commission to study the matter, and the members denied the request. Instead, the ICC recommended a federal takeover of the railroads for the duration of the war.

Perhaps this was the best way to proceed, not only for the wartime period, but afterwards as well. If railroads were vital to the nation—and everyone involved said they were—and the users could not or would not pay rates sufficient to keep them in good shape, why not look upon them as an important part of the infrastructure that was needed to assist in creating the general prosperity? This was the view taken in Europe and other parts of the world, where not only railroads, but telephone and telegraph companies and later airlines were run at losses by governments, often through their postal services.

A debate on the matter was in order but did not take place. Instead, under the terms of the Federal Possession and Control Act, on December 29, 1917, Wilson seized the railroads and placed command of them in the hands of the United States Railroad Administration (USRA). The lines would be paid for their services, and ownership would not change. After the war the properties were to be returned to private control "substantially in good repair." Congress established a fund of $500 million for this purpose, and one of the first acts of the USRA was to increase rates by 28 percent, and later an additional 32 percent. Thus, the government conceded it could not run the lines profitably without such boosts.

The matter of public ownership cropped up after the war, when the railroad brotherhoods and prewar progressives, led by Glenn Plumb, a lawyer who was special counsel for the brotherhoods, backed what was known as the Plumb Plan. Plumb calculated the railroads were worth $18 billion. He would have the government sell that amount of bonds, purchase the equity in the railroads at a price it would set, and then run them in much the same way as they had during the war. The plan was rejected. Instead, in 1920, Congress passed the Esch-Cummins Act, which was the first railroad legislation since the formation of the ICC that conceded the railroaders had made some telling points. One provision of the act was to guarantee the railroads a return of at least 5.5 percent on equity, with the understanding that anything above 6 percent could be recovered by the government and distributed to those lines that earned less than 6 percent. The ICC was also encouraged to consider mergers favorably, since the feeling was that with these would come important economies of scale. The concept was sound enough, but there was little action on this during the interwar period.

The railroads were drowning in a sea of paperwork. In some cases they were required to keep as many as three sets of books: one for the ICC, another for the Department of Internal Revenue, and a third for the shareholders. In the 1930s a fourth set was needed for the Securities and Exchange Commission. It was difficult to discover just how much money a railroad made or lost or its book value, and so calculations regarding margins were as much matters of conjecture as anything else.

The industry's available technology and techniques were changing, and the railroads hoped to profit from these. The railroads petitioned the ICC for permission to switch to containerized freight, which not only would have resulted in economies, but would have cut down on pilferage. The request was turned down. Further attempts to realize savings were also rejected.

By then, too, there was competition from other carriers, cars and trucks on land and the beginning of air transport. At one time railroads attracted some of the finest managerial talents in the nation. No longer. There was too much grief in running a railroad. Far more attractive for those interested in transportation were automobiles and airlines, both of which received government assistance in the forms of highways, contracts, airport construction, and related support. The competition from cars, buses, and trucks was becoming troublesome. In 1920 cars and trucks had accounted for less than 1 percent of all intercity freight movements. Ten years later they took 4 percent of the business, while the railroads' share fell from 77 percent to 74 percent. Clearly motor vehicles were not yet a major problem, but there were clear signs that this could change. The situation was even more striking in the area of passenger traffic. By 1930 one in five people who traveled from rural areas or cities to other cities went by bus.

Most railroads ignored the challenge, but not the Pennsylvania. Beginning in 1922 that railroad purchased or originated several bus and trucking companies. At first this was a matter of economy. The company would attempt to abandon lightly used commuter lines and replace them with buses, while where appropriate commercial customers might be served by trucks. There was the added advantage that in this period buses and trucks were not regulated by the ICC. The operation grew, and in 1927 the Pennsylvania organized several companies to service isolated communities, something like the way today's commuter airlines fly out of hubs. Two years later it organized American Contract & Trust as a holding company for these lines, and then it purchased People's Rapid Transit, which operated a scheduled service between Philadelphia and small New Jersey towns. Other acquisitions followed, and the Pennsylvania became one of the largest motor-vehicle operators in the nation.

The company also entered the air travel business in 1928, through a one-fifth share in Transcontinental Air Transport (TAT). Passengers would board a Pennsylvania Pullman in New York in the early evening and arrive in Port Columbus, Ohio, by early morning. They then would board a Ford Trimotor that would take them to Watnoka, Oklahoma, the western terminus of the Acheson, Topeka, and Santa Fe, where they would board the train to dine and then sleep, awakening in Clovis, New Mexico, in time for a flight from there to Los Angeles. The trip took 48 hours and cost $351 one-way. The service was never popular and didn't last for long.

The Pennsylvania was still primarily a railroad, but these new forms of transportation were tempting, especially when the company's executives reflected on how much assistance they were receiving from government. Then the government ruled that railroads could not own airlines, thus closing that window of opportunity. TAT would reorganize as Transcontinental & Western, or TWA, and in time become part of one of the nation's major airlines.

The railroads were in poorer shape when war erupted in Europe in 1939 than they had been on the eve of entry into World War I in 1917. Because of the inadequate highway system and rubber shortages, trucks and buses could be used only sparingly, and the airlines were not up to the tasks of large-scale transport—the planes were too small, and in any case, all production was geared to supplying the Air Corp and the Allies. This time the government did not attempt to take control of the lines, and rate increases were permitted. Under the terms of the Transportation Act of 1940, cooperation between railroads was encouraged, and Washington indicated it would smile on mergers undertaken in the name of efficiency. The ICC opposed this law, interpreting the Clayton Antitrust Act as a barrier against mergers. The matter was taken to the courts, which were indecisive on the issue. For the time being, the necessities of war dictated cooperation between the lines, and this was achieved.

The railroads came out of the war in 1945 in better condition than when they entered. The ICC took note of this and now seemed intent on blocking mergers and rate increases, saying they no longer were needed. For the moment these matters were not of primary concern. Rather, the railroads had to meet the challenge posed by the airlines.

This was a major period for airline expansion. Route mileage, which had been 39,000 miles in 1945, rose to 114,000 ten years later, and in the same period revenue miles flown went from 32.6 million to 131.6 million and passengers carried from 475,000 to 3.4 million. From 1945 to 1955 railroad revenues rose from $9 billion to $10.2 billion; in contrast, during this span domestic airline revenues went from $214 million to $1.2 billion. By 1954 airliners were making the coast-to-coast trip nonstop in less than seven hours, and one in four intercity travelers went by air.

It seemed clear that airplanes in time could supersede passenger trains for long trips. Thrown into the mix was government aid. The airlines benefited from the throwoff of military technology and from assistance in the form of airport construction, air controllers, and more. In 1958 alone the federal government spent $431 million in supporting airlines and airports. (That year the railroads spent close to $1 billion on maintenance, $232 million on construction, and paid taxes of $180 million.) Around the corner was shuttle service in the Northeast corridor and then elsewhere as well.

Automobiles were serious rivals for shorter trips. The middle-class American way of life was changing after the war. The automobile brought Americans to the suburbs; two-car families had come into being, along with drive-in fast-food operations. Motel construction soared. The Federal Highway Act of 1944 authorized the expenditure of $1.5 billion over a three-year period on interstate highways, while the states proceeded on their own to develop toll superhighways. Dwight Eisenhower, who became president in 1953, was a strong sup-porter of highway programs, and during his first years in office the federal government provided more than half a billion dollars annually for such programs. Under the terms of the Federal Highway Act of 1956 the nation committed itself to constructing a 41,000-mile net-work of controlled-access superhighways to link all cities with popula-tions of more than 50,000 over a 13- to 16-year period. This was to be the largest civilian government construction program in history. Even before it was completed, the superhighways would challenge the rail-roads for longer trips. To compound the problem for the eastern lines, Eisenhower asked for and got appropriations for the St. Lawrence Seaway, which would open the Great Lakes area to the Atlantic for much of the year, and that, too, would cut into railroad freight traffic.

Given the interstates and the Seaway, Detroit's autos and Chicago's grain would no longer be shipped via the New York Central to New York for transshipment to Europe. If Henry Ford's automo-biles indirectly destroyed the passenger business, Dwight Eisen-hower's programs seemed to be doing the same for the freight operations of the eastern trunk lines.

In retrospect it seems clear the time had arrived for mergers and government assistance, at least for those lines east of the Mississippi that did not carry bulky, low-cost items. Soon it would become impos-sible to make a profit on commuter lines, but the ICC refused to per-mit abandonment or have Congress and the states provide financial support. By the 1950s and certainly the early 1960s, most in the industry realized that mergers would be needed if the passenger lines were to survive.

On November 1, 1957, the Pennsylvania and New York Central announced that they had decided to study the viability of a merger. The announcement hit the industry with the force of a thunderbolt. These two lines had been intense competitors since before the Civil War. The Pennsylvania's Broadway Limited and the Central's Twentieth Century had slugged it out for the prized Chicago-New York passenger run for more than half a century. Now, of course, both were being made obsolete by the superhighway and the airliner.

If the symbolism of such a merger was important, the economics were impressive. According to one newspaper story, if united, the new company would have assets of $5 billion, making it the tenth largest American company. It would have revenues of $1.5 billion and would carry 80 million passengers and 378 million tons of freight annually. In reporting the story, the newspapers made it sound like the second coming of U.S. Steel, the first billion-dollar corporation organized shortly after the turn of the century. At the time few noted the problems involved and the difficulties of the match.

The Central was an important carrier of manufactured goods, and by means of lines that extended southward, it carried coal as well. The company had been in poor financial shape as recently as 1954, when it was drowning in debt. In desperation, the Central's CEO, Robert Young, turned to Alfred Perlman, who agreed to become president. Perlman was one of the most highly regarded railroad men in the country. After earning a degree at MIT and studying railroading at the Harvard Graduate School of Business, during which time he helped salvage the Burlington Northern, he worked as a consultant, and in 1936 he took over at the defunct Denver and Rio Grande Western, which he not only saved, but modernized and made a viable road. One of the reasons he had not earlier been tapped for greater position was the fact that he not only was a Jew, but was irascible and imperious.

Perlman knew from the start that turning the Central around would be difficult. He also suspected that his real task was to whip the railroad into shape so that it could make a plausible merger partner. Within three years he had done just that, by scrapping Young's plans for increased passenger business and concentrating instead on making the Central attractive to shippers. At one point, when the ICC refused to permit Perlman to abandon a particularly unprofitable passenger line, he offered to purchase every commuter his or her own automobile if permitted to leave the business. He dieselized the entire locomotive fleet and expanded and modernized the freight cars and was even able to raise the dividend. But then came the recession of 1957, which hit the Central hard, and it appeared to be on the way down once again. The previous year the Central had reported earnings of $39 million on revenues of $780 million. The company had lost money on operations, however; the profits came from investments, some in other dividend-paying railroads.

In contrast, the Pennsylvania appeared in good shape, and in CEO James Symes it had a leader with long experience at the line and a profound understanding of the industry and its problems. Sixty years old in 1957 and five years away from retirement, he had come to the Pennsylvania in 1916 as a clerk in the traffic department, and as was not unusual at the time, worked his way up the managerial ladder. The previous year the Pennsylvania had reported earnings of $41 million on revenues of $991 million. Most of those earnings came from dividends, especially from the Norfolk & Western, a profitable railroad in which it had a major stake.

Under Symes the Pennsylvania had worked out alliances with other railroads besides the N&W. At that time he was proposing that the area south of New England and north of Virginia have three major systems, the C&O-B&O, the N&W, and the union of the Pennsylvania and the Central, in which the Pennsylvania would be the senior partner. Such was the situation in January 1958, when Symes and Young met to discuss the situation. Nothing came of the talks at the time. On January 25, 1958, Young committed suicide, which put everything on hold.

Meanwhile, a veritable mergermania was beginning in eastern railroading. While some of the mergers worked out well, others were failures. One success was the Norfolk & Western-Virginian merger that took place in 1959, with ICC and union blessings. This was a merger that was attempted in the 1920s when it was turned down by the ICC. The change was taken as a sign that future amalgamations might be possible.

The Norfolk & Western was one of the so-called "Pocahontas" bituminous coal roads that serviced the West Virginia and eastern Kentucky mines, and as indicated, was controlled by the Pennsylvania. Bituminous coal was used in power generation, and its market was good and expanding, making the line highly profitable. The Virginian was a smaller railroad in the same area and also carried bituminous coal. Significant savings were realized, and the merger was applauded both within the industry and on Wall Street.

The N&W's CEO, Stuart Saunders, now came to be seen as a coming executive in the industry, the heir apparent to Symes at the Pennsylvania. A medium-sized, stocky, balding man with a bulldog expression, Saunders could be very impressive when talking with outsiders, but those within the industry had a low opinion of the man. A Harvard Law School graduate, he had worked as an attorney at the road, but was not considered particularly knowledgeable about operations. The actual running of the N&W was left to others, while Saunders devoted himself to strategic planning.

At the time there were many other possible combinations in the East, which befuddled all but close students of the industry. Each of the five major players there—the B&O, the C&O, the Central, the Pennsylvania, and N&W—had two possible merger partners, or at least that was the way it seemed from their respective board rooms. The B&O could have united with the C&O or the Central; the C&O with the N&W or the B&O; the N&W with the Pennsylvania or the C&O; the Central with the B&O; the Pennsylvania with the N&W. Finally, to complete the circle, the Pennsylvania and Central still perceived advantages in a merger. To complicate matters further, several chronically ill lines, including the Erie Lackawanna, were exploring means of uniting with the N&W, even while that strong line rejected such overtures.

There was another possibility that was never seriously considered: a merger of all the lines into a single railroad, with the government permitting the new entity to abandon passenger lines that could never be profitable, or subsidizing the service. Something like this was eventually done, but not before there was much grief and losses.

Perlman attempted unsuccessfully to enter several combinations—that of the C&O-B&O and then the unification of the N&W and the Nickel Plate. Rebuffed, he reluctantly came to realize that the

Central could not survive on its own and that the Pennsylvania was his logical partner.

Symes and Perlman did not particularly care for one another, but each man respected the other's ability and knowledge. The relationship between Saunders and Perlman, even before Saunders became the Pennsylvania's CEO, was quite different. Even before they met Saunders resented Perlman's attempts to muscle his way into mergers with other firms and viewed him as an outsider and an arrogant newcomer to eastern railroading. For his part, Perlman did not think much of Saunders's competence. As far as he was concerned, anyone could have amassed a good record at so sound a line as the N&W. To further complicate matters, David Bevan, chairman of the Pennsylvania's finance committee, disliked Perlman but shared his contempt for Saunders and had spoken openly of his feelings.

Perlman was accurate in assessing Saunders as one who did not share his passions for railroading. Milton Shapp, who at the time was an aspiring Pennsylvania politician who would take office as governor in 1971, was convinced Saunders had little interest in railroading. Speaking to reporters, he said:

> There's no doubt that Saunders wanted to get out of the railroad business, even during the merger controversy. I've been to several parties with him where he had a few drinks, and he was always talking about Litton Industries and how Litton and other conglomerates had cash coming in and were putting it to good use, getting good returns. He said he wanted to keep the money for real estate investments instead of putting it in the fucking railroad. That's what he said, the fucking railroad.

In itself there was nothing unusual about this. Astute businessmen have always withdrawn from money losers to stress new opportunities. We have seen how Peter Grace's willingness to abandon Latin America for chemicals invigorated W. R. Grace. But Grace did not have the ICC to deal with. Attempts to cut back on railroad services in favor of diversification could be blocked by that powerful agency.

There were problems in such a merger other than those of personality. The two lines had differing forms of organization. The Pennsylvania had a divisional structure, in which branch managers had a large degree of autonomy, while at the Central there departments were managerial rather than administrative. In other words, from the New York office the Central's officers were responsible for a single department throughout the railroad, while the Pennsylvania's managers in the field took charge of a geographic area. In addition, their billing systems were different. The companies had differing accounting systems, and their computer systems were incompatible. As discussions and negotiations with the ICC progressed, nothing was done to deal with these problems.

For all of these reasons the merger made little sense. That the talks continued in the face of them was the first of a series of blunders involved with the creation of the Penn Central. That managements would not recognize or deal with the troubles was the next.

As he prepared to assume the Pennsylvania's mantle, Saunders amassed a war chest by disposing of most of Pennsylvania's large holdings in other railroads, including the valuable block of stock in the N&W. Among his plans was the razing of Pennsylvania Station in New York City and then the creation of a new Madison Square Garden plus twin office towers on the site. In return for its property, the Pennsylvania was to receive a quarter ownership in the complex. Saunders planned similar operations in Philadelphia and Chicago. In the 1963 *Annual Report* it was noted that the Pennsylvania owned close to 11,000 acres of land that it meant to develop. The company already had coal mines; there would be more of them, and perhaps a chemical subsidiary as well. On coming to office in 1962, Saunders indicated he would build upon this base.

Already there was a model for such an effort. Another attorney-turned-railroader, Ben Heineman, had taken over at the failing Chicago & North Western in 1956. He turned it around, but realized there was little future in railroading in its territory, so he purchased two chemical companies and shopped Chicago & North Western. Eventually he would form Northwest Industries as a holding company for the railroad and other properties, and he finally merged the railroad with the Chicago Great Western, leaving Heineman the head of a $350 million conglomerate with interests in chemicals and ownership of Philadelphia & Reading, a coal company that itself had diversified into underwear and boots. All of this was in the future, of course, but Heineman's strategy was already well-known in 1963. This was, after all, the age of the conglomerate, and Jimmy Ling, not Alfred

Perlman, was Heineman's exemplar. He would serve as one for Saunders as well.

Saunders's vehicle for diversification would be the wholly owned Pennsylvania Company, an entity formed shortly after the Civil War to take control of trackage west of Pittsburgh and which in 1918 had become the repository for all the corporation's miscellaneous properties, including its shares in the N&W. So Saunders was prepared to take the plunge and had the vehicle with which to perform the task. All that was lacking was the person who could perform the actual mechanics of the takeovers, isolate likely properties, and above all, provide him with a plausible rationale and strategy.

He found all of these attributes in Bevan, who possessed the instincts and the proper connections to make investments. In 1962 he had organized Penphil, an investment company into which several associates placed $16,000 each, and which turned out to be highly profitable, due in large part to investment advice provided by Bevan's friend, Charles Hodge, who was chairman of the executive committee of the investment bank of Glore, Forgan & Co.

Bevan was prepared to cooperate in the diversification scheme. In 1963 the Pennsylvania Company purchased a one-third interest in the Buckeye Pipe Line for $28 million in cash and preferred stock, and the rest of the shares were acquired in the next two years. The eighth largest processor of crude oil in the nation and one of the most important suppliers of jet fuel to the airlines, Buckeye was a sound company in a growing industry. It could be counted on to provide a boost to Pennsylvania's earnings, which in turn could enhance the value of its stock, making it the currency Saunders could use for future takeovers.

The following year Saunders purchased a 60 percent interest in the Great Southwest Corp., a land developer with several properties, the most important being an amusement park, Six Flags Over Texas. Great Southwest was planning more of them, and at a time when Disneyland was doing well amusement parks seemed attractive. In 1965 he purchased an additional 20 percent. Saunders clearly believed that real estate and related activities were the future for the Pennsylvania. Thus, he purchased a controlling interest in Arvida, which owned approximately 100,000 acres of land in Florida. Macco Realty, a California-based company came next. Then, in a flurry of activity, Saunders acquired Strick Holding Co., a manufacturer of aluminum trailers and containers with an interest in mobile homes, and made loans to Executive Jet Aviation, which hoped to develop a large charter business. To cap things off, Saunders sold the Long Island Railroad to New York State for $65 million, ridding the Pennsylvania of a commuter line that like all such operations was incapable of turning a profit.

It was later learned that some of these properties had come into the Pennsylvania Co. through Penphil, so Bevan was in on both sides of the deal.

Meanwhile, the ICC continued its investigation of the proposed merger. Astonishingly, some of the critics asserted that the new company would be a powerhouse that would dominate its region and crush competition, and so should be disallowed on antitrust grounds. Others were willing to allow the merger to go through on condition it include the decrepit New York, New Haven & Hartford, which after a struggle Saunders and Perlman acceded to. In late 1965 the ICC examiners recommended approval, but there were more objections, including an appeal to the Supreme Court, which approved the merger on January 15, 1968. Now all agreed the date for the inaugural of the new company would be February 1 of that year.

From the first there were clear signs of problems ahead in the management area. Saunders was to be chairman and CEO, while Perlman was president and COO. The first annual report was released in late March—the traditional day for the Pennsylvania. It was prepared by the Pennsylvania's staff, and the Central's staff had no input in the document. It was subtitled: "121st Annual Report," indicating the new company was building on the Pennsylvania's tradition and excluding the Central. The name of the New York Central Building was altered to the New York General Building, the etched letters "C" and "T" changed to "G" and "E." Perlman and his staff remained in New York; Saunders stayed in Philadelphia.

The Penn Central was structured with three levels of ownership and operation. At the apex was the Penn Central Transportation Co., which owned and operated the railroad properties and was charged with the development of railroad-controlled real estate. It also owned all the stock of the Pennsylvania Co, which in turn owned the shares of the newly acquired nonrailroad properties. Most of the Central's executives worked for the Transportation Co. and had nothing to do with the Pennsylvania Co., another indication Penn Central was really the Pennsylvania's takeover of the Central.

The Penn Central was management mess. It had a chairman more interested in nonrailroad activities than in the company's main business, a president who was ignored, and a chairman of the finance committee whose outside interests conflicted with his main job. The three leaders seemed cheerful enough at the annual stockholders' meeting on April 1, 1968. Saunders did almost all of the talking. He conceded the wedding had its problems, but these had been anticipated, and the Penn Central had set aside a fund of $275 million to provide for the changeover. The railroad had been hurt by the continuing recession, he said; operating revenues had fallen from $1.7 billion to $1.6 billion, while return on investment had gone from 2.7 percent to 0.8 percent. True enough, but the earnings resulted from "creative accounting" and dividends from subsidiaries, and not railroad operations, which were in the red. The Penn Central's operating losses were formidable. In 1968 they would come to $140 million. In addition, the dividends from the new companies were less than what had been received from those sold. Then there was the matter of the New York, New Haven & Hartford, which cost $128 million and whose deficit in 1968 alone was $22.3 million, and rising. The unions were another problem. In order to obtain union support for the merger and assure labor peace, the railroad had to guarantee employment to all existing workers.

Dissension in the corporate suites didn't help. David Smucker of the Pennsylvania became Perlman's deputy in New York. The two men clashed from the first, to the point where they were not on speaking terms. The animosity showed in the field as well. The Pennsylvania crews were used to hauling coal, which was fungible, so one carload could be substituted for another. The Central crews were accustomed to handling manufactured goods, for which accurate and prompt delivery was essential. The Central people accused their Pennsylvania counterparts of being slovenly, and the Pennsylvania personnel resented what they took as the arrogance of the Central people.

As a result of all of this there were foul-ups, misroutings, bottlenecks, and utter confusion. Trains were sent to the wrong cities; some were misplaced for days. One customer protested that the new company combined the worst aspects of each railroad, and he switched to trucks. Another noted that a good deal of the fresh-meat traffic had been lost to the Erie Lackawanna, itself hardly a model of efficiency. So it went. "Shippers are dissatisfied with our service," wrote one executive to Saunders, who did not reply. There were floods of complaints from major industrial customers such as Allied Chemical, Stauffer Chemical, and the New York Perishable Dealers' Association. Eastman Kodak's piggyback vans missed connections in St. Louis three quarters of the time. Perlman complained to Saunders that Smucker either was sabotaging operations or simply was not up to the job. Then he informed Saunders and Bevan he would need $1.5 billion to create the Metroliner service for the Boston-New York-Washington run.

Strapped for funds, Penn Central started selling off holdings. Six Flags Over Georgia, one of the new properties, was sold in 1968, and Six Flags Over Texas went the following year. This coincided with a managerial shakeup. Perlman was forced to accept the insignificant post of vice chairman and was replaced as COO by Paul Gorman, the recently retired president of Western Electric, who had a fine record, especially in the area of cost controls, but knew nothing about railroads and in any event wouldn't be able to take over for a few months. Gorman hadn't a clear idea of what he was getting into. Shocked by what he found, he responded by cutting costs, not knowing, however, what was fat and what was meat and bone.

Transportation revenues for 1969 came to $1.9 billion. According to the Annual Report, railroad costs and expenses were about the same. As far as the casual reader was concerned, under trying conditions the Penn Central's railroad operations just about broke even. But lower down on the earnings statement was a "special item," an extraordinary loss, most of which was due to "investment in long-haul passenger service facilities," which came to $126 million. This looked like a charge for merger costs, something stockholders and analysts had come to expect. Late in the year, Bevan had decided to write off that amount against the complete depreciation of old passenger cars and stations. Since it was reported as an extraordinary item, it did not affect earnings, but it did reduce depreciation charges by more than $4.5 million, which was reflected in the final earnings statement provided the public and so made the company appear better managed than really had been the case.

Bevan also had several subsidiaries remit special dividends to the parent. This enabled the Penn Central to report decent earnings while stripping the subsidiaries' treasuries. Merchant's Despatch Transportation, a trucking company, reported a 1969 profit of $2.8 million and remitted $4.7 million. Another trucking subsidiary, New York Central Transport, had profits of only $4.2 million and yet paid $14.5 million in dividends. So it went with the others as well. Yet the Penn Central paid a dividend of $1.80 per share in 1969, against $2.40 the previous year. Saunders apologized for the cut, but pledged to restore the dividend as soon as he could.

It later was learned that in this period Penn Central insiders were selling the company's stock and bonds.

In a move he advertised as recognizing the altered nature of the company, Saunders announced the formation of the Penn Central Co., which acquired the stock of Penn Central Transportation on a share-for-share basis. He said the new company would be an umbrella for both the Transportation and Pennsylvania companies and "future acquisitions." There would be none of the latter. Rather, Saunders was attempting to create a structure in which the Transportation Co. and the Pennsylvania Co. might be distanced from each other. Then, if the Transportation Co. fell into bankruptcy, the Pennsylvania Co. might survive. It was an interesting ploy, which didn't work out, since in time the Pennsylvania Co. was stripped of all its assets.

The situation at the Transportation Co. didn't improve. In March, knowing that $100 million in debt was due to mature in 1970, Bevan suggested the company issue that amount in new bonds. Before this could be done the first quarter's report came out, showing losses from railroad operations of $102 million. Still, the company went ahead with its bond offering. The bonds carried a premium rate of 10.5 percent, but even so, it failed to attract buyers, and the offering was withdrawn. Saunders and Bevan approached the company's lead bank, First National City, asking for a loan, and they were turned down. Similar approaches to Secretary of Transportation John Volpe met with the same response.

By late April newspapers started to run stories about the problems. The common stock, which was at 17¾ on May 11, dropped 2½ points the next day on heavy volume. On May 29 Penn Central closed at 12⅝. The word was out that the banks were dumping the stock.

Gorman informed the board of the parlous situation at the company on June 8. He also advised the members that Secretary Volpe had relented and would support legislation providing $750 million to help financially troubled railroads, with some $300 million earmarked for the Penn Central. In addition, the government would guarantee $200 million of Penn Central notes for six months, or until the legislation passed. The government would decide how the money would be allocated, and there would have to be a switch in management. In the end, Saunders, Bevan, and Perlman were dismissed. Assuming the legislation passed, the Penn Central would become a ward of the government.

This did not happen. In the face of congressional opposition the Nixon Administration withdrew its support for loans, the announcement being made after the stock market closed on Friday, June 19. On Sunday, June 21, the Penn Central Transportation Company filed for bankruptcy protection under Section 77 of the 1933 Bankruptcy Act. In effect, it would become a ward of the court.

In the days and weeks that followed there were autopsies galore, with discussions centering on mismanagement and blunders. Some of the commentaries mentioned the European and Japanese train operations, which seemed modern and efficient compared to their American counterparts. Americans who had traveled on the foreign trains noted they were cleaner, the schedules were maintained, and the crews seemed in good cheer.

Little note was taken of the fact that abandonment of poorly used lines was quite common: Almost half of the United Kingdom's mileage of 1945 was no longer in use in 1970. True enough, the crack lines did run on time, but the others were as dismal as the American carriers. Moreover, none were profitable, and they carried only 10 percent of Europe's freight. Had they used American accounting practices, they would have shown losses.

In contrast, outside the Northeast, the American railroad companies were making money while carrying two fifths of the freight, and their efficiency was beyond that of most European government-controlled lines. In 1973 the American railroads would report profits of $19 million, while the German Federal Railway, one of the continent's best, had a deficit of close to $2.7 billion. The privately owned Canadian Pacific had a slim profit that year, while the Canadian National Railway reported a loss of $174 million. The speedy Tokyo to Osaka train was a money loser: In 1973 the Japanese National Railway posted a $2 billion loss. The solution of the eastern railroad mess, then, was not to imitate the foreign lines.

In order to bring some kind of order out of the chaos the government established the United States Railroad Association (USRA), financed initially with $1.5 billion, which was mandated to create a unified railroad system from the Penn Central and other bankrupt lines. To accomplish this, the USRA was authorized to abandon 12,000 miles of main track from the 30,000 then in operation. From the Penn Central and the other failed eastern lines, including the Erie Lackawanna, came Consolidated Rail Corporation (Conrail) and Amtrak, the former a freight hauler, the latter running passenger services, both of which received heavy government subsidies and began operations in 1976. In 1976 also Congress passed and the President signed the Railroad Revitalization and Regulatory Reform Act, which gave the ICC more flexibility in rate making. Conrail was awarded $2.1 billion from the USRA. After all of those years, the government was in the railroad business, and it wasn't making a go of it. From the time of its formation to 1981, Conrail lost $1.5 billion. The Penn Central collapse finally alerted Washington to the fact that the railroads had been stifled and further failures were in the making.

In 1980, as railroad bankruptcies mounted and it appeared the freight lines might be unable to service the nation's industrial heartland, an alarmed Congress passed the Staggars Rail Act and the Motor Carrier Act, which ended the ICC's control over freight rates over a three-year period and gave regulatory power to the Surface Transportation Board, located in the Department of Transportation, which looked more kindly on rate increases. With this, railroading started to turn around. Now capable of earning decent profits, once-abandoned tracks were refurbished and put back into service. New lines were constructed. Truckers faced stiff competition from the railroads, especially for long-haul business. Railroad shipments, as measured by cars loaded, rose from 19.5 million in 1985 to more than 24 million in 1997. In the latter year the government sold 85 percent of its stake in Conrail to the team of CSX and Norfolk Southern in what was the largest initial public offering to that time, $1.6 billion, with the rest going to the employees. The industry shows signs of new life, too late for the Penn Central, however.

CHAPTER ELEVEN

PAN AMERICAN WORLD AIRWAYS: THE BLUNDER OF DEPENDENCY

Regulation used to be considered the panacea for societal ailments. Not so today, when many more Americans extol the virtues of free enterprise and minimal government. It became fashionable in the late 1970s, and especially the 1980s and 1990s, to find solutions to economic, social, and political problems through resorts to the marketplace. The gospel has spread overseas, where Great Britain's Labour Party all but abandoned socialism and became New Labour. Similar developments have occurred elsewhere.

Critics of free enterprise, who in the 1970s looked to Japan and other economies in which the government played a leading role in guiding business, felt quite different when foreign businesspeople flocked to Silicon Valley and other technology centers to learn how Americans developed entrepreneurial skills. The 1997 collapse of Southeast Asian economies was generally blamed on the strong nexus there of government and business, while the success of America was credited to the more open nature of the economy and society.

While there certainly is some truth in this diagnosis, it also flies in the face of much of American history. Indeed, government's role in and assistance to business is embedded in the Constitution itself. In Article I, Section 8, in which Congress's power is enumerated, that body is given the responsibility of providing for "the general welfare" of the nation, and this specifically included such matters of concern to business as the coining of money and the promotion of science. Governments were instrumental in the development of transportation and communication, ranging from the operation of the postal service, assistance to the merchant marine, and the creation of canals and railroads to the space program and the development of the Internet. The Federal Highway Program alone has cost more money than what was expended in recovery programs during the Great Depression, another example of government intrusion in the economy. The huge defense program, the basis of the "military-industrial complex," has been one of the striking examples of government's role in the economy.

How could it be otherwise? Who would purchase an automobile if there were no roads, provided by governments? There might be some private turnpikes, but not the system automobiles require. Who would purchase radios and television sets if broadcasting frequencies were not allocated, so that clear signals could be received? Thus, we needed the Radio Commission and then the Federal Communications Commission. This is not to suggest that government need play a major role in all, or even most, industries. Rather, its presence is required in some of them, some of the time, especially in the beginning.

The presence might take one or more of several forms. Subsidies, land grants, the provision of desired services at nominal or no costs, protection against foreign competition and regulation are some of the leading ways governments help or control industries. Of all of these, regulation is the most visible. It can be beneficial or punitive, depending on the direction it takes. As has been seen, government helped make the railroads possible, but then the ICC's policies prior to World War I caused them to decline, and they have never recovered from the penurious attitude that agency adopted in that period. In contrast, the Federal Aviation Administration (FAA) and its predecessors created an umbrella under which the airlines thrived.

This having been said, what might happen if and when that presence is removed and competition is permitted, even encouraged? The new paradigm may bring many blessings, but it also causes pain and failure. It had happened in industries as disparate as electric utilities and trucking.

Commercial aviation was one of those industries most impacted by deregulation. In the early days, airline officials realized that without government assistance at many levels their businesses would have developed much more slowly than was the case. Deregulation, but not an end to government assistance, began in the 1970s and blossomed in 1987, and with this the companies that had learned how to thrive under the umbrella of rate protection had to discover how to compete on a price and service basis.

With deregulation the price of travel plummeted, without an immediate substantial pickup in travelers. The major carriers experienced a wave of red ink. In the new competitive environment the airline industry lost more money during the first five years of the 1990s than was made in all the rest of its history. New airlines appeared, and old ones went belly-up. Eastern, once one of the four top domestic lines, is no more. TWA, another of the top four, went in and out of bankruptcy, and is a pale shadow of what it once was. United and American, the other two, remain strong, but suffered through years of red ink. Delta, which adjusted to the competition and was able to capitalize on the distress of others, thrived. Pan American, which began its life as America's "chosen instrument" in the international field, the largest airline in the world, vanished without causing much of a stir.

Was deregulation by the government a blunder? Or were the blunders made by the airlines? What did the survivors and the successful newcomers do right that Pan Am did wrong?

There is a long and a short response to this question. The short one was that Pan Am and the government worked out a set of rules and practices that enabled that airline to become a spectacular performer, one of the greatest transportation companies in history. Pan Am liked the arrangement it had helped create, and so did Washington. Later on, Pan Am led in the founding of a quasi-cartel with the national airlines of other countries. Then the playing field changed to such an extent that the company was unable to adjust. Because of this, the blame for failure is difficult to assess, but it is more complicated than simply the matter of regulation.

There is another, more contentious explanation that requires elucidation. Pan Am's founder and longtime leader, Juan Trippe, was one of the most astute, clear-sighted, and venturesome businesspeople of the twentieth century. He assumed great risks to realize his vision, and most of the time they worked out well. One of these was planning a global airline at a time when aviation was in its commercial infancy, and he won that gamble. Another was his role in taking the world into the commercial jet age, and that, too, he accomplished brilliantly. Finally, Trippe hoped to make intercontinental travel inexpensive, comfortable, and rapid. To do so he needed a different kind of airliner, and to induce the manufacturers to produce them he had to place the largest order in industry history. He did so, and as it happened, the timing was wrong, something he could not have foreseen. Soon after, Trippe stepped down, and one of his successors made one of the industry's most botched takeovers. The crippled company lingered on for more than a decade, and then it was no more.

The story begins with the birth of aviation itself. Aviation appealed to the romantic and adventuresome, such as Teddy Roosevelt, the first President to fly. The air aces of World War I were the only glamorous group to emerge from that carnage. Still, at a time when the planes were barely faster than trains and far more dangerous, the idea that ordinary people would fly was not taken seriously. Besides, the planes of that period couldn't carry much weight, and so it appeared that to actually make money sky-high fares would have to be charged. Why pay premium prices to risk your life? Perhaps airplanes might be used for some commercial activities. Carrying the mail seemed possible, but not much more than that.

Some European countries had organized airlines in the post–World War I period. Germany had the Deutsche Luft Reederei, the predecessor of Lufthansa, and there were several French lines, some of which later became the backbone for Air France. British Aircraft and Transport actually began during the war. All had major financial support from their governments.

Although Congress voted an appropriation of $100,000 for an experimental air service for the Post Office Department, which carried mail between Chicago and New York, Presidents Woodrow Wilson and Warren Harding were not willing to make much more of a commitment. There were some private passenger lines, such as one between Albany and New York, which carried mail as well, but these amounted to very little.

Most improbably, Calvin Coolidge, whose prime goal while in office was to cut taxes, slash spending, and pay off the national debt, supported aviation with money as well as words. Coolidge was intrigued by aviation, in part because it held out the promise of defense on the cheap. He had received reports that the large battleships that had performed poorly during the war might not be as important as the navy believed. "If battleships become obsolete we wouldn't want to spend a lot of money on them," he said at a September 16, 1924, press conference. "And if aviation becomes more efficient perhaps it is reasonable to spend more money on aviation."

Accordingly, Coolidge supported the Kelly Air Mail Act of 1925, named after Congressman Clyde Kelly, and additional legislation in 1928, which provided subsidies for American carriers. The latter act mandated the Postal Service to award contracts to "the lowest responsible bidders that can satisfactorily perform the service." In addition, Coolidge backed the Air Commerce Act of 1926, which gave the Department of Commerce control over the nascent air-transport industry and provided it with government patronage. That year, too, he signed a law creating the Army Air Corps, inspired in part by the sensational Billy Mitchell court-martial trial, in which the Colonel charged that military aviation was antiquated and the country in danger should war erupt.

By then Juan Trippe had almost three years of experience with air transport, some of it in the Caribbean. Despite his name, which he disliked but which served him well in dealings with Latin Americans, Trippe had English antecedents. A Trippe had arrived in England with William the Conqueror in 1066, and Trippes had been businessmen and soldiers ever since. Lieutenant Henry Trippe arrived in Maryland in 1663, where he became a tobacco planter. The family then migrated to New Jersey, and in the midnineteenth century Frederick Trippe became a wealthy merchant. His son, Charles Trippe, was an engineer who married an heiress, Juanita Terry, and Juan was their son. Juan was named after his mother's stepfather, a Cuban with a fortune based on sugar.

Juan Trippe had a fashionable education, including a degree from Yale, and during his student days his father was a wealthy Wall Street banker, the head of the firm of Trippe & Co. Juan had learned to fly during the war, but did so too late for action in France. So he completed his degree requirements and appeared set to join his father's firm and, like him, become an investment banker. Then Charles Trippe died suddenly. Juan and his mother were shocked to learn that he had left an estate of only $30,000 and that Trippe & Co. was on the verge of bankruptcy. Working for a living was not an option, for young Juan, but a requirement.

Upon graduation Trippe accepted a banking post at Lee, Higginson, but was on the prowl for opportunities in aviation. While there he met John Hambleton, who had been a flyer in the war, and in 1922 they purchased surplus Navy seaplanes for $500 each and launched an airline, a charter service that took people to and from

New York and Long Island resorts. This lasted for two years but was never more than a hobby. In 1925, after passage of the Kelly Act offered a glimmer of hope for those who wanted airmail contracts, Trippe joined with Cornelius Whitney, Percy Rockefeller, and William Vanderbilt, classmates at Yale, and organized Eastern Air Transport. After merging with a rival, Colonial Air Transport, and taking that company's name, he won one of the first contracts and in 1926 started carrying the mail between New York and Boston.

Trippe had wider ambitions than that of being a postman, however. By then he had conceived of a worldwide airline, operated with the assistance and cooperation of the government. In this period it was generally assumed that each major country would have a "flag carrier," and Trippe intended to operate the entry of the United States. Most European countries had good business reasons to want such services, but Trippe believed such an airline was even more important for America, which had emerged from World War I the most powerful nation in the world, its largest creditor, eager to spread its business interests in other lands. Moreover, an English or French national airline could come into being by offering services to nearby European countries. The United States, between two oceans, with Latin America to the South, could have a larger, even global reach. Just as transportation had been important in making the United States a continental power, so it would be essential if it were to realize its worldwide ambitions.

Finally, throughout his life Trippe avoided competition whenever possible. He reasoned that there would be a great deal of rivalry for domestic services, but the nation could afford only one international airline. If his company became that airline, he could work out deals with politicians and not have to worry unduly about jostling with other would-be aviation tycoons.

A corollary to this was his conviction that airlines would have to have government assistance and be regulated so as to prevent cutthroat competition. Airlines would require protected routes and would be provided with terminals, controllers, weather information, and more. What would be needed was a friendly version of the ICC. Unlike the railroaders, who for the most part disliked the ICC, Trippe felt airlines would require an entity to furnish needed services. Such thoughts informed his activities during the next half century.

Trippe's first step outside the country was to be Cuba. He quickly arranged to obtain landing rights in Havana, and hoped to carry mail and passengers to and from there and Key West, Florida. Before this could be arranged, however, Trippe lost a power struggle at Colonial and was forced from the company, whereupon he organized the Aviation Corporation of America (AVCO), which retained the rights to land in Cuba. Then, to go with those rights, Trippe attempted to win the airmail contract between Key West and Havana. He was one of three bidders. Pan American Airways, headed by war aces Eddie Rickenbacker and Henry "Hap" Arnold, was one of the competitors, and the other was Atlantic, Gulf and Caribbean Airways.

Each had something the other needed. AVCO had landing rights in Havana, Pan Am had them in America, and AG&C had financing in place. AG&C's leader, Richard Hoyt, agreed with Trippe about competition. He arranged for a meeting with Assistant Postmaster General Irving Glover, who had concluded that only a merged airline could be awarded the contract. The merger took place, with Atlantic becoming a holding company for Pan Am, which was to be the operating company, and Trippe its president and general manager. In October 1927, Pan Am began its runs to and from Havana.

The service arrived just in time to capitalize on Charles A. Lindbergh's flight to Paris, which sparked an interest in aviation. Trippe had known Lindbergh before he became famous, and the two men liked and trusted each other. Now they joined in a long-term business alliance, which would benefit both men, Trippe more than Lindbergh.

Trippe's next challenge was to convince potential passengers that the overwater flight to Cuba was not only fast, but safe. This he did by first offering free flights and then charging for tickets when the service became popular. One of the early paying customers was "Scarface Al" Capone who, on purchasing his ticket, reportedly told the agent, "Better see that it's a *safe* plane. If anything happens to us, it won't be so healthy for you."

In 1928 Trippe met a fraternity brother's father-in-law, Secretary of the Treasury Andrew Mellon, who in turn introduced him to Congressman Kelly. At the time, Kelly was drafting that second piece of legislation to govern international mail policy and the awarding of contracts. By dint of skillful lobbying, Pan Am was granted an airmail contract between Puerto Rico and the mainland.

Trippe next tried to expand his routes into South America, joining with W. R. Grace in 1929 to form Panagra. Trippe didn't need
Grace's money as much as its knowledge of the area and political and
business contacts. He wasn't pleased with the idea of having a partner,
but knew that Grace, which dominated the western coast of South
America, was considering starting an airline of its own to complement
the Grace Line steamships. Trippe was simply heading off CEO
Joseph Grace at the pass.

Panagra began operations with a 795-mile run between Lima and
Talara in Peru, and it swiftly spread throughout the South American
west coast into Ecuador, Bolivia, Chile, and Argentina. In this period
it took four days to fly from New York to Chile. W. R. Grace did not
consider Panagra to be in competition with the Grace Line, which
made the trip in more than two weeks. Businessmen—those were the
ones for whom the service was designed—had to be adventuresome
and short of time to take the perceived risks of flying and forgo the
comforts of an ocean liner.

Within a few years Panagra had the longest route structure of
any airline, with airmail providing the bulk of the earnings. It was in
direct competition on some routes with Pan Am itself. In fact, travelers to Buenos Aires from Balboa in the Canal Zone generally preferred the shorter Panagra route to Pan Am's.

Herbert Hoover became president in 1929, and he named Walter
Folger Brown his postmaster general. Brown, who had been assistant
secretary of commerce in the Coolidge Administration and Hoover's
campaign manager, was if anything more averse to competition than
were Kelly and Glover. He awarded domestic mail contracts to American, Eastern, Trans World Airways, and United, enabling these four to
obtain a leadership in the domestic arena they would enjoy for half a
century. Brown thought to do the same in the Latin American business,
with Pan Am and the New York, Rio, and Buenos Aires Airline
(NYRBA), which was backed by a consortium that included Ford
Motors, Irving Trust, and James Rand of Remington Rand, as well as
having powerful connections within the Hoover Administration.

Though not as experienced as Pan Am, NYRBA was well
financed and had an edge in the form of its modern fleet of planes. For
his part, Trippe had strong allies within the postal department, such as
Walter Brown. In addition, Francis White, Yale 1913, was in charge of

Latin American affairs in the State Department. Finally, NYRBA was attempting to work out an alliance with France's Aeropostale, which didn't sit well in Washington. By waiting it out, while NYRBA suffered losses due to a lack of business, Trippe not only won the contract, but was able to buy out NYRBA at the knockdown price of $2 million in AVCO stock. The Americas belonged to Juan Trippe.

The 1930s was the decade of the Great Depression in the United States, but for Pan Am it was a time of major growth. Pan Am's passengers were international businesspeople and wealthy tourists, for whom money wasn't a problem. In 1930 the company carried 40,000 passengers; by the end of the decade the figure was up to 246,000. Even so, in none of the years of the 1930s did passengers account for more than half of Pan Am's revenues. The mail contracts remained crucial.

Trippe next hoped to offer service to Europe. There was no thought of using Lindbergh's route as a template. Rather, he considered flights from New York to Bermuda, and from there to the Azores, and then on to Lisbon, a route that Lindbergh, on a Pan Am commission, advocated. Another route ran from New York to Newfoundland, next to Ireland, and then to London and other European capitals, but could not be used during the winter season, since part of it was ice locked at that time of year. When land-based planes had sufficient range, thought Lindbergh, this would be the better route.

For the time being, for several reasons, amphibians were required. For one, they could land at sea in case of problems, though how safe that would be was questionable. Still, the thought might calm passengers. In a period when any flight took daring and nerves of steel, those over water—especially an ocean—were deemed on the same level as those facing astronauts today. More important, however, was the simple fact that in 1932 there were no hard-surface runways long enough to accommodate large, long-distance passenger planes. In any case, Europe would have to wait. To fly either route would require permissions, and the British were reluctant to grant rights in Bermuda, although the French had obtained rights in the Azores from Portugal and would cooperate. So Trippe turned westward instead.

In 1932 Trippe announced his intention to offer passenger and mail flights across the Pacific, to the Philippines. The service began three years later with the Martin M-130s, the soon-to-become-famous Clippers. The name was chosen deliberately, to evoke images of the nineteenth century clipper ships, pictures of which adorned the walls at Pan Am offices. The crew would be dressed in uniforms copied from those used by the navy, and the pilots and copilots were called captains and first officers.

The Clippers looked impressive, but were slow, with a maximum speed of 180 mph, and corrosion from salt water was always a problem. There would be one scheduled flight every two weeks. The Clippers had room for 41 passengers, but on the Pacific run could carry only half that amount, because the rest of the space was needed for extra fuel tanks. Occasionally, there would be too many passengers, or the weight would be too high, in which case a passenger or two would be bumped and would have to wait another two weeks before boarding. That first year Pan Am carried a total of 106 passengers. The planes would take off without a single passenger, however, because not to do so would be to forgo $10,000 in airmail revenues.

Trippe's authoritarian ways resulted in troubles with the Roosevelt Administration. Roosevelt, a Harvard graduate, had an instinctive mistrust of "Yalies." "Juan Trippe is the most fascinating Yale gangster I ever met," he once observed. The President had decided that civil aviation had to be regulated by a single agency. This did not seem to bother Trippe, who continued to consider regulation as potentially favorable to Pan Am. He had proven adept at handling bureaucrats, and felt reasonably certain that even the Roosevelt appointees to such a body could be swayed into annealing Pan Am's domination of international traffic. The Civil Aeronautics Authority (CAA) was approved in 1938, but before anything consequential could be done, World War II erupted.

At the time the European national airlines had come to look upon Pan Am as America's entry into the competition. Like Trippe, their leaders disliked rivalry and so were prepared to cooperate. Even so, they feared Pan Am's clout, Trippe's cleverness, and a reputation that Pan Am had earned by experience in other parts of the world.

For several years Trippe had persisted in his attempt to crack into Europe, with no success. In order to get routes there Trippe petitioned the Roosevelt Administration for assistance. For national security reasons if no other, such help was provided. Secretary of State Cordell Hull intervened in Pan Am's behalf and worked out a deal with the British whereby that country's Imperial Airways and Pan Am would cooperate in opening the Atlantic, pooling passengers and cargo. Trippe then obtained landing rights in the Azores, in a deal that forbade any other airline except Pan Am from using the base for a period of 15 years. This violated American antitrust laws, and Trippe was obliged to back down on this clause, whereupon the objections were dropped.

With this out of the way, Trippe was able to make flights to Europe in 1939, on the eve of World War II, using Clippers produced by Boeing and designated the 314s. These had a range of 3,500 miles and were one and a half times the size of the earlier Clippers. They had a crew of 14 and a load of airmail, but at first, no passengers. Service began in June, and soon after passengers were accommodated. Fully loaded, the Clippers could carry 74 passengers, but rarely had half that many; on the maiden voyage to Marseilles on June 24 there were only 22 of them, who paid $375 for their tickets. Without passengers, the planes could carry a ton of mail, and this helped considerably, since the government subsidized the shipments. Also important was the CAA's willingness to permit Trippe to boost rates, as well as the opening of LaGuardia Airport in the autumn.

The future of transoceanic flight was to be with land-based planes, but for the time being the Clippers ruled the skies over the Atlantic Ocean. It was not a profitable route at first. Weather was a problem; of the 87 scheduled flights that first winter, only 40 were completed. Profits from Panagra would subsidize oceanic traffic for quite a while.

All of this came at a price. Pan Am was debt-laden as a result of airliner purchases and Trippe's willingness to take losses on passenger travel in order to establish the service. A palace coup removed him as CEO in 1939, but he remained as president and was back as CEO less than a year later.

In late 1941, shortly before the Japanese attack on Pearl Harbor, Roosevelt learned of Trippe's attempts to win for Pan Am a monopoly to operate all overseas routes during the war. According to the Pan Am plan, the government would provide financing for the company's expansion, for which it would receive ownership rights but no participation in management. If accepted, this would realize Trippe's ambitions for Pan Am to be the nation's flag carrier and eliminate any possibility of competition.

Roosevelt would have none of this. He continued to mistrust Trippe, though he had no choice but to have the government work with Pan Am. "In government and in war, you have to use scoundrels."

Others in the Administration agreed with this point of view. Secretary of the Interior Harold Ickes said, "Trippe is an unscrupulous person who cajoles and buys his way." "I have never liked the idea of Pan American having a world monopoly of our airlines," presidential adviser Harry Hopkins told Edward R. Stettinius, the Lend-Lease administrator who was also Trippe's brother-in-law. By then, however, Trippe had succeeded in placing allies on the CAA and would continue this practice with other regulatory agencies.

Instead of a Pan Am monopoly, the War Department organized the Air Transport Command (ATC), which awarded contracts to Pan Am—and other airlines as well. Pan Am received more business than any other carrier, but during the war rival airlines became factors in the overseas business. A frustrated Trippe saw American and Trans World flying the North Atlantic to London, while United went into the Pacific and Eastern and Braniff flew to Latin America. Key government officials opposed Trippe's attempts to monopolize the business, and so did the Allies. General George Marshall noted "the recurring resentments of the British to Pan Am's expansion into the Middle East and the fact that Pan American tends to regard a military effort as a commercial operation." That Washington preferred competition on international routes to the prewar Pan Am monopoly was quite clear. Whether or not the Roosevelt Administration would get it was uncertain.

In 1943 the 19 airlines that had ATC contracts were called to Washington for a meeting and were told the government had no intention of remaining in the transport business after the war. It was up to the airline executives to determine the shape of this part of the industry. Trippe had little to fear from them. From the vantage point of 1943, transcontinental airline growth seemed a chimera. United had commissioned a study, which concluded that few first-class steamship passengers—believed the only possible customers—would find the long, chancy passage appealing. After the war, thought the United's economists, 43 passenger planes would be needed for the North Atlantic run. Since eight countries had indicated interest, that came to an average of little more than five per country. Perhaps two American companies could make a profit given such numbers, and Pan Am, the most experienced and best known, would certainly be one of these. United had a coast-to-coast route system, a natural feeder for travelers from other parts of the country wanting to fly to Europe, but declined to submit a bid. The domestic business seemed more appealing than anything trans-Atlantic passage could offer.

Roosevelt thought Trippe had the edge when it came to overseas flight. "I don't think that anyone other than Trippe could be successful in running a worldwide system," he told one associate, but to another he confided, "Juan Trippe can't have it all." The answer for him was to have the other airlines enter different areas, such as Latin America, Asia, and Europe. Pan Am would be all over the globe, but in each segment, said Roosevelt, it would face American competition.

As it happened, 17 American carriers eventually filed route requests with the Civil Aeronautics Board (CAB), which had taken over some of the duties of the CAA. Trippe's allies there could not block them, but he was prepared for something like this, and in April 1945 sprung his plan. Since before the war the European state airlines had banded together in the International Air Traffic Association, through which they set fares and cooperated in other matters. Pan Am was a junior member, nothing more, since price fixing was against American law. Now, together with those foreign airlines that flew oceanic routes, Trippe led in the establishment of the International Air Transport Association (IATA), which intended to fix prices and set rules and policy, one of which was to restrict entry. It had the appearance of a cartel, if not the ironclad ability to exclude outsiders. Since prices would be set in such a way as to assure profits to all members, these would be quite high. Interest in air travel was growing, and if the trend continued, decent profits might be realized by the efficient lines.

Washington instantly complained that the IATA was in violation of the antitrust laws, but this was gotten around when British Overseas Airways (BOAC) agreed to permit other carriers to enter London, and in return the American government accepted IATA. From then on, IATA was more important in regulating fares and practices for transnational carriers than were governments.

While a wholehearted supporter of IATA, there was one aspect of it Trippe disliked, and that was the matter of price. Trippe wanted sharp reductions, not only to encourage traffic, but also because Pan Am, being by far the most efficient line, could do very well with lower charges. In October, when a one-way trip between New York and London cost $375 and the Europeans wanted to boost it to $572, he proposed a $275 rate. A compromise was reached at keeping the old rate, but Trippe would continue to fight for the lower charges.

Trans World Airlines, which has been seen in the preceding chapter, once was Transcontinental & Western and changed its name to represent its new ambitions, challenged Pan Am for the New York-to-London route. Now headed by Howard Hughes, who had deeper pockets than Trippe, it was a formidable competitor, the first the Pan Am CEO had ever had to face. In addition, TWA had a strong national network, including the New York-to-Los Angeles route. Moreover, TWA was using the faster land-based planes, which meant that Pan Am had to follow suit, and the end of World War II saw the last of the Clipper flights.

In 1946, the first postwar year, what was now Pan American World Airways had revenues of $113 million, on which it earned $3 million, while TWA posted revenues of $57 million, on which it had a loss of $14 million. (By way of comparison, United had $65 million in revenues and $1 million in earnings that year, while the figures for American were $68 million, on which it had a loss of less than half a million dollars, and Eastern had $42 million in revenues and a profit of more than $3 million.)

Trippe foresaw a new era in travel once the war ended, one in which airlines would play an ever more important role. He planned for a truly global airline that conducted business on all continents and provided for all necessities. As part of his program, starting in 1946 Trippe purchased and then constructed hotels, known as the Intercontinentals, where travelers on the Pan Am flights might stay, this being accomplished with government assistance in the form of loans from the Export-Import Bank for 90 percent of the hotel prices. His objective was to bring into the life of the average person those amenities that had once been the privilege of only the fortunate few. "That person's holiday has, in the past, been the prisoner of two grim keepers—money and time," he said. "Their enjoyment of the world has been circumscribed by the high walls of an economic jail. We can level these prison walls only by bringing travel costs way down and by shortening travel time."

This did not mean that Trippe was prepared to take the next step, however, that of asking the IATA and CAB to permit competition in rates, landing slots, and all else. Pan Am had grown up with regulation, and Trippe wanted this to continue. Rather, he desired cooperation between the carriers and government to lower fares and provide more assistance in the form of airport construction and services.

He was as good as his word. Trippe approached the CAB with a proposal to fly what amounted to a shuttle between New York and San Juan, Puerto Rico. The fare was to be $75 and could be paid on an installment plan. By restructuring the seating, the planes would carry 63 passengers. There would be no galley and but one flight attendant for the 14-hour flight.

As Trippe had expected, after the war there was a boom in passenger travel across the Atlantic, especially to London. Here Pan Am faced competition, not only from TWA and the foreign airlines, but from the old way of making the journey: passenger liners, which were offering round-trip tourist-class service for around $350, while more lavish passage cost upward of $700. Trippe wanted to charge less than $500 for air service, and he obtained permission to do so with cooperation from the other IATA members and the government. All the while he urged Douglas, Boeing, and Lockheed to produce planes that could make the trip nonstop. So they did, this being made possible by government aid in the form of military contracts, with the airliners using technology developed for the Air Force.

The ocean liners' passenger rosters increased till 1957, when more than one million passengers crossed the Atlantic by ship. Airliner service increased at a more rapid rate, however, and as a result of $450 fares for economy class, more passengers crossed by air than by ship that year. The early postwar growth continued until 1951, when high airline prices caused a slowdown and taught IATA the lesson of the dangers of monopoly pricing. Accordingly, the fare was reduced, whereupon business picked up.

These were Pan Am's glory years. In 1955 the company posted revenues of $238 million, on which it earned more than $10 million. It was the class of the field and by then had also taken an interest in several foreign airlines.

Pan Am was also the technological pioneer; late in the year Trippe announced his intention to purchase jetliners. At the time the manufacturers of passenger planes hoped to make and sell turbojets, a hybrid Trippe thought made no sense. He talked Douglas's Donald Douglas into producing designs for the jet DC-8s that fitted his needs. When Boeing's William Allen refused to enlarge his planned 707, Trippe placed orders for both planes, preparing to take 21 707s and 24 DC-8s, which would cost $269 million, a purchase that dwarfed all previous ones.

Angered at seeing Douglas receive the larger order and continue its string of successes in the civilian market that began with the DC-3, Allen reluctantly agreed to redesign the 707s to meet Pan Am's specifications and assured Trippe that Pan Am would get the first deliveries. The foreign airlines had no option but to accept his dictates, knowing that once Pan Am entered the field with jets, they would have to follow.

The 707s made their appearances in 1958. They had a range of 3,000 miles, traveled at 600 mph, and could carry from 60 to 120 passengers, depending upon the configuration. The DC-8s followed two years later, and these planes had an even longer range. They were expensive, coming in at more than $5 million apiece, close to ten times the prices of those prewar 314s. They were profitable, however, and Trippe responded by leading IATA into new rounds of price cuts, made possible by the faster flights and the new plane's larger capacity. With this, nonstop travel from New York to London became a reality.

By 1966 Pan Am was operating 115 passenger planes and had become an $841 million company with $72 million in earnings. It was the prime contractor for the Cape Kennedy Missile Range and had fingers in other pies. Trippe moved his offices from the Chrysler Building to a new edifice arising behind Grand Central Station, which was to be called the Pan Am Building. The name in large metal letters couldn't be missed by anyone driving or walking north on Park Avenue below 42nd Street. Trippe insisted a heliport be installed on the roof, from which helicopters could whisk important travelers from the airports to midtown in a matter of minutes.

In Hollywood the motion picture 2001 was in the planning stages. When the time came to make the film, the space shuttle bore the Pan Am logo. None other would have been plausible.

Adjusted for a 2–1 stock split, Pan Am common had gone from 10 in late 1962 to 40 in mid-1966 and had the cachet of being both a blue-chip and a glamour stock.

It was then that things started turning sour for Pan Am. It began with Panagra. Neither partner had thought the airline would become as successful as it was, and this caused tensions between Trippe and Peter Grace. Before the war Trippe had tried unsuccessfully to buy out the Grace interests, and when that failed, he refused to permit Panagra to enter Miami and New York. In retaliation, Grace had become cofounder of and stockholder in Eastern Airlines. When that company was unable to get landing rights, Grace formed a partnership with National Airlines, hoping to merge it with his half of Panagra. Trippe blocked this. "How can you let a boathouse get into the airline business?" he asked. As has been seen, Peter Grace wanted to sell his half-interest in Panagra to Pan Am for $15 million, but that fell through. In 1967 he sold Braniff the Grace half, whereupon Trippe also sold that company his share. By then, Pan Am's attentions had turned elsewhere, and the loss of Panagra was not considered of major consequence.

There were two more important blows. The first was technological and the second, economic. Just as in the late 1950s the airline industry was invigorated by the arrival of the first jets, so it appeared another new day was coming with the development by a British-French consortium of the first supersonic airplane, designed to fly at 1,800 mph and carry 200 passengers. Air France and BOAC intended to take the planes, and Pan Am was the first foreign company to do so, signing up for 15 copies. That the Soviets had announced their intention to build the TU-144 supersonic seemed to clinch the creation of an American entry.

There followed a long debate in the United States regarding the feasibility of an American supersonic carrier. Of course, no such plane was ever built. In time, the American and foreign carriers went instead for another, quite different design, the Boeing 747, one of the new generation of superliners then being planned by the industry, which included entries from Douglas (DC-10) and Lockheed (L-1011). At the time Boeing was in the lead, and it appeared its launch would come first.

Unlike the supersonic, which was to be called the Concorde, the 747 would not fly at supersonic speeds, but it could carry up to 400 passengers and fly 5,500 miles without refueling; and the 747SP's range was 7,000 miles. Not only would flights to Europe be comfortable, but with refueling in Hawaii, the Asian mainland could be reached as well. Moreover, the economics of the 747 versus the Concorde were compelling. Would sufficient passengers pay a premium price in order to land in New York *before* they took off from London or Paris due to time zone changes?

In those years Pan Am and other airlines also flew the Boeing Stratocruiser, a transport version of the World War II B-29, which was a double-decker. There was talk of another double-decker, with a cocktail lounge complete with a piano player, with two aisles and nine-abreast seating. Trippe thought such a configuration possible for the 747s and DC-10s. The Concorde was cramped in comparison to first class in the 747, while the ticket-price differences were minimal.

At least, this was the way Trippe seemed to analyze the situation. In April 1966 he signed an agreement with Boeing to take 25 of the 747s at a price from $17 million to $20 million each, on condition the planes be delivered between September 1969 and May 1970 and that Pan Am get delivery before any other airline. The price for the planes and spare parts came to more than $530 million, the biggest commercial airplane sale in history.

The contract called for a down payment of 2.5 percent of the price and half the total amount in quarterly payments, the last of which would be made six months prior to delivery of the first planes. Thus, for this order alone Pan Am would have to ante $265 million before having seen the 747 fly commercially. In addition to the 747s, Pan Am had orders for 19 more 707s, which would double Pan Am's indebtedness. To cover himself, Trippe had options for eight Concordes and 15 for a planned Boeing SST.

It was the biggest gamble in airline history, one Pan Am need not have taken. The company could have proceeded more slowly, since its competition was far behind in all overseas markets. But Trippe gloried in being the pacesetter. Just as he had been first with jets, so he wanted to be first with the superliner. Moreover, he was now 67 years old and knew his career had to end soon. It would be a dramatic way to make an exit.

In 1967, Trippe's last year at the helm, Pan Am posted revenues of $950 million and earnings of $65 million, the former figure a record, the latter second best in Pan Am history after 1966's $72 million. Assuming the trend continued, Trippe might look back at these figures as the springboard for the next stage in Pan Am's history. If airline usage declined, however, Pan Am would be in a serious financial bind.

Signs of decline in air travel soon appeared and then came with a vengeance. There could scarcely have been a worst time for the purchases. The economy fell into recession, and airline traffic dropped. Pan Am lost money in the first quarter of 1968 and the red ink continued. Trippe might have sensed the going was about to get rough. He announced his intention to retire and named his longtime second in command and president, Harold Gray, as his successor. Newcomer and Washington insider Najeeb Halaby would be president. Gray had cancer and lasted only a year and a half before retiring and turning the company over to Halaby.

Trippe had left Gray and Halaby headaches galore, including $120 million in losses for the three years from 1969 to 1971. There were troubles with the 747s as well. Servicing the debt became difficult. Other problems surfaced. Ever since the days of the Clippers Pan Am had a monopoly over Pacific flights. TWA received Pacific rights and became America's second global airline.

This situation struck Pan Am at its core. The other Atlantic and Pacific carriers, such as TWA, United, Northwest, and American, had strong domestic routes and could offer passengers bargains when taking them from their homes or offices outside New York to Europe or Asia. Moreover, transfers often could be in the same terminal. Not so Pan Am, which lacked those domestic routes. In addition, since IATA had lost the power to set prices as a result of deregulation, Pan Am's position as its leader no longer mattered for much.

Halaby knew he had to do something about this, and the most obvious path was a merger or working relationship with one or more domestic carriers. There was an attempt to forge a Pan Am-American Airlines partnership, which would unite American's domestic routes with Pan Am's overseas operations. Nothing came of this, or of subsequent negotiations with Eastern, United, and Delta. By 1971 Halaby was talking with TWA about a merger that would result in annual savings on the order of $200 million. Not only did the airlines match, but the combination of Pan Am's Intercontinental and TWA's International Hotels would make it a major factor in that field as well. Again, failure, as the plan was blocked by the Justice Department's Anti-Trust Division.

For 1971 Pan Am was expected to report a loss of around $46 million, and within inner circles there was some fear the company's line of credit might not be extended. That just about sealed Halaby's fate. On December 1, 1971, Pan Am announced his replacement by William Seawell, formerly president of Rolls-Royce Aero, the American subsidiary of the English company and a former Air Force general.

Seawell did the expected. He fired employees left and right. There were 42,000 of them when he arrived, and the number fell to 27,000 by the time he was through. This meant route abandonment.

Americans who flew from New York to Paris, Moscow, and Vienna had to find new carriers, as did those who made the trip from Seattle and Portland to Hawaii.

In 1974 the industry was hit by increases in the price of petroleum, the first of two major blows to the industry, the other, as will be seen, being deregulation. An explosion in the money supply pushed interest rates higher, with some Pan Am bonds carrying double-digit coupons. Losses that year came to $85 million. Pan Am continued to seek a partner, and now came the most astonishing offer of all. The Shah of Iran wanted to buy Pan Am and merge it with Iranian Air. This fortunately was not done, for had the offer been accepted, the Ayatollah would have controlled the American flag carrier during the hostage crisis in the Carter Administration.

When Pan Am was no more it was revealed that in 1975 Seawell had called an emergency meeting to draw up a contingency plan for taking the company into bankruptcy. That was the year Trippe left the board and finally retired for good, amid whispers that his 747 program had been responsible for Seawell's problems.

From 1968 to 1976 Pan Am's total deficits had come to $318 million, which was more than the company had earned in its entire history. Nor was this the end. There was a second fuel crisis in 1978, and the company was obliged to take large writeoffs. At the end of the year it reported that net working capital was a negative $288 million.

The blunders continued. Seawell hoped that a merger with a domestic company would help resolve Pan Am's problems. Several of these were on the ropes, and their prices were attractive. National Airlines was one such company. It had a strong network along the East Coast and also went into New Orleans, Houston, and was a minor force on the West Coast as well. Among the negatives was an aging airliner fleet and a generous union contract. Seawell went after National, but so did Frank Lorenzo, then in the process of trying to transform his Texas International Airlines into a major carrier. TIA and Pan Am entered into a bidding war in 1979, in which the price of National common was pushed from 20 to 50, by which time Eastern had also entered the bidding. Pan Am won, for a total cost of $400 million. Then the 747 experience repeated itself. The nation was hit with another recession and still higher interest rates, causing all companies having to finance debt to borrow at rates that went over 20 percent.

Of course, Pan Am was not alone among the airlines that suffered from these hammer blows. TWA, United, Eastern, and American also had negative working capital. The glamour industry of the 1950s and early 1960s had become a basket case, due in part to matters beyond the control of the companies' leaders.

Deregulation was the second shock to hit the industry. The key figure in deregulation, not only of airlines, but of other parts of the economy as well, was Cornell economist Alfred Kahn, who for years had been arguing for the elimination of such controls and the total dismantling of regulatory agencies. Kahn was named to the CAB in 1977 by President Carter and immediately indicated his desire to bring competition to a previously noncompetitive industry. He began by inviting the airline executives to apply for discount and special fares, and he pressed for legislation making it easier for new carriers to become certified. When several of the weaker lines complained they could not stand up to the competition, Kahn remarked, "No businessman protected from competition ever believed that competition is anything but destructive," and in any case, his job was "to protect competition, not companies." As far as he was concerned, the era of government-industry cooperation to fix prices was over.

Kahn's star was on the rise in Washington, and he was named to membership on the Economic Policy Group and he became chairman of the Council on Wage and Price Stability. He had a congressional ally in Senator Edward Kennedy, who charged the airlines with rigging ticket prices in collusion with the CAB. By then, too, the Penn Central collapse had prompted a debate as to the ICC's complicity in weakening the nation's railroads.

Under Kahn's aegis the Carter Administration was free and loose in awarding routes to other carriers. Delta got Atlanta to London, National obtained Miami to Paris and Amsterdam, and Northwest was able to fly into Copenhagen and Stockholm. Foreign airlines also obtained rights, and more and more KLM, British Airways, and Lufthansa flights arrived, with Pan Am in no condition to ask for a quid pro quo.

At about the same time Kahn arrived in office, Freddie Laker, whose British charter airline had applied for permission to operate "Skytrain," with inexpensive fares between New York and London, received CAB approval, posing another threat to Pan Am. Laker's no-frills operation was a huge success, and other similar lines appeared both domestically and in the overseas markets. Pan Am and other IATA members responded by cutting their fares to his level, but Laker continued to grow nonetheless, and others joined in. Then came passage of the Airline Deregulation Act of 1978, which ended regulation of domestic air fares and further eased entry for new carriers. As far as the old established lines were concerned, this was deregulation run amok.

Deregulation turned the industry upside down. The airlines had previously made a practice of overbooking their flights, which sometimes worked out well, since no-shows were fairly common, but on other occasions caused customer anger. It had been the task of staff to move people to other flights. One of the dark secrets of the industry was that older people and those in the armed forces were least likely to complain, so they were bumped first. Under Kahn's leadership the airlines started auctioning seats, offering free trips and cash for those booked passengers who voluntarily accepted seats on later flights. None of this could have been imagined by Trippe in his wildest dreams. By then Kahn was proposing the CAB, of which he had become the head, itself shut down.

In their attempts to become more economical and survive the airlines abandoned unprofitable routes, or if they were retained, were able to do so by using hub-and-spoke techniques. Passengers in the 1980s became accustomed to the airline's version of musical chairs. Dozens of planes would land at the hub from the spokes, and passengers would alight and rush to the next plane, which would take them to their final destinations. Thus, a passenger might leave College Station, Texas, for Dallas, and then take a plane to San Francisco, where he or she would transfer to a plane to Hawaii—along with passengers bound for Hawaii from Boston, Chicago, Minneapolis, Miami, and dozens of other cities. Likewise, passengers from these cities might fly to New York and then transfer to planes going to London, Paris, and Rome.

The airlines searched for other ways to economize. By the 1990s cutbacks in meals became common, with complete abandonment of poorly booked flights not unusual. Passengers were now encouraged to bring their own food for some flights, and all of this was accepted quite calmly. This resulted in savings of some $500 million annually for the airlines. The competition prior to deregulation was to provide the preponderance of amenities. In the 1990s it was to provide the least—at the most savings.

Most of the old airline executives were unable to cope with the new dispensation. Fortunately for American, it already had in Robert Crandall, an executive who not only had a proper and realistic vision of the future but also the nerve to create and implement a winning strategy. Crandall, the closest the industry would have to latter-day Juan Trippe, had joined American as senior vice president for marketing in 1973, after stints at a variety of companies, including Hallmark Greeting Cards, where he directed that company's computer-programming division.

As it happened, Crandall had the kind of experiences airline executives needed in this period. He formed an alliance with IBM to produce the Semi-Automatic Business Research Environment (Sabre) ticket-reservation system, which gave American the lead in three major areas: discount fares, management of pricing, and filling empty seats. Crandall also introduced the frequent-flyer program, Advantage, the first in the industry. While initially opposed to deregulation, he soon changed his mind, and almost alone of the leaders at the old-line carriers, he welcomed deregulation as an opportunity to win market share. Trippe was made for a regulated environment, since he knew how to capitalize on it. Crandall told reporters, "The problem isn't deregulation; it was regulation. For forty years the government regulated the airlines and did a perfectly awful job of it." Just as Trippe had been a near-perfect airline executive for the age of regulation, so Crandall was the kind of CEO needed in the deregulatory atmosphere of the 1980s and 1990s. Under his leadership American adjusted nicely; Pan Am's leaders blundered.

Pan Am was clearly in trouble in early 1980, its bonds downgraded, its stock selling for $4 a share. Survival would be possible only through sales of assets, which were begun soon after. It resembled the scene in the motion picture, *Around the World in Eighty Days*, where Phineus Fogg orders the captain of his ship to dismantle it and feed the wood to the steam engine to keep it afloat. Or the divestitures and maneuverings during the final days of the Penn Central. That year Pan Am sold the Pan Am Building to Metropolitan Life for $400 million, at the time the highest price ever paid for Manhattan property. Metropolitan permitted the Pan Am sign to remain, and the company continued to maintain offices in the building. Pan Am's profit came to $294 million and enabled the company to report "earnings" of $80 million, indicating that operating costs for the airline were enormous. Pan Am's banks canceled its $470 million line of credit. That did it. In August 1981 the company announced Seawell's resignation as CEO, though he would remain as chairman.

Trippe wasn't around to see this. He had a massive cerebral hemorrhage in September 1980 and died on April 3, 1981.

Seawell was replaced by William Waltrip, the company's executive vice president who was to report to the board, not to Seawell, and serve as interim Pan Am leader while the board searched for a permanent replacement. Soon thereafter Waltrip announced a major corporate restructuring. Now there were to be three Pan Ams under a single corporate umbrella: Pan American World Airways, which would be Waltrip's responsibility; Intercontinental Hotels, to be headed by Paul Sheeline; and Pan Am World Services, managed by Thomas Flanigan. Sheeline hadn't even taken office when his company was sold from under him. Intercontinental Hotels went to Grand Metropolitan for $500 million. Airliner purchases were canceled or postponed. Pan Am's debt was downgraded, and its subordinated bonds fell to junk status.

That summer the board found its next leader. C. Edward Acker had been president of Braniff and more recently had transformed Air Florida from a minuscule factor in the industry into a regional power. Acker tried to infuse optimism in Pan Am, but it was too far gone by then to be saved. There were no important divestitures in 1982, and absent these, Pan Am reported a loss of $495 million, with working capital now at minus $340 million. The unions agreed to wage freezes, a sure sign of distress, and management also accepted cuts in salaries.

Pan Am next started disposing of parts of its fleet; Crandall led the way and purchased 15 DC10s. Then the routes went. There was a crippling pilot strike in 1985 that all but did in the company. United purchased the Pacific routes and 18 airliners that year for $750 million and also took 2,700 relieved Pan Am employees, including 410 pilots. All the while intense competition from European airlines hurt Pan Am on its Atlantic routes. To exacerbate the problems, the strong dollar made it difficult for Pan Am to compete on a price basis. The Pan Am fire sale recalled the disposal by RCA of its computer business to Sperry Rand.

In 1987 Pan Am was being shopped around, not only by management, but also by the pilot's union, which hoped for someone to come in and save their jobs. Sir James Goldsmith was interested for a while, and then it was Kirk Kirkorian's turn, to be followed by Jay Prizker. Rumors were bandied about that Carl Icahn, who was doing poorly with TWA, might want another chance to run an airline. All the while, the board was seeking a replacement for Acker. They found him in Thomas Plaskett, who had once headed Continental, and who arrived in January 1988.

Miracle of miracle, Pan Am turned around. By summer Plaskett was predicting a modest profit and a positive cash flow. Then, on December 21, Flight 103 was blown up by politically inspired saboteurs over Lockerbie, Scotland. Of course it could have happened to any airline, but Pan Am bungled the matter incredibly. The airline released the wrong telephone number for family members to call; one family was informed of the death of their daughter by a message on their answering machine. Some of those families that telephoned were put on hold and had to listen to a recording of "I'll be Home for Christmas." Pan Am advised the media that all the families had been notified when this was not true. So it went, with one blunder after another, and in the process Pan Am lost both credibility and any sympathy it might have had. Even so, the search for a partner continued. There were talks with Northwest, which came to nothing. There were more sales.

In 1990–1991, when the airline industry in the aggregate lost $6.5 billion, Pan Am threw in the towel. On January 8, 1991, the company filed for Chapter 11 bankruptcy. The old Pan Am was no more. The disposals continued, with the London operations sold for $290 million to United. The Atlantic routes, with hubs at New York, London, and Frankfurt went to Delta. The Pan Am Shuttle, which had once competed with the Eastern Shuttle, was sold to Delta, which also provided Pan Am with a $140 million line of credit.

With this, Pan Am emerged as a Miami-based airline with flights to Latin America. It was back to where it had been when Juan Trippe started out.

Delta was a powerful force in the Atlantic, due in large part to its acquisitions of Pan Am's businesses in that part of the world. It obtained greater might by allying itself with the likes of Swissair, Sabena, Aer Lingus, Austrian, Aeromexico, TAP Air Portugal, and others. More powerful still was United, in alliance with, among others, Air Canada, Scandinavian, Varig, Lufthansa, Thai Airways International, and Singapore. American, which had joined with Canadian, British Airways, LOT, and Qantas and then formed an alliance with U.S. Airways and British Airways, while Northwest took control of Continental. That the industry is part of the globalization movement current in the late 1990s is evident. But globalization was taking place without the company that once had been the symbol of global travel: Pan Am.

It might be argued that the problems at Pan Am originated in the 1920s, when for perfectly sound and sensible reasons the United States government decided to regulate the airlines industry, in order to help it develop at a time when private enterprise could not do the job. This was a period when it appeared the public would never take to air travel, and if the industry were to develop it, it would have to do so with government assistance in the form of subsidies and generous airmail contracts. So the companies grew and prospered under the umbrella of a benevolent CAA and CAB. By the 1950s the airlines no longer had to rely upon airmail to break even and make money. That was the time to recognize the time for deregulation had arrived, and had this taken place then, rather than 20 years later, the old dogs of the airlines might have learned new tricks in a more favorable business environment, and Pan Am, as well as Eastern, a strong TWA, and some other companies of the period might be with us today.

Everything usually seems quite clear in retrospect, but not in prospect. We must always remember that businesspeople function in what one historian called "a cloud of information." From today's vantage point it might appear Trippe blundered in making the huge 747 purchases in the late 1960s, and after Pan Am failed, quite a few analysts said this was the beginning of the end for the company. But in so doing they failed to realize that the same arguments had been used when Trippe blazed the way for jet travel across the Atlantic, one of his greatest successes. True blunders occur when business leaders falter when the evidence at hand argues against actions and paths taken. In sum, Pan Am erred on several occasions, but whether Trippe blundered is at least arguable. That Seawell's misbegotten takeover of National sounded the company's death knell was conceded within the industry at the time and soon after in the investment community as well.

CHAPTER TWELVE

MONTGOMERY WARD: THE BLUNDER OF THE STOPPED CLOCK

I ndividuals and products superbly suited for a specific time, place, and function may prove deficient when the passage of time and unanticipated developments alter the situation, and then they may become harmful or inappropriate. The CEO who was ideal for a period of growth may falter when retrenchment is demanded. The financially oriented leader may do poorly when technological expertise is required. We have seen how Pan Am's CEOs in the 1970s, 1980s, and 1990s were unable to come to terms with a new dispensation. Wise boards understand this. When the current CEO departs, the members assess the company's probable needs and only then make their selection for a successor. If due to changes in the business climate the CEO does not fill the bill, they ease him out.

Now and then a fine product, service, or even company falls of its own weight, and there is little management can do to rectify the situation. Once Keuffell and Esser produced the best slide rules in the world. In came the pocket calculator, out went the slide rule, and K & E was gone as well. Management saw it coming, knew the company was doomed, and simply gave up.

Usually the end comes more slowly and less dramatically. The seventh largest American corporation in 1909 was Central Leather, the leading supplier of industrial belting to factories, where leather straps were used to transmit steam power from the generator to the assembly lines. The factories electrified in the 1920s, and Central Leather was shuttered by the end of the decade. In the early 1960s Republic Steel saw a key customer, the canning industry, turn to the aluminum version, while foreign manufacturers were eroding its other markets. Management appeared paralyzed. At a time when several aluminum companies might have been purchased at reasonable prices, the CEOs spoke of aluminum as "the weak metal," adding Republic would never give up on steel. Today Republic is no more, doomed by unimaginative and timid leaders.

What might these companies have done? K&E had a skilled labor force and a staff of top-notch designers. Entry into the instrumentation field would not have been impossible. Central Leather owned forests (from which to extract tannin), glue works, and had several factories at which chemicals were manufactured. The sales force was tops in its field, and the balance sheet strong. To remain in the leather business made no sense at all, but Central Leather might have stressed forest products or adhesives, or found some other outlet for its assets. For this company to have failed indicates an obvious lack of imagination and paralysis of will.

Changes in corporate direction can be made, and often are. In 1909 Pullman was the eighth largest American industrial corporation. There was a time when it was virtually alone as a manufacturer and leaser of railroad sleeping cars. Indeed, just as today Xerox has become synonymous with office copiers ("I'll xerox this and send you a copy."), so Pullman was generic for sleepers. In came the airplane, the passenger railroads declined, and Pullman suffered sales losses.

Pullman had a happier fate than did Central Leather. Management saw what was coming and made adjustments. Even before placements of sleeping cars declined it expanded into freight carriers. During World War II Pullman purchased M. W. Kellogg and expanded into plant-and-process engineering for the oil and chemical industries. Then it acquired Trailmobile and became a major factor in truck trailers. Today little is left of the old Pullman. Likewise, of course, the W. R. Grace that Peter Grace bequeathed to his successor was completely different from the one he had inherited.

Frequently the decline and fall of a once-proud product results from the business blunders of managements frozen in time and space, unable to adjust intelligently to change. Safe in their niches, secure in their market share, managements are blindsided by new technologies and customers. Such was the situation with Montgomery Ward at the end of World War II.

Since the late nineteenth century Montgomery Ward and its arch rival, Sears Roebuck, had engaged in a vigorous competition, second in retailing history only to that of Macy's and Gimbel's in New York. Between them the two companies dominated the mail-order business. Sears had the edge prior to World War I, and after the war both companies suffered through a sharp though short depression of the kind that often follows cutbacks of military spending. Sales for Montgomery Ward fell from $102 million in 1920 to $69 million in 1921, when the company posted a loss of $8 million. Then, with the arrival of economic recovery, Montgomery Ward expanded exponentially under the leadership of CEO Theodore Merseles and his second in command, Robert Wood, who had arrived in retailing with a background that made him unique in the field. Wood had made a reputation as the West Point-trained director of the Panama Railroad Co. during the construction of the Panama Canal. He had been quartermaster general during World War I, after which one of his assistants, Robert Thorne, recruited him for the company. Wood took to the business, bringing to it a fine intelligence and a fresh point of view.

At the time Montgomery Ward was closing in on Sears Roebuck. Merseles, who had come up the ladder in mail order, was convinced he could pass his rival in a decade. Wood had other ambitions. He knew the mail-order business was booming, but saw it as a relic of rural America that was bound to decline as farmers in their Model Ts came to the cities to shop. In his view the future of the industry rested in retail department stores, not in mail order. "We can beat the chain stores at their own game," he told Merseles in 1921. "We can easily and profitably engage in the chain-store business ourselves with a relatively small amount of capital." With Montgomery Ward's franchise name and reputation, Wood wanted to establish stores in and around large cities.

Merseles rejected the idea, but the two worked well together during the next few years. Sears Roebuck had large sales, but Montgomery Ward's profit margin was much higher and was growing more rapidly. By 1924 Montgomery Ward's revenues were three quarters those of Sears Roebuck. Despite this, Wood continued to argue for stores, and Merseles always rejected the notion.

Knowing of the differences at Montgomery Ward headquarters and hoping to snare an outstanding leader, Julius Rosenwald of Sears

Roebuck approached Wood with the offer of the top operational position there. Angered on learning of this, Merseles fired Wood, who promptly accepted the Sears offer and went on to become one of the industry's legends.

Letting Wood go was one of many Montgomery Ward mistakes. Yet this could not be seen as a blunder. After all, Merseles was able to show strong growth in catalog sales. Once at Sears, Wood started putting up those stores, and he took other steps as well. Enamored as he was with the automobile, he founded Allstate as a wholly owned subsidiary to insure them.

Reflecting on the successes of the stores and recognizing his error, Merseles switched position and two years later opened the first Montgomery Ward store, in Plymouth, Indiana. This was not to be a department store, however, but rather a showcase for catalog goods. He was surprised to discover that customers did not want to purchase those goods from catalogs, but rather from inventory. Somewhat reluctantly he gave in. Montgomery Ward had ten stores in 1926, which rose to 248 in 1928 and on to 554 in 1930. Merseles still considered himself a mail-order merchant, but was sufficiently flexible not to fight the trend.

As it did practically all American industries, the Great Depression crippled retailing, and the optimistic Merseles was not the right man for the times. He continued opening stores in 1931, even though most of the existing ones were starting to show losses and the company was deep in red ink. Montgomery Ward common, which sold as high as 157 in 1929, was less than 7 in late 1931.

J. P. Morgan & Co., Montgomery Ward's banker, thought it was time for a change at the top and replaced Merseles with Sewell Avery, who arrived at the Chicago headquarters in November 1931. As U. S. Gypsum's CEO from 1905 on, Avery had been a capable and imaginative leader, especially when it came to cutting costs. In the process he created an enterprise that was the pioneer in its field. While other companies that produced materials used in construction suffered during the economic falloffs that came with the end of World War I , Gypsum did very well. There were several minor slumps in the 1920s, during which Avery pushed Gypsum into new markets and increased its share of the business. If anyone could manage in bad times it was Sewell Avery.

Avery, who was 54 years old, tackled the task with verve and intelligence, which made up for his lack of experience in retailing. At the time virtually everyone in the industry agreed that partnerships were necessary in order to survive in the poor business environment of the period, but the top retailers were convinced they could make it on their own. For a while there was talk of a merger of Montgomery Ward and Sears, which would enable the united entity to realize economies. Avery would have none of this. Nor would Wood, but the Sears board pressed him to move ahead on the matter. Avery, who dominated his board, had no such worries. Sears then turned to J. C. Penney as a possible partner, but nothing came of this either.

The selection of Avery at that particular time was fortuitous, for during the Depression Avery proved as good if not better a manager as Wood. While remaining as Gypsum's CEO, he introduced efficiencies, upgraded the merchandise, and refurbished the stores. Avery closed almost 100 old stores and opened nearly twice as many new ones. Recognizing that the mail-order mentality still existed at the stores, he brought in new managers who were rewarded on the basis of performance. In the process he cut the 1931 loss of $8.7 million to one of $5.6 million by 1933, and the following year Montgomery Ward reported a profit of $2 million, followed by one of $9 million in 1935. The dividend, omitted in the beginning of the Depression, was restored in 1936.

Montgomery Ward did better than anyone could have imagined. Wood recognized this challenge. In a speech delivered to his sales force at Sears in 1939 he said, "I believe there still lingers in some, not all, of Sears's buying force a trace of that feeling of smugness or superiority which was quite noticeable ten or fifteen years ago. Montgomery Ward's volume fifteen years ago was nearly half of Sears's; today it is 80 percent of Sears's. If you have such feeling, get rid of it, for you don't deserve it after 1937 and 1938. Learn from your competition, examine yourself to see what are your weak spots, and see if you can't discover new ways in your line to make sales and profits." Wood had good reason to feel this way. When in 1939 it appeared the Depression was ending, Avery started building new stores in downtown areas, and Wood followed suit.

For a while it appeared the old rivalry for top spot in the industry had resumed, but it did not last for long. War was approaching, and

Avery realized expansion would not be possible or even desirable in the kind of economy this would bring. Avery believed the war would take the nation out of the economic doldrums, as it had during the Great War of the previous generation, but the demands of the military meant peacetime goods would not be produced. Furthermore, when the war ended there would be massive dislocation and a return to the Depression atmosphere of the 1930s. This had been the reaction after the Great War, and Avery saw no reason why this should not be so this time. With this in mind Avery generated a strategy for the postwar period, when he hoped to surpass Sears, not by expanding, but by retrenching. Montgomery Ward stopped opening stores in 1941.

Avery was a difficult man to get along with and had few friends. He was an unreconstructed reactionary in many things, hating government and inveighing against the income tax. His actions caused Montgomery Ward to be fined $35,000 for violations of National Recovery Administration codes. Avery refused to pay the fine, and because of this the Montgomery Ward stores were denied the right to display the NRA Blue Eagle. In 1944, with the nation at war, he refused to renew a union contract and continued to do so even when countermanded by the War Labor Board. President Roosevelt ordered the company seized, and a defiant, scowling Avery was carried out the door by soldiers. A photograph of this event, captured by a *Life* magazine photographer, was anchored in the national imagination.

Avery's stubbornness and disinclination to listen to the views of others were to result in the resignations of four presidents and 30 vice presidents, several of whom went to work at Sears. It got worse as he aged. Associates cringed when he entered the room.

Montgomery Ward came out of World War II in superb financial condition, and Avery meant it to stay that way. Having learned the lessons of prudence in 1921 and then again in 1931, he was prepared to await that anticipated economic slowdown before undertaking expansion. In his 1945 message to shareholders, Avery predicted that massive unemployment and deflation would accompany the end of the war. He assured them that Montgomery Ward would weather the coming economic storm.

There was no new economic crisis. Although postwar government purchases declined by a sum equal to one quarter of the GNP, this did not cause a return to the Depression levels. There was unemployment, as the military released its personnel into the work-force. In 1944 there had been 670,000 reported unemployed workers, which rose to slightly more than one million in 1945 and then leaped to 2.3 million in 1946. The figure kept rising, peaking at 3.6 million in 1949 before declining. But economic experts had anticipated 8–9 million would be out of work, and this dire prediction proved far off the mark.

The reasonably harmonious economic conversion resulted from a postwar outburst of demand, which led to inflation as wartime wage-and-price controls were lightened and consumers rushed to purchase those goods they had gone without during the Depression and war, paying for them with savings from their wartime jobs. Avery took note of this, but assured reporters and others this was a bubble that would be followed, he thought, by a crash.

Where had he gotten such ideas? Avery learned of the work of Geoffrey Moore, a distinguished business-cycle theorist, who noted startling similarities between credit growth in the 1920s and what occurred in the post-World War II period. Moore pointed this expansion of credit purchases and mortgage loans, leading him to conclude a bust was in the making. His writings reenforced Avery's proclivities toward fiscal conservatism. Avery kept charts and statistics on his desk going back to the Napoleonic Wars, prepared to show and explain them to any and all. After doing so he would invariably ask, "Who am I to argue with history?"

Refusing to recognize signs of prosperity in the economy, Avery accelerated his hoarding of capital, starving operations. Meanwhile, Wood had set out on what he called "the biggest gamble of my career." From 1945 to 1954, as Avery added to his pile of cash and securities, Sears invested $300 million in more than 100 new stores and support systems. By 1954 Montgomery Ward had cut its number of stores to 568, from the 628 in 1946, and hadn't opened a new one in 14 years. The company's large paint factory, its fence factory, warehouses, and other minor operations were deprived of capital needed for expansion. At the end of World War II Montgomery Ward's sales were 58 percent those of Sears; by 1954 they were less than 29 percent.

Though there was to be no depression, Montgomery Ward's performance was outstanding during the immediate postwar period. This was not the result of Avery's strategy, however. Rather, the company's prosperity was due to that explosion of consumer spending, which impacted on all retailers. Without increasing the number of its stores, Montgomery Ward's revenues expanded, rising from $974 million in 1946 to $1.2 billion in 1948, while earnings advanced from $42.2 million, or $6.30 a share, to $68.2 million, which came to $10.28 per share. Even so, the price of Montgomery Ward common fell by close to half. In the same period Sears's earnings went from $4.18 to $5.70 per share, while the common traded in a narrow range in the 50s. The investing public clearly preferred Wood's approach to that of Avery's.

By 1948 some of the Montgomery Ward executives spoke guardedly of the need for the 74-year-old Avery to retire. This came at a time when Montgomery Ward had been swept by departures; there had been 12 vice presidential resignations in the previous year. President Wilbur Norton and eight vice presidents told Avery and the board that unless they were given greater responsibilities—at least those their titles indicated they should have—all would resign. Avery responded by firing them. Those directors who supported the insurgents were also dismissed, as Avery cut the board by three. With this, the two Morgan partners on the board, Henry Davison and George Whitney, submitted their resignations. The revolt at Montgomery Ward spread to U.S. Gypsum. That company's president, William Kreader, resigned, obliging Avery to take over day-to-day management for a while. There followed more departures at Montgomery Ward. For a while it seemed the company was stocking America's executive suites. Frank Folsom left for the presidency of Radio Corporation of America, and Walter Baumhogger became president of United Cigar. More of the Montgomery Ward alumni went to its direct and indirect competitors. Walter Hoving went from Montgomery Ward to Tiffany. Retailer W. T. Grant made Raymond Fogler its president. Henry Johnson went to Spiegel.

Meanwhile, challenges were appearing hot and heavy. Discount operations such as E. J. Korvette were making their marks, and both Sears and Montgomery Ward had to slash prices to remain competitive. Suburbia was becoming the new center of American life; Sears responded by erecting stores there, while Montgomery Ward proceeded cautiously.

In his single-minded quest for liquidity, Avery even refused to take advantage of federal laws to minimize taxes. From 1946 to 1953,

Montgomery Ward paid $357.6 million in income and excess-profits taxes. Had Avery established a profit-sharing and employee-pension plan these would have slashed this figure considerably, while enhancing employee morale and loyalty. Avery always had been penurious, so this failure to act came as no surprise. An executive once noted the CEO's name was S. L. Avery, and slavery was what life there was like.

It had become apparent to those who worked with him that Avery had lost his sense of reality. In 1953 some of the firm's directors tried to maneuver him into retirement. When this failed, they talked of a merger with Allied Stores, with Avery kicked upstairs to become "honorary chairman." The news was bruited around the industry and gave further credence to talk that something portentous was afoot at Montgomery Ward; the stock started to stir. Wall Street had concluded Avery had become a liability. When in 1954 he entered the hospital for an operation, Montgomery Ward common rose by five points, only to collapse when he was released.

By then the decline had begun. In 1955 revenues had dwindled to $970 million and earnings to $35.4 million, or $5.22 per share, most of which went into the bank. In 1949 cash and securities had amounted to $87 million; in 1955 it was more than $320 million, the largest liquid position of any American corporation. Current assets that year were $690 million against current liabilities of only $82 million, for an extraordinary ratio of 8:37 to 1 (in 1949 the ratio had been 4.87 to 1), and the percentage of current assets represented by cash and securities went from 17 to 47. In the decade following the end of World War II, Sears's sales had doubled, while Montgomery Ward's were down by 10 percent, this in the midst of a consumer-driven boom Avery tried to brush aside. Montgomery Ward was being called "the bank with the department-store front," and there was talk of a "significant development" coming out of the Chicago headquarters.

That was not a merger or acquisition, but instead a hostile takeover bid, a singular development in this period. Indeed, so unusual was the struggle that it easily qualified as the business story of the year, which in 1955 caused the price of Montgomery Ward's stock to rise spectacularly in the face of sluggish performance. The "raider," to use a term that was to be familiar to business writers of the 1980s, was Louis Wolfson, the most flamboyant businessperson of the mid-1950s.

The son of an immigrant junk man, the darkly handsome Wolfson had amassed his fortune by purchasing surplus shipyards and other properties at distress prices, selling off portions, using his profits to purchase other similarly underpriced assets and repeating the operation. He was a precursor of the raiders of the 1980s, though he operated on a smaller scale.

In 1954, Wolfson was CEO of Merritt-Chapman-Scott, a major shipbuilder, and Capital Transit, which operated the Washington, D.C., transportation system. He also had a collection of other, smaller interests that had one thing in common: They had been purchased at discounted prices and then turned around. Wolfson by then had targeted Montgomery Ward, which he hoped to take over in a proxy contest and to unlock the assets Avery had permitted to dwindle.

When the Montgomery Ward battle was a memory, Wolfson wrote an article on what to look for in a company to be acquired. In it he sketched the characteristics of takeover candidates that fit Montgomery Ward quite well:

> The business sought should have a larger profit potential than appears on the surface. To determine whether this is so, ask these questions:
>
> Is the company owned by elderly persons who are close to retiring and who have not been able to pour sufficient vigor into the enterprise?
>
> Are the owners ultraconservative, hoarding their profits and thus bottling up needed expansion?
>
> Are sales and production methods obsolete?
>
> Does the present management siphon off too much of the profits for personal use?
>
> In short, do the operators lack the vision, imagination, or energy needed to bring the business up to its highest possible level?
>
> Throughout the country there are many firms which fit this description. Sometimes they are found on the edges of a town, fabricating specialized articles. Progress has passed them by. They are doing business in old-fashioned ways and keeping afloat by serving a few, old faithful customers. New blood, new ideas, can do a great deal with them.

Then the would-be acquirer has to answer another set of questions. Can the product be repackaged? Does it perform a service that can be improved? If all can be answered in the affirmative, "you have found your business."

For Wolfson, that company was Montgomery Ward.

In early 1954 Wolfson and his associates gathered information about Montgomery Ward and its competitors. They pored over documents, analyzed balance sheets, and held frequent discussions. The more they looked, the more attractive Montgomery Ward appeared and the more likely it seemed a raid would succeed. Whatever happened—even if he did not gain control—the figures indicated Wolfson couldn't lose.

When he started accumulating shares, Montgomery Ward common was selling in the high 40s, having fallen to that level from the 1946 peak of 104. The stock's average ratio of price to earnings (P/E) the previous year had been less than 10, indicating just how out of favor the shares had become. The company had $50 a share in cash and securities alone. Armed with this knowledge, Wolfson started buying. By September he had more than 200,000 Montgomery Ward shares and claimed to be the company's largest shareholder.

Central to the Wolfson campaign were assertions that Avery had permitted Montgomery Ward to stagnate while other retailers expanded vigorously and successfully. Wolfson noted that although the Pacific Coast states were among the fastest growing in the country, Montgomery Ward closed 5 stores there, while Sears Roebuck opened 17. "Twelve years ago, Montgomery Ward had 18 percent of the business done by the top ten companies," he remarked. "Now its share is 11 percent." Moreover, if Avery and his associates truly believed they were doing so fine a job, how could they explain the fact that management owned very few shares in the company?

If he won the contest, Wolfson would require the president to purchase 10,000 shares at market value and each of the five executive vice presidents 5,000 shares, paying with 10 percent down and the rest out of dividends that would repay interest-free loans made to them by the company. In effect, Wolfson wanted managers to be owners.

Wolfson put forth a ten-point program to demonstrate how he would use part of the Montgomery Ward cash hoard. He pledged to offer shareholders the right to tender 2 million shares at book value, which worked out to around $93 a share, 12 points higher than the stock stood in late February, when he mailed his proxy material. Wolfson further pledged that he, his family, and the 13 members of the "Wolfson-Montgomery Ward Stockholders Committee," which he led, would not tender any of their shares. He maintained this would have the immediate effect of boosting per-share earnings. Wolfson realized that even if he lost, management might be forced to carry out parts of the program, or do something else to bolster shareholder values.

Wolfson also would split the stock three-for-one and boost the dividend. He intended to institute a profit-sharing bonus plan for the employees, but not until stockholders achieved a 6 percent return. As had been the case at his shipyards, there would be a large bonus for managers and smaller ones for salespeople with outstanding records. Montgomery Ward would increase its advertising and concentrate on the construction and acquisition of factories to manufacture goods for sale in the stores.

Management criticized the plan. They noted that on the one hand Wolfson was promising to distribute a large part of the cash in the Montgomery Ward treasury to shareholders, and on the other he planned a large-scale construction program. This seemed contradictory and harmed Wolfson's plausibility.

Possibly seeking to counter this, Wolfson presented an ingenious program for restructuring Montgomery Ward. He would organize a separate company, initially capitalized at $50 million, to which would be transferred Montgomery Ward's fixed assets plus $18 million in cash. Shares of this new company would be distributed on a pro rata basis to Montgomery Ward's shareholders, who now would own two certificates, one in the operating company, the other in the real-estate firm. The latter, which had the hard assets, would be permitted to borrow up to $200 million, to help finance his program of construction and renovation. Wolfson expected to open no fewer than 24 new stores in his first year. Existing stores would be modernized, and like those of competitors, would be air-conditioned. This plan had to be abandoned, however, when it was learned it would have adverse tax consequences for shareholders.

Montgomery Ward common rose immediately after Wolfson made his announcement, and by December was close to 80. The reason was evident. Speculators purchased shares in the expectation they would rise during the struggle for control, after which they would sell. This often happened in such circumstances and didn't necessarily aid one side or the other.

Apparently out of fear Wolfson might actually succeed, Montgomery Ward took account of some of his recommendations. Avery raised the quarterly dividend from 50 cents to 75 cents and declared a year-end extra payout of $1.75. Some of the stores received their first coats of paint in years. The board seemed to be saying that Wolfson was correct in charging disregard of shareholders' interests, but anything he might do for them could be done by current management.

The board tried to keep Avery off the stump, assigning the role of company spokesmen to President Edmund A. Krider and Vice President for Finance and Secretary John Barr, who met with Montgomery Ward shareholders, telling them Wolfson was an adventurer who if given a victory would squeeze their company dry. Other CEOs joined in the attack, fearing perhaps that a Wolfson success would encourage raiders like him to take a look at their companies. For his part, Wolfson spoke of fumbles at Montgomery Ward and his ability to uncover values at the company. He took credit for the rise in the price of the stock and promised it would go even higher once he assumed command.

Throughout the contest Montgomery Ward spokesmen talked of Wolfson's lack of experience in department stores. Wolfson acknowledged this, saying he would not take a managerial role at Montgomery Ward, but rather would seek an experienced person to place at the helm, and it soon was rumored he was negotiating with a top Sears executive to take over as chief operating officer when and if he won the proxy contest.

The showdown in the Wolfson-Avery battle took place at the Medinah Temple, a garish Shrine auditorium on Chicago's North Side. Medinah often was the locale for circuses, and the 1955 Montgomery Ward meeting was just that. On Saturday, April 20, two days prior to the meeting, Wolfson sent a telegram to Avery demanding the directors make their annual presentations before the balloting, and not after, as had been traditional. Krider rejected the suggestion and then told reporters that Wolfson's plan to have Montgomery Ward officers purchase shares with interest-free loans constituted a criminal act under Illinois law. "It again reflects his lack of appreciation of legitimate business practices," he said. "Such a deal, if carried through, would likely put Mr. Wolfson and other members of the board in the penitentiary."

The Temple was packed for the meeting. Those who hoped for high drama were not disappointed, for there were several such moments during the three-hour session. The contrast between the two major protagonists was striking. On the one side was the young, glamorous Floridian, who was a liberal Democrat. On the other was the aged conservative Republican. Avery seemed tired and befuddled throughout, flying off on tangents during his replies to barbed questions from the Wolfson forces. He didn't seem to know where he was and instead of facing the audience spoke with his back turned. John Brooks, who later would achieve fame as a business writer, was at the meeting. He described Avery as "a frail old man with snow-white hair and a blue suit, looking vulnerable rather than commanding."

> He mumbled about "when the economic rain arrives"; he was silent for long, agonizing pauses, and sometimes he appeared about to topple over bodily; he snapped back querulous answers to taunts from the floor; and only once, when he spoke of the $700 million, debt-free, that Montgomery Ward had put away in its treasury, did his voice rise to a semblance of strength. When the scene became almost too much to bear, a subordinate [Krider] gently escorted the old man to a seat and took over the meeting himself.

Wolfson was courteous, pulling his punches, perhaps realizing Avery was indicting himself by his actions. Even so, by then Wolfson must have known he didn't have the votes. His slate did receive 31 percent of the ballots, which under the Montgomery Ward bylaws entitled them to three board seats. Wolfson and two lieutenants joined the board. Two other board members indicated they might vote with Wolfson if Avery insisted on remaining at the helm.

Avery had made more than a normal share of blunders since the end of World War II. Now it was the turn of those shareholders who supported him to make their missteps. With Wolfson's proposed changes, Montgomery Ward common would have risen substantially. Absent them, the company would continue to decay.

Several months later *Trends in Management-Stockholder Relations* released an analysis of the votes. The banks were overwhelmingly for management—92 percent of the shares were voted for the Avery group, and only 8 percent for the Wolfson slate. The educational institutions were also for management, with 96 percent of their votes.

More than 73 percent of shares in brokerage accounts went to Wolfson. In this period most small shareholders took actual possession of their securities, so it may be assumed the broker accounts represented those who had made purchases in hope of a Wolfson victory, in which case Montgomery Ward's prospects and the price of its stock would improve. That the number of broker-held shares increased from 500,000 to one million from March of 1954 to March of 1955 would appear to support this conclusion. A surprising 27 percent of the individual shareholders who had possession of their shares came down for Wolfson, a strikingly large number in that period of shareholder loyalty to management. In this regard, at least, Wolfson had a symbolic victory.

Wolfson had the ill fortune to appear on the corporate scene at the wrong time, when opportunities for individuals with his talents, concerns, and viewpoint were uncommon and usually minor. His attempted takeover was of the kind that would appear often in the 1960s and 1980s, but stood out starkly in 1955, when it seemed not only bold and dramatic, but somewhat exotic. His appeal to shareholders was forceful, to be sure, but did not succeed. Wolfson had been unable to persuade small shareholders, who held the balance of power, of his abilities to run what many still considered part of their family. So long as shareholders received their dividend checks and the price of their holdings did not decline significantly they tended to support management—*their* management, as shareholders of the time tended to think. In a later period, when shareholders looked upon their stock as a means of obtaining dividends and especially capital gains, the result might have been different.

Wolfson attempted to win Montgomery Ward without the aid of a major Wall Street bank. This, too, was not unusual in this period. Banks didn't get into the messy work of raids at that time. In 1955 no bank would have extended financing for such an undertaking.

Try to imagine what a bank officer would have thought when Wolfson sketched the true value of Montgomery Ward, suggesting there would be a successful tender at, say, 60 for the 6.5 million shares, coming to $390 million or so. Wolfson could then have pointed to the $320 million in cash and equivalents in the treasury. The banker might have reflected that once in control, Wolfson expected to sell $500 million or so in bonds, which would be low-rated by Moody's and Standard & Poor's. Given the mind set of the period those commercial bankers probably would have been aghast at such a proposition. Even if the loan were granted, who would buy such bonds? Certainly not the institutions or the conservative mutual funds or even individuals with deep pockets. The deal would not have flown.

Attempting to make the best of the situation, a subdued Lou Wolfson told reporters wanting to know what would happen next that "The Avery tea party is over." He planned to attend every board meeting and make his own reports to the shareholders. Moreover, he said that he intended to renew the struggle in 1956. Both Avery and Krider resigned soon after, the news causing the price of Montgomery Ward's stock to rise five points.

With only a few seasoned hands at headquarters, the board turned the company over to John Barr, who had no experience in retailing, even though he had been with the company for more than 20 years. He did as good a job as might have been expected. Barr started by bringing in new management, some of whom had been dismissed by Avery, and others from Sears Roebuck, to whom he gave broad authority. Morgan's John Davison returned to the board. Barr closed unprofitable stores and started a refurbishing program for the others, using part of the cash hoard accumulated by Avery. He moved aggressively into the suburbs, paying much higher prices for land and construction than had Sears when it went there a decade earlier. Montgomery Ward common was split two for one, and the dividend increased. Barr strove mightily to turn Montgomery Ward around. Wolfson recognized this and attended the next shareholders' meeting to say as much. In retrospect it can be seen that Montgomery Ward had little chance of regaining the momentum it had generated under Avery during the Depression and had lost when it retrenched after World War II and lost its key personnel.

Even so, in spite of the better performance and positive news stories, absent the proxy fight the price of Montgomery Ward shares fell. So did earnings, which never again reached their 1953 level. In 1958 the company earned $2.08 per share, less than the $2.25 dividend, and the stock sold for as low as 28 before turning around, due largely to Barr's successes. Revenues that year were $1.1 billion, against Sears's $3.6 billion. J. C. Penney, with sales of $1.4 billion, had edged past Montgomery Ward and now was the nation's second largest retailer.

Barr proclaimed his intention to regain the number-two slot and continued building stores. "Once lethargic Montgomery Ward has embarked on an ambitious expansion program which envisions a substantial increase in sales and earnings," wrote *Forbes* in 1959. True, in Barr's three years at the helm revenues had increased by close to $200 million, but had achieved this result by spending $160 million, and net income was down to $30.6 million.

The company was in trouble. Barr still lacked the kind of personnel that directed Sears and Penney. Like Gene Ferkauf would a few years later, though in a quite different circumstances, Barr sought talent through merger. There was talk of one with Interstate Department Stores, whose galaxy included White Front and Topps and was doing well in discounting. In 1959 Interstate had revenues of only $90 million and earnings of $1.4 million. The thought was that Interstate's Sol Cantor would become vice president of the new company and would, in a couple of years, succeed Barr. The union did not take place. Instead, in 1961, Tom Brooker, an engineer and production man, became president, and four years later took over as chairman as well.

Brooker was considered a fine manufacturing hand, but did not have experience in retailing. What he did have was the support of a group that had purchased $1 million worth of Montgomery Ward common. By then Montgomery Ward's cash position was down to $31 million. Recall that in 1955 Montgomery Ward had $320 million in cash. Debt-free during the Avery years, Montgomery Ward now had to consider floating a large bond issue in order to continue its expansion program.

The company, which once had had a strong identity, was by the late 1960s seemingly without a real mission. In 1966 it purchased Pioneer Trust & Savings, a smallish unit, for reasons no one seemed able to explain. That year Montgomery Ward had revenues of $1.9 million and earnings of $16.5 million, the latter less than half of what they had been in 1956. The following year Brooker made an even stranger purchase,

Hydro Conduit Co., a minor force in the concrete water-pipe business, which had revenues of $20 million. Then there was the formation of the Montgomery Ward Life Insurance Co., perhaps in the hope that it might perform in insurance as Allstate did for Sears Roebuck.

This was the age of the conglomerateur, and several of them cast their eyes on Montgomery Ward. As it had been when Wolfson had eyed the company in 1954, given the price of the stock, the company might easily be taken over and then, if no recovery took place, carved up as Jimmy Ling had done with his properties and sold off piecemeal, or offered to another retailer as a merger possibility. One thing appeared fairly certain: Montgomery Ward either would die a lingering death, as was to be the case with E. J. Korvette, or would disappear in some other fashion.

Brooker must have recognized this, because he started casting about for a merger. Rumors flew, and in 1967 discussions began between the Montgomery Ward team and one from Container Corporation of America.

The thought of a union of a mail-order department-store retailer with revenues of $1.9 billion and earnings of $17 million and the largest cardboard container company in the world whose sales were $463 million and whose earnings were $33 million did not raise eyebrows. If Ling could unite a meatpacker with a steel company and an electronics operation, why couldn't Brooker entertain notions of a meeting of minds with Leo Schoenhofen of Container Corp.? He might even have talked of synergies, that magic word of mergers: Container's boxes could be used to pack Montgomery Ward's merchandise.

This merger, however, resulted more from the vagaries of the federal tax code than from hopes for a good business fit. Like all department stores, Montgomery Ward offered installment-credit sales, and because of this was able to defer tax payments on earnings for several years, or until the payments were actually made. As a result it could shelter some of Container Corp.'s earnings. So the merger took place. Brooker would become chairman, but Schoenhofen would be chief operating officer and would succeed to the chairmanship in two years. From the first it was clear that Schoenhofen would be the dominant figure at what was to be called Marcor and that Container Corp.'s capital needs would take precedence over those of Montgomery Ward.

Even so, the recovery continued at the stores. By 1972 both ends of Marcor were doing well, which led to the next transformation. The Organization of Petroleum Exporting Countries boosted the price of oil in 1973, leading to higher profits for those companies with large reserves, but also to uncertainty as to what might happen next. This prompted the oil giants to search for diversification. At Mobil this took the form of a 5 percent investment in Marcor, and later in the year came a purchase of another 51 percent of the shares. In an over-heating economy, Marcor looked quite attractive, so in 1976 Mobil purchased the rest of the company.

Montgomery Ward received a large cash infusion from Mobil, which did little good. It had become even more of a cyclical company than earlier, clearly behind the times, as other retailers displaced it. The stores seemed dowdy, as though out of another era. In the mid-1980s the company tried to redesign itself as a collection of specialty shops, "The Seven Worlds of Ward," which included the likes of Rooms & More, Home Ideas, Gold 'N' Gems, Auto Express, and Electric Avenue, and this led to a short-lived revival. That year too, Montgomery Ward dis-continued its catalog operation. By then Mobil was searching for a way out, having forgiven $500 million of the loans to its ailing subsidiary.

This was the heyday of the hostile takeover, as investment banks, led by Drexel Burnham Lambert, were providing billions of dollars to takeover artists on the prowl for bloated properties and managements wanting to affect leveraged buyouts. In 1988 Montgomery Ward's management availed itself of such a device, and with Mobil's enthusi-astic support engineered a $3.8 billion LBO, with the participation of General Electric Capital, which received half the ownership for $180 million. Thus, Montgomery Ward became privately owned with an immense debt.

It was the season for such activities. In 1986 Canadian real-estate developer Robert Campeau had acquired Allied Stores for $4.1 billion. While Campeau had some trouble putting the deal together, in the end the money was there. Less than two years later he purchased Fed-erated Department Stores for $6.8 billion. All of this was made possi-ble through junk-bond financing. In the light of such deals, the Montgomery Ward LBO did not appear so immense.

Shortly after taking over at Federated, Campeau filed for bank-ruptcy. The Montgomery Ward people did better. GE Capital infused additional funds into Montgomery Ward, which according to whom one believed, came to somewhere between $300 million and $900 million.

In early summer 1997 Montgomery Ward's suppliers started complaining about late payments of bills. The company was in dire financial straits. Montgomery Ward filed for Chapter 11 bankruptcy protection on July 7, 1997. In making the announcement, Montgomery Ward said it had lost $249 million the previous year. CEO Roger Gaddu tried to put up a brave front. "Although a Chapter 11 bankruptcy filing was not our desired course of action, we believe that with the cooperation of our vendors and our associates, it will allow us to concentrate on implementing our merchandising strategy and emerge as a healthier and more contemporary retailer." There wasn't much of a chance for this to happen.

The company was all but finished. Industry analyst Kurt Barnard thought salvage impossible. "Ward has lost its reason for being."

What might have saved Montgomery Ward? Had Sewell Avery been correct in his projections of a post-World War II depression and had then followed through with his strategy to expand, the company might have pushed passed the debt-laden Sears Roebuck and survived. Had Louis Wolfson been able to take over and implement his program, the same might have occurred. Had the rumored merger with Sears Roebuck gone through, Montgomery Ward would have disappeared into the larger and more successful company. There are many more "ifs" in the Montgomery Ward story, but there also is the matter of the mortality of retailing operations. This is a harsh and demanding industry. Sears itself, once considered the premier company in the field, went through a rough patch in the 1980s and even now is struggling. The Department Store Hall of Fame has, among its members, Frank Woolworth, A. T. Stewart, and Adam Gimbel, and for a while, Gene Ferkauf. None of their stores exist today. Sebastian Kresge is a member; his S. S. Kresge, as noted, is no longer a true department-store chain. Rowland Macy is a member; Macy's underwent a humiliating bankruptcy. True enough, Avery and the others blundered, but in retailing, which is so unforgiving, perhaps criticism has to be tempered with compassion.

CHAPTER THIRTEEN

AMERICAN TOBACCO: THE BLUNDER OF STANDING PAT

T wo of the iconic phrases of the 1920s were "What will they think of next?" and "New and improved." The former was an almost reflexive reaction to the flood of consumer goods, from electric irons to radios to celluloid collars, that came to market during that decade. The latter also referred to those products, the thought being that progress was foreseeable and inevitable. Whatever was new, be it next year's car, refrigerator, or fountain pen, was bound to be better than this year's model. Ever since then—and even before, for that matter—merchandisers who ignored these concepts often suffered loss of sales and market share.

This is not to suggest that change and novelty for its own sake necessarily brings success. As Schlitz learned to its sorrow, there are products that consumers cling to, and they will resent any attempts to meddle with a successful formula. The same holds true for other drinks—Coca-Cola comes to mind—and foodstuffs. Producers tread carefully when altering the components and images of such products. Not so, however, for most other products and services.

Two of the most often told stories around IBM deal with Tom Watson, Jr.'s, attempt to win over his father to computers that would replace the IBM calculators, and his subsequent "bet-the-company" decision to go ahead with the 360 family of computers that would replace many computers then in use. In both cases Watson, Jr., was willing to engage in Schumpetersque "creative destruction," and in both cases the gamble paid off. Had they not, there might not be an IBM to consider today, and Watson would be a footnote in business history. Moreover, were it not for the strengths of the company he had created, IBM might not have been able to salvage as much as it did when Watson's successors erred initially in their approach to personal computers, stumbling badly before redeeming a measure of success as it attempted to remake itself.

One such failure by a major company was the inability of American Tobacco in the 1950s to recognize that changes were taking place in cigarette demand. Like Watson, Sr., the executives there thought their Pall Mall, the leader in king sized cigarettes, the dominant category at the time, could not be dislodged, and they rejected suggestions that might have affected that brand. In a way their refusal to change was understandable. The cigarette executives had been reared in an atmosphere of brand loyalty, which they also thought would continue. As it happened, they were wrong, and the signs were there to be seen and acted upon. Like Sewell Avery at Montgomery Ward, American Tobacco's executives refused to recognize that their old beliefs had been overcome by events.

The dominance today in cigarettes of king-sized and filter brands, and especially the combination, king-sized filters, has been the result of a large-scale anticigarette campaign, which continues to this day. There was nothing new about this. A century ago, as cigarettes came to the fore as the preferred tobacco product, opposition to them intensified. The key figure in the anticigarette crusade of that period was Lucy Page Gaston, who had been raised in an abolitionist family and had previously been active in the temperance movement. Gaston was convinced that the inhalation of cigarette tobacco smoke could be lethal due to the presence in it of furfural, which she said was produced by the burning of the glycerine in the cured tobacco. She thought smoking also altered physical development, causing what she called "cigarette face," and claimed she could always spot a habitual cigarette smoker.

In 1899 Gaston established the Chicago Anti-Cigarette League, and branches were organized for other cities. The League and similar organizations opened clinics to which smokers could repair for cures. Dr. D. H. Kress, the League's general secretary, patented a mouthwash containing a weak solution of silver nitrate, the use of which, he claimed, combined with warm baths and a bland diet, would cure all craving for cigarettes. There were other specifics, including No-to-bac, which was supposed to end the desire for all forms of tobacco. Its motto: "Don't tobacco-spit your life away."

Anticigarette lobbying in Washington was effective. In 1897, in an amendment to the Dingley Tariff, the federal government forbade the use of coupons, cards, and other inducements for smoking in tobacco packages. The following year the government increased the cigarette tax from 50 cents per thousand to $1 per thousand.

The crusade was a qualified success with the public. Cigarette production peaked at 4.9 billion units in 1897 and then started to decline. By 1901 fewer than 3.5 billion were being smoked. By then a flood of anticigarette statutes were passed in the states and localities. New Hampshire had strict legislation, in 1901 making it illegal to manufacture, sell, or smoke cigarettes, and Illinois followed suit in 1907. By 1909 Iowa, North Dakota, Tennessee, Arkansas, Indiana, Kansas, Minnesota, Nebraska, Oklahoma, South Dakota, and Wisconsin had laws prohibiting or limiting the use of cigarettes. New York State prohibited public smoking by anyone under the age of 16. In time anticigarette laws were passed in every state except Wyoming and Louisiana. Many cities also passed statutes against cigarettes. In 1908 New York City's Sullivan Ordnance prohibited women from smoking in public, and other municipalities followed. Generally speaking, however, in this period anticigarette sentiment was strongest in the Midwest, had some vigor in the Far West, and was weakest in the East.

The industry retaliated. One way was to advertise "the fixings," meaning smoking tobacco and cigarette paper. In those states where the sale of cigarettes was illegal but the actual smoking was permitted, the companies would suggest merchants give them away and charge the price for matches instead. And of course there was an amount of cigarette bootlegging into states that banned them.

Prominent public figures came forth with their observations. David Starr Jordan, chancellor of Stanford University, thought "Boys who smoke cigarettes are like wormy apples that fall from the tree before they are ripe." Jordan later asserted "The boy who smokes cigarettes need not be anxious about his future. He has none." Similar expressions were heard from other anticigarette crusaders. Elinor Glyn, the author of several steamy novels, thought smoking robbed people of their virility. "Every smoke is a tiny drop of old age, so small that for a long time it is unnoticed." Others were attracted to the campaign, including such luminaries as Thomas Alvah Edison and Henry

Ford. Scientists testified as to the harm. Gaston importuned railroads to ban the smoking of cigarettes, and some did. The campaign was effective. Cigarette smoking declined.

While the fight against the cigarette was spearheaded by social reformers such as these, others who hoped to cripple the industry had a different motivation. Allied with the anticigarette forces was a combination of progressive reformers who saw in the industry's domination by a single entity a combination in restraint of trade that had to be smashed. The "Tobacco Trust," a creation of James Buchanan "Buck" Duke, consisted of two large companies, American Tobacco and Continental Tobacco, under an umbrella company, Consolidated Tobacco. The trust not only dominated the American market, but shipped more than a billion cigarettes annually overseas. The empire underwent many changes, and toward the end of its existence was once again known as American Tobacco.

In 1911 the reformers succeeded in destroying the Trust, which was superseded by four large enterprises: Liggett & Myers, American, Lorillard, and Reynolds. L&M received a third of the chewing-tobacco businesses and close to half that in snuff. In cigarettes it had Fatima, American Beauty, Home Run, and several others. American would lead in cigarettes, with such brands as Pall Mall, Sweet Caporal, and Mecca, none of which had national distribution, however, since in this period no cigarette had achieved such status. American also had a strong position in pipe tobaccos. Lorillard was a balanced firm, whose major stake was in cigars, and that was second to American in pipe tobaccos. Its cigarettes had a foreign tinge—Turkish Trophies, Murad, Helmar, and the like, that were favored by esthetes in large eastern cities.

Richard J. Reynolds received no cigarette brands, instead was given positions in chewing and pipe tobaccos, including the nation's leading brand, Prince Albert. His R. J. Reynolds was the smallest of the four, but he was not complaining. Reynolds had an abiding hatred of Buck Duke, who had cobbled together the old trust and now headed American Tobacco. Reynolds considered independence more important than size. All he had was two small factories, what seemed a mountain of debt, and a determination to smash Duke.

At the time the received wisdom in cigarettes was that brand proliferation was the way to go. The thought that a single brand appealing across the boards to all kinds of Americans in all parts of the country seemed audacious. Such was the way with chewing tobacco, cigars, and other forms of tobacco. Why should it be different with cigarettes? Duke had a wide variety of cigarettes in the days of the trust, from economy brands selling for 5 cents for a pack of 20, to upscale smokes at 15 cents, and some exotic brands that went for 20 and 25 cents.

Whether or not Reynolds thought to put all of his money on a single brand or did so because he lacked the wherewithal to have many is unknown, although after the fact he would claim that had been his plan from the first. In any case, he had plenty of competition, for in the aftermath of the breakup all the companies came out with new brands.

After several false starts, Reynolds hit upon the idea of naming a cigarette for an animal. There was a small independent company that had a brand called Red Kamel, which had been discontinued. For $300 he purchased the name and set about creating the cigarette he planned to call Camel. Some of the cigarettes of this period came with cards and other extras geared to winning customers. There would be no prizes or cards with Camel. On the back of the pack were the words, "Don't look for premiums or coupons, as the cost of the tobaccos blended in CAMEL Cigarettes prohibits the use of them." To help publicize the brand, Reynolds purchased a camel, which was called "Old Joe." He was not used for long, but of course resurfaced in a different configuration in 1988. As for the tobacco, Camels were made of Carolina bright, a highly flavored white burley, to which was added some Virginia leaf and a touch of Latakia. It looked and tasted like a 20-cent brand, but Reynolds decided to charge 10 cents and go for the larger market.

In 1914 Reynolds earmarked $1.3 million for advertising and promotion, with most of this going for Camel. The effort worked. That year Camel became one of the nation's best-selling brands, with 3 percent of the market. Now Reynolds spent even more on advertising. At the end of 1915 Camel was available nationally, with a 13 percent market share. The following year Reynolds outsold L&M and became the nation's second-largest tobacco company. By 1918 more than one out of every three American cigarettes was a Camel. Dick Reynolds died that year, knowing he had bested Buck Duke. More important, perhaps, he had obliged the other cigarette companies to rethink their strategies.

American Tobacco resurrected the name of a pipe tobacco that was supposed to recollect the California gold rush and came up with Lucky Strike as its entry in the national race. L&M already had Chesterfields and now concentrated its attention on that brand. Lorillard held back and didn't come out with Old Gold until 1926. Philip Morris, which had not been a member of the trust, was represented by Philip Morris. Brown & Williamson, a subsidiary of British American Tobacco, offered Raleigh.

The turnabout in cigarette sales began with the introduction of Camel, but America's entry into World War I marked the real end of the drop, as the country's leaders actually encouraged soldiers to smoke. In a rush of patriotic zeal, the YMCA distributed free cigarettes to soldiers and sailors, who before the war had been deterred by their officers from smoking. Servicemen didn't have to be encouraged to smoke. The tensions of war had always fostered smoking and drinking, and this conflict was no exception.

The former servicemen continued to smoke after the war, and during the 1920s the practice caught on with women and was taken as a sign of sophistication and liberation. During the Great Depression smoking was considered an inexpensive method to deal with despair. The fact that so many motion pictures presented smokers as heroes—and villains—added an impetus to smoking. From 1917 to 1949, cigarette sales increased from 10 billion units to 393 billion, and per capita consumption rose 20-fold. This was the highest growth rate for any industry in this period.

Health issues continued to be discussed, but so long as nothing conclusive had been proven, and smokers liked what they were getting, there appeared no reason for the manufacturers to make changes. The Big Three companies—American, Reynolds, and L&M—turned out their Lucky Strikes, Camels, and Chesterfields, while the smaller ones, including Lorillard, Philip Morris, and Brown & Williamson trailed the leaders. At a time of brand loyalty when switching was uncommon, it seemed these three cigarettes, which by 1925 accounted for more than 80 percent of sales, were destined to dominate the mass market. By 1941 the figure had fallen to slightly less than 70 percent, but Chesterfield, then in third place with 37.5 billion units, was far ahead of the fourth-largest seller, Philip Morris, at 17.5 billion. In all, Reynolds had a 32.7 percent market share, American a 25.6 percent share, and L&M a 10.7 percent share.

As they had during World War I, cigarette sales increased in World War II. Shortages in the civilian market were chronic in this period, as manufacturers couldn't keep up with demand. Sales increased 66 percent during the wartime years of 1940–1945, and while slowing down after peace returned, rose by 12 percent from 1945 to 1950.

Smoking continued to expand in 1953, but then the industry hit a brick wall, placed there by the revival of the anticigarette movement. This crusade, which is now close to half a century old and is still intense, usually is dated to a 1952 *Reader's Digest* article, "Cancer by the Carton." It was a powerful indictment, claiming that smoking caused lung cancer. Over the years the magazine had published more than a dozen articles on the same subject, but this one hit home. The industry responded by noting the article hadn't mentioned that the previous year fewer than 20,000 deaths in America had been attributed to lung cancer, 1.3 percent of all deaths and 9.2 percent of cancer deaths. Moreover, tobacco spokesmen asserted that the linkage was purely statistical in nature and that correlation did not prove causation.

Some students of the anticigarette crusade argue that more important than the article and others that followed, was the 1964 surgeon general's report, which asserted there was a link between cigarette smoking and lung cancer in men. But the impact on sales started in 1953, when there was a 2 percent decline, attributed to health fears. This was the first falloff in two decades. Herbert Brean's book, *How to Stop Smoking*, published by a vanity press in 1951 when it had virtually no sales, became a best-seller, and before it was remaindered more than 500,000 copies were sold, most in a new paperback edition. In mid-1955 the government claimed that in the past year and a half, more than 1.5 million Americans had stopped smoking. Then sales rose 15 percent in the next five-year segment, as the health fears subsided.

One reason for this sales increase was the doubts some studies threw on the cigarette-cancer link. *Consumer Reports* printed several articles on the subject. In early 1955 the magazine stated there were clear associations with such ailments as vascular disorders of the extremities and of the eyes, and that smoking caused peptic ulcers. "As for cancer of the lung, the most reasonable view at this time relates its phenomenal and alarming rise in frequency in industrial countries partly to the diffusion into the air of carcinogens derived from industry and transportation, partly to unusual exposures to carcinogens in many occupations, and partly to excessive cigarette smoking."

Another, even more important factor, was the cigarette companies' apparently successful response to the health challenge. Increasingly they turned to products the public wanted because it seemed reasonable that they were safer than the old Big Three brands: king-sized and filtered smokes, and to a lesser extent, mentholated brands.

Pall Mall, the biggest winner in the king-sized category, had been around since before the turn of the century, as an all-Turkish tobacco cigarette. As noted, when the Tobacco Trust was dissolved, it was assigned to American Tobacco. George Washington Hill, on his way to becoming the industry's dominant figure, had his first success as brand manager for Pall Mall, which he took to leadership in the upscale market. In 1936 Hill, who by then headed the company, was still enamored with the brand. He reformulated the mixture, replacing most of the Turkish leaf with flavored white burley, this to make it an "American" cigarette. Hill took Pall Mall out of its cardboard box, put the cigarettes in a classy carmine-red soft package, and most important, extended its length from 70 mm to 85 mm. Paul Hahn, who was Hill's heir apparent, was given the brand with orders to make it the nation's best-seller in its premium category. As will be seen, Hahn did better than that.

As the company's Lucky Strike declined, Pall Mall sales rose. Elated, Hill transformed another of his stable of cigarettes, Herbert Tareyton, into a king brand, gave it a new package and an advertising campaign that stressed elegance and quality. For whom? The answer was that Tareyton was supposed to appeal to the purchasers of premium cigarettes. Like Pall Mall, it carried a higher price tag than the standards.

If Pall Mall was geared to be the Cadillac of the American Tobacco line, Tareyton was designed to be its Rolls-Royce. It also was successful, and American now dominated the market for this configuration of cigarettes. Other companies attempted to enter the field, but none could match Pall Mall, which by 1951 was the nation's fifth most popular seller, inching past Old Gold. The following year it would surpass Philip Morris and go to fourth position. By then it was American Tobacco's best seller, doing better than Lucky Strike, and Tareyton was coming up fast. At American Tobacco headquarters it appeared king-sized smokes were the future of cigarettes, and the company had two of the top brands in that category.

The other tobacco companies continued to seek responses to Pall Mall and Tareyton. L&M revived Fatima in a king-sized version with Turkish tobacco, and it did surprisingly well, though clearly it would not become a best-seller. Lorillard's entry was Embassy. Brown & Williamson, which had the nation's leading mentholated brand in Kool, transformed Wings and Avalon into larger smokes, and smallish Larus did the same with Domino and Alligator. Reynolds, which until then had had nothing but Camel, came in with the king-sized Cavalier, which had a strong start but then fizzled.

The popularity of the king-sized brands was such that in 1952 L&M announced that Chesterfield, in third position in sales, would henceforth be available in regular and king sizes. The kings would carry a slightly higher price. In New York, where regular Chesterfields sold for 23 cents, kings were to go for 25 cents.

This brand extension, which was to become familiar, at the time was considered daring. The company tried to play this down, noting that different-sized packages were common for a variety of consumer products, from cereals to drugs. Yet, while it was one thing to revive an old languishing brand in a new configuration, tampering with a successful one was unusual. As it happened, smokers took to the longer Chesterfields, which quickly reached third place in its category behind the two American Tobacco entries. Now the others imitated L&M and also were successful. By early 1954 all the major companies were considering phasing out the regular-sized smokes and switching over to kings, but they held back, for this was considered too radical a step. But it did seem the time of the Big Three brands was over and that diversity, not uniformity, would be the rule within the industry in the future. However, Pall Mall, Tareyton, and Chesterfield kings would never dominate the market as had Camel, Lucky Strike, and Chesterfield a generation earlier.

Why did the kings have such success? Some within the industry attributed it to the fact that they seemed more elegant. Others noted that in the good times that came after World War II smokers didn't mind spending a few cents more for their cigarettes. Surveys indicated that Chesterfield smokers were switching to the kings because they thought longer cigarettes were milder, offered less of a health risk, and were more economical. Of these, the health issue seemed the most plausible. Cigarette manufacturers had often made claims of smoothness for their brands, so they were accustomed to taking this line. They had done so in the past because, as has been seen, health issues had plagued the industry since it began. Now the companies asserted the kings delivered fewer potentially harmful substances. Pall Mall, for example, laid claim to be a "longer and finer and milder smoke." What produced this mildness? The company appeared to be saying it was the greater length, "to travel the smoke further—to make it cooler and sweeter for you." This was so because Pall Mall's "richly flavored tobaccos" were "the finest quality money can buy," and "fine tobacco is its own best filter." American Tobacco continued to trumpet the mildness of Pall Mall and the use of tobacco as a natural filter.

In 1954 *Consumer Reports* wrote that "King-size cigarettes, provided they are smoked no further down than ordinary cigarettes, allow generally less nicotine and tar to enter the smoke than the shorter cigarette." Soon after, however, the magazine changed its mind on this score, and other impartial authorities indicated such was not the case. Additional tests showed that Pall Mall was among the leaders in other areas—tars and nicotine. At a time when it was possible to "program" the amounts of both substances in cigarettes, American refused to do so. The company had a winner, and it intended to stand pat with what it had.

If kings had natural filters, wouldn't artificial ones, designed for that purpose, do even better? There had been some filtered cigarettes before the war, and some had cardboard mouthpieces as well. L&M had Imperials and Obaks, and B&W experimented with Viceroy filters in 1936, but these were considered too exotic and unconventional to win much of a market in the United States.

Benson & Hedges, a specialty tobacco company, had manufactured Parliament and Virginia Rounds since 1931, selling them along with other expensive cigarettes from the company's exclusive Fifth

Avenue store in New York, which had a resplendent doorman and a staff that served tea and cucumber sandwiches to an elite clientele. Virginia Rounds was a cork-tip cigarette, made from the Virginia tobacco preferred by the English, that sold for 25 cents for a package of 20, a super-premium price for the time. Parliament had a blend of Virginia, burley, and Turkish tobaccos and contained a minimum of moistening agents and flavorings. It had a cardboard mouthpiece and a recessed cotton filter and came in a cardboard slide-and-shell box. The filter wasn't there for health reasons, however, but to keep the bits of tobacco from the smoker's mouth. Parliament sold initially for 25 cents for 20, but in 1932 the price was boosted to 30 cents, twice the price of ordinary smokes.

Benson & Hedges did little advertising, and that in upscale magazines. The cigarettes weren't available outside New York and a few other big cities and resorts favored by the wealthy, such as Newport and Palm Springs. In 1944, at a time when Americans would smoke anything they could find and shortages were constant, Parliament accounted for one tenth of one percent of the market. Two years later, when smokers returned to their old brands, sales fell to half that amount. Then, in 1946, without advertising or promotions, sales increased sharply, to the point where B&H couldn't keep up with demand. In 1951 Parliament was the twelfth-best-selling brand, with one half of one percent of the market.

Joseph Cullman, Jr., the president of B&H, and his son, Joseph III, were baffled by this showing. Joseph, Jr., who had been wedded to cigars, had purchased B&H through an investment trust he controlled and had been content to settle for the carriage trade, selling cigars as well as cigarettes at the store. Now, without an effort on his part, he controlled the fastest-growing cigarette in the industry. What caused that upsurge in demand? He discovered that some New York doctors, who had read scientific papers dealing with the relationship of smoking and diseases, were recommending filtered cigarettes to their patients. Virginia Rounds did not appeal to smokers of Camel and Lucky Strike, but Parliament did. By 1960 B&H's two brands were selling in the 600,000 range—out of an industry total of 353 billion.

Did filtered cigarettes have a future in America? The major companies thought not, believing filters were affectations and perhaps effeminate. They might appeal to some women, but certainly not to men, who still accounted for a majority of sales. Finally, filters had no track record in modern America. Unsurprisingly, American and L&M had opted to concentrate on kings. B&W was in an unusual situation. It had three unique brands: Kool; Raleigh, which gave out coupons that could be redeemed for merchandise, with each pack; and Viceroy, a regular-size filtered cigarette. At this juncture B&W decided to pin its hopes on Kool. Nothing special would be done for Viceroy.

Philip Morris had several ailing brands and by the early 1950s was losing market share. The company considered coming out with a king-sized version of Philip Morris, but instead reformulated an old brand, Dunhill, making it King Dunhill, which flopped. Reynolds, with the nation's top brands, hoped there would be no changes in the industry.

Lorillard was at a loss as to what to do. King-sized Embassy offered some promise, but not enough. So in February 1952, several months before the publication of the *Reader's Digest* article, Lorillard released Kent, with what was called a "micronite" filter, which had been "developed by researchers in atomic energy plants," and backed it with a national advertising campaign, claiming it "removes seven times more tars and nicotine than any other cigarette." This was not strictly correct. John Alden, an "off-brand," removed more tar and nicotine from its tobacco without recourse to filters, and Sano, which was a king-sized filter brand put out by smallish United States Tobacco, had half the nicotine as Kent and the same amount of tar. But Kent did deliver less tar and nicotine than was to be found in the more popular cigarettes. At a time when standard cigarettes delivered more than 3 milligrams of nicotine, Kent had 0.5 milligrams. The standards had 20 milligrams of tar, and Pall Mall had a rating of 25— Kent initially had 2 milligrams.

Sales for the next eight months were half a billion, far less than the 2.7 billion sold by Viceroy for the full year but way ahead of Parliament's 1.6 million. By industry standards, Kent was not doing particularly well. Lorillard commissioned a study of those who had switched to Kent and then dropped it, the results of which startled the company's leaders. Smokers complained there was no "kick" in Kent because the filter removed so much of the tars and nicotine. There were other problems. Because the filter was so fine it took more effort for smokers to draw on it than on other cigarettes. The filter was reformulated, and the amount of tar was boosted to 12 milligrams. Sales expanded, though not as much as to cheer those in the corporate offices.

In 1957 *Reader's Digest* published another of its articles on smoking, entitled "The Facts Behind Filter-Tip Cigarettes," in which it maintained there was no "reasonable doubt" that smoking was a cause of cancer. The article went on to assert that the substances that caused cancer were tars and nicotine. It listed the contents for popular brands, and Kent was at the bottom of the lists for both tar and nicotine. Another *Reader's Digest* article the following month, "Wanted—and Available—Filter Tips that Really Filter," was practically an endorsement of Kent.

Kent sales skyrocketed. The factories worked around the clock and still had to allocate them to retailers, who on their part would not sell them by the carton, to make certain all their customers could get packs. Lorillard's 1957 sales were 50 percent higher than those for 1956. Lorillard's stock, which had hovered in the low 20s for the past five years, rose to more than 80 in 1959, whereupon it was split. The new shares went on to top 70 in 1961.

By then Kent had plenty of competition. New filters came to market shortly after Lorillard took the plunge. These utilized cellulose filters, not much different from those employed in Parliaments. Liggett & Myers came out with L&M, which had "the Pure White Miracle Tip of Alpha-Cellulose," which was "Just What the Doctor Ordered." Reynolds offered Winston, a filtered brand, in the spring of 1954, with the slogan, "Winston Tastes Good—Like a Cigarette Should," which offended language purists who did not approve of the use of the word "like" rather than "as." The cigarette's blend was formulated for the tastes of nonfiltered smokers, which is to say, the vast majority of cigarette users. Winston sold 7.5 billion units in its first year, making it the thirteenth best-seller in the entire field and one of the top performers in its segment. It rose to fifth place in 1955 with 23 billion units and shot ahead of Kent in 1958.

Philip Morris transformed Philip Morris into a king, and that failed, but the company was already working on a reformulation of Marlboro. Until that was ready the company would purchase Benson & Hedges, primarily to get Parliament. Into Philip Morris came the B&H team, headed by Joseph Cullman III, who would assume leadership of the Marlboro campaign and soon after become CEO. By 1957 filters had close to 40 percent of the market. All the major cigarette companies had filter brands—except for American Tobacco.

In the light of this showing why did American Tobacco hold back? Paul Hahn was not strongly opposed to filters. "If we can find a good filter—a really good one that doesn't take all the taste and flavor out of the cigarette—we'll have a serious look at it," he said in 1953, thinking perhaps of the early failure of Kent. In any case Dick Reynolds had demonstrated the importance of placing major bets on one national brand. Of course, companies would have several others as well, but the leader merited the most attention, and at American Tobacco, the flagship brand was still Pall Mall. The following year, as filters became more popular, Hahn approved adding cellulose filters with a bit of activated charcoal to Tareyton, which performed poorly. Pall Mall was doing very well; by 1958 it was the nation's second best-seller, behind Camel. Three years later it was the top seller by a wide margin, followed by Camel and Winston, both Reynolds products. American's Lucky Strike was in fourth place, and then came Salem, which was Reynolds' mentholated brand, ahead of B&W's fading Chesterfields.

Clearly the industry had changed from what it had been in the previous generation, and at that point it appeared American and Reynolds had been the biggest winners. Hahn seemed to be thinking, "Why take chances?" As the industry rushed to filters, American, which commanded one third of its sales, pinned its hopes on the king-size Pall Mall. There would be no American Tobacco filter cigarette while Hahn was in office. Even so, there was one move he might have made to resolve the issue, and that would be to put out Pall Mall in both a filtered and a nonfiltered version. This wouldn't be as daring as the appearance of Chesterfield kings. One could purchase L&M and Kent in both regular filter and king filters. Philip Morris was available in regular and king, Kool in both regular and king filter, and Old Gold in regular, king, and king filter. In all of these cases sales rose when the new version appeared. That American did not recognize this and produce a Pall Mall filter is puzzling. Equally so was the failure of the company to attempt to bring down Pall Mall's very high nicotine and tar figures. Of the top 39 sellers, only Raleigh King and Chesterfield King had more tar and nicotine than Pall Mall. Might it have been that American Tobacco thought that the higher concentrations made

Pall Mall more appealing and that this would be considered attractive when and if the cancer scare subsided? This hardly seems likely, since all the manufacturers, bowing to consumer preferences, were lowering the amounts of tar and nicotine in their cigarettes. According to the American Cancer Society, in 1954, 95 percent of all cigarettes had tar in the range between 35 and 53 milligrams. By 1960 the range had fallen to between 19 and 35 milligrams.

In 1963 Robert Barney Walker took over as American Tobacco CEO and president. A colorful, talkative character, eager to place his mark on the company, Walker also hoped to become an industry spokesman, blasting away at those who claimed cigarettes were injurious to health. More important, however, was rectifying mistakes at American. By the time of Walker's promotion the company had already started its decline, and the executives there finally conceded this was because of the failure to enter the filter- and mentholated-brand areas. A marketing man all of his professional life who had started out as a route salesman in the Bronx, Walker was confident of his abilities to affect a turnaround.

Hahn had approached the market with a rifle, carefully aiming his shot (Pall Mall) at the quarry. Walker used the shotgun, firing a load of buckshot at the market hoping some of the pellets would find their targets. He believed that the days were over when a single brand could capture a quarter of the market for cigarettes. He also realized that if a new cigarette could capture 1 percent of the market after two years it could be judged a success. Thus, if American could release a great many brands, and some of them did well, the total market share could increase substantially.

In January 1964, Walker finally released Carlton, a king filter that had its low-tar and nicotine figures—2.4 milligrams of tar, 0.4 milligrams of nicotine—printed on the package. American achieved this by using a duel cellulose and charcoal filter, porous paper, and two rows of small vent holes. Walker thought that by offering about a sixth as much tar and nicotine as Kent, Carlton could cut into that cigarette's sales. It didn't. As one of the earliest high-filtration brands (known within the industry as "hi-fi") Carlton demonstrated that there was a level below which smokers would not purchase cigarettes.

In March American released Roi-Tan, a hybrid cigar-cigarette. The anticigarette people had not attacked cigars, which usually were not inhaled. Roi-Tan was an American Tobacco cigar. Now it emerged as a small cigar or cigarette, with a filter and packaged 20 to a pack. Was it to be inhaled? The advertising didn't say. Roi-Tan didn't appeal to cigar smokers or to cigarette smokers. It didn't last.

In April Walker made his play for pipe smokers with Half and Half, named after and based on an American tobacco-pipe mixture. "Enjoy America's Best-Tasting Pipe Tobacco in a Filter Cigarette!" was its unimaginative slogan. But like Roi-Tan, was it supposed to be inhaled? Half and Half was another of Walker's failures.

In May the man who was becoming known in the industry as "Brand a Month Barney" released Montclair, a mentholated version of Carlton. Another failure. In August he offered Lucky Strike Filters, and then several other mutations, so that within two years smokers could get Luckies in seven different formulations. In January 1965 American offered Waterford, whose filter was impregnated with encapsulated droplets of water that were released when the filter was squeezed. So it went. Walker even revived Sweet Caporal, that best-seller of the pre-Camel era. "Sweet News for You From 1870!" read the ad. If Hahn had attempted to copy Dick Reynolds, Walker was a throwback to the Buck Duke of the time of the trust.

Walker's only significant success came with Pall Mall 100 mm, which prompted a host of imitators in 1967, including Chesterfield 101s, advertised as being a "tiny millimeter" longer. The American Tobacco CEO had fired his buckshot, but only one of the pellets found the target.

In 1971 Reynolds still had the largest market share, 32.3 percent, but the runner-up by then was Philip Morris, with 17.5 percent, while the share of what was now designated as American Brands as a result of its entry into nontobacco areas had gone from 25.6 percent to 17.5 percent. Once the industry's leader, it now was a fading company. In 1977 American's Pall Mall, still the company's leading seller, was in fifth place in industry sales, behind Marlboro, Winston, Kool, and Salem. The first two cigarettes were filters, the next two mentholated brands. Seven of the top ten were filtered; none of them came out of American.

Joseph Cullman III was the person who came up with the best way to operate in the new environment, and he did so by blending aspects of both Buck Duke and Dick Reynolds. It will be recalled that Cullman arrived at Philip Morris when that company acquired Benson

& Hedges and that he took charge of the Marlboro campaign. He directed a talented team that reformulated the blend, which was smoother than Winston's, and working with America Enka, devised the "selectrate" filter, which was an improvement over those already in the field. With the help of the Leo Burnett Agency his team designed the package, which was to be cardboard with a flip-top, rather than the conventional paper, and created the Marlboro Man commercials, some of the most effective in television history. Most people remember the Marlboro Cowboy, but there also were the naval officer, the athlete, and others. Even after cigarette advertising on television and radio was discontinued on January 1, 1970, memories of the ads remained. Moreover, Philip Morris assayed the switch to more print ads very well, and the Marlboro Man was still in sight on billboards.

Then Cullman did something novel. American cigarettes were smoked overseas, but no American manufacturer in recent times had made a concerted effort in other countries. The reasons were cultural as much as anything else, but there were historical roots as well that went back to the Buck Duke era.

Duke had been known to have global ambitions, and he had purchased Ogden Ltd. of Liverpool as his vehicle to seize control of the English market as the start of his campaign to bring American tobacco products to the rest of the world. The English had responded by organizing Imperial Tobacco to meet the Duke challenge. A fierce battle then erupted, which ended in a draw. Duke sold Ogden to Imperial for a stock interest in the English concern, and together they formed British-American Tobacco (BAT) to sell both the Imperial and Consolidated brands in the rest of the world outside the United States and England. Duke was to receive two thirds of BAT's shares and so took direction of the firm. Finally, American and Imperial agreed not to sell cigarettes in the other's backyard. Ever since, the American tobacco companies had shown little interest in overseas markets.

The new American Tobacco of Richard Reynolds had not been concerned with foreign sales. Reynolds rarely set foot out of North Carolina, was xenophobic, and impressed this attitude on his company; the imprint was still there after World War II. In contrast, the Cullman cigar business had taken Joseph Cullman, Jr., to European and Cuban tobacco markets, and Joseph Cullman III knew the world, having served on a cruiser in the Pacific during World War II and traveling to Europe and elsewhere both before and after the war. He had seen firsthand how Australians and others had taken to American cigarettes. He also knew that in postwar Germany American cigarettes virtually replaced currencies, being used to purchase goods and services. Besides, Philip Morris's culture was based in New York, not the Carolinas and Virginia, and was far more cosmopolitan than that at the other companies. So Cullman was prepared to take Marlboro overseas, and in the process made it the world's best-selling cigarette by far. This was the most important and most successful move by an American cigarette company since the end of World War II.

By 1975, 20 years after Marlboro was introduced, Philip Morris had 25 percent of domestic sales, behind Reynolds, which had a 33 percent market share. But Cullman could boast that Philip Morris was the largest cigarette company in the world in unit sales as a result of international sales, which accounted for 20 percent of the business. The following year, Marlboro outsold Winston in the domestic market for the first time. The reason was not only that Marlboro had better advertising, but that smokers' tastes had changed. They appeared to prefer Marlboro's smoother taste to the bite that came with Winstons. Moreover, Winston was using more reconstituted leaf, which degraded the product in a fashion akin to the changes that had damaged Schlitz in beer. Winston mentholated and Winston Lights were marketed in an insipid, unoriginal fashion. Reynolds remained a powerful firm, but it was no match for Philip Morris.

Like Reynolds, Philip Morris also put out variants of Marlboro, the first of which was Marlboro Lights, which in time outsold the original, and under Cullman's successors there were others to follow, both in mixes and packages. When the need was felt for an even lower-tar-and-nicotine cigarette, Cullman brought forth Merit, which soon outsold Marlboro Lights. Asked whether Merit was cannibalizing sales from Marlboro Lights, Cullman shrugged and replied that he would just as soon sell Merits as Marlboros. Cullman also came up with a cigarette geared specifically for women, Virginia Slims, and in it had another success.

Cullman even demonstrated that moribund brands might be revived with the proper packaging and advertising. It is possible to invigorate a cigarette brand, assuming interest, intelligence, drive, imagination, and funding. Reynolds did it with Camel in the 1980s, and in 1966 Philip Morris revived Benson & Hedges by presenting it in a new configuration while keeping the old to retain existing customers. The cigarette was lengthened to 120 mm and was given the Parliament-type cardboard shell-and-slide box. The new B&H package was wood-grained gold and looked elegant. The advertising firm of Wells Rich Greene came up with an unusual, successful campaign. Until then the companies had stressed the advantages of length. B&H would hit upon disadvantages. The TV ads featured people trying to smoke a B&H in an elevator (permitted at the time, as were TV ads) and how the door closed on the cigarette, and a man seated in a VW Beetle turning to look at a woman and mashing the cigarette against the window. The campaign was a success, and B&H became the leader in its segment of the market. When the so-called economy brands appeared, Marlboro's Basic became one of that segment's leaders.

This is not to suggest that Cullman and Philip Morris did not experience its share of flops. What smoker can remember Cambridge, Alpine, Paxton, Players, or even Saratoga, which had some small success for a while? The absence of failures usually indicates the company was risk-averse and probably missed many opportunities as well. Rather, Cullman was not trapped by the past as was Hahn or going off in all directions at once, the problem that befell Walker. As a result, he became the most successful tobacco man of his time. Moreover, he accomplished all of this in the face of the assault against cigarettes mounted by government and private interests. When Cullman stepped down as CEO in 1978 Philip Morris was the leading tobacco company in the United States, with 29 percent of the market, and had 6 percent of the foreign market as well.

American Brands gave up the ghost in the United States in 1994 and sold its domestic tobacco business to Brown & Williamson. It was left with a hodgepodge of companies in sporting goods, office supplies, liquor, and hardware, as well as Gallahers, the largest tobacco company in the United Kingdom, purchased in 1968 in a belated attempt to imitate Philip Morris's overseas success. On October 6, 1996, American Brands announced it would split in two. Gallahers would go its own way, while what remained would be renamed Fortune Brands. And with this, the last vestige of American Tobacco, once the nation's leading tobacco company, vanished from the business scene.

At this writing the jury is out on whether this disappearance due to earlier blunders was or was not fortuitous. The tobacco litigation that heated up in the 1990s continues. That the former American Tobacco interests will have to participate in the settlement is clear. How this will affect a company that is no longer in the business remains to be seen.

CHAPTER FOURTEEN

THE NEW YORK STOCK EXCHANGE: THE BLUNDER OF THE NARROW VIEW

While today The New York Stock Exchange (NYSE) is the most important financial market in the world, its position as such is no longer what it had been during the 1920s, when New York superseded London as the major capital market, or in the 1950s and 1960s, when it was the undisputed centerpiece of trading activity. In those years the NYSE was monitored and tracked by the rest of the world. Today a global marketplace has come into being. When New York closes down for the day the financial baton is passed to Tokyo and then to London and back to New York. Other exchanges such as the ones in Singapore, Hong Kong, Frankfurt, and Paris are more important than they used to be.

The American markets, too, have changed drastically. At one time almost all newly issued American stocks would be traded over the counter by broker-dealers. The dealers would work from their offices, pencil and pad at the ready, scanning the "green sheets" to learn current prices. They would maintain bid-and-ask prices on the stocks they handled and await telephone calls from brokers seeking to either buy or sell. Many stocks would have several dealers making markets in them, but some seldom-traded stocks would have only one. Theoretically the broker would call several or perhaps all the dealers and obtain for his customer the best price, but in practice this seldom was done, since it involved more time and effort than appeared worthwhile.

When the stock fulfilled certain requirements, the company that issued its shares might apply for listing at the American Stock Exchange (Amex), known to some as the "Little Board" and then switch to the NYSE—the "Big Board"—when they met that market's standards, whereupon the Amex would cease trading its shares.

No more. Today the Amex tries to hold onto its stocks. Furthermore, there are many unlisted stocks, including those for stellar companies such as Intel, Microsoft, Liz Claiborne, Sun Microsystems, Cisco, and Oracle that qualify for NYSE listing and prefer to remain where they are, which often is NASDAQ (the acronym for National Association of Securities Dealers Automated Quotation System), an automated market. Trading in domestic stocks and bonds is still concentrated in New York, however, but other markets have sprung up to trade NYSE-listed securities, both in the United States and overseas. That this is so results as much from technology as from any other cause. Telecommunications and computerization are such that this situation is all but mandated.

The huge financial derivative market is centered in Chicago, where the Chicago Board of Trade's Chicago Board Options Exchange (CBOE) is central. Its successes are another sign that the NYSE's near-monopoly has been shattered for good. This need not have happened. Given farsighted leadership, there might today be no NASDAQ or CBOE, or if they did exist, they would not nearly be as important and successful as they are. The NYSE's centrality could have been greater than it now is.

As it has been since the 1930s, the NYSE is controlled by the specialists, people who "make markets" in listed securities. Unlike bankers, who have to satisfy customers and clients, and brokers who cater to the needs of their accounts, the specialists have obligations only to their securities, the Securities and Exchange Commission (SEC), the Board of Governors of the NYSE, and each other. While momentous changes were taking place involving technologies and markets, they had a stake in maintaining the status quo. In time the current crop of specialists arrived at terms with technology and are engaged in attempting to rectify blunders made by them and their predecessors, but this came reluctantly and late in the game. They are doing quite well, even while changes have occurred to erode the power and position of the Exchange itself.

That the NYSE has survived and flourished for more than two centuries has been due more to good fortune than to superior vision and clearheaded leadership. The good fortune continues to this day, as the NYSE is undergoing a renaissance of sorts resulting from the failure of its rivals to capitalize on their advantages and from making a few blunders of their own. Moreover, the exchange picture today is more complicated than at any time in history.

The NYSE's good fortune began in 1825, when the market that it was to become benefited from the opening of the Erie Canal, which in the words of Oliver Wendell Holmes made New York "the tip of the tongue that laps up the cream of the commerce of a continent." Within a relatively few years Manhattan was boosted into commercial supremacy over the likes of Boston and Philadelphia. Then the telegraph started to bind the nation together, opening the New York financial market to much of the country. By the time of the Civil War, Wall Street had become the preeminent capital center, through no exceptional or extraordinary effort of its own. Leaders of the New York marketplace, which in this period were the brokerages, welcomed the telegraph, recognizing its implications almost immediately. The same was true of the ticker and the telephone, which appeared later. All of these served to increase the business of those who made an aftermarket in securities issued by companies and governments. At one time the United States had approximately 250 securities markets; today, depending on how one measures such things, there are fewer than 20.

During the Civil War a rival exchange, the Open Board of Stock Brokers, did a larger business than what then was the New York Stock and Exchange Board. As its name indicates, the Open Board was accessible to all who would pay its fee. At that time the Stock and Exchange Board utilized outcry auctions, in which the seller would deposit his shares with the auctioneer and the potential buyers would bid against each other. This was acceptable when volume was low, but made little sense in busy periods, when traders required continuous action, which also involved lower transaction costs and more rapid trading. The Open Board utilized continuous trading, but was so crowded that buyers and sellers had a difficult time locating each other. They swiftly realized that the problem might be solved by agreeing that each stock would be traded at a different location on the floor. In time some brokers stopped trading for customers, but rather "made markets" in stocks. They stood prepared to buy and sell and to arrange for cross-sales. These were the first specialists, whose methods were far more efficient than those auctions at the Stock and Exchange Board. Only through a merger in 1869, which created the NYSE, did the older exchange manage to survive, doing so by first utilizing both trading methods and then by abandoning the auctions. In that period the new NYSE had a strong instinct for survival and awareness of a clearly superior method of transacting business.

Not completely, however. The NYSE refused to trade stocks of industrial companies when these appeared in larger numbers during the post-Civil War period. As a result, the Boston Stock Exchange, which did list them, once again became an important rival. Finally, in 1887 the NYSE started trading these securities, but only at what was called the "unlisted department."

At the turn of the century there were some one hundred stock exchanges in the United States, but their numbers were dwindling. So long as telegraph and long-distance telephone charges were high and getting through was time consuming in a period when coordination between two or three companies and operators was difficult, the locals could eke out livings. As costs came down, they were forced to close, unable to realize the economies of scale enjoyed in New York and the more liquid markets to be had there.

If the NYSE had less competition from regional exchanges, this was not the case in the city. There, for a dozen years the Consolidated Stock Exchange (CSE) was the NYSE's major rival. The CSE attempted to innovate and so win business from the NYSE. Brokers affiliated with this exchange did a brisk business in odd lots (sales and purchases of fewer than 100 shares), something the NYSE commission brokers grudgingly accepted shortly after the turn of the century. At CSE brokerages it was possible for a customer to put up as little as 10 percent of the price of an order, which would not be filled, but rather would be placed in the ledger as though a wager on the stock. The customer could sell whenever he wanted and receive the proceeds, without the underlying stock being affected in the least. These brokerages, known as "bucket shops," were attacked vigorously by the NYSE's leaders.

In the eyes of the Big Board, the Consolidated was guilty of another major offense, that of trading NYSE-listed stocks at lower commissions than those of the Exchange, thus competing in an area in which the members believed they deserved to have a monopoly. The

NYSE demanded investigations, removed its tickers from the CSE, and NYSE members were forbidden from conducting business with any brokerage that had anything to do with it. The CSE closed down in the late 1920s, ending this kind of competition for more than a generation.

During the glory days of the 1920s investment bankers were the most powerful figures in the district. To them, the secondary markets—the exchanges—were critical for the liquidity they provided, little else. The real action was in the board rooms, where money was raised for clients by selling their newly issued paper to customers. The investment bankers, the more important of whom were Thomas Lamont of Morgan, Albert Wiggin of Chase, William Potter of Guaranty Trust, and Seward Prosser of Bankers Trust were in control of affairs in the district during that decade. The great J. P. Morgan and his successors worked across the street from the NYSE; they never set foot on its floor. That was for the lesser lights at Morgan, such as NYSE vice president and then president, Richard Whitney, the not particularly bright brother of George Whitney, who was an investment banker at the firm. Even so, the investment bankers wielded power at the NYSE.

The stock market crashed in October 1929, and business dried up soon after. From the peak of 1.1 billion shares set in 1929, volume fell irregularly, bottoming out at 125.6 million shares in 1942 before rising once more. In this same span the price of a NYSE seat declined from $625,000 to $39,000. Wall Street had become a stagnant backwater.

During the 1930s most of the talented bankers, brokers, traders, and salesmen left for other occupations, and when the United States entered World War II, those who remained departed for government jobs or service in the Armed Forces. "When the crash came in the thirties, no banker would admit where he worked," recalled Citibank's CEO Walter Wriston. "Nobody wanted to work for a bank from 1933 to 1939. Then the war started. So there was nobody coming into the business from 1933 to 1946."

In 1940 only 5,855 people worked in the financial district. By 1946 the labor force had declined to 4,343.

Richard Whitney had been succeeded as NYSE president by quite a different kind of person. Charles Gay did not live on Park

Avenue, but rather in a middle-class Brooklyn neighborhood, not far from the botanical gardens, where he liked to take walks on weekends. He was a partner at the firm of Whitehouse & Co., an old but minor commission house that did not engage in investment banking. He led a quiet but comfortable life. Gay did not have a country estate, and membership in a golf club was his only indulgence.

At that, Gay was better off than most investment bankers. Underwriting securities, their major occupation, and fallen off sharply. By the mid-1930s most of the money earned on Wall Street came from commissions and trading, not client services. The focus of attention had turned from the board rooms to the NYSE floor, where the specialists ruled, having taken over when the investment bankers and their representatives left a vacuum in leadership. Wall Street's past had been dominated by bankers such as Morgan and Jacob Schiff. Its immediate future seemed to rest with commission brokers such as Gay, but even more so, with specialists such as John Coleman.

After the full impact of the Crash was felt, Coleman, who was virtually unknown outside Wall Street and the hierarchy of the Catholic Church, became by far the dominant figure at the NYSE. The investment bankers in their peak years may have had powers far beyond the narrow confines of the financial district, but during the 1930s and afterwards, not at the NYSE; Coleman's power was there, and not in the corporate boardrooms and political salons. This suited him fine. He would leave his Park Avenue apartment at 7:00 A.M., attend church services, arrive at his office at 9:00 A.M., and 15 minutes later would appear on the trading floor, his throne room. By the time Coleman died in 1977 he had become a legend.

Coleman was the son of an Irish-American policeman whose beat was the financial district. He left school at the age of 14 to help support his family and the following year worked as a page at E. H. Stern & Co., a member of the New York Curb Market. In time he became a partner at the firm and a floor broker. Coleman moved to the NYSE in 1924, where he was the youngest specialist. Stern retired in 1928, and Coleman and Paul Adler, the second in command, reorganized the firm as Adler, Coleman & Co.

The tall, powerfully built Coleman ranged the floor and like his policeman father made certain everyone was living up to his strict standards. He was on the board of governors and served as chairman from 1943 to 1947. More important, he dominated the Committee on Stock List, which determined which specialist unit received new listings or inherited them from units that were found wanting. Unsurprisingly, Adler, Coleman became a paramount specialist unit; by the late 1940s it was handling 47 stocks, including the likes of American Tobacco, Armour, Wilson, Liggett & Myers, International Minerals, Curtiss Wright, and General Public Service. Once, when a client threatened to complain to the Securities and Exchange Commission about Coleman's disdainful behavior, the great man snapped, "The hell with the SEC. If they don't like the way my stocks are traded, let them come down here and trade them with their money."

As noted, John Coleman's beloved specialists still control the NYSE, a central fact of life there. They have approximately one third of the total votes, and they influence most of the others. Their livelihoods and fortunes, often for three and four generations, are bound up in the retention of the current ways of doing business. Once tight-lipped and secretive, today the specialists defend what they still call their "auction" market against its rivals with vigor and reason.

By auction the NYSE does not mean the common use of the term, which is to say, it is quite different from the auctions of the pre-1869 period or those at Christie's. Rather, orders are taken to the specialist on the Exchange floor, where he attempts to bring together buyer and seller at a mutually agreeable price, determined by supply and demand. They contrast this to the dealer market, in which the dealer buys and sells from inventory. In practice, however, when buyer and seller cannot be brought together at the NYSE, the specialist comes in and buys or sells the shares himself, attempting to maintain orderly markets, raising the prices when demand increases more rapidly than supply, and lowering them when the reverse occurs. Such transactions account for approximately a quarter of the NYSE volume.

The specialist also takes orders to sell at prices higher than those quoted and to buy at lower prices, which are known as "limit orders." These he enters in his "book," to be triggered when the prices are reached. Finally, the specialist buys and sells for his own account, in order to maintain an orderly market. In the words of the NYSE, "The absolute obligation of the specialists is to place and execute public investor orders ahead of their own—to yield at all times to public orders. However, if public customers cannot get together, the specialists have a second obligation—to make the market as continuous as possible by providing their own capital or inventory to complete a transaction."

The NYSE contrasts the public obligations of the specialists with lack of them for the dealers, which is true enough. Beneath the talk of the superiority of the specialist system over the dealers, however, is the simple fact that without the auction market there would be no need for specialists. Self-preservation is a powerful motive, and the specialists' desire to survive certainly is understandable.

One of the threats to both the system and the NYSE itself after World War II came from the so-called "Third Market," a group of brokers, not NYSE members, who traded in NYSE-listed stocks over telephones from their offices, offering lower commissions, as had the CSE a half century earlier. These brokers received the same kind of treatment meted to the CSE: removal of their tickers and threats of reprisal and investigation. The Big Board also enacted Rule 394. Ratified in 1955, it forbade members from dealing as principals or agents in affecting off-NYSE transactions in listed securities with nonmembers. The Board passed the word to the members: transgressions would be dealt with severely.

The NYSE asserted the Third Market was narrow and the brokers themselves little more than marginal. Unsurprisingly, the brokers fought back, and in the 1962 case of *Silver* v. *New York Stock Exchange* won the right to continue their practices. This marked the beginning of the end of the NYSE's hegemony.

In the years that followed the Third Market dealers attempted to lower costs by substituting computers for telephones, and they largely succeeded in so doing, a development that was not lost on the OTC dealers. They recognized the increased trading volume there required a shift toward the new technologies. As early as 1961 William Claflin, chairman of the board of the National Association of Securities Dealers (NASD), the government-created governing body for the OTC, told his colleagues that "other electronic devices, as they become available, will make push-button execution feasible, and were they here today there would be no problem in handling trading volume." This did not trouble the market makers at the OTC who, unlike the specialists, stood to benefit, not lose, by automation.

Of course, the NYSE also had computers, but not for the actual trading, still overseen by the specialists, who were not about to allow themselves to be replaced by machines. In a 1963 report the SEC declared, "The floor of the NYSE has been untouched by most of the technological developments of the twentieth century."

During the early 1960s, when there was talk of forthcoming 50-million-share sessions, some consideration was given to the erection of a new building on landfill in the East River. There would be all sorts of devices installed to assist traders, representatives of the wire houses, and the specialists. The NYSE's leaders knew that something would have to be done to facilitate the settlements of trades, but the essential structure would not change. The specialist was to remain the heart of the system.

There was a market "event" in May 1962 that put some veteran brokers in mind of 1929. President Kennedy had reacted sharply when, in defiance of him and in violation of their pledges, the major steel companies had raised their prices. Kennedy's harsh treatment of the companies forced them to back down, but now there was talk of an antibusiness vendetta, and this made the markets skittish. Stocks drifted downward, and on May 23, when volume reached 5.4 million shares and stocks declined from Dow 636 to 627, the tickers ran more than 143 minutes late at one point, the greatest gap since the 1929 crash. Prices continued to plummet, reaching 612 on Friday, May 25. Then, on Monday, May 28, they collapsed from the start of trading, ending the session at 577, for a decline of 6 percent.

This was the worst point loss since the 1929 crash. Volume that day reached 9.3 million shares, the seventh largest in history. It was a stunning blow, mitigated when prices rebounded on an even wilder Tuesday session, when volume reached the incredible 14.7 million level. The Dow slid during the morning but moved upward during the afternoon to close at 603, and then went on to end the next day at 613, wiping out the losses.

A subsequent investigation by the SEC indicated that the OTC's market makers had abandoned many of their stocks during the decline, while the NYSE specialists did not act to stabilize their shares. The market makers had no obligation to stabilize prices, but the specialists did, and they had failed in a moment of distress, providing the NYSE's critics with more ammunition. At one point on May 28 the disparity between prices bid and asked was so great that the specialists were unable to cross trades and were unwilling to make purchases of their own. It was learned that an order to purchase AT&T at the market price reached the trading floor at the same time as a sell order arrived there. The seller received 102, while the buyer made his purchase at 108. Clearly that specialist had fouled up.

By 1966 sessions where more than 10 million shares were traded were no longer unusual The NYSE's clearing operations were strained to the hilt, while volume continued to expand. In December 1967 there were only two sessions in which fewer than 10 million shares were traded and six in which more than 12 million were traded. There even was one 14-million-share day. Interest in securities continued to grow. In April 1968 the lowest volume day was 12.5 million shares, the highest, 20.4 million.

In desperation the NYSE experimented with earlier closings and extended the delivery period for securities and payments from four to five days. On June 12, 1968, the Big Board closed on Wednesdays to permit the clerks time to catch up with paperwork. Now even the most vigorous opponents of change conceded that computerization would be needed, not because it was wanted, but rather because there was no other way to continue transacting business. During the 1960s the NYSE was being dragged kicking and screaming into the computer age, and the specialists were alarmed.

In 1967 Exchange President Keith Funston retired, and in his place the board selected Robert Haack, the CEO of the NASD. This was rather unusual, for Haack was known to favor dealer markets. At the time it was thought he got the job as a NYSE attempt to convince the SEC it was prepared to accept reforms. One of the more important of these involved negotiated commissions on stock trades, which would have slashed the incomes of the brokerages. In this period customers paid ten times as much for the purchase or sale of 10,000 shares of a stock as they did for 1,000 shares; there were no volume discounts. As a result, the NYSE lost business to the Third Market, which provided discounts to institutions interested in trading large blocks, which meant 10,000 shares or more. Since institutional ownership of stocks was increasing rapidly, it meant that the mutual funds, trusts accounts, pension funds, and the like looked there for lower costs. This was one change specialists were prepared to accept, since it would not affect their business. Indeed, lower commissions might lure some business from the Third Market.

The brokerages received support from highly respected former Chairman William McChesney Martin, who in a 1971 report opposed negotiated commissions, which he said would result in the shuttering of hundreds of small brokerages, at a time when many already had fallen. Martin also came out in favor of the specialists over the dealers, although he wanted them to boost their capitalizations.

Part of the Martin Report dealt with the thorny matter of a national securities market. As noted, local securities markets closed down as better communications permitted lower transaction costs and economies of scale. There really was no need for them. The existence in New York of two stock markets, the NYSE and the American Stock Exchange (ASE), occurred because at one time the so-called "curbstone brokers," who dealt out of doors in securities not traded at the Exchange, banded together to form a more formal market, which in 1921 moved into its new building at Trinity Place. Such a situation may have once made sense, but no longer. Likewise, the presence of exchanges in Boston and Philadelphia could hardly be justified unless they had something different to offer, while the Pacific Coast Exchange's only excuse for existence was that it traded securities after the NYSE closed down. This could be easily remedied with around-the-clock trading, which had been spoken of at the Amex in the 1950s and which was disdained by the NYSE. By the 1970s American securities were traded in London, Tokyo, and elsewhere when New York was closed. Such a situation could be resolved by a national, or even an international, centralized securities market.

Martin would not go that far. He advocated cooperation, not unification. For example, he wanted a "consolidated tape," which would report all transactions on all exchanges, even those of NYSE's rivals. He asserted that "consolidation of certain computer facilities of the New York Stock Exchange and the American Stock Exchange will provide maximum economy in their use."

Nothing came of this, but publication of the Martin Report stirred debate on the matter of a national market, and the NYSE and Amex did unite to form the Securities Industry Automation Corporation, two thirds owned by the NYSE, and one third by the Amex, to obtain and operate the core computers used in transactions and other business. One SEC member, James Needham, called for the creation of a "United States Stock Exchange," with all the exchanges transferring their assets to the new entity and receiving shares in proportion to the value of their seats. Under such an arrangement, the Third Market would go out of existence and the USSE would be dominated by the former NYSE members, meaning the specialists. The new exchange would determine standards for listing, meaning the old OTC would not become part of the system. Unsurprisingly, Needham's proposal was welcomed at the NYSE and played a part in his being selected as the Exchange's leader in 1972.

While this debate proceeded events that would prove more important were taking place outside the Wall Street community. In 1968 Alan Kay, a computer designer with no formal knowledge of the securities business, designed AutEx, a computerized trading system, with the hope of selling it to the NYSE. The operator at an AutEx console could transmit messages regarding the willingness to buy and sell specified amounts of stock. The offer would go out to all subscribers to the service, and should one or more be interested, he could telephone the operator and consummate the deal. It was a crude system, most adaptable to OTC trades in large blocks and not to the specialists.

Kay, who knew nothing of specialists and dealers, was rather surprised when the NYSE refused to consider AutEx. Undeterred, on his own he established the system and by mid-1969 was signing up subscribers who traded NYSE-listed stocks as well as those on the OTC market. Within a year Kay had 140 subscribers, 30 of whom were NYSE members.

Kay's success encouraged former securities analyst Jerome Pustilnik to take AutEx one step further. Ever since the mid-1960s his company, Institutional Networks, had been attempting to create an automated exchange. Pustilnik's "Instinet" not only preserved the anonymity of the buyers and sellers, but permitted the actual execution of orders via the consoles. The program went into operation in 1970. As was to have been expected, the NYSE put pressures on members to remain true to the Exchange floor. Instinet did not become a national marketplace as Pustilnik hoped, but it survived for the usual reason—it filled a need and for some customers and some trades provided a better market than did the NYSE.

Without meaning to do so, Kay and Pustilnik had created a Fourth Market, another rival with which the NYSE would have to contend. The Fourth Market did not compete with the Third, at least not directly. Rather, it provided vehicles through which the Third Market's traders could function more efficiently.

All the while the NASD leaders made plans of their own for a more formal market structure. Instinet intrigued them. They realized that unless they moved and did so quickly, many of the OTC members would be attracted to the new electronic networks and so would create complications in that sector of the industry. There was no way of predicting the reactions of the NASD members who had seats on the NYSE. Some already had issued complaints regarding the way the NYSE was being managed, and there was at least a chance that some would migrate to Instinet, which would create conflicts with the specialists.

Both the NYSE and the NASD were being threatened by automation. The NYSE chose to ignore the technological imperative it faced, while the NASD did not. Being a federally chartered organization headquartered in Washington, not in New York, bureaucrats, and not the members, held the decision-making power. There was no large and powerful special-interest group among the members, but rather a varied and independent lot, running all the way from New York-based investment banks to notary publics who sold mutual funds to customers in small towns.

There were three distinct constituencies within the NASD with differing attitudes toward a much discussed new market. First were the OTC dealers whose business was solely in unlisted stocks. To them, an electronic marketplace was an interesting but hardly vital idea. They were doing quite well without it, but they were willing to give it a try, in the expectation that a workable system would provide better communications and swifter executions. The second group was those who comprised the Third Market. These people embraced the concept enthusiastically. Not only did it appear more efficient and less expensive than the NYSE, but an electronic marketplace would be a powerful weapon in a confrontation with the NYSE. They dreamed of a time when such a system might displace the specialists, just as the specialists, responding to a need, had a century earlier displaced the scheduled auctions. Finally, there were those NASD members who also belonged to the NYSE. They remained loyal to the old organization, but not necessarily to the specialists. While less enthusiastic than those who fell into the first two groups, they were at least willing to suspend judgment and see how matters developed.

The idea of an electronic marketplace was not new to the NASD in 1970. Two years earlier the Association had entered into an agreement with Bunker-Ramo, a relatively small electronics concern, whereby it would create a model for the electronic marketplace that, if accepted, would be put into place and operated by the company. The NASD would receive a portion of the profits and would have an option to purchase the system in 1976 or afterwards. The system was ready to go into operation by 1970.

The decision whether or not to proceed was in the hands of Gordon Macklin, who had become president of the NASD the previous year. Macklin came from the Midwest, where at the time of his appointment he was in charge of sales management and syndication at McDonald & Co., a Cleveland-based bank. He had been active in the NASD in District Nine and he understood the situation on Wall Street. However, he was unknown to the district's leaders and they to him, and so lacked the contacts required and the experience to work out some kind of arrangement with the NYSE.

Macklin wasn't certain of the capabilities of the electronic marketplace, or where such a system could lead. Like his predecessors at the NASD, he lacked a mandate for change. Even so, he decided to go ahead with the project, out of which NASDAQ emerged.

NASDAQ is, perhaps, technologically the kind of exchange that would be created *de novo* today. In time the NYSE would realize this and would expend hundreds of millions of dollars to catch up in terms of automation of operations, while retaining the specialist system. But as will be seen, NASDAQ also had flaws that had nothing to do with technology, and these provided the NYSE with breathing space.

Initially, NASDAQ was to deal only in unlisted stocks. Thus, the first chance for a national or even an international market and the end of the specialist system (and perhaps the NYSE itself) passed. In time this would change, and NASDAQ would compete with the NYSE for NYSE-listed stocks.

NASDAQ went into operation on February 5, 1971, providing information on 2,400 unlisted securities to more than 800 dealers. There was some confusion in those early days, even among NASDAQ participants, as to just what this new market was. Some thought it was a variety of automated stock exchange for OTC stocks, which would eliminate the human factor. This thought troubled the dealers as much as it might the specialists had they been presented with such a change. Most believed NASDAQ was only a replacement for the telephone and typewriter, with dealers spending their workdays peering at computer screens, learning the bids and asks of rivals, and adjusting their own prices accordingly. Likewise, the stockbrokers might also have access to the screens and would thus be able to select the best prices for their customers. What this inferred was more competitive prices and narrower spreads between the bids and asks for stocks.

There were to be three levels to NASDAQ. Level I enabled the dealers to obtain median bid-and-ask prices, which usually came through existing systems, such as Quotron. Level II subscribers received all bids and asks and were free to act upon them through existing channels, meaning the telephone. Level III terminals received all the information in the system, the bids and asks, the amounts of stock offered and requested, the names of the houses involved, as well as the price and volume statistics for the day.

The specialists had read about NASDAQ, listened to rumors, and had started quite a few of their own. They were curious and troubled. A handful of them managed to visit Third Market and OTC firms and witness the machines and their operators in action. The sight was at the same time confusing and awesome. There, in a room not much larger than a dining facility at a good club, were several dozen traders at desks, each equipped with a console, and all facing displays. There was some shouting and badinage, but the traders were not talking to one another and making deals, as was done on the NYSE floor. Rather, they were addressing their machines, as they had previously their telephones.

At the turn of the century J. P. Morgan had said the most important attribute for a Wall Streeter was character. The electronic gear knew nothing of character. Specialists had to know their stocks better than anyone else on the floor and had to have a feel for the market. Traders on NASDAQ had to know their stocks and possess the instincts required of traders. But operators on Levels II and III could be clerks or junior partners. To the specialists who watched, it appeared a congenial blend of man and machine. It worked—too well by half to please the NYSE members.

In conversations with the dealers, they also learned that there was no reason for them to work from New York. Given electronics, they could function anywhere. Rooms in low-rent districts. Their homes. Or they could move to a resort area and operate from poolside or the ski chalets. Or even outside of the country.

A year later the NASD had $25 million in equipment, not in lower Manhattan, but rather in Trumbull, Connecticut. Most of the machines came from suppliers such as Bunker-Ramo. Some were revamped systems first tested in Las Vegas gaming houses and at race-tracks. Central to it all were several computers operated by technicians. By then NASDAQ daily volume was 8 million shares, more than the total for the Amex and the regionals combined, though still far behind the NYSE.

All of this revived talk of a USSE, which might have utilized NASDAQ technology. There was to be no USSE. Rather, under the terms of the Securities Act Amendments of 1975, a national market system was established that retained the independence of the individual exchanges. Three years later the Intermarket Trading System (ITS) went into operation, with the NYSE and Philadelphia Stock Exchange trading 11 stocks simultaneously. During the next four years other exchanges and stocks were added. Linked together over the ITS were the NYSE, the American Stock Exchange, the over-the-counter market, NASDAQ, and the regional stock exchanges. Under this scheme, traders were able to buy and sell securities traded anywhere at the best available price. However, there was to be no consolidated limit-order book, which would have carried the system further than the NYSE wanted. Finally, there was to be a consolidated tape for trades in NYSE-listed securities no matter where they were traded and a consolidated quote system.

Clearly ITS was a compromise. "There was enormous pressure for a national market system," said NYSE Chief Economist William Freund. "The Exchange didn't want fragmented markets, but it didn't want a consolidated limit-order book either." The SEC, however, took a different stand on ITS. One commissioner, Irving Pollack, called it "this Rube Goldberg system," and many students of the subject agreed.

The SEC prevailed in one area. Commissions on trades above $300,000 in value were deregulated on April 14, 1973, and in a series of steps other commissions also fell. On May 1, 1975, all commissions were negotiated, and brokerage hasn't been the same since. It was the first of only several blows that would alter the exchange community. Virtually all of them would be opposed or initially ignored by the NYSE.

The technology would not go away. As computerization proceeded in other businesses, there still was little of it on the NYSE trading floor. Although they grumbled about costs, Coleman and his associates were not averse to automation. They were willing to accept computers in those areas of NYSE business that did not affect the actual specialist auctions. Why not at the trading posts? In 1974 one governor, a specialist, blandly told a writer that he couldn't support the introduction of such devices because they wouldn't fit into the "furniture." Of course, this was not the reason. The fear was that computers would render the specialists obsolete, which indeed could have been the case.

Its back to the wall, and recognizing the survival of the specialist system was at stake, the NYSE reacted. In 1971 Haack asked Alan Loss, who had worked on trading systems at the NASD, to come to the Exchange and help modernize its trading operations. Within six months Loss had developed a system for executing 100 share trades without the direct input by specialists. "If an order reached New York from Los Angeles electronically," said Loss, "you really shouldn't need a human being to take the order the last 100 yards."

The specialists were not amused.

Loss had produced the Automated Trading System, which enabled clerks to transmit 100 share orders via teletype machines to the specialists, who would execute the orders. It was introduced as a pilot program, and workers were called in to modify the post where the test would occur on a Monday morning. Before the opening Loss was summoned to the trading floor, where he found the manager and a group of bystanders around the test area. Someone had come in over the weekend and demolished the new platform. Just who did the deed remains unknown, but clearly someone or a group at the Exchange didn't care to have established ways of conducting business changed. In any case the system proved unworkable and was abandoned. In its place came the Block Automation System (BAS), by which institutional buyers and sellers would match orders for 10,000 shares or more and then bring them to the floor—and the specialists—for execution. Of course, the specialist would not be needed in such a trade, but he or she had to be there nonetheless, somewhat akin to the firefighter remaining in diesel locomotives. No one particularly liked or needed the system, and it, too, was abandoned.

The NYSE tried the Registered Representative Rapid Response, a cumbersome system that, as the name indicates, provided a faster execution of orders, again through the specialist. It wasn't popular. More successful was the Designated Order Turnaround, or DOT, which was based on systems developed at regional exchanges. Essentially, DOT was the electronic entry and execution of trades at the specialist's post, through an "electronic book" and without hands-on intervention or the use of floor brokers to take the transaction physically to the post. DOT was followed by an expanded version, Super-DoT. The floor brokers lost business, but the specialists remained in the saddle. In the process, the old auction market was modified in such a way as to make the NYSE system appear more like the dealer operations, but the specialists were untouched. This put one in mind of Microsoft recognizing the superiority of the Apple operating system over DOS and creating Windows as an overlay on DOS to give the appearance of an Apple screen and its ease of use. It might be acceptable, but it clearly is an inferior alternative to the original.

The NYSE finally started to change in earnest in 1976, when William Batten was named to head the Exchange. Batten, the former head of J. C. Penney, was the first to occupy that office who had a background in a competitive business. As a member of the NYSE board he had authored the Batten Report, which criticized both the specialists and the specialist system. As chairman Batten defended the system, but also poured millions into modernization programs, which were continued by his successor, John Phelan. Yet the NYSE no longer was the center of the investment universe. In 1990 NYSE President Richard Grasso was obliged to concede that "our principal competition these days is the NASD." It needn't have been the case. Such was the price of preserving the specialist system.

Even then, after the rise of NASDAQ and the presence there of so many stocks that qualified for NYSE listing but elected to remain there, the Big Board continued to maintain the superiority of the specialist system. The specialists truly believed this and offered arguments to support their view. But then, there are tobacco-company executives who deny cigarettes constitute any kind of health hazard. When your economic well being is so closely identified with your vocation, such is to be expected.

The NYSE missed out on other opportunities in this period. During the late 1960s there was a small options business in the country, centered in lower New York. Options give the holder the right to purchase or sell a specified number of shares in a particular stock at a set price on or before a certain date. They are akin to placing a wager on the stock, that it will either rise or fall. Options are almost as old as civilization itself, but the business, which was important in the post-Civil War era, was less so in the 1960s. In those years the person who purchased an option usually held it until it was exercised or expired. The options dealers comprised a small and close-knit community. Their organization, the Put & Call Brokers & Dealers Association, was barely known outside the district.

Some at the NYSE, Phelan among them, tried to interest the members in developing an options exchange, but they were met with indifference. Meanwhile in Chicago, commodities traders at the Chicago Board of Trade (CBT) considered creating such a market. During the late 1980s the commodity-futures business was in one of the worst doldrums in history, and the members there were desperate for new instruments. These were colorful markets, using the outcry system to buy and sell contracts. In its own way the outcry system was as outmoded as the specialists, but like the specialists in New York, the local people in Chicago were in control, and they, too, feared computerization would render them redundant.

In 1935 the CBT had received permission to function as a stock exchange, and it studied options, which were not too different from futures contracts on commodities. They liked what they then saw as little more than an opportunistic move, so on April 26, 1973, the CBOE opened for business in the smokers' lounge at the CBT, with most of the traders members who usually dealt in such commodities as grains and pork bellies.

Seats at the CBOE initially sold for $10,000, to 284 individuals representing 1,211 firms. The initial instruments to be traded were calls on only 16 stocks. The CBOE lost $1 million its first year, but showed a small profit the next.

Options had obstacles to overcome before being accepted. For one thing, new financial instruments usually have difficulties, and at the time potential customers didn't have a method of pricing them. The first matter would be taken care of by the passage of time. The second was rectified by the propitious appearance of two articles dealing with pricing: Fischer Black's and Myron Sholes's, "The Pricing of Options and Corporate Liabilities," and Robert Merton's, "Theory of Rational Option Pricing." Each of these arcane essays appeared in relatively inaccessible publications, the first in the *Journal of Political Economy* (May–June 1973) and the Merton piece in *Bell Journal of Economics and Management* (Spring 1973). It wasn't long, however, before lucid explanations of what came to be called "Black-Sholes" became well-known to more sophisticated customers as well as options dealers.

It took a few years for the public to become familiar with the instruments, and then the CBOE traded put options as well. The price of a seat rose to a high of $80,000 in 1975, slightly more than one at the NYSE. By 1980 there were 120 options traded, and in 1983 the CBOE introduced options on the Standard & Poor's 100 Index; by 1993 this Index, which enabled the buyer or seller to place a wager on the market itself, averaged 253,000 shares a day, and seats were changing hands at upward of half a million dollars.

In this same period the Chicago Mercantile Exchange, another commodity market whose best-known product was pork-belly futures, also considered new business. When the United States abandoned the last vestige of gold backing for the dollar in 1971, currencies started to move against one another based on supply-and-demand considerations, making it difficult for commercial interests to make contracts for future deliveries. Moving swiftly, the "Merc" organized the International Monetary Market in 1972, which started dealing in seven currencies. Like the CBOE, the Merc moved into other areas of trading.

The NYSE initially failed to embrace currency trading and options on currencies, enabling not only the Merc but the Philadelphia Exchange to enter the field and flourish. Part of the reason for these failures to respond is that currency trading does not lend itself to specialist markets, and so the NYSE simply neglected the field, which is far larger than that for equities. But in 1980 it opened the New York Futures Exchange and began trading contracts in financial futures and its own NYSE index. This market never went anywhere and was discontinued. The NYSE indicated that "at some future time" the exchange would consider options trading, but this hardly was possible given the specialist system. Clearly, specialists could not deal in options written on their stocks: The possibilities of manipulation in such a situation would have been tremendous, and the SEC would never have approved of such an arrangement. Nor could other specialists—or a new group of specialists on the floor—deal in the options, for the proximity to the stock trading would have presented similar difficulties.

What of those companies that did not desire options to be traded against their stocks? The CBOE could afford to ignore them. It would have been different at the NYSE, where the companies could retaliate by delisting their stocks and using NASDAQ instead. The establishment of a New York Options Exchange might have resolved the matter. The NYSE might have controlled such a market, which could have had facilities a distance from the Exchange. There is some indication that this was considered. Needham consulted with Marsh, Block & Co., a major put-and-call dealer, but did not follow through. Instead, the Amex entered the field, welcoming a new product for its small exchange.

Repeatedly in the 1970s and 1980s, it seemed other exchanges entered new businesses before the NYSE got wind of them. A revived Amex later created instruments based on indexes, such as "Spiders" (based on the Standard & Poor's 500) and "Diamonds" (after the Dow-Jones Industrials), and then WEBS (World Equity Benchmark Securities), a hybrid group of single-country index funds. In those decades the NYSE resembled nothing more than a lumbering elephant chasing after gazelles, most of which came from Chicago.

This isn't to suggest Chicago is about to displace New York as the nation's—and world's—financial capital. Rather, these developments indicated that Chicago instead of New York had become the locus of the options and other derivative-securities market. Then, in the swiftly moving securities-trading industry, the Amex, which a decade ago seemed on the ropes, revived and planned mergers with NASDAQ and the Philadelphia Stock Exchange, with the new entity challenging Chicago for leadership in options trading. That the NYSE permitted a commodities exchange in another city to become the leader in financial derivatives and the Amex to innovate so successfully without a response were other blunders. How long might this continue?

Meanwhile, new threats to both the NYSE and NASDAQ are on the horizon. Sharp entrepreneurs have figured out ways to trade stocks on the Internet. By the spring of 1998 there were more than 70 online brokerages, led by E*Trade, and their businesses were growing. For good reason. E*Trade offered $20 trades, compared with the $60 and more charged by the other discount brokerages. According to Credit Suisse First Boston, in 1997 the number of customers using Internet trading doubled, to 3.3 million. Already the small firm of Direct IPO plans to take companies public on the Internet. Is there a new CSE—the Cyberspace Stock Exchange—in the securities trading future?

CHAPTER FIFTEEN

SCHWINN: MULTIPLE BLUNDERS

I n previous chapters I have attempted to demonstrate how a company and its leaders erred in one way or another and suffered as a result. In all I have indicated that while other mistakes were made, in each case one was paramount.

Is it not possible that a company can commit multiple blunders that bring it down over a fairly long period, because other factors are present to buoy even the more incompetent firms? For example, while there is no way to demonstrate the "might have beens" of history, the NYSE would have had a tougher time competing with its new rivals were it not for the buoyant financial atmosphere of the period during which the transformation of the market system occurred.

Such was the case in the bicycle industry during the post-World War II years. When the war ended, Schwinn was not only the industry's leader, but its most celebrated company, poised to capitalize on the growing market for bicycles. For a while it did. Then came a series of blunders and errors that ultimately brought it down. Some of these will be familiar by now and will not be dwelled upon here. Others will be new, such as undue dependence on suppliers, the failure to exploit the relationships, and unwise plant location. Financial errors were made, and the company didn't expand when virtually everyone else in the industry was doing so. New domestic and foreign companies appeared to exploit on changing tastes that Schwinn ignored. Schwinn failed to recognize that after those golden years the bicycle markets segmented, with new populations arriving to take to alternate forms of the sport. If the companies wouldn't provide them with desired forms of bikes, they would cobble them together on their own.

For many years bicycling had been pretty well confined to youngsters. By the 1960s this had changed. For recreational and health reasons, adults returned to biking. This presented the manufacturers with golden opportunities. Children's bikes were typically low priced; adults would pay much more for their models, with some of the high-performance ones costing as much as a decent used car.

Schwinn did not move into this market rapidly enough. Its relationships with the retailers eroded, and then the company went off on its own, marketing through dealers, who were controlled badly when at all. A misbegotten attempt to structure a dealership relationship that more closely resembled that enjoyed by the auto companies backfired. Schwinn's relations with its Asian suppliers, who in time eclipsed the company, were inept. If RCA provided the Japanese with the needed patents and know-how to best the Americans, Schwinn more than any other American bicycle company tutored the Taiwanese and Chinese in the ways of bike design and manufacture.

Then there was the "Not invented here" (NIH) syndrome. It stems from a conceit bred of success, in which the company's leaders, having achieved dominance in an industry or niche, assume they have little to learn from the competition. Schwinn provides examples of NIH and many other errors. Finally, there was the matter of family dynasties. To the end Schwinn was led by men bearing the name of the founder, when far more able managers were available and ignored. Among the "rules" Peter Drucker set down for managing family businesses, was this one:

> The first rule is that family members do not work in the business unless they are at least as able as any nonfamily employee, and work at least as hard. It is much cheaper to pay a lazy nephew not to come to work than to keep him on the payroll. In a family-managed company family members are always "top management" whatever their official job or title. . . . If mediocre or lazy family members are kept on the payroll, respect for top management and for the business altogether rapidly erodes within the entire workforce. Capable nonfamily people will not stay. And the ones who do soon become courtiers and toadies.

As will be seen, Drucker might have been thinking of Schwinn when writing these words. Some of the Schwinns were competent and even superb; the last of the line was a disaster. Such often is the fate in dynasties. Yet most businesses can mitigate this problem by making public stock offerings when the moment seemed right. The Schwinns might have done this easily and still retained control of the company. That none of the Schwinns appeared to have considered this route until it was too late to do so was an indication either of naivete or arrogance.

In the late 1940s Schwinn was at the top of the bicycle heap. For a while it seemed impregnable. Indeed, so powerful was the company that in 1962 it was the object of an antitrust suit that dragged out for five years and ended with Schwinn having to alter its method of conducting business. In 1992 Schwinn filed for Chapter 11 bankruptcy protection. All of these aforementioned strategic, production, marketing, financing, acquisitions, and personnel blunders came in this period. That Schwinn lasted as long as it did was due to the franchise the name provided and the booming market for a wide variety of bikes.

For a while it appeared Schwinn might disappear, and this saddened those adults who as children and teenagers pleaded not for a bike, but for a Schwinn, and did not realize that at the time of its failure, most Schwinn bikes were made by others in the Far East. The company that once sold Schwinns to chain stores that slapped on their own nameplates was now engaged in the same practice.

The reason the Schwinn story did not attract as much attention as, say, the Chrysler bailout, is no secret. While bicycling is popular, in recent years the industry hasn't attracted much scholarly or journalistic attention. Outside of a substantial cadre of aficionados, the bicycle business is not considered as "essential" as autos, aviation, and electronics, to name a few whose leading companies are household names, well-known even by those who have no interest in driving, flying, or purchasing a computer. Yet there was a time when Schwinn was just that: a franchise name. No more.

Outside of scholars and those concerned with bicycling, few know the power of the bicycle and the public fascination with the machine during the last decade of the nineteenth century. Yet virtually all of those who as youngsters owned a bicycle (as opposed to a tricycle) while in their teens may recall the sense of freedom obtained by having one at their disposal. Those who can recall the feeling also know it was a step toward a still more powerful vehicle, the automobile. Such was not the case in the 1890s, when as has been seen in the chapter on

Packard, the auto was in its infancy and considered a rich man's toy, while the bicycle was perceived as the average person's transportation of the future. Bicycles were clean, swift, easily maneuvered, compact, and silent. They required no fuel and were easy to repair. While it could not have been realized at the time, the bicycle as it eventually evolved was to be the most energy-efficient vehicle ever developed.

In the 1890s a white-collar worker who drove a horse and buggy to work had to worry about caring for the horse, feeding it, the elements, and a host of other matters. In traffic horses might bolt and cause serious damage, and the horse and buggy were not particularly agile. Little wonder, then, that the bicycle was so popular—or that in 1899 a writer confidently predicted that "the ordinary 'horseless carriage' is at present a luxury for the wealthy; and although its price will probably fall in the future, it will never, of course, come into as common use as the bicycle."

It took a while before the bicycle arrived at this status. Devices resembling bicycles were playthings for the nobility in the early years of the nineteenth century. Kirkpatrick MacMillan, a Scots blacksmith, created a wooden contraption that operated like a bicycle in 1839, and in some histories he is credited with the invention. Some 20 years later two Frenchmen, Pierre Michaux and Pierre Lallement, working independently, constructed their *veloces*, which provided the basis for the generic term "velocipede," the common designation at the time. Lallement introduced the velocipede to America in 1865, where it attracted little attention at first, but then the interests of hobbyists not unlike those who created the radio, automobile, and personal computer industries.

The machines featured a large front wheel and a small rear one, with pedals attached to the front axle providing the means for the rider to power them. The higher the front wheel, the more distance might be covered by a single rotation, but the size also made the bicycles unstable. So long as these "high wheelers" were the norm, it took some skill and courage to attempt to ride them on city streets. In this period races conducted on horse tracks became a sport, the meets attended by people who considered riding bikes and others who would never dare to do so, and certainly not in the city streets.

In the next few years the design was refined, and soon carriage makers were cobbling together machines for those eager to test themselves on the devices. Eschewing the open roads, some went to large halls, where alert entrepreneurs rented bikes to those wanting to try them out. By 1870 there were 5,000 bikers in Boston alone, and *Scientific American* was suggesting that 30-foot-long tricycles, peddled by passengers, might replace trolleys. Then, as might have been expected, the fad died down. How might it be otherwise until paved roads and sturdier machines appeared?

Improvements were not long in coming, and these arrived from England, where bicycling had become more popular than it was in the United States. Manufacturers there replaced the wooden frames with those made of steel tubing, employed ball bearings to reduce wheel friction, and used tires of solid rubber around the wheels, all of which cut down on weight.

Several of these machines, which came to be known as "ordinaries," were demonstrated at the Philadelphia Centennial Exposition, where architect Frank Weston and Colonel Albert Pope, a Union Army veteran and industrialist who owned and operated a shoe factory in Boston, became interested in them. Weston prodded a friend, Arthur Cunningham, into forming the firm of Cunningham, Heath & Co. to import English bikes. The firm did well enough for Pope to purchase the Lallement patent as well as others. With this he positioned himself to become, if he so desired, a virtual monopolist. This was not his intent, however. Pope was more interested in promoting bicycles than in dominating the industry. He probably thought that without the creation of a broad market, control of the minuscule market wouldn't be worth much, so he licensed his patents for modest fees.

The first bikes Pope sold were English imports, but soon he engaged Weed Sewing Machine Co., based in Hartford, Connecticut, to manufacture the Colombia, which weighed 70 pounds and cost $313, a year's salary for a skilled worker in this period. One of the reasons Pope was able to sell at that price was because he managed to convinced local legislators to support a 35 percent tariff on imports. He organized a riding school that offered free lessons. By 1884 he was turning out bicycles at the rate of 5,000 a year. Now priced at around $125, they remained wealthy people's toys. In 1890 Pope helped organize the League of American Wheelmen, which lobbied for improved streets and endowed a professorship of highway engineering at the Massachusetts Institute of Technology.

In 1880 more than 60 percent of the nation's roads were unpaved, and of those that were, more than half were of macadam and gravel, hardly ideal for bicycling. In 1900 fewer than half the roads were unpaved, and 10 percent of the paved roads were asphalt or concrete. The bicycle had changed the nature of the American street and road. Of course, in time this would redound to the benefit of the automobile, which would drive many bicycles off the road and lead their riders into car purchases.

Even with the tariff the English bikes found customers. "The machines in England are lighter than those made in this country," wrote *The Bicycling World*, a Boston-based fan magazine in 1884. "I think the greatest drawback experienced by American riders is the machine used by them. It is impossible for a man to race and make fast time on a thirty-pound machine, and compete successfully with his English cousin on a twenty-two pound racer." True enough, but if racing were to be the most significant part of the market for bicycles, they would hardly become popular. What was needed more than a drop in weight was a device the average person could manage without toppling over due to the height of that front wheel, a common enough experience, especially when the rider attempted to stop suddenly.

The English realized this and tested geared bicycles, known as "geared ordinaries," in which the large front wheel was replaced by a smaller one, and power was transmitted to the front wheel by means of a large front gear and a smaller rear one connected by a skip-tooth metal chain. Others experimented with small front wheels and larger rear ones, in which the pedal was on the rear wheel. A few moved the pedal from the axle onto the large gear. Finally, in 1885 Englishman James Kemp Starley produced a model that would be familiar to today's bikers. The two wheels were the same size, about 30 inches in diameter, and the rider sat in a seat above the front of the rear wheel. The handlebars were shorter than current ones, but still recognizable as such. Power was provided to the rear wheel by the chain and gear arrangement. This bike had solid rubber tires and a crude shock absorber for the front wheel. Three years later Dr. J. B. Dunlap of Belfast, Ireland, produced a hollow rubber tire that had to be inflated by means of a pump. The pneumatic tire had been born. By then Columbia had introduced the Light Roadster Safety in the United States.

The public took to the "safety bike," and soon the other manufac-turers switched production to this version. It is difficult to compare the impact of the new bike configuration on the industry to that of a simi-lar development in other fields, but perhaps one would be the introduc-tion of automatic transmissions in automobiles in the late 1930s, or perhaps smoother shifting in the previous decade. Even so, the safety bike had a greater impact on bicycling. After testing one, *The Bicycling World* reported, "The element of safety is rather distasteful to a good many riders that prefer to run some risk as it gives zest to the sport for them; to such the ordinary must ever be preferable." But the writer con-ceded, "The ordinary has a future, and will never be an obsolete pattern. It has too many splendid qualities for that. On the other hand, the rear-driving safety has come to stay, and while it is bound to run the old timer for honors on the road, it can never hope to crowd it entirely out." Which is precisely what it did. The last ordinary was produced in 1893.

Other improvements followed—children's bikes and bikes with frames designed to permit women to ride more easily. In fact, biking became so popular with women that the sport led to the abandonment of corsets and bustles. Bikes became lighter, falling to 20 pounds by 1895, by which time there were more than 400 American manufactur-ers, many of them in the Midwest, with Chicago becoming for bicy-cles what Detroit would later be for automobiles. There were good reasons for the bike's popularity at that time. A skilled rider on decent roads could travel twice as fast as a horse and carriage. It was the beginning of a national mania, and middle-class people lined up to purchase bikes, which not only were a means of transportation, but were the status symbol of the time. The craze had unanticipated con-sequences. Book and musical-instrument sales declined sharply, as cycling replaced reading and music as a diversion. Attendance at the theaters and vaudeville fell off as well. Not even the coming of a major depression could affect bicycle sales.

With economies of scale, prices dropped to an average of $100 in 1895, and to $50 in 1898, this at a time when the average weekly wage was approximately half that amount. By then there were more than 4 million bikes on America's roads, and with the pressures applied by bicyclers, those roads were improved, and automobile sales climbed.

Pope realized what was happening; he began making cars in 1897, and after selling $4.2 million worth of new stock started producing them in small bicycles plants in Toledo, Hartford, and Indianapolis. Meanwhile the bicycle factories he had organized in New England continued turning out those vehicles. For a brief period Pope was the nation's largest manufacturer of cars as well as bicycles. "I predict that inside of ten years there will be more automobiles in use in the large cities of the United States than there are now horses in these cities."

He was one of several automakers who began in bicycles. Among the others were John Willys and Charles Duryea. William Knudson, later a president of General Motors, started in bicycles. We have seen how Alexander Winton, who sold James Packard that lemon of a car, was primarily a bicycle manufacturer at the time. Among the foreign bike companies that later turned to automobiles were Germany's Opel, England's Rover, Humber, and Morris, France's Peugeot and Darracq. The auto pioneers borrowed chain drives and shock absorbers from the bikes, so the relationship between the two industries was fairly close. Aviation pioneers began in bicycles. Wilbur and Orville Wright were bicycle mechanics, as was Glenn Curtiss. The bicycle industry could lay claim to being the incubator of twentieth century transportation.

Reliable statistics for this period are hard to come by, but it appears American manufacturers produced and sold 2 million bicycles in 1897, when the population was 72 million. That was the high point for bicycles. Not until the post-World War II period, when the population was 146 million, would sales again exceed 2 million.

One of the early bike companies was founded by a German immigrant, Ignatius Schwinn, more commonly called Ignaz. Schwinn arrived in America in 1891 at the age of 31 and headed to Chicago. He was an experienced bicycle mechanic, having designed and built ordinaries and safeties in Germany, and helped to create a factory for what became the Adler Works. A person with such qualifications had no trouble finding employment, and so he did, flitting from job to job, all the while thinking of starting his own business. That would require capital, not much to be sure, but he had next to nothing.

Schwinn found a backer in Adolph Arnold, like him a German immigrant, who made a good living from a meatpacking establishment and had also become a bank president. Arnold liked the prospects for bicycles and saw in Schwinn the right person to back. In 1895 they organized Arnold, Schwinn & Co. to manufacture bicycles, wagons, carriages, and parts. It could not have dented Arnold's bank account too severely, since the "factory" was not much more than a storefront. Schwinn would purchase parts from suppliers and then assemble them into bicycles, which initially were sold to a walk-in trade in Chicago and to hardware and chain stores elsewhere.

The company was an immediate success, appearing as it did at a time when there were long waiting lists for bicycles. Arnold, Schwinn produced and sold the "World," which was a premium model, but its biggest business was in lower-priced bicycles for Sears Roebuck, which sold them under its own nameplate. According to company records, the company's sales for its first full year came to 25,000 units, hardly spectacular, but Schwinn claimed this made it an industry leader.

The good times were soon to end. As greater numbers of automobiles took to the roads made possible by bikes in greater numbers, sales slumped, output falling to 230,000 by 1905. Of those 300 manufacturers barely 20 or so survived. Arnold, Schwinn was one of these, due largely to the fact that it was still small with low overhead. The troubles of others were turned to its benefit. Arnold, Schwinn took over a bankrupt firm in 1901 and moved operations to its larger facility.

Albert Pope also thought to take advantage of the decline in sales. He approached sporting-goods tycoon Albert Spaulding with a plan to gobble as many of the bankrupt companies as might be resurrected, along with some of the survivors, to form the American Bicycle Co. This they did, and in March 1899, having raised $40 million, Spaulding claimed to have 75 percent of the business. As happened, the "Bicycle Trust" would fail because of inept leadership and rickety financing, but mostly due to the nature of the market.

Faced with a market that adults were leaving in droves and with limited sales for children's bikes, in 1908 Arnold sold his share of the partnership to Schwinn. The company was still formally called Arnold, Schwinn, and this would remain the case for another half century, but to the general public and its suppliers, it was now Schwinn & Co.

The bicycle business was hardly dead, but it was ailing. In 1910 sales came to a mere 170,000, and increasingly these were to parents who purchased them for their children. The figure was twice that in 1915 and rose irregularly, getting close to the half-million mark some years during the 1920s.

Schwinn survived due to the combination of leadership, product, and price. On the average it had 15 to 20 percent of the market in this period. The company took whatever other business was available. During World War I Arnold, Schwinn manufactured aircraft engines, which provided it with a financial cushion. The company flirted with motorcycles, acquiring the Excelsior Motor Manufacturing & Supply Co. for a small amount of cash, since that firm was close to bankruptcy. Ignaz Schwinn redesigned its "X" model, which was the first to go 100 miles per hour. Sales soared, enabling Schwinn to purchase the Henderson Motorcycle Co. in 1917 for $285,000, hiring the Henderson brothers to manage it and design new products. Soon they quarreled, as the Hendersons were prepared to sacrifice heavy frames for speed, while Schwinn preferred strength to the light frames. So the Hendersons left, but not before instructing Schwinn in the finer arts of motorcycle design. Ignaz then united Excelsior and Henderson, making Schwinn the third-largest factor in the industry behind Harley-Davidson and Indian. Bicycles may have been in the doldrums, but motorcycles, now Schwinn's more important business, were doing quite well. Ignaz had become more interested in them, leaving the bicycle business to his eldest son, 36-year-old Frank W. Schwinn.

The coming of the Great Depression hit both bicycles and motorcycles hard. Excelsior was closed down, while Henderson laid off workers and cut back sharply. National bike sales slumped to 194,000 in 1932, and Schwinn's output fell to less than 20,000 units in this period. Now more than 70 years old, dejected and worn out, Ignaz stepped aside from day-to-day management, although retaining the title of president, and Frank W. took over as CEO. It was he who transformed Schwinn from a company that was one of a host of the more prominent manufacturers into the industry leader.

Schwinn and the other manufacturers were scrambling for customers. None of them had thought to imitate the automobile industry by setting up dealerships and dictating terms to them. Rather, they sold much of their output to the chain department stores such as Sears and Montgomery Ward and the rest to independents, which usually operated out of small, shabby storefronts with repair shops in the rear, or to hardware stores, which carried a few bikes as a sideline. One could hardly lay down conditions to such marginal operations, which catered primarily to children and teenagers, the latter often using their bikes to deliver newspapers in the morning and after school. The only significant large customer was Western Union, which delivered telegrams via an army of uniformed delivery boys, and Western Union could dictate terms to the manufacturers.

The bicycle manufacturers had difficulties with suppliers. Unlike the major auto companies, which manufactured most of their parts, the bicycle companies continued to purchase a great deal of what went into a bike from specialized suppliers. New Departure provided brake systems to most of the manufacturers, while spokes and handlebars came from Torrington. U.S. Rubber was the prime supplier of tires. There were many bicycle companies and few suppliers, and so they could dictate terms to Schwinn and the others.

While his father accepted this situation, Frank W. Schwinn railed against it. How might the company differentiate its products if it had the same components as did competitors? His experience with motorcycles, where competition on the basis of quality and performance was the accepted way of conducting business, may have spurred him in this direction, or it may have been that he had felt this way from the time he entered the business. Then there was the matter of personality. Ignaz had been a hard case, but Frank W. was tougher still. He was a fierce competitor, who would not accept second place to anyone.

Frank W. set out to remake the American bicycle and the business. In the early 1930s the wheel rims were made of wood covered by metal, while tires were only one and a half inches wide and cheaply made, so flats were problems, and more often than not, the tire could not be repaired. Frank W. called these "glorified pieces of garden hose." In contrast, tires on European bikes were wider, constructed on a cord casing, and were thicker; these were called "balloons." Knowing this, wealthy Americans interested in cycling would purchase the much more expensive European models, especially the Raleigh, considered the class of the field.

In 1932 Schwinn traveled to England and Germany, made contacts with tire manufacturers, and arranged for shipments to his factory. On his return he went to U.S. Rubber's Akron headquarters to tell executives that unless they provided him with similar tires, he would turn all of his business over to the foreign manufacturers. Knowing that if Schwinn did this the other manufacturers would probably follow his lead and not wanting to lose any business at a time that proved the bottom of the Great Depression, U.S. Rubber bowed, and produced 5,000 two-inch balloon tires with rubber knobs that gripped the pavement and also lasted longer, for Schwinn. Then Schwinn went to Firestone, which equipped rims for the Excelsior motorcycles, and asked that company to manufacture them for the bicycles as well. All the while the Schwinn factory was widening its frames and forks to go with the wider tires. The next step was to convince dealers and Sears and Montgomery Ward that the new product would far outsell the old.

It worked. Schwinn's "Super Balloon Tire Bicycle," which would evolve into the Excelsior, was released in 1933 and was an instant success. It was the most important change since the Safety had replaced the Ordinary four decades earlier, and the other manufacturers scrambled to adopt the new standard.

There was more to come. Schwinn produced the Streamline Aero Cycle the following year. This bike featured a "tank," housing for the wheels and cost $35, which was a much higher price than bikes offered by competitors. In 1935 Schwinn released the Cycle Plane, which sold for less than $30 and had a lifetime guarantee. In 1935 Schwinn sold more than 100,000 Cycle Planes alone, a year when the total industry output came to 660,000.

Frank W. had revived the industry during the tough years of the Great Depression. The market for his bikes was clear enough: middle-class teenagers. The more affluent would purchase Schwinns, while those who could not afford them would have to settle for Huffeys, Roadmasters, Columbias, and other lesser products from companies that learned they could not compete with Schwinn on image and quality and had to do so on the basis of price.

Lacking the funds to purchase a new or even a used bike, enterprising teenagers would create them from discarded parts. This wasn't particularly difficult, since bikes were relatively simple affairs in those prehand-brake and prederailleur days (a derailleur "derails" the chain from one combination of sprockets and "rerails" it to another). A discarded frame, bent wheels straightened out for small change at the neighborhood bike store, new tires, and a few other accessories, and the amateur mechanic could have a serviceable bike for around $10. This was not deemed an important part of the industry, however, and took only minor sales from the retailers, which occupied most of Frank W.'s attention as he strove to push his company into leadership position.

As the Schwinn reputation grew, the chain stores no longer insisted on placing their own nameplates on bicycles purchased from the company; they were more than happy to sell them as Schwinns. Retailers knew they had no choice in the matter. Schwinn was able to command premium prices for its bikes. The advertising of the period proclaimed, "Don't get a bike, get a Schwinn." Schwinn advertisements appeared on the inside back cover of many comic books, this being the best way to reach its kind of audience. Schwinn was the biggest advertiser in *Boy's Life* magazine. The company's ads featured smiling Hollywood stars, among them Ronald Reagan, on its bikes. Schwinn had become one of the best known names in the country, along with Coke and Lucky Strike. It had opted for a strategy similar to that employed by Packard in its early years. It wanted to be top of the line and to enjoy the prices that such status entailed.

Ignaz died in 1948, and Frank W. took the title of president. That year also marked the shipment of the last private-label bike manufactured by Schwinn. The chain stores turned to other manufacturers for their product and offered them to old customers who couldn't tell the difference between a Schwinn Sears from one of the others.

The postwar period saw the rise of suburbia. The 1960 census indicated that more Americans lived in suburbs than in cities and farms combined, and the trend was still growing. The suburbs spawned the two-car and the one-bike-per-youngster family, and whenever possible financially, that bike would be a Schwinn. In 1950 Schwinn had a quarter of the American bike market. Its prime model early in the decade was the Black Phantom, which fairly dripped with chrome and weighed in at more than 62 pounds. It featured hand brakes and a shock absorber, as well as a headlight. In addition, the Black Phantom had a guarantee for one year against theft, a welcome feature as the bike cost upward of $80.

This was the period in which the family autos were palaces of chrome, the age of what has been called "Detroit Baroque," and children wanted their version. The Black Phantom filled the bill. This was the high point for Schwinn. Frank W. knew the market could only grow. The baby boom began in the late 1940s and continued into the early 1950s. In 1940 there were 22 million Americans between the ages of 5 and 15, the prime age for bicycle purchases. By 1950 the cohort was 24 million and in 1960, 35 million. With the coming of television, Schwinn sponsored the popular *Captain Kangaroo Show*, and the Captain became a company spokesperson.

While the prospects for selling bikes to youngsters were enticing, that for their parents was starting to look promising as well. President Eisenhower suffered a heart attack in 1955, and his physician, Dr. Paul Dudley White, who hailed from Boston, instantly achieved celebrity status. As it happened, White was a lifelong cylicist, who not only was convinced the sport offered positive health benefits, but was prepared to act as spokesperson for it. White prescribed exercise on a stationary bike for Eisenhower and suggested out-of-shape Americans might consider taking to the roads on their bikes—and if they didn't have them, purchase them.

For the first time since the 1890s municipalities felt pressure to create bike paths. Chicago announced the creation of 36 bike paths, and other cities followed suit. Boston created the Charles River Bicycle Path and named it after White. The Department of the Interior earmarked a token $2 million for paths. Bicycle production, which had been 1.75 million units in 1954, rose to more than 2 million by 1958 and continued upward, to 3.7 million in 1960.

Schwinn's sales did not rise correspondingly. Due to a variety of reasons, company's market share had slid from approximately a quarter of the market in 1950 to 14 percent in 1955. For one thing the Chicago factory, not much changed since the early years, was outdated and too small to meet the demand. It was not unusual for Schwinn to fill orders months after they were received. With an army of relatives working at the factory and demanding high dividends, Frank W. would not invest in expansion. In frustration dealers turned to the domestic and foreign competitors, which were hungry, eager, and more efficient than Schwinn. In an attempt to stimulate European economies during the early years of the Cold War, tariffs on imported bicycles were lowered. By the mid-1950s imports accounted for four out of every ten sales. The percentage would decline once the tariffs were raised, but by the 1970s Asian imports were making inroads into the American markets.

The foreign companies introduced Americans to the three-speed hubs manufactured by Sturmey-Archer, which the American companies accepted somewhat reluctantly. Noting that lightweight bikes accounted for a substantial number of the imports, Schwinn attributed part of the success to the eight-speed derailleur gears they sported—two sprockets in front, four in the rear. The company purchased 1,000 gear sets and mounted them on its lightweight models. The bikes were failures, and the project had to be scrapped. Much of the failure could be attributed to the reluctance of dealers to learn how to service the models. By the mid-1950s, when sales were still good, it had become evident that an industry that hadn't altered its ways of doing business or its designs for a generation was out of touch with the public. What automobiles would experience in the 1960s, bicycles encountered a decade earlier.

Now in his mid-sixties, Frank W. had started easing out of active management. Most of the work was done by his son, Frank V., and by Ray Burch, the marketing vice president, and Al Fritz, who was in charge of product design and manufacturing. Fritz had started out as a factory hand and rose rapidly through hard work and intelligence, and by then he was recognized as one of the ablest executives in the industry. Burch had a background in retailing and in aircraft manufacturing. He had marketed motorcycles successfully and was considered the savviest salesperson in the business.

In this period Schwinn distributed most of its products through 22 independent distributors, who in turn sold them to the dealers. In investigating the situation, Burch found some dealers who purchased one or perhaps two bikes a year, clearly for their own use or for those of friends and relatives, had gotten on the list in order to buy them wholesale. One distributor serviced 1,200 dealers and sold them only around 600 bikes a year. There were dealers who didn't know the first thing about repairs and hundreds of inactive ones. Burch reasoned that most dealers couldn't make a living on Schwinn sales and so ignored them for other products. Such was the case with some grocery-store owners and barbershops who had somehow gotten on the dealership roster. Burch purged the list ruthlessly, retaining only the best producers, and then made certain their operations were up to snuff.

Schwinn paid a price for these actions. The Justice Department started investigating the program and charged the company with antitrust violations, citing its apportionment of distributors' territories, the requirement for distributors to sell bikes to specified dealers, and price fixing. Schwinn was exonerated in the lower court, where U.S. District Court Judge J. Sam Perry found that by so acting

Schwinn actually enhance competition by providing more viable alternative retail outlets to the chain stores. The government appealed, and in 1967, in a 5–2 decision, the Supreme Court ruled that Schwinn could not dictate terms as it did to the distributors. Writing for the majority, Justice Abe Fortas said, "Such restraints are so obviously destructive of competition that their mere existence is enough. Once the manufacturer has parted with title and risk, he has parted with domination over product."

The company had been prepared for this and promptly announced it would open its own company-run distribution centers and so control the supplies to dealers through them rather than through the distributors. This action backfired. The former Schwinn distributors, some of whom were among the most knowledgeable people in the field, switched to other manufacturers and took their dealers with them. The big winner in this was Murray Ohio, which despite the name was based in an up-to-date factory in Nashville, Tennessee, where labor costs were lower than those in Chicago. Murray's bikes were every bit as good as the Schwinns and were priced lower.

In 1963, while Burch concentrated on shaping up the dealerships, Fritz attempted to fashion a strategy to deal with a grassroots movement originating in California. Teenagers there were purchasing discarded bikes with the small 20-inch wheels that had been popular for a while a generation earlier and were replacing the bikes' conventional handlebars with the higher, much wider ones favored by newspaper deliverers of that era. A few years earlier Richard Person, whose family was in the saddle business, had come up with such a bike, often called "the high-riser," which because of its wheel size was easily maneuverable. The Person version featured a "banana seat," as well. Person attempted to convince Schwinn these bikes could be used by children to play what he called "bicycle polo." Nothing came of this at the time, and Person unloaded his seats on California parts distributor Peter Mole, who sold them to those experimenters. How did they come up with such an idea? Those Californians might have had the same idea as Person, since they called the seats "Polo Solo." But Fritz was intrigued with these bikes and had his Schwinn team create a prototype of its own.

All of this occurred at a time when the company's attention was focused on the matter of succession. Frank W. was ailing, suffering from prostate cancer, and he died on April 19, 1963, at the age of 69. By then Frank V. had taken over, while his younger brother, Edward, became executive vice president. Both men had grown up in the shadow of their domineering father, who had become the leading figure in the industry. The situation was somewhat like what had happened at RCA when Bob Sarnoff took over from the General, but there were some differences. Schwinn was a much smaller family business, and while the tradition was for the eldest son to succeed, all the other sons, as well as sons-in-laws, cousins, and uncles could work for Schwinn if they were of a mind to do so. They comprised a mixed bag at best, and their presence caused dissension among the nonfamily employees . Moreover, all the Schwinns were taken care of financially, and so there often was little money left over for modernization. In good years there would be large surpluses that would be distributed in the form of dividends, but in poor ones the company would suffer.

Frank V. was an adequate CEO who turned in a decent performance but was unable to match his father's record. Edward was incompetent. He had little interest in the business, neglected his work, and preferred sports to bikes. Frank W. had fired him at least twice, but was obliged to take him back when his wife protested, "You can't fire your son."

Frank V. and Edward learned of Fritz's efforts with what he now called the "Sting Ray," and didn't think much of it. The bikes didn't seem stable, and this might frighten parents. But after the funeral Fritz invited some of the distributors who had come to pay their respects to visit the factory, where he showed them several models of the new bike and invited them to try them out. At first skeptical, they quickly turned enthusiastic. Perhaps the Sting Ray would be only a short-term craze, but it could be good for a few thousand sales. Besides, development costs would be low, and even with modest volume the bikes could prove profitable. Frank V. reluctantly went along with the experiment, betting that Fritz wouldn't be able to sell 5,000 of them that year. He lost: Sting Ray sales came to 47,000. The Sting Ray phenomenon quickly went national, and it was not flash-in-the-pan either; the industry as a whole sold 7.5 million bicycles in 1968, with American Machine & Foundry selling its imported model as Avenger, Murray Ohio as the Eliminator, and the others selling with equally grim names. The companies vied for the most garish paint jobs and accessories.

In 1968 Schwinn introduced its "Krate" series—with the likes of Orange Krate, Apple Krate, and Lemon Peeler, among others. These were the first true "off-road" bikes, which had banana seats, 16-inch front wheels and 20-inch wheels in the rear, a springer front end, rear shocks, and on the crossbar, a five-speed shift. The initial retail price was $86.95. Frank V. continued to be troubled about the matter of safety and in 1974 set down stricter standards that tamed the bikes and made them less appealing than the racier ones the competition provided.

Those bikers who liked the original version made similar models on their own that were for competitions known as "Bicycle Moto-Cross," which were competition races even more dangerous than street biking. "BMX" bikes became phenomenal sellers, and all the companies except Schwinn, with Murray Ohio in the lead, participated in the boom. Schwinn had done the pioneering with Sting-Ray and might easily have converted them to BMXs. Some dealers wanted to alter Sting Rays to sell to customers who wanted BMXs. Schwinn warned that if they did this, the warranties would be voided. Frank V. told them that BMX was a fad, but he was mistaken. By midsummer of 1974 there were more than 100 tracks in California alone, and due to the BMXs, and for the first time since World War I, more bicycles than automobiles were sold in the United States. Schwinn finally got back into the BMX market in 1975 with the Scrambler, which was too heavy and made little impact.

By the late 1960s cyclists had their choice of a variety of different bikes, but there were three basic configurations. The high riser, such as the Krates, the hot-rods of the industry, priced between $35 and $80, were the favorites of the young and accounted for three quarters of all sales. The middleweights were the familiar models that went back to the 1930s. Rugged, with balloon tires, they weighed around 45 pounds and could be had for as little as $30. Finally, lightweight bikes, with slim tires and ten-speed gears made possible through the use of two sprockets on the chainwheel and five on the rear-wheel gear cone, were coming into favor. While not racing bikes, they approximated the feel provided by such machines. The ten-speeders cost anywhere from $130 to $250 when fully equipped, with Iverson, a small Long-Island-based bike company, offering a stripped-down model for as low as $85. Schwinn had well-regarded, competitive entries—when you could find them—and went against the likes of Fuji, Peugeut, Atala,

Itoh, and Raleigh among the imports and against Murray Ohio, the Sears bikes manufactured by Huffman, Roadmaster, and the others. They weighed ten pounds less than the middleweights, and with a ten-gear speed shift could cost as little as $60. As adults returned to cycling in larger numbers, these models were to grow in popularity.

Schwinn remained the best-selling brand during the 1970s and 1980s, but Huffman and Murray Ohio, which moved forcefully into the privately branded segment of the market and were selling their products to Sears, Penney, Western Auto Supply, and others, were growing more rapidly. Perhaps it would have been otherwise had Schwinn been able to turn out more bikes. In 1971 the company produced 1.1 million of them, but took its last orders in May. Christmas season in this period accounted for a quarter of sales, and that year potential buyers had to settle for other brands. Families that had purchased Schwinns for generations now learned that the competition turned out pretty good products and at lower prices. They were also starting to realize that some of the privately branded bikes were made in Japan. The family that warily purchased its first Toyota or Datsun and was pleasantly surprised at the quality available at such low prices was prepared to buy Japanese bikes. In 1972 imports accounted for one third of the 13.9 million bicycles sold in the United States.

Twice as many bikes were manufactured in the United States in 1973 than in 1970. Most of the other manufacturers had enlarged their facilities, but not Schwinn. Outside of a $2.5 million satellite plant where frames were welded and a rim mill and warehouse, the Schwinns continued to come from that one outmoded Chicago plant.

In 1973 Schwinn shipped fewer than 1.5 million bikes, placing it fourth in the industry behind Murray Ohio (2.4 million), Huffman (2.3 million), and AMF (1.8 million). Frank V. certainly realized that Schwinn was losing market share, but he refused to modernize the factory or expend large sums on refurbishing it. His reasoning was somewhat puzzling. "We lost a degree of quality," he said. "We had to catch up on that. The volume of work entailed in answering consumer complaints was staggering compared with what it had been."

The reputation for quality remained, even as the reality had changed. In a 1974 survey of the industry, *Fortune* writer Arthur Lewis called Schwinn "the aristocrat of the industry," whose "fetish of quality" had been created by Ignaz and had been "passed along to his son, Frank

W. Schwinn, and to his grandson, Frank V." But the company was a laggard. In the mid-1970s bikes manufactured of exotic materials such as titanium appeared; these could weigh less than four pounds and cost more than $1,000. Teledyne, a newcomer whose parent was a conglomerate, was a big player in this specialty area, which Schwinn ignored.

Matters got worse during the 1974 Christmas season, at the peak of a boom fueled in part by the Arab oil boycott and subsequent rises in gasoline prices, which as has been seen also affected Pan Am and helped fuel the hostile takeover mania of the next decade. Dealers who in the past had been warned to carry at least 50 percent of their inventory in Schwinns pleaded for product, which the factory could not supply. They went on allocation a month before Christmas. Other companies had problems with meeting demand and reacted by importing foreign product, much of which came from Japan. Frank V. held back, insisting that only Schwinn would manufacture bikes with that name affixed to them.

Shortly afterward, Frank V. had a heart attack and seemed to lose interest in the business. Edward Schwinn had died two years earlier. and his young son, Edward, Jr., had joined the firm on his graduation from college in 1972. Two years later he was elevated to the post of vice president for corporate development. So the Schwinn dynasty was to continue, while seasoned veterans like Fritz and Burch soldiered on, knowing that while at other companies they might have hoped for the post of CEO, it was impossible at Schwinn.

On his recovery Frank V. told the dealers they could suspend the 50 percent rule, so they would be permitted to take on many more other bikes from other manufacturers so long as the shortages continued. Then, bowing to the inevitable, Frank V. quietly began importing Japanese bikes, although they initially did not have the Schwinn name on them. The following year Schwinn was bringing them in 200,000 at a clip.

The situation in the domestic bicycle industry presented Japanese, Taiwanese, British, French, and West German companies with a superb opportunity to make further inroads into the American market. The boom seemed endless. In 1978 the Bicycle Institute of America claimed there were 65 million bikes on the roads, compared with 93 million registered automobiles. Soon they would pass the number of cars. By then the proportion of the market taken by the foreigners reached more than one third.

In 1976, in its well-followed evaluations, *Consumer Reports* reported as "very good" seven foreign models, ranging in price from $149 to $220. Two Schwinns were in the "good to very good" category, and these retailed for $170 and $210. The lower-end bike was manufactured for Schwinn by Japanese firms.

Frank V. stepped down as CEO in October 1979, but remained as chairman. He was replaced by Edward, Jr., who was still in his twenties and had worked only seven years at the firm. Youth and inexperience aside, Edward, Jr. did not possess either the temperament or the skills required for such a position. More like his father than his grandfather or uncle, Edward, Jr., blundered his way through the company. He dismissed many of the old hands at the firm, believing that Schwinn's poor performance was due more to corporate deadwood than to the inefficient plant, outdated design, and poor quality control. Ray Burch was shoved into retirement and was succeeded by John Nielsen, who lacked his experience and ability. Others followed. Edward, Jr., wanted to make it clear that a new era had dawned at Schwinn, but he didn't seem to have a strategy for it. Al Fritz, who was the Schwinn executive best prepared to take over, watched in dismay.

Around the plant Edward, Jr., acted as though to the manor born. He delighted in arrogant surprises, such as arriving at formal dinners in shorts and polo shirts. Edward, Jr., insulted veteran dealers and refused to listen to Fritz and others at the plant who had many more years of experience than he. There was something childlike about him, which didn't sit well with executives and the distributors.

The company, which had had a good labor record under Ignatz, Frank W., and Frank V., faced discontent. In March 1980 the workers voted to unionize, and now the United Auto Workers represented the workforce. Soon after, the company had its first strike.

At the time Schwinn had been supplied with 20 percent of its bikes from Japanese manufacturers. The chief non-Japanese supplier was Taiwan's Giant Manufacturing, which despite its name was quite small. Giant was one of those young, aggressive firms that would enable Taiwan to become a business powerhouse. It had been founded in 1971 by an engineer, King Liu, with a stake of $100,000. Soon after, the company purchased a trading company to act as its marketing outlet, and with it came Tony Lo, an aggressive, imaginative, and shrewd businessman who spoke fluent English. Taiwan was next door to mainland China, where bikes were the common means of transportation. China was a huge market, but it was virtually closed to Taiwan in this period. Across the ocean was the United States, where the Japanese automobile invasion had just commenced. American boys and girls were wedded to bicycles, but their parents were less inclined to purchase and use them. But this, too, was changing, as adults were taking to the BMXs and then the ten-speeders. Lo contacted Schwinn in the mid-1970s and invited company leaders, including Al Fritz, to visit the Giant factory. Lo offered to provide Schwinn with better-quality bikes at lower prices, this made possible by the higher Japanese labor costs. Fritz accepted the offer.

The strike obliged Schwinn to find new suppliers. Edward, Jr., wanted to know if Giant could provide more bikes, and Lo leaped at the chance to expand its American sales. During the next five months Giant shipped 70,000 bikes to Schwinn, and it turned out they were less expensive and better constructed than the American models. The strike ended in February 1981, but the relationship with Giant remained as strong as it had been during the walkout. In 1981 Schwinn was bringing in 100,000 Giants a year and selling them as Schwinns.

The strike soured Edward, Jr., on the Chicago workforce, and he considered the construction of a new plant. This was not a new idea; in 1977 he had contemplated a move to Tulsa, to a plant that would have cost $50 million. The amount was small change to automakers, but quite a lot of money for a privately owned bicycle manufacturer with so many relatives to provide for. This time he wanted to move to Greenville, Mississippi. The reason for this unusual choice was labor costs and the fact that Mississippi was a right-to-work state. The plant was quickly approved and opened for business in the summer of 1981.

The Greenville plant was a disaster on all levels. Start with the fact it was located 75 miles from the nearest interstate highway. To get to Greenville from Chicago one had to fly into Memphis and take an infrequently scheduled twin-propeller commuter plane to a small airport near Greenville. The workforce there received lower wages than their Chicago counterparts, but also were less productive, and quality control was even poorer there than at the old plant. Few executives were willing to relocate to the backwater town, all of which meant that Schwinn was obliged to rely increasingly upon its foreign suppliers.

In late 1981 William Austin became vice president for marketing, succeeding Nielsen. Austin was a gruff, plain-spoken bicycle man who was prepared to face down Edward, Jr. He worked well with Jay Townley, a Schwinn marketing veteran. Together they surveyed the situation. When completed, Austin recommended increased importation of bikes from Giant. Schwinn agreed, and a flood of orders were sent to Giant, along with Schwinn personnel, plans, dies, and more. It was clear the Schwinn meant to use Giant as its main supplier in the future. By 1984 Giant was providing Schwinn with 500,000 bikes a year. Lo was grateful and realized Giant's growth was dependent on the Schwinn connection.

This was the time for Schwinn to demand the right to purchase a minority stake in Giant. When the proposal was made, Lo countered with an offer to purchase Schwinn. The matter was dropped as Schwinn looked for other suppliers. Schwinn had Murray Ohio produce some of its lower-priced models. Increasingly, the company was becoming a wholesaler of bikes, not a producer. The company closed its Chicago plant. The result of all these changes was salutary. Sales and profits rebounded, and by 1986 Schwinn had a profit of $7 million on sales of $174 million. It wouldn't last.

New bicycle configurations were coming to market. By the mid-1980s it was the turn of mountain bikes, a balloon-tire model. These were sturdy models, built to be used off the roads as well as on them. It seemed a return to the street bikes Schwinn had pioneered during the 1930s. These made up 2.6 million of 1987's 12.6 million in sales, and market share was increasing, to the point that mountains soon would account for half of all sales.

Just as it had failed to lead with BMXs, Schwinn did not originate mountain bikes and held back initially. A California Schwinn dealer hit upon the reason. "If they didn't think it up, it wasn't worth making," thought John Lewis. Trek, a leader in the high end of this category, expanded rapidly, and in the process signed up some of the top Schwinn dealers. There were other reasons. The Schwinns considered the bikes inherently dangerous; like with the BMXs, the riders were susceptible to injuries, which in turn would result in lawsuits.

Fritz had wanted Schwinn to get into mountain bikes immediately, but was stopped by Frank V. and then Edward, Jr. When he protested Fritz was shunted aside to become president of Excelsior Exercise Co., a wholly owned subsidiary that as its name indicates, manufactured and sold that equipment. Exerciser production was transferred to Taiwan. Under Fritz's leadership Excelsior became quite profitable, selling 67,000 of its Air-Dyne machines for $595 per copy by 1986, while Schwinn languished, an indication of what might have been at the parent company. By then Fritz was on the way out, forced to retire by Edward, Jr., at the age of 60.

There were other errors of judgment. When Schwinn had been strong, the dealers were weak, because the company could withhold product. So they were required to accept the 50 percent rule. When the company was weak, the dealers would be strong, because they could take competitors' product. In 1988 Schwinn finally started opening company stores, but this foreclosed pushes into Kmart and Wal Mart, a missed opportunity. Nothing Edward, Jr., did seemed to work out right.

"Schwinn had the best bike engineers in the country," noted J. C. McCullough of *Bicycling* magazine, "but it lost its edge because its management didn't respond quickly enough. They didn't talk to Generation X the way the other companies did," which is to say, they failed to make a strong enough push in those bikes adults wanted. It was more than that. The relationship with Giant had turned around. While supplying Schwinn, Giant had expanded operations into Europe and in the process was soon to become an industry leader. Schwinn ignored the European market.

The failure to export carried other costs. Trek, which established beachheads in Europe and Asia, profited from the competition. According to Paul Brodek, director of Trek Japan, "We've learned things in Germany and Japan, the most demanding markets, that have improved the quality of our bikes in the United States." Said another competitor, "Schwinn was obsessed with cutting costs instead of innovation." By the time Schwinn got around to mounting an important overseas move, it did so with bikes manufactured by others, including Giant. Why buy a Schwinn that was really a Giant when you could get the identical bike, with a Giant label, for 10 percent less? Another competitor told a reporter, "Schwinn gave the franchise to Giant on a silver platter."*

---

*Might it be that history is repeating itself in the 1990s? Taiwanese firms such as Acer, Inventec, and Mitac were producing computers for Compaq, Dell, and IBM. All of Dell's notebook computers are put together in Taiwan, and in 1998 IBM outsourced $1.8 billion worth of orders to Taiwanese firms. The time may come—and soon—when the Taiwanese firms will undercut American prices (on their own machines) with their own brand names, as they did in bicycles in the 1980s.

Taken aback by Giant's success, Schwinn looked for other partners. There was a minor venture into Hungary, but the more important connection was one with China Bicycles Co. (CBC), based in
Shenzhen province and owned by a Hong Kong businessman, Jerome
Sze, who supplied bikes to Sears Roebuck. This time Schwinn insisted
on being given an equity position in return for placing orders with the
company and was permitted to buy a one-third stake. Now the Giant
experience was recapitulated. Schwinn sent to China a team of engineers, designers, and mechanics and helped CBC reorganize its operations. "CBC came light years in a short period of time because of a
lot of technology transfer from Schwinn," said *Bicycling's* McCullough.
CBC did not intend to become a satellite of Schwinn in the United
States. In 1990 it purchased an American distributor and started selling its Diamond Back bikes at lower prices than the same bikes it provided Schwinn. By then Schwinn was being engulfed in an ocean of
red ink. Key personnel left. William Austin became president of
Giant's American subsidiary, Giant Bicycle, Inc.

Throughout all of this Edward, Jr., was strangely composed and
inactive. Schwinn was still a respected nameplate, and Edward
Schwinn could have played Giant against CBC. He failed to do this,
and both companies came to depend less and less on Schwinn sales.
Nor did he do anything consequential to improve matters at the
Greenville plant, which was never profitable. He insisted on keeping
it open, perhaps in order to maintain the thought that Schwinn was
still a manufacturer, not just a distributor. Finally, in 1991 he closed
down Greenville, a bungled experiment that had cost the company
more than $30 million.

It was as though his will were paralyzed. This became evident to
Judith Crown and Glenn Coleman, reporters at *Crain's Chicago Business*, who covered Schwinn. They would later write the only book that
dealt with the company, entitled *No Hands: The Rise and Fall of the
Schwinn Bicycle Company, An American Institution*. Clearly, the "no
hands" in the title had a double meaning, the way children rode with
no hands on the handlebars and referring to Edward, Jr.'s, stewardship.

In 1991, largely because of Greenville, Schwinn posted a loss of
$23 million. In the first half of 1992, with the closing of Greenville, it
bounded back to profitability. This was the time to attempt to find a
buyer, or at least to take the company public, before the red ink

returned. The Finkelstein brothers of Grand Rapids, Michigan, who had just sold their business, offered the ridiculously high sum of more than $100 million for a majority position in Schwinn. It was rejected; no one could displace the Schwinns at Schwinn thought Edward, Jr. By then he was willing to accept a minority partner, but the family had to remain in charge. Nothing more was heard from the Finkelsteins. Then Schwinn turned in a string of losses, and it became less attractive.

The investment banking firm of Donaldson, Lufkin, Jenrette was hired to work out a leveraged buyout. DLJ had in mind a $90 million deal for around 85 percent of the company, which would net the family around $60 million. The family would retain those shares in China Bicycles, which were worth some $15 million. Edward Jr. rejected this deal. Other offers rolled in, each lower than the previous one, and all were turned down. Finally, in September Edward, Jr., came to his senses and indicated to Continental Partners, which had been engaged to find an investor, that he was prepared to talk with some of those he had earlier refused. They no longer were interested.

The beginning of the end was signaled during the summer of 1992, when Giant and China refused to ship bicycles unless paid for them first with letters of credit. Vendors would not return telephone calls from Edward Schwinn, Jr., and other executives. Dealers were deserting.

On October 7, 1992, Schwinn was obliged to file for a Chapter 11 bankruptcy. At the time the company owed its banks more than $50 million and its suppliers another $32 million. Schwinn's debt to Giant came to $9 million and to CBC, $18 million. Tony Lo took it in stride. Giant had become the world's largest bike exporter. "Without Schwinn we never would have grown to where we are today," said Lo. "We learned many basic things from them: quality, value, service." He had the grace not to add that these were matters Schwinn had somehow failed to maintain.

CONCLUSION

Abraham Lincoln, in a morose moment during the Civil War, said, "I claim not to have controlled events, but confess plainly that events have controlled me. The pilots on our Western rivers steer from point to point, as they call it—setting the course of the boat no farther than they can see." But from Mark Twain's *Life on the Mississippi* we learn that Lincoln was mistaken, that the pilots knew every bend on the route and learned when sand bars shifted, as they so often did and still do. Twain also realized just what it is one can learn from studying the past. "History does not repeat itself," he wrote, "but it rhymes." This is about as far as one can go. There are some things one can learn from history, and one of these is that it does not repeat itself. Winston Churchill, who of all twentieth-century public figures knew more of the way chance determines the outcomes of important events, wrote, "History with its flickering lamp stumbles along the trail of the past."

Of course, the study of business blunders is not on the same level as the study of the Civil War and World War II. The future of the United States and of Western civilization did not hinge on the success or failure of any of the companies discussed in this book. Nonetheless, the foul ups caused a great deal of grief in the lives of those they affected. Of the 15 companies discussed in these pages, eight have not survived fumbles of their leaders—Osborne, E. J. Korvette, Kaiser-Frazer, Packard, Drexel Burnham, Penn Central, Pan American, and American Tobacco. RCA exists as a subsidiary of General Electric. Schlitz and Pabst as shadows of their old selves; once available wherever beers were sold, they can't be found in some parts of the country.

LTV is a turgid steel company with inefficient facilities; Montgomery Ward is a bankrupted department-store chain with no mission or purpose. W. R. Grace remains the world's largest specialty chemicals company with interests in several other fields, having survived its expensive forays into merchandising, restaurants, foods, and those other businesses that captured Peter Grace's roving eyes, which included the gathering and marketing of bull semen. Schwinn is a small factor in a bicycle industry dominated by foreign concerns. The New York Stock Exchange is still there, and is thriving, but its success is due more to a roaring bull market and a just-in-time willingness to bow to some of the technological imperatives of the age than to the superiority of its specialist system.

What lessons can be gleaned from this record of failures? We should start by noting that each case was different from the others, which can be seen in the titles of the chapters. If there is any single moral to the tales it is that for all but one of these entities failure was preceded by great success. Then, too, what happened to these firms and companies after the blunder resulted in anything from declines to disasters.

Osborne Computer was the king of the transportables when Adam Osborne stumbled. Osborne remained on the periphery of life in Silicon Valley; he never again was a player of consequence after his two-year meteorlike rise and fall. Instead, he returned to writing and became a director of Silicon Valley Technologies. In April 1991 *Dataquest* published an article by him entitled, "Be Proud to Be an Indian," in which he talked about his roots in that country and predicted that if Indians were proud of their heritage, they would go on to greatness.

Gene Ferkauf had revolutionized merchandising with his discount stores when he took that step into department stores that ended in disaster. The shuttering of Korvette in 1980 was not the end of the story. There were clearance sales, the filing for Chapter 11 bankruptcy, and a slew of lawsuits. During this period executives and journalists conducted autopsies of the company, and all seemed to agree on the causes. E. J. Korvette had been a pioneer and had performed well so long as it stuck to its formula and had few competitors. As Robert Warner, a Macy's executive who joined Korvette as a senior vice president, put it: "The reality was that Korvette found great success for two reasons. One was that it could sell cheaper, and people go crazy when you can do that. The other was that it had big assortments. With both of those, people became aware of Korvette and flocked to it. But it also attracted rivals who started copying it."

Kaiser-Frazer's initial offerings were greeted with enthusiasm, and the dealers had full order books before the first model appeared. Then Kaiser fumbled, and Frazer left the firm. Disaster lay ahead; it didn't take an automobile industry expert to realize this. Not all of the company's products vanished, however. American Motors would purchase Jeep from Kaiser Industries in 1970 and then it would become part of Chrysler in 1987. As it turned out, the Jeep was a major reason for Chrysler's revival. Joe Frazer had the last laugh after all. Henry Kaiser's automobile legacy is a few hundred aging cars prized by collectors. The Jeep, which in part at least was Frazer's creation, survives and prospers.

RCA went on to recover some of its old patina under the management of General Electric. Bob Sarnoff was not as fortunate. He faded into obscurity, and when he died in 1997 many hadn't realized he was still around. With proper training and better handling, Bob might have been able to compete with IBM's Tom Watson Jr., and other humans, but he knew he hadn't a chance in a competition with RCA for his father's attention. Clearly, he should not have become the RCA CEO.

In 1939 N.S.B. Gras, one of the first systemic business historians, divided businessmen into three groups: the playboys, the energetic and competent businessmen, and the inheritors. Of the last he wrote, "The individuals who make up this group have been born into business or married into it or have grown sour in administration. They may make sundry unpromising experiments in their business or branch out to invest in other enterprises. Rather logically, they end by impairing the financial position of the very business that they should nourish and cherish."

Peter Grace had his share of triumphs with specialty chemicals and other businesses when he opted to enter the food, restaurant, and retailer areas; in his case successes followed these missteps, but his end was tragic. Within weeks of his departure other ugly stories surfaced regarding Grace's relationship with J. P. Bolduc. It seemed the two men had had a falling out in 1994, involving Bolduc's fast-and-loose

financial dealings, in particular in awarding contracts and in his intention to dispose of some of Grace's prize companies. In addition, it
appeared Grace's son, Peter III, had misused company funds to purchase a W. R. Grace unit, which resulted in his sudden resignation.

W. R. Grace became a stormy battlefield, pitting Constantine
Hampers, who had been allied with Grace in the struggle against
Bolduc, against the man who succeeded Bolduc two weeks after
Grace's death, Albert Costello. Much of the struggle revolved around
continuing rumors of a massive restructuring and sales of assets, and it
is there that the scope of Peter Grace's accomplishments should be
gauged. When they toted up the numbers on Wall Street, after Peter
Grace's death, analysts calculated National Medical alone was worth
$4 billion. Grace Packaging, which grew out of Dewey & Almay,
would fetch another $2.4 billion, and Grace Davison, $1.1 billion. The
rest of the corporation could bring in as much as $1.3 billion. So alto-
gether, W. R. Grace was worth an estimated $8.8 billion.

Packard was the class of its field before producing cars for the
parvenue, and even then it went on to successes in that area for a
while. At the time of its downfall its failure was taken as a sign that
niche players had no place in the automobile marketplace. But this
wasn't so. Even as Packard folded, another car with a single model
aimed at a specific market was soaring: Volkswagen. It might be
argued that VW was aimed at the mass market and so could apply
Packard lessons—slow model changes and a reputation for quality—
profitably. Significantly, the other car produced by VW, upscale
sports-car Porsche, wasn't anything like the famed Beetle.

Schlitz had half a century of success, years when it was the
nation's best-selling brew, and then blundered by cutting corners.
Taste and image, which Gussie and August Busch understood, prevailed over economics and technology, the path taken by Schlitz and
Pabst. This is a moral that applies in several of the chapters. Packard
cheapened its image and declined. Schlitz and Pabst degraded their
product and fell into obscurity.

LTV was the nation's fastest-growing large company; and then
came the run-in with the government. Plagued by inefficient plants
and a generally uncompetitive position, LTV filed for Chapter 11
bankruptcy protection on July 17, 1986, the largest industrial bankruptcy in American history to that time. When an attempt to sell its

defense business to France's Thomson-CSF was blocked by the government, that part of the company was sold to a consortium of Loral and Northrop/Carlyle in 1992. The company emerged from bankruptcy in 1993, whereupon Sumitomo Metal Industries purchased a 10 percent stake. In 1980, when it had been a premier conglomerate, LTV was an $8 billion company. Today, as the nation's third-largest steel company, it is half that size. But it has survived and is once again profitable.

As for Ling, he attempted several comebacks. In 1980 he organized Matrix Energy, which explored for oil and natural gas in Oklahoma and Texas without much success. Then, in 1981 Ling was stricken by Guillain-Barré syndrome, a little-known debilitating illness. While still recovering, he became involved with L. G. Williams, another exploration company, and for a while seemed on the way back, but this amounted to little. Then he vanished from sight. There was a rumor that he had become a minister in eastern Texas, under a different name. His father, Hugo, would have understood. The greatest of the conglomerateurs was a forgotten man.

Drexel Burnham Lambert was the most exciting and successful investment bank in the nation prior to the reaction to its financings of hostile takeovers, and Michael Milken was the star of the decade. For a while there was some talk of reviving the firm under the name of Drexel Harriman, but this was never seriously acted upon. After Milken was released from prison on probation in 1993 he learned he had prostate cancer. Then, aided by treatments he helped devise, the cancer fell into remission. He set up a publishing company and an institute that studied world problems and continued his longtime interest in education. But Milken no longer is in finance, being barred from such endeavors under the terms of his sentence. Even so, he continued to advise some former clients, and in 1998 the SEC went after him, charging violations of the conditions of his parole. Milken denied that he had engaged in activities barred by the parole, and in time the Justice Department conceded that the evidence that he did so was "conflicting." Milken settled with the government by paying a $42 million fine, the amount of his fees plus interest. In return the government agreed to drop the charges and his probation was ended.

Pan Am was the class of the skies before Trippe's gamble with the 747; of course, other errors followed, and then it died. Ironically, Pan

Am was reborn in a new guise in 1996. Financier and former Assistant Secretary of Commerce Charles Cobb had purchased the right to the name for $1.3 million in 1993, and three years later, together with former Pan Am COO Martin Shugrue, resurrected the company, actually two companies, under the Pan American Corporation umbrella, Pan Am World Airways and Pan American Airways. The start-up capital came to $30 million, or little more than one of those 747s cost Trippe in the old Pan Am's glory days. Shugrue, who had also worked at Eastern and Continental, had originally wanted to resuscitate the Eastern name, but accepted Pan Am when market research indicated that despite the Lockerbie tragedy, the public still held it in some affection. The new Pan Am leased three old Airbus transports and entered the long-distance-discount business, while Pan American ran a charter operation

What might the new company hope for? In January 1996 industry analyst Ray Neidl thought, given some breaks, it could become the "ValueJet of the long-haul market." Alas, Neidl had it wrong. Instead, ValueJet became the Pan Am of the short-haul market. Four months later ValueJet Flight 592 crashed in the Everglades. That company soon vanished from the scene, reemerging later as AirTran, thus joining the pantheon of failed airlines, including, of course, the old Pan Am.

In late 1987 Pan Am absorbed the much larger Carnival, which operated between New York and Florida. By January 1998 it was carrying 5,000 passengers daily to 14 cities, covering Florida, the Northeast, the Midwest, and Puerto Rico. Not for long. In late February 1998 Pan Am (but not the parent company) suspended its services, filing once more for bankruptcy protection, with assets of $50 million and $147 million in debt. This did not mean the airline suffered a second death, however. Rather, under court protection it entered the charter business and searched for means to restart. At that point Carl Icahn indicated he indeed might make a bid for Pan Am, talking to reporters about infusing $43 million into the line, but he withdrew in March, just when another bidder appeared in the form of Milan Mandaric, a Yugoslavia-born investor in high-technology companies and "distressed situations," the latter term most descriptive of Pan Am during its last years in the air.

Montgomery Ward gave Sears Roebuck a run for it and had a better record than Sears during the Depression. But after World War

II Sewell Avery's blunders all but doomed the company to decline. After the bankruptcy filing Chairman Roger Gaddu tried to sound an optimistic note. "Although a Chapter 11 bankruptcy filing was not our desired course of action, we believe that with the cooperation of our vendors and our associates, it will allow us to concentrate on implementing our merchandising strategy and emerge as a healthier and more contemporary retailer." That strategy consisted of selling off or closing additional stores and turning the rest into low-priced outlets. Kurt Barnard, president of *Barnard's Retailing Marketing Report*, which monitored the industry, was not sanguine regarding prospects. "Ward has lost its reason for being. In simplest terms, they bumped up against Sears, and management hasn't helped with its lack of a definitive strategy." The company shuttered 54 stores in 1997. A handful of them are still in operation, but probably will be liquidated by the turn of the century.

American Tobacco's failure to enter the filter-cigarette field faster than it did came after it had conquered king-sized brands. There is no American Tobacco today, and this may prove a blessing to the shareholders of Fortune Brands, its successor.

The NYSE was the world's dominant exchange when it failed to perceive the opportunities in options and the need for automation. With all of this, the NYSE not only survived, but in 1997 set records for volume and earnings. In early 1998 a seat there changed hands at a record $2 million. By then average daily volume had risen to well over 500 million shares. An intensive drive to obtain listings paid off; 279 companies came to the NYSE that year. Even so, on a typical day NASDAQ will trade 10 percent or so of the volume of the NYSE in listed stocks, while other organized exchanges—the Chicago, Pacific, Boston, Cincinnati, and Philadelphia exchanges—trade a comparable amount, with Chicago in the lead.

So it isn't exactly a case of "change or die." In the heady atmosphere of the great bull market of the 1990s not to have done so well would have been unusual. The NYSE will be there for a long while even if it doesn't alter its present course substantially, which is to say, retain the specialist system in its current state. Even so, the designation of "Big Board" seems outdated given its slippage. The moral would appear to be, "accommodate to new technologies and markets or suffer the consequences."

Schwinn was the most famous and desired bicycle in America before the fall. As has been seen in the case of Pan Am, Chapter 11 filing does not mean the company's life comes to an end. Schwinn had liabilities, to be sure, but also assets that did not make their way to the company's balance sheet. For one thing, there was the name itself, still well regarded by bikers, and for another, there remained some top-notch people at headquarters. Schwinn went on the block, and among the bidders were Trek and Giant. The contest was won by Sam Zell, who headed Zell/Chilmark Fund, which specialized in taking over distressed firms, in alliance with ski-accessory-manufacturer Scott USA. Together they formed Scott Sporting Goods, whose bid of $43 million was accepted. Much of this went to pay creditors. When it was all over, the Schwinns, who had worked at the plant and counted on those jobs, were out on the street and if not exactly penniless, had joined the middle class.

Scott infused the company with another $7 million and moved the company to Boulder, Colorado, an indication that it was going to make a big move into mountain bikes. It had a long way to go. In 1993 Schwinn sold fewer than 300,000 bikes, out of industry sales of 12 million units. It is still around and doing quite well. It is a smaller though more respected firm than it had been in the last days of Edward Schwinn, Jr.'s, regime. But given better management—and wiser decisions—it could have remained the industry leader it once had been.

One might argue that the Penn Central was the exception, that it was doomed from the start. Had it been able to hold on the company might still be with us today. With the revival of railroading during the good times of the 1980s and 1990s, Conrail performed well, and in 1997 became the target of two takeover bids, one from CSX, the other from Norfolk Southern. CFX was based on the old C&O, while Norfolk Southern evolved out of N&W. The struggle ended in a compromise: Norfolk Southern and CSX will share the assets of Conrail, the final form to be announced before the end of 1998. The price for this once-seemingly worthless property was $10.3 billion. Railroading will never be what it was in the pre-ICC days, or what it could have been absent that agency.

Apparently CSX will receive what once had been much of the Central, while Norfolk Southern will take over many Pennsylvania lines, while both companies will share some lines, specifically the mileage between New York and Philadelphia. This was done with relative ease, indicating that the glue that bound the Pennsylvania and the Central was not very strong. Ironically, the old contest between the two cities climaxed with the rail path between them shared by two other railroads. So the mergers continue, with the descendants of the old players the most important new ones.

Another lesson is that companies would be wise to reconsider forays into areas beyond their expertise and that failures to adjust to changing markets and technologies can bring a company down. Inadequate funding can present problems even when all goes well. Businesspeople have to be solicitous of their customers, for unless they are, they will lose them. The government can be a friend and supporter, but it also can be an enemy to those who cross the paths of politicians and bureaucrats, as Michael Milken and James Ling learned to their sorrow, along with scores of now-departed railroad executives. But for each Milken and Ling there are the likes of Juan Trippe and David Sarnoff who benefited from government assistance in several forms. Exceptions do not prove rules; they demolish them. And there are few rules in avoiding business blunders other than these.

SELECTED BIBLIOGRAPHY

Adams, Steven. *Mr. Kaiser Goes to Washington*. U. of North Carolina, 1997.

Ahl, David. "Fourteen Notebook Computers in Brief." *Creative Computing*, January 1984.

——. "Osborne Computer Company." *Creative Computing*, March 1984.

Alderson, Frederick. *Bicycling: A History*. David & Charles, 1972.

Allen, Oliver. *The Airline Builders*. Time-Life, 1981.

"All Terrain Bicycles." *Consumer Reports*.

Anderson, Rudolph. *The Story of the American Automobile*. Public Affairs, 1950.

Anon. *Fifty Years of Schwinn-Built Bicycles*. Arnold, Schwinn, 1945.

Bailey, Fenton. *Fall from Grace: The Untold Story of Michael Milken*. Birch Lane, 1992.

"Ball Point Bonanza." *Business Week*. February 22, 1947.

Barmash, Isadore. *More Than They Bargained For*. Lebhar-Friedman, 1981.

"Battle of the Pens." *Business Week*, May 4, 1946.

Beatty, David. *The Water Jump*. Harper & Row, 1979.

Bender, Marylin, and Selig Altschul. *The Chosen Instrument*. Simon & Schuster, 1982.

Bernstein, Marver. *Regulating Business by Independent Commissions*. Princeton, 1955.

"Bike Boom: A Way Out for Commuters?" *U.S. News & World Report*, December 6, 1971.

"Bicycle Boom Pedals into High Gear." *U.S. News & World Report*, December 19, 1977.

"Bicycle Boom Still in High Gear." *U.S. News & World Report*, November 5, 1973.

Biddle, Wayne. *Barons of the Sky*. Simon & Schuster, 1991.

"Bike Boom Rises to Its Christmas Best." *Business Week*, December 21, 1968.

Blume, Marshall, Jeremy Seigel, and Dan Rottenberg. *Revolution on Wall Street*, Norton. 1993.

Brenner, Melvin, James Leete, and Elihu Schott. *Airline Deregulation*. Eno, 1985.

Brenner, Marie. "The Man Who Fell to Earth." *Vanity Fair*, August, 1989.

Brooks, John. *Business Adventures*. Weybright & Talley, 1969.

Brown, Stanley. *Ling: The Rise, Fall, and Return of a Texas Tycoon*. 1972.

Bruck, Connie. *The Predator's Ball*. Simon & Schuster, 1988.

Carosso, Vincent. *Investment Banking in America*. Cambridge, 1970.

Carson, Robert. *Main Line to Oblivion*. Kennicatt, 1971.

Christensen, Clayton. *The Innovators Dilemma: When New Technologies Cause Great Firms to Fail*. Harvard Business School, 1977.

Coll, Steve, and David Vice. *Eagle on the Street*. Scribners, 1991.

Crown, Judith, and Glenn Coleman. *No Hands*. Holt, 1996.

Daley, Robert. *An American Saga: Juan Trippe and His Pan Am Empire*. Random House, 1980.

Daughen, Joseph, and Peter Bitzen. *The Wreck of the Penn Central*. Little Brown, 1971.

Davies, R. E. G. *Pan Am: An Airline and Its Aircraft*. Orion, 1987.

Dawes, Nathaniel. *The Packard: 1942–1962*. A. S. Barnes, 1975.

Dershowitz, Alan. *Reversal of Fortune*. Random House, 1986.

Dreher, Carl. *Sarnoff*. Quadrangle, 1977.

Drucker, Peter. *Managing in a Time of Great Change*. Truman Talley/Plume, 1995.

Ehbar, Al. "Have Takeovers Gone Too Far?" *Fortune*, May 27, 1985.

"Elegant Wheels for a New American Fad." *Fortune*, March, 1974.

"Fountain Pen Scramble." *Fortune*, July, 1946.

Freiberger, Paul, and Michael Swaine. *Fire in the Valley*. Osborne/McGraw-Hill, 1984.

Freiberger, Stephan, and Paul Chew. *A Consumer's Guide to Personal Computing and Microcomputers*. Hayden, 1980.

"Furor over Pens." *Business Week*, March 2, 1946.

Gandt, Robert. *Skygods: The Fall of Pan Am*. Morrow, 1995.

Garten, Michael. *Riding the Pennsy to Ruin*. Dow-Jones, 1971.

Giovannini, Joseph. "A Sturdy Mountain Bike Wins Hearts in the City." *New York Times*, July 30, 1983.

Gras, N. S. B. *Business and Capitalism*. Crofts, 1939.

Gunther, John. *Inside U.S.A.* Harper, 1947.

Gwynn-Jones, Terry. *Wings Across the Pacific*. Orion, 1991.

Halberstam, David. *The Reckoning*. Morrow, 1986.

Hand, A. J. "Big Boom in the Hot New Bikes." *Popular Science*, July 1971.

Hawthorne, Fran. "Could Drexel Have Been Saved?" *Institutional Investor*, March 1990.

Hayes, Samuel. "The Transformation of Investment Banking." *Harvard Business Review*, March–April 1979.

Heimann, Robert. *Tobacco and Americans*. McGraw-Hill, 1960.

Heppenheimer, T. A. "How They Derailed the Penn Central." *Audacity*, Summer 1993.

——. "The Only Way to Fly," *Audacity*, Spring 1955.

——. *Turbulent Skies*. Wiley, 1995.

Herlihy, David. "The Bicycle Story." *American Heritage of Invention & Technology*, Spring 1992.

Herndon, Boonton. *Satisfaction Guaranteed*. McGraw-Hill, 1972.

"High-Rise Bikes." *Consumer Reports*, January 1975.

Hoge, Cecil. *The First Hundred Years Are the Toughest*. Ten Speed, 1988.

Holbrook, Giovanna. "With Pan Am Gone, Spirits No Longer Soar." *Travel Weekly*, Spring 1992.

Horwitch, Mel. *Clipped Wings: The American SST Conflict*. MIT, 1982.

Johnstone, Bob. "Riding High: Business Booms for Bicycle-Maker Shimano Industries." *Far Eastern Economic Review*, December 14, 1989.

Kichen, Steve. "A Buyer's Guide to Home Computers." *Forbes*, October 10, 1983.

Kluger, Richard. *Ashes to Ashes*. Knopf, 1996.

Kohlmeier, Louis. *The Regulators*. Harper & Row, 1969.

Kolko, Gabriel. *The Triumph of Conservatism*. Free Press, 1963.

Kornbluth, Jesse. *Highly Confident: The Crime and Punishment of Michael Milken*. Morrow, 1992.

Kukoda, John. "Birth of a Bike." *Cycling*, April 1990.

Kuter, Lawrence. *The Great Gamble: The Boeing 747*. University of Alabama, 1973.

Lardner, James. *Fast Forward*. Norton, 1987.

Louis, Arthur. "How the Customers Thrust Unexpected Prosperity on the Bicycle Industry." *Fortune*, March 1974.

Lyons, Eugene. *David Sarnoff*. Harper, 1966.

McClellan, Stephen. *The Coming Computer Industry Shakeout*. Wiley, 1984.

McGlynn, Daniel. *Personal Computing*. Wiley, 1979.

McShane, Clay. *Down the Asphalt Path*. Columbia UP, 1994.

McWilliams, Peter. *The Personal Computer Book*. Ballantine, 1982.

Magnet, Myron. "The Little Computer that Could." *Fortune*, March 8, 1982.

Martin, Albro. *Enterprise Denied*. Columbia, 1971.

Melamed, Leo. *Leo Melamed: Escape to the Futures*. Wiley, 1996.

Meyer, John. *Lung Cancer Chronicles*. Rutgers, 1990.

Norris, Floyd. "Phelan Leaves a Remolded Exchange." *New York Times*, December 10, 1990.

O'Neill, Ralph. *A Dream of Eagles*. Houghton Mifflin, 1973.

Options Institute, ed. *Options: Essential Concepts and Trading Strategies*. Irwin, 1995.

Osborne, Adam. *An Introduction to Microcomputers. Volume O, The Beginner's Book*. Osborne, 1977.

———. *An Introduction to Microcomputers: Volume I, Basic Concepts*. Osborne, 1976.

———.and John Dvorak. *Hypergrowth: The Rise and Fall of Osborne Computer*. Idthekkethan, 1984.

———. with Susann Jacobson, and Jerry Kane. *An Introduction to Microcomputers: Vol. II, Some Real Products, June 1977 Revision*. Osborne, 1977.

"Osborne: From Brags to Riches." *Business Week*, February 22, 1982.

"Osborne Goes Down." *Fortune*, October 17, 1983.

"Packard." *Fortune*, January 1937.

"Packard's Road Back." *Fortune*, November 1952.

Palmer, Arthur. *Riding High: The Story of the Bicycle*. Dutton, 1956.

Patrick, Kevin. "Mountain Bikes and the Baby Boomers." *Journal of American Culture*, Summer 1988.

Patton, Phil. "Champion of the Adequate." *Audacity*, Spring 1993.

Picker, Ida. "Picking Up the Pieces at Drexel." *Institutional Investor*, April 1992.

Poser, Norman. "Restructuring the Stock Markets." *New York University Law School Review*, November/December 1981.

Pridmore, Jay, and Jim Hurd. *The American Bicycle*. Motorbooks International, 1995.

Rae, John. *Climb to Greatness*. MIT, 1968.

———. *The Road and Car in American Life*. MIT, 1971.

"Reyonlds Offers Model 2." *Business Week*, April 20, 1946.

Reynolds, Patrick, and Tom Shachtman. *The Gilded Leaf. Triumph, Tragedy, and Tobacco. Three Generations of the R. J. Reynolds Family and Fortune.* Little, Brown, 1989.

Robert, Joseph. *The Story of Tobacco in America.* Knopf, 1949.

Rosenberg, Hilary. *The Vulture Investors.* HarperCollins, 1992.

Rottenberg, Dan. "The Explosive New World of Wall Street." *Town & Country*, March 1988.

———. "LaSalle Street vs. Wall Street." *Town & Country*, March 1988.

Salisbury, Stephan. *No Way to Run a Railroad.* McGraw-Hill, 1982.

Sampson, Anthony. *Empires of the Sky.* Random House, 1984.

Saunders, Richard. *The Railroad Mergers and the Coming of Conrail.* Greenwood, 1978.

Schroeder, Otto. *Packard: Ask the Man Who Owned One.* Post-Era Books, 1974

Scott, Michael. *Packard: The Complete Story.* Tab, 1985.

Seligman, Joel. "The Future of the National Market System." *Journal of Corporation Law*, Fall 1984.

Serling, Robert. *The Only Way to Fly.* Doubleday, 1976.

———. "Pan Am: The First Fifty Years." *Airline Executive*, Summer 1977.

Sheeline, William. "Who Needs the Stock Exchange?" *Fortune*, November 19, 1990.

Simon, Michael, and Robert Colby. "The National Market System for Over-The-Counter Stocks." *George Washington Law Review*, 1986.

Sloan, Allan "A Chat with Michael Milken." *Forbes*, July 13, 1987.

Sloane, Eugene. *The New Complete Book of Cycling.* Simon & Schuster, 1974.

Slutsker, Gary. "If You Can't Beat 'Em." *Forbes*, January 6, 1992.

Smith, Adam. *The Roaring Eighties.* Summit, 1988.

Smith, Robert. *A Social History of the Bicycle.* American Heritage, 1972.

Stern, Richard. "Living Off the Spread." *Forbes*, July 10, 1989.

———. "A Dwindling Monopoly." *Forbes*, May 13, 1991.

"Smoking on the Rise Despite Warnings." *U.S. News & World Report*, December 17, 1973.

Sobel, Robert. *Dangerous Dreamers.* Wiley, 1993.

———. "How James Ling Made 1+1+1=13." *Audacity*, Winter 1995.

———. *Inside Wall Street.* Norton, 1977.

———. *NYSE: A History of the New York Stock Exchange.* Weybright & Talley, 1977.

———. "Peter's Grace." *Audacity*, Spring 1997.

——. *RCA*. Stein & Day, 1986.

——. "The $150 Million Lemon." *Audacity*, Winter 1997.

——. "The Son of the Father of Television." *Audacity*, Spring 1996.

——. *They Satisfy*. Doubleday, 1978.

——. "Why Pay More?" *Audacity*, Spring 1994.

Solberg, Carl. *Conquest of the Skies*. Little Brown, 1979.

Sorell, Lewis. *Government Ownership and Operation of Railways for the United States*. Prentice-Hall, 1937.

Stewart, James. *Den of Thieves*. Simon & Schuster, 1991.

Stover, John. *The Life and Decline of the American Railroad*. Oxford, 1971.

Tanser, Andrew. "Bury Thy Teacher." *Forbes*, December 21, 1992.

Tennant, Richard. *The American Cigarette Industry*. Yale, 1950.

"10-Speed Bikes." *Consumer Reports*. February, 1976.

Tilley, Nannie. *The R. J. Reynolds Tobacco Company*. U. of North Carolina, 1948.

Turnquist, Robert. *The Packard Story: The Car and the Company*. Barnes, 1965.

Uttal, Bro. "A Computer Gadfly's Triumph." *Fortune*, March 8, 1982.

Van Doren, Carlton. "Pan Am's Legacy to World Tourism." *Journal of Travel Research*, Summer 1993.

Velocci, Anthony. "New Pan Am Tries Again." *Aviation Week and Space Technology*, February 5, 1996.

Wagner, Susan. *Tobacco Country*. Praeger, 1971.

Ward, James. *The Fall of the Packard Motor Car Company*. Stanford UP, 1995.

Wells, Chris. *The Last Days of the Club*. Dutton, 1975.

——. and Monica Roman. "The Future of Wall Street: Why Our Financial System Will Never Be the Same." *Business Week*, November 5, 1990.

Wiegner, Kathleen. "Can Osborne Do It Again?" *Forbes*, October 15, 1983.

Wigmore, Barrie. *Securities Markets in the 1980s*. Oxford UP, 1997.

Wilson, S. S. "Bicycle Technology." *Scientific American*, March 1973.

Woodford, John. *The Story of the Bicycle*. Universe, 1971.

"Writes Anywhere." *Business Week*, May 26, 1945.

Yago, Glenn. *Junk Bonds*. Oxford, 1991.

Young, Jeffrey. *Forbes Greatest Technology Stories*. Wiley, 1998.

INDEX